Cox:
Personal Recollections of the Civil War

Volume 1

Cox:
Personal Recollections of the Civil War
West Virginia, Kanawha Valley
Gauley Bridge, Cotton Mountain,
South Mountain, Antietam,
the Morgan Raid & the
East Tennessee Campaign

VOLUME 1

Jacob Dolson Cox

LEONAUR

Cox: *Personal Recollections of the Civil War—West Virginia, Kanawha Valley Gauley Bridge, Cotton Mountain, South Mountain, Antietam, the Morgan Raid & the East Tennessee Campaign Volume 1*
by Jacob Dolson Cox

Published by Leonaur Ltd

Text in this form copyright © 2007 Leonaur Ltd

Originally published in 1900 under the title
Military Reminiscences of the Civil War: Volume 1

ISBN: 978-1-84677-227-6 (hardcover)
ISBN: 978-1-84677-228-3 (softcover)

http://www.leonaur.com

Publisher's Note

The opinions expressed in this book are those of the author and are not necessarily those of the publisher.

Contents

Preface	7
The Outbreak of the War	9
Camp Dennison	26
McClellan in West Virginia	42
The Kanawha Valley	56
Gauley Bridge	73
Carnifex Ferry—to Sewell Mountain and Back	93
Cotton Mountain	112
Winter-Quarters	127
Volunteers And Regulars	143
The Mountain Department—Spring Campaign	165
Pope in Command—Transfer to Washington	185
Retreat Within the Lines	202
South Mountain	220
Antietam: Preliminary Movements	244
Antietam: the Fight on the Right	258
Antietam: The Fight on the Left	274
McClellan and Politics	292
Personal Relations of McClellan, Burnside and Porter	309
Return to West Virginia	323
Winter Quarters, 1862-63	347
Farewell to West Virginia	364
The Vallandigham Case—The Holmes County War	377
Burnside and Rosecrans—The Summer's Delays	390
The Morgan Raid	404
The Liberation of East Tennessee	420
Burnside in East Tennessee	436

Preface

My aim in this book has been to reproduce my own experience in our Civil War in such a way as to help the reader understand just how the duties and the problems of that great conflict presented themselves successively to one man who had an active part in it from the beginning to the end. In my military service I was so conscious of the benefit it was to me to get the personal view of men who had served in our own or other wars, as distinguished from the general or formal history, that I formed the purpose, soon after peace was restored, to write such a narrative of my own army life. My relations to many prominent officers and civilians were such as to give opportunities for intimate knowledge of their personal qualities as well as their public conduct. It has seemed to me that it might be useful to share with others what I thus learned, and to throw what light I could upon the events and the men of that time.

As I have written historical accounts of some campaigns separately, it may be proper to say that I have in this book avoided repetition, and have tried to make the personal narrative supplement and lend new interest to the more formal story. Some of the earlier chapters appeared in an abridged form in *Battles and Leaders of the Civil War*, and the closing chapter was read before the Ohio Commandery of the Loyal Legion. By arrangements courteously made by the Century Company and the Commandery, these chapters, partly re-written, are here found in their proper connection.

Though my private memoranda are full enough to give me reasonable confidence in the accuracy of these reminiscences, I have made it a duty to test my memory by constant reference to the original contemporaneous material so abundantly preserved in the government publication of the Official Records of the Union and Confederate Armies. Where the series of these records is not given, my references are to the First Series, with the abbreviation O. R., and I have preferred to adhere to the official designation of the volumes in parts, as each volume then includes the documents of a single campaign.

J. D. C.

Chapter 1

The Outbreak of the War

On Friday the twelfth day of April, 1861, the Senate of Ohio was in session, trying to go on in the ordinary routine of business, but with a sense of anxiety and strain which was caused by the troubled condition of national affairs. The passage of Ordinances of Secession by one after another of the Southern States, and even the assembling of a provisional Confederate government at Montgomery, had not wholly destroyed the hope that some peaceful way out of our troubles would be found; yet the gathering of an army on the sands opposite Fort Sumter was really war, and if a hostile gun were fired, we knew it would mean the end of all effort at arrangement. Hoping almost against hope that blood would not be shed, and that the pageant of military array and of a rebel government would pass by and soon be reckoned among the disused scenes and properties of a political drama that never pretended to be more than acting, we tried to give our thoughts to business; but there was no heart in it, and the morning hour lagged, for we could not work in earnest and we were unwilling to adjourn.

Suddenly a senator came in from the lobby in an excited way, and catching the chairman's eye, exclaimed, "Mr. President, the telegraph announces that the secessionists are bombarding Fort Sumter!" There was a solemn and painful hush, but it was broken in a moment by a woman's shrill voice from the spectators' seats, crying, "Glory to God!" It startled every one, almost as if the enemy were in the midst. But it was the voice of a radical friend of the slave, who after a lifetime of public agitation believed that only through blood could freedom be won. Abby Kelly Foster had been attending the session of the Assembly, urging the passage of some measures enlarging the legal rights of married women, and, sitting beyond the railing when the news came in, shouted a fierce cry of joy that oppression had submitted its cause to the decision of the sword. With most of us, the gloomy thought that civil war had begun in our own land overshadowed everything, and seemed too great a price to pay for any good; a scourge to be borne only in preference to yielding the very groundwork of our republicanism,—the right to enforce a fair interpretation of the Constitution through the election of President and Congress.

The next day we learned that Major Anderson had surrendered, and the telegraphic news from all the Northern States showed plain evidence of a popular outburst of loyalty to the Union, following a brief moment of dismay. Judge Thomas M. Key of Cincinnati, chairman of the Judiciary Committee, was the recognized leader of the Democratic party in the Senate, and at an early hour moved an adjournment to the following Tuesday, in order, as he said, that the senators might have the opportunity to go home and consult their constituents in the perilous crisis of public affairs. No objection was made to the adjournment, and the representatives took a similar recess. All were in a state of most anxious suspense,—the Republicans to know what initiative the Administration at Washington would take, and the Democrats to determine what course they should follow if the President should call for troops to put down the insurrection.

Before we meet again, Mr. Lincoln's proclamation and call for seventy-five thousand militia for three months' service were out, and the great mass of the people of the North, forgetting all party distinctions, answered with an enthusiastic patriotism that swept politicians off their feet. When we met again on Tuesday morning, Judge Key, taking my arm and pacing the floor outside the railing in the Senate chamber, broke out impetuously, "Mr. Cox, the people have gone stark mad!" "I knew they would if a blow was struck against the flag," said I, reminding him of some previous conversations we had had on the subject. He, with most of the politicians of the day, partly by sympathy with the overwhelming current of public opinion, and partly by reaction of their own hearts against the false theories which had encouraged the secessionists, determined to support the war measures of the government, and to make no factious opposition to such state legislation as might be necessary to sustain the federal administration.

The attitude of Mr. Key is only a type of many others, and makers one of the most striking features of the time. On the 8th of January the usual Democratic convention and celebration of the Battle of New Orleans had taken place, and a series of resolutions had been passed, which were drafted, as was understood, by Judge Thurman. In these, professing to speak in the name of "two hundred thousand Democrats of Ohio," the convention had very significantly intimated that this vast organization of men would be found in the way of any attempt to put down secession until the demands of the South in respect to slavery were complied with. A few days afterward I was returning to Columbus from my home in Trumbull County, and meeting upon the railway train with David Tod, then an active Democratic politician, but afterward one of our loyal "war governors," the conversation turned on the action of the convention which had just adjourned. Mr. Tod and I were personal friends and neighbours, and I freely expressed my surprise that the convention should have committed itself to what must be interpreted as a threat of insurrection in the North if the administration should, in opposing secession by force, follow the example of Andrew Jackson, in whose honour they had assembled. He rather vehemently reasserted the substance of the resolution, saying that we Republicans would find the two hundred thousand Ohio Democrats in front of us, if we attempted to cross the Ohio River. My answer was, "We will give up the contest if we cannot carry your two hundred thousand over the heads of your leaders."

The result proved how hollow the party professions had been; or perhaps I should say how superficial was the hold of such party doctrines upon the mass of men in a great political organization. In the excitement of political campaigns they had cheered the extravagant language of party platforms with very little reflection, and the leaders had imagined that the people were really and earnestly indoctrinated into the political creed of Calhoun; but at the first shot from Beauregard's guns in Charleston harbour their latent patriotism sprang into vigorous life, and they crowded to the recruiting stations to enlist for the defence of the national flag and the national Union. It was a popular torrent which no leaders could resist; but many of these should be credited with the same patriotic impulse, and it made them nobly oblivious of party consistency. Stephen A. Douglas passed through Columbus on his way to Washington a few days after the surrender of Sumter, and in response to the calls of a spontaneous gathering of people, spoke to them from his bedroom window in the American House. There had been no thought for any of the common surroundings of a public meeting. There were no torches, no music. A dark crowd of men filled full the dim-lit street, and called for Douglas with an earnestness of tone wholly different from the enthusiasm of common political gatherings. He came half-dressed to his window, and without any light near him, spoke solemnly to the people upon the terrible crisis which had come upon the nation. Men of all parties were there: his own followers to get some light as to their duty; the Breckinridge Democrats ready, most of them, repentantly to follow a Northern leader, now that their recent candidate was in the rebellion; the Republicans eagerly anxious to know whether so potent an influence was to be unreservedly on the side of the country. I remember well the serious solicitude with which I listened to his opening sentences as I leaned against the railing of the State House park, trying in vain to get more than a dim outline of the man as he stood at the unlighted window. His deep sonorous voice rolled down through the darkness from above us,—an earnest, measured voice, the more solemn, the more impressive, because we could not see the speaker, and it came to us literally as "a voice in the night,"—the night of our country's unspeakable trial. There was no uncertainty in his tone: the Union must be preserved and the insurrection must be crushed,—he pledged his hearty support to Mr. Lincoln's administration in doing this. Other questions must stand aside till the national authority should be everywhere recognized. I do not think we greatly cheered him,—it was rather a deep Amen that went up from the crowd. We went home breathing freer in the assurance we now felt that, for a time at least, no organized opposition to the federal government and its policy of coercion would be formidable in the North. We did not look for unanimity. Bitter and narrow men there were whose sympathies were with their country's enemies. Others equally narrow were still in the chains of the secession logic they had learned from the Calhounists; but the broader-minded men found themselves happy in being free from disloyal theories, and threw themselves sincerely and earnestly into the popular movement. There was no more doubt where Douglas or Tod or Key would be found, or any of the great class they represented.

Yet the situation hung upon us like a nightmare. Garfield and I were lodging together at the time, our wives being kept at home by family cares, and when we reached our sitting-room, after an evening session of the Senate, we often found ourselves involuntarily groaning, "Civil war in *our* land!" The shame, the outrage, the folly, seemed too great to believe, and we half hoped to wake from it as from a dream. Among the painful remembrances of those days is the ever-present weight at the heart which never left me till I found relief in the active duties of camp life at the close of the month. I went about my duties (and I am sure most of those I associated with did the same) with the half-choking sense of a grief I dared not think of: like one who is dragging himself to the ordinary labours of life from some terrible and recent bereavement.

We talked of our personal duty, and though both Garfield and myself had young families, we were agreed that our activity in the organization and support of the Republican party made the duty of supporting the government by military service come peculiarly home to us. He was, for the moment, somewhat trammelled by his half-clerical position, but he very soon cut the knot. My own path seemed unmistakably clear. He, more careful for his friend than for himself, urged upon me his doubts whether my physical strength was equal to the strain that would be put upon it. "I," said he, "am big and strong, and if my relations to the church and the college can be broken, I shall have no excuse for not enlisting; but you are slender and will break down." It was true that I looked slender for a man six feet high (though it would hardly be suspected now that it was so), yet I had assured confidence in the elasticity of my constitution; and the result justified me, whilst it also showed how liable to mistake one is in such things. Garfield found that he had a tendency to weakness of the alimentary system which broke him down on every campaign in which he served and led to his retiring from the army much earlier than he had intended. My own health, on the other hand, was strengthened by out-door life and exposure, and I served to the end with growing physical vigour.

When Mr. Lincoln issued his first call for troops, the existing laws made it necessary that these should be fully organized and officered by the several States. Then, the treasury was in no condition to bear the burden of war expenditures, and till Congress could assemble, the President was forced to rely on the States to furnish the means necessary for the equipment and transportation of their own troops. This threw upon the governors and legislatures of the loyal States responsibilities of a kind wholly unprecedented. A long period of profound peace had made every military organization seem almost farcical. A few independent military companies formed the merest shadow of an army; the state militia proper was only a nominal thing. It happened, however, that I held a commission as Brigadier in this state militia, and my intimacy with Governor Dennison led him to call upon me for such assistance as I could render in the first enrolment and organization of the Ohio quota. Arranging to be called to the Senate chamber when my vote might be needed upon important legislation, I gave my time chiefly to such military matters as the governor appointed. Although, as I have said, my military commission had been a nominal thing, and in fact I had never worn a uniform, I had not wholly neglected theoretic preparation for such work.

For some years the possibility of a war of secession had been one of the things which would force itself upon the thoughts of reflecting people, and I had been led to give some careful study to such books of tactics and of strategy as were within easy reach. I had especially been led to read military history with critical care, and had carried away many valuable ideas from this most useful means of military education. I had therefore some notion of the work before us, and could approach its problems with less loss of time, at least, than if I had been wholly ignorant.

My commission as Brigadier-General in the Ohio quota in national service was dated on the 23d of April, though it had been understood for several days that my tender of service in the field would be accepted. Just about the same time Captain George B. McClellan was requested by Governor Dennison to come to Columbus for consultation, and by the governor's request I met him at the railway station and took him to the State House. I think Mr. Larz Anderson (brother of Major Robert Anderson) and Mr. L'Hommedieu of Cincinnati were with him. The intimation had been given me that he would probably be made major-general and commandant of our Ohio contingent, and this, naturally, made me scan him closely. He was rather under the medium height, but muscularly formed, with broad shoulders and a well-poised head, active and graceful in motion. His whole appearance was quiet and modest, but when drawn out he showed no lack of confidence in himself. He was dressed in a plain travelling suit, with a narrow-rimmed soft felt hat. In short, he seemed what he was, a railway superintendent in his business clothes. At the time his name was a good deal associated with that of Beauregard; they were spoken of as young men of similar standing in the Engineer Corps of the Army, and great things were expected of them both because of their scientific knowledge of their profession, though McClellan had been in civil life for some years. His report on the Crimean War was one of the few important memoirs our old army had produced, and was valuable enough to give a just reputation for comprehensive understanding of military organization, and the promise of ability to conduct the operations of an army.

I was present at the interview which the governor had with him. The destitution of the State of everything like military material and equipment was very plainly put, and the magnitude of the task of building up a small army out of nothing was not blinked. The governor spoke of the embarrassment he felt at every step from the lack of practical military experience in his staff, and of his desire to have some one on whom he could properly throw the details of military work. McClellan showed that he fully understood the difficulties there would be before him, and said that no man could wholly master them at once, although he had confidence that if a few weeks' time for preparation were given, he would be able to put the Ohio division into reasonable form for taking the field. The command was then formally tendered and accepted. All of us who were present felt that the selection was one full of promise and hope, and that the governor had done the wisest thing practicable at the time.

The next morning McClellan requested me to accompany him to the State Arsenal, to see what arms and material might be there. We found a few boxes of smooth-bore muskets which had once been issued to militia companies and had been returned rusted and damaged. No belts, cartridge-boxes, or other accoutrements were with them. There were two or three smooth-bore brass fieldpieces, six-pounders, which had been honeycombed by firing salutes, and of which the vents had been worn out, bushed, and worn out again. In a heap in one corner lay a confused pile of mildewed harness, which had probably been once used for artillery horses, but was now not worth carrying away. There had for many years been no money appropriated to buy military material or even to protect the little the State had. The federal government had occasionally distributed some arms which were in the hands of the independent uniformed militia, and the arsenal was simply an empty storehouse. It did not take long to complete our inspection. At the door, as we were leaving the building, McClellan turned, and looking back into its emptiness, remarked, half humorously and half sadly, "A fine stock of munitions on which to begin a great war!" We went back to the State House, where a room in the Secretary of State's department was assigned us, and we sat down to work. The first task was to make out detailed schedules and estimates of what would be needed to equip ten thousand men for the field. This was a unit which could be used by the governor and legislature in estimating the appropriations needed then or subsequently. Intervals in this labour were used in discussing the general situation and plans of campaign. Before the close of the week McClellan drew up a paper embodying his own views, and forwarded it to Lieutenant-General Scott. He read it to me, and my recollection of it is that he suggested two principal lines of movement in the West,—one, to move eastward by the Kanawha valley with a heavy column to co-operate with an army in front of Washington; the other, to march directly southward and to open the valley of the Mississippi. Scott's answer was appreciative and flattering, without distinctly approving his plan; and I have never doubted that the paper prepared the way for his appointment in the regular army which followed at so early a day.

During this week McClellan was invited to take the command of the troops to be raised in Pennsylvania, his native State. Some things beside his natural attachment to Pennsylvania made the proposal an attractive one to him. It was already evident that the army which might be organized near Washington would be peculiarly in the public eye, and would give to its leading officers greater opportunities of prompt recognition and promotion than would be likely to occur in the West. The close association with the government would also be a source of power if he were successful, and the way to a chief command would be more open there than elsewhere. McClellan told me frankly that if the offer had come before he had assumed the Ohio command, he would have accepted it; but he promptly decided that he was honourably bound to serve under the commission he had already received and which, like my own, was dated April 23.

My own first assignment to a military command was during the same week, on the completion of our estimates, when I was for a few days put in charge of Camp Jackson, the depot of recruits which Governor Dennison had established in the northern suburb of Columbus and had named in honour of the first squelcher of secessionism. McClellan soon determined, however, that a separate camp of instruction should be formed for the troops mustered into the United States service, and should be so placed as to be free from the temptations and inconveniences of too close neighbourhood to a large city, whilst it should also be reasonably well placed for speedy defence of the southern frontier of the State. Other camps could be under state control and used only for the organization of regiments which could afterward be sent to the camp of instruction or elsewhere. Railway lines and connections indicated some point in the Little Miami valley as the proper place for such a camp; and Mr. Woodward, the chief engineer of the Little Miami Railroad, being taken into consultation, suggested a spot on the line of that railway about thirteen miles from Cincinnati, where a considerable bend of the Little Miami River encloses wide and level fields, backed on the west by gently rising hills. I was invited to accompany the general in making the inspection of the site, and I think we were accompanied by Captain Rosecrans, an officer who had resigned from the regular army to seek a career as civil engineer, and had lately been in charge of some coal mines in the Kanawha valley. Mr. Woodward was also of the party, and furnished a special train to enable us to stop at as many eligible points as it might be thought desirable to examine. There was no doubt that the point suggested was best adapted for our work, and although the owners of the land made rather hard terms, McClellan was authorized to close a contract for the use of the military camp, which, in honour of the governor, he named Camp Dennison.

But in trying to give a connected idea of the first military organization of the State, I have outrun some incidents of those days which are worth recollection. From the hour the call for troops was published, enlistments began, and recruits were parading the streets continually. At the Capitol the restless impulse to be doing something military seized even upon the members of the legislature, and a large number of them assembled every evening upon the east terrace of the State House to be drilled in marching and facing, by one or two of their own number who had some knowledge of company tactics. Most of the uniformed independent companies in the cities of the State immediately tendered their services, and began to recruit their numbers to the hundred men required for acceptance. There was no time to procure uniform, nor was it desirable; for these independent companies had chosen their own, and would have to change it for that of the United States as soon as this could be furnished. For some days companies could be seen marching and drilling, of which part would be uniformed in some gaudy style, such as is apt to prevail in holiday parades in time of peace, whilst another part would be dressed in the ordinary working garb of citizens of all degrees. The uniformed files would also be armed and accoutred; the others would be without arms or equipments, and as awkward a squad as could well be imagined. The material, however, was magnificent, and soon began to take shape. The fancy uniforms were left at home, and some approximation to a simple and useful costume was made. The recent popular outburst in Italy furnished a useful idea, and the "Garibaldi uniform" of a red flannel shirt with broad falling collar, with blue trousers held by a leathern waist-belt, and a soft felt hat for the head, was extensively copied, and served an excellent purpose. It could be made by the wives and sisters at home, and was all the more acceptable for that. The spring was opening, and a heavy coat would not be much needed, so that with some sort of overcoat and a good blanket in an improvised knapsack, the new company was not badly provided. The warm scarlet colour, reflected from their enthusiastic faces as they stood in line, made a picture that never failed to impress the mustering officers with the splendid character of the men.

The officering of these new troops was a difficult and delicate task, and so far as company officers were concerned, there seemed no better way at the beginning than to let the enlisted men elect their own, as was in fact done. In most cases where entirely new companies were raised, it had been by the enthusiastic efforts of some energetic volunteers who were naturally made the commissioned officers. But not always. There were numerous examples of self-denying patriotism which stayed in the ranks after expending much labour and money in recruiting, modestly refusing the honours, and giving way to some one supposed to have military knowledge or experience. The war in Mexico in 1847 was the latest conflict with a civilized people, and to have served in it was a sure passport to confidence. It had often been a service more in name than in fact; but the young volunteers felt so deeply their own ignorance that they were ready to yield to any pretence of superior knowledge, and generously to trust themselves to any one who would offer to lead them. Hosts of charlatans and incompetents were thus put into responsible places at the beginning, but the sifting work went on fast after the troops were once in the field. The election of field officers, however, ought not to have been allowed. Companies were necessarily regimented together, of which each could have but little personal knowledge of the officers of the others; intrigue and demagogy soon came into play, and almost fatal mistakes were made in selection. After a time the evil worked its own cure, but the ill effects of it were long visible.

The immediate need of troops to protect Washington caused most of the uniformed companies to be united into the first two regiments, which were quickly despatched to the East. It was a curious study to watch the indications of character as the officers commanding companies reported to the governor, and were told that the pressing demand from Washington made it necessary to organize a regiment or two and forward them at once, without waiting to arm or equip the recruits. Some promptly recognized the necessity and took the undesirable features as part of the duty they had assumed. Others were querulous, wishing some one else to stand first in the breach, leaving them time for drill, equipment, and preparation. One figure impressed itself very strongly on my memory. A sturdy form, a head with more than ordinary marks of intelligence, but a bearing with more of swagger than of self-poised courage, yet evidently a man of some importance in his own community, stood before the seat of the governor, the bright lights of the chandelier over the table lighting strongly both their figures. The officer was wrapped in a heavy blanket or carriage lap-robe, spotted like a leopard skin, which gave him a brigandish air. He was disposed to protest. "If my men were hellions," said he, with strong emphasis on the word (a new one to me), "I wouldn't mind; but to send off the best young fellows of the county in such a way looks like murder." The governor, sitting with pale, delicate features, but resolute air, answered that the way to Washington was not supposed to be dangerous, and the men could be armed and equipped, he was assured, as soon as they reached there. It would be done at Harrisburg, if possible, and certainly if any hostility should be shown in Maryland. The President wanted the regiments at once, and Ohio's volunteers were quite as ready to go as any. He had no choice, therefore, but to order them off. The order was obeyed; but the obedience was with bad grace, and I felt misgivings as to the officer's fitness to command,—misgivings which about a year afterward were vividly recalled with the scene I have described.

No sooner were these regiments off than companies began to stream in from all parts of the State. On their first arrival they were quartered wherever shelter could be had, as there were no tents or sheds to make a camp for them. Going to my evening work at the State House, as I crossed the rotunda, I saw a company marching in by the south door, and another disposing itself for the night upon the marble pavement near the east entrance; as I passed on to the north hall, I saw another, that had come a little earlier, holding a prayer-meeting, the stone arches echoing with the excited supplications of some one who was borne out of himself by the terrible pressure of events around him, whilst, mingling with his pathetic, beseeching tones as he prayed for his country, came the shrill notes of the fife, and the thundering din of the inevitable bass drum from the company marching in on the other side. In the Senate chamber a company was quartered, and the senators were there supplying them with paper and pens, with which the boys were writing their farewells to mothers and sweethearts whom they hardly dared hope they should see again. A similar scene was going on in the Representatives' hall, another in the Supreme Court room. In the executive office sat the governor, the unwonted noises, when the door was opened, breaking in on the quiet business-like air of the room,—he meanwhile dictating despatches, indicating answers to others, receiving committees of citizens, giving directions to officers of companies and regiments, accommodating himself to the wilful democracy of our institutions which insists upon seeing the man in chief command and will not take its answer from a subordinate, until in the small hours of the night the noises were hushed, and after a brief hour of effective, undisturbed work upon the matters of chief importance, he could leave the glare of his gas-lighted office, and seek a few hours' rest, only to renew the same wearing labours on the morrow.

On the streets the excitement was of a rougher if not more intense character. A minority of unthinking partisans could not understand the strength and sweep of the great popular movement, and would sometimes venture to speak out their sympathy with the rebellion or their sneers at some party friend who had enlisted. In the boiling temper of the time the quick answer was a blow; and it was one of the common incidents of the day for those who came into the State House to tell of a knockdown that had occurred here or there, when this popular punishment had been administered to some indiscreet "rebel sympathizer."

Various duties brought young army officers of the regular service to the state capital, and others sought a brief leave of absence to come and offer their services to the governor of their native State. General Scott, too much bound up in his experience of the Mexican War, and not foreseeing the totally different proportions which this must assume, planted himself firmly on the theory that the regular army must be the principal reliance for severe work, and that the volunteers could only be auxiliaries around this solid nucleus which would show them the way to perform their duty and take the brunt of every encounter. The young regulars who asked leave to accept commissions in state regiments were therefore refused, and were ordered to their own subaltern positions and posts. There can be no doubt that the true policy would have been to encourage the whole of this younger class to enter at once the volunteer service. They would have been the field officers of the new regiments, and would have impressed discipline and system upon the organization from the beginning. The Confederacy really profited by having no regular army. They gave to the officers who left our service, it is true, commissions in their so-called "provisional army," to encourage them in the assurance that they would have permanent military positions if the war should end in the independence of the South; but this was only a nominal organization, and their real army was made up (as ours turned out practically to be) from the regiments of state volunteers. Less than a year afterward we changed our policy, but it was then too late to induce many of the regular officers to take regimental positions in the volunteer troops. I hesitate to declare that this did not turn out for the best; for although the organization of our army would have been more rapidly perfected, there are other considerations which have much weight. The army would not have been the popular thing it was, its close identification with the people's movement would have been weakened, and it perhaps would not so readily have melted again into the mass of the nation at the close of the war.

Among the first of the young regular officers who came to Columbus was Alexander McCook. He was ordered there as inspection and mustering officer, and one of my earliest duties was to accompany him to Camp Jackson to inspect the cooked rations which the contractors were furnishing the new troops. I warmed to his earnest, breezy way, and his business-like activity in performing his duty. As a makeshift, before camp equipage and cooking utensils could be issued to the troops, the contractors placed long trestle tables under an improvised shed, and the soldiers came to these and ate, as at a country picnic. It was not a bad arrangement to bridge over the interval between home life and regular soldiers' fare, and the outcry about it at the time was senseless, as all of us know who saw real service afterward. McCook bustled along from table to table, sticking a long skewer into a boiled ham, smelling of it to see if the interior of the meat was tainted; breaking open a loaf of bread and smelling of it to see if it was sour; examining the coffee before it was put into the kettles, and after it was made; passing his judgment on each, in prompt, peremptory manner as we went on. The food was, in the main, excellent, though, as a way of supporting an army, it was quite too costly to last long.

While mustering in the recruits, McCook was elected colonel of the First Regiment Ohio Volunteers, which had, I believe, already gone to Washington. He was eager to accept, and telegraphed to Washington for permission. Adjutant-General Thomas replied that it was not the policy of the War Department to permit it. McCook cut the knot in gallant style. He immediately tendered his resignation in the regular army, taking care to say that he did so, not to avoid his country's service or to aid her enemies, but because he believed he could serve her much more effectively by drilling and leading a regiment of Union volunteers. He notified the governor of his acceptance of the colonelcy, and his *coup-de-main* was a success; for the department did not like to accept a resignation under such circumstances, and he had the exceptional luck to keep his regular commission and gain prestige as well, by his bold energy in the matter.

Orlando Poe came about the same time, for all this was occurring in the last ten days of April. He was a lieutenant of topographical engineers, and was stationed with General (then Captain) Meade at Detroit, doing duty upon the coast survey of the lakes. He was in person the model for a young athlete, tall, dark, and strong, with frank, open countenance, looking fit to repeat his ancestor Adam Poe's adventurous conflicts with the Indians as told in the frontier traditions of Ohio. He too was eager for service; but the same rule was applied to him, and the argument that the engineers would be especially necessary to the army organization kept him for a time from insisting upon taking volunteer service, as McCook had done. He was indefatigable in his labours, assisting the governor in organizing the regiments, smoothing the difficulties constantly arising from lack of familiarity with the details of the administrative service of the army, and giving wise advice to the volunteer officers who made his acquaintance. I asked him, one day, in my pursuit of practical ideas from all who I thought could help me, what he would advise as the most useful means of becoming familiar with my duties. Study the Army Regulations, said he, as if it were your Bible! There was a world of wisdom in this: much more than I appreciated at the time, though it set me earnestly to work in a right direction. An officer in a responsible command, who had already a fair knowledge of tactics, might trust his common sense for guidance in an action on the field; but the administrative duties of the army as a machine must be thoroughly learned, if he would hope to make the management of its complicated organization an easy thing to him.

Major Sidney Burbank came to take McCook's place as mustering officer: a grave, earnest man, of more age and more varied experience than the men I have named. Captain John Pope also visited the governor for consultation, and possibly others came also, though I saw them only in passing, and did not then get far in making their acquaintance.

Chapter 2
Camp Dennison

On the 29th of April I was ordered by McClellan to proceed next morning to Camp Dennison, with the Eleventh and half of the Third Ohio regiments. The day was a fair one, and when about noon our railway train reached the camping ground, it seemed an excellent place for our work. The drawback was that very little of the land was in meadow or pasture, part being in wheat and part in Indian corn, which was just coming up. Captain Rosecrans met us, as McClellan's engineer (later the well-known general), coming from Cincinnati with a train-load of lumber. He had with him his compass and chain, and by the help of a small detail of men soon laid off the ground for the two regimental camps, and the general lines of the whole encampment for a dozen regiments. It was McClellan's purpose to put in two brigades on the west side of the railway, and one on the east. My own brigade camp was assigned to the west side, and nearest to Cincinnati. The men of the two regiments shouldered their pine boards and carried them up to the line of the company streets, which were close to the hills skirting the valley, and which opened into the parade and drill ground along the railway.

A general plan was given to the company officers by which the huts should be made uniform in size and shape. The huts of each company faced each other, three or four on each side, making the street between, in which the company assembled before marching to its place on the regimental colour line. At the head of each street were the quarters of the company officers, and those of the "field and staff" still further in rear. The Regulations were followed in this plan as closely as the style of barracks and nature of the ground would permit. Vigorous work housed all the men before night, and it was well that it did so, for the weather changed in the evening, a cold rain came on, and the next morning was a chill and dreary one. My own headquarters were in a little brick schoolhouse of one story, which stood (and I think still stands) on the east side of the track close to the railway. My improvised camp equipage consisted of a common trestle cot and a pair of blankets, and I made my bed in the open space in front of the teacher's desk or pulpit. My only staff officer was an aide-de-camp, Captain Bascom (afterward of the regular army), who had graduated at an Eastern military school, and proved himself a faithful and efficient assistant. He slept on the floor in one of the little aisles between the pupils' seats. One lesson learned that night remained permanently fixed in my memory, and I had no need of a repetition of it. I found that, having no mattress on my cot, the cold was much more annoying below than above me, and that if one can't keep the under side warm, it doesn't matter how many blankets he may have atop. I procured later an army cot with low legs, the whole of which could be taken apart and packed in a very small parcel, and with this I carried a small quilted mattress of cotton batting. It would have been warmer to have made my bed on the ground with a heap of straw or leaves under me; but as my tent had to be used for office work whenever a tent could be pitched, I preferred the neater and more orderly interior which this arrangement permitted. This, however, is anticipating. The comfortless night passed without much refreshing sleep, the strange situation doing perhaps as much as the limbs aching from cold to keep me awake. The storm beat through broken window-panes, and the gale howled about us, but day at last began to break, and with its dawning light came our first reveille in camp. I shall never forget the peculiar plaintive sound of the fifes as they shrilled out on the damp air. The melody was destined to become very familiar, but to this day I can't help wondering how it happened that so melancholy a strain was chosen for the waking tune of the soldiers' camp. The bugle reveille is quite different; it is even cheery and inspiriting; but the regulation music for the drums and fifes is better fitted to waken longings for home and all the sadder emotions than to stir the host from sleep to the active duties of the day. I lay for a while listening to it, finding its notes suggesting many things and becoming a thread to string my reveries upon, as I thought of the past which was separated from me by a great gulf, the present with its serious duties, and the future likely to come to a sudden end in the shock of battle. We roused ourselves; a dash of cold water put an end to dreaming; we ate a breakfast from a box of cooked provisions we had brought with us, and resumed the duty of organizing and instructing the camp. The depression which had weighed upon me since the news of the opening guns at Sumter passed away, never to return. The consciousness of having important work to do, and the absorption in the work itself, proved the best of all mental tonics. The Rubicon was crossed, and from this time out, vigorous bodily action, our wild outdoor life, and the strenuous use of all the faculties, mental and physical, in meeting the daily exigencies, made up an existence which, in spite of all its hardships and all its discouragements, still seems a most exhilarating one as I look back on it across a long vista of years.

The first of May proved, instead, a true April day, of the most fickle and changeable type. Gusts of rain and wind alternated with flashes of bright sunshine. The second battalion of the Third Regiment arrived, and the work of completing the cantonments went on. The huts which were half finished yesterday were now put in good order, and in building the new ones the men profited by the experience of their comrades. We were however suddenly thrown into one of those small tempests which it is so easy to get up in a new camp, and which for the moment always seems to have an importance out of all proportion to its real consequence. Captain Rosecrans, as engineer, was superintending the work of building, and finding that the companies were putting floors and bunks in their huts, he peremptorily ordered that these should be taken out, insisting that the huts were only intended to take the place of tents and give such shelter as tents could give. The company and regimental officers loudly protested, and the men were swelling with indignation and wrath. Soon both parties were before me; Rosecrans hot and impetuous, holding a high tone, and making use of General McClellan's name in demanding, as an officer of his staff, that the floors should be torn out, and the officers of the regiments held responsible for obedience to the order that no more should be made. He fairly bubbled with anger at the presumption of those who questioned his authority. As soon as a little quiet could be got, I asked Rosecrans if he had specific orders from the general that the huts should have no floors. No, he had not, but his staff position as engineer gave him sufficient control of the subject. I said I would examine the matter and submit it to General McClellan, and meanwhile the floors already built might remain, though no new ones should be made till the question was decided. I reported to the general that, in my judgment, the huts should have floors and bunks, because the ground was wet when they were built,—they could not be struck like tents to dry and air the earth, and they were meant to be permanent quarters for the rendezvous of troops for an indefinite time. The decision of McClellan was in accordance with the report. Rosecrans acquiesced, and indeed seemed rather to like me the better on finding that I was not carried away by the assumption of indefinite power by a staff officer.

This little flurry over, the quarters were soon got in as comfortable shape as rough lumber could make them, and the work of drill and instruction was systematized. The men were not yet armed, so there was no temptation to begin too soon with the manual of the musket, and they were kept industriously employed in marching in single line, by file, in changing direction, in forming columns of fours from double line, etc., before their guns were put in their hands. Each regiment was treated as a separate camp, with its own chain of sentinels, and the officers of the guard were constantly busy teaching guard and picket duty theoretically to the reliefs off duty, and inspecting the sentinels on post. Schools were established in each regiment for field and staff and for the company officers, and Hardee's Tactics was in the hands of everybody who could procure a copy. It was one of our great inconveniences that the supply of the authorized Tactics was soon exhausted, and it was difficult to get the means of instruction in the company schools. An abridgment was made and published in a very few days by Thomas Worthington, a graduate of West Point in one of the earliest classes,—of 1827, I think,—a son of one of the first governors of Ohio. This eccentric officer had served in the regular army and in the Mexican War, and was full of ideas, but was of so irascible and impetuous a temper that he was always in collision with the powers that be, and spoiled his own usefulness. He was employed to furnish water to the camp by contract, and whilst he ruined himself in his efforts to do it well, he was in perpetual conflict with the troops, who capsized his carts, emptied his barrels, and made life a burden to him. The quarrel was based on his taking the water from the river just opposite the camp, though there was a slaughter-house some distance above. Worthington argued that the distance was such that the running water purified itself; but the men wouldn't listen to his science, vigorously enforced as it was by idiomatic expletives, and there was no safety for his water-carts till he yielded. He then made a reservoir on one of the hills, filled it by a steam-pump, and carried the water by pipes to the regimental camps at an expense beyond his means, and which, as it was claimed that the scheme was unauthorized, was never half paid for. His subsequent career as colonel of a regiment was no more happy, and talents that seemed fit for highest responsibilities were wasted in chafing against circumstances which made him and fate seem to be perpetually playing at cross purposes.

A very different character was Joshua W. Sill, who was sent to us as ordnance officer. He too had been a regular army officer, but of the younger class. Rather small and delicate in person, gentle and refined in manner, he had about him little that answered to the popular notion of a soldier. He had resigned from the army some years before, and was a professor in an important educational institution in Brooklyn, N.Y., when at the first act of hostility he offered his services to the governor of Ohio, his native State. After our day's work, we walked together along the railway, discussing the political and military situation, and especially the means of making most quickly an army out of the splendid but untutored material that was collecting about us. Under his modest and scholarly exterior I quickly discerned a fine temper in the metal, that made his after career no enigma to me, and his heroic death at the head of his division in the thickest of the strife at Stone's River no surprise.

The two regiments which began the encampment were quickly followed by others, and the arriving regiments sometimes had their first taste of camp life under circumstances well calculated to dampen their ardour. The Fourth Ohio, under Colonel Lorin Andrews, President of Kenyon College, came just before a thunderstorm one evening, and the bivouac that night was as rough a one as his men were likely to experience for many a day. They made shelter by placing boards from the fence tops to the ground, but the fields were level and soon became a mire, so that they were a queer-looking lot when they crawled out next morning. The sun was then shining bright, however, and they had better cover for their heads by the next night. The Seventh Ohio, which was recruited in Cleveland and on the Western Reserve, sent a party in advance to build some of their huts, and though they too came in a rain-storm, they were less uncomfortable than some of the others. Three brigades were organized from the regiments of the Ohio contingent, exclusive of the two which had been hurried to Washington. The brigadiers, beside myself, were Generals Joshua H. Bates and Newton Schleich. General Bates, who was the senior, was a graduate of West Point, who had served some years in the regular army, but had resigned and adopted the profession of the law. He lived at Cincinnati, and organized his brigade in that city. They marched to Camp Dennison on the 20th of May, when, by virtue of his seniority, General Bates assumed command of the camp in McClellan's absence. His brigade consisted of the Fifth, Sixth, Ninth, and Tenth regiments, and encamped on the east side of the railroad in the bend of the river. General Schleich was a Democratic senator, who had been in the state militia, and was also one of the drill-masters of the legislative squad which had drilled upon the Capitol terrace. His brigade included the Third, Twelfth, and Thirteenth regiments, and, with mine, occupied the fields on the west side of the railroad close to the slopes of the hills. My own brigade was made up of the Fourth, Seventh, Eighth, and Eleventh regiments, and our position was the southernmost in the general camp. McClellan had intended to make his own headquarters in the camp; but the convenience of attending to official business in Cincinnati kept him in the city. His purpose was to make the brigade organizations permanent, and to take them as a division to the field when they were a little prepared for the work. Like many other good plans, it failed to be carried out. I was the only one of the brigadiers who remained in the service after the first enlistment for ninety days, and it was my fate to take the field with new regiments, only one of which had been in my brigade in camp. Schleich did not show adaptation to field work, and though taken into West Virginia with McClellan in June, he was relieved of active service in a few weeks. He afterward sought and obtained the colonelcy of the Sixty-first Ohio; but his service with it did not prove a success, and he resigned in September, 1862, under charges. General Bates had some reason to expect an assignment to staff duty with McClellan, and therefore declined a colonelcy in the line at the end of the three months' service. He was disappointed in this expectation after waiting some time for it, and returned to civil life with the regrets of his comrades. There were some disappointments, also, in the choice of regimental officers who were elected in the regiments first organized, but were afterward appointed by the governor. The companies were organized and assigned to regiments before they came to camp, but the regimental elections were held after the companies were assembled. Garfield was a candidate for the colonelcy of the Seventh Regiment, but as he was still engaged in important public duties and was not connected with any company, he was at a disadvantage in the sort of competition which was then rife. He was defeated,—a greater disappointment to me than to him, for I had hoped that our close friendship would be made still closer by comradeship in the field. In a few weeks he was made colonel of the Forty-second Ohio, in the second levy.

Up to the time that General Bates relieved me of the command of the camp, and indeed for two or three days longer, the little schoolhouse was my quarters as well as telegraph and express office. We had cleared out most of the desks and benches, but were still crowded together, day and night, in a way which was anything but comfortable or desirable. Sheds for quartermaster's and subsistence stores were of first necessity, and the building of a hut for myself and staff had to be postponed till these were up. On the arrival of General Bates with two or three staff officers, the necessity for more room could not be longer ignored, and my own hut was built on the slope of the hillside behind my brigade, close under the wooded ridge, and here for the next six weeks was my home. The morning brought its hour of business correspondence relating to the command; then came the drill, when the parade ground was full of marching companies and squads. Officers' drill followed, with sword exercise and pistol practice. The day closed with the inspection of the regiments in turn at dress parade, and the evening was allotted to schools of theoretic tactics, outpost duty, and the like. Besides their copies of the regulation tactics, officers supplied themselves with such manuals as Mahan's books on Field Fortifications and on Outpost Duty. I adopted at the beginning a rule to have some military work in course of reading, and kept it up even in the field, sending home one volume and getting another by mail. In this way I gradually went through all the leading books I could find both in English and in French, including the whole of Jomini's works, his histories as well as his *Napoleon* and his *Grandes Opérations Militaires*. I know of no intellectual stimulus so valuable to the soldier as the reading of military history narrated by an acknowledged master in the art of war. To see what others have done in important junctures, and to have both their merits and their mistakes analyzed by a competent critic, rouses one's mind to grapple with the problem before it, and begets a generous determination to try to rival in one's own sphere of action the brilliant deeds of soldiers who have made a name in other times. Then the example of the vigorous way in which history will at last deal with those who fail when the pinch comes, tends to keep a man up to his work and to make him avoid the rock on which so many have split, the disposition to take refuge in doing nothing when he finds it difficult to decide what should be done.

The first fortnight in camp was the hardest for the troops. The ploughed fields became deep with mud, which nothing could remove but the good weather which should allow them to pack hard under the continued tramp of thousands of men. The organization of the camp kitchens had to be learned by the hardest also, and the men in each company who had some aptitude for cooking had to be found by a slow process of natural selection, during which many an unpalatable meal had to be eaten. A disagreeable bit of information came to us in the proof that more than half the men had never had the contagious diseases of infancy. The measles broke out, and we had to organize a camp hospital at once. A large barn near by was taken for this purpose, and the surgeons had their hands full of cases which, however trivial they might seem at home, were here aggravated into dangerous illness by the unwonted surroundings and the impossibility of securing the needed protection from exposure. As soon as the increase of sickness in the camp was known in Cincinnati, the good women of that city took promptly in hand the task of providing nurses for the sick, and proper diet and delicacies for hospital uses. The Sisters of Charity, under the lead of Sister Anthony, a noble woman, came out in force, and their black and white robes harmonized picturesquely with the military surroundings, as they flitted about under the rough timber framing of the old barn, carrying comfort and hope from one rude couch to another. As to supplies, hardly a man in a regiment knew how to make out a requisition for rations or for clothing, and easy as it is to rail at "red tape," the necessity of keeping a check upon embezzlement and wastefulness justified the staff bureaus at Washington in insisting upon regular vouchers to support the quartermaster's and commissary's accounts. But here, too, men were gradually found who had special talent for the work.

The infallible newspapers had no lack of material for criticism. There were plenty of real blunders to invite it, but the severest blame was quite as likely to be visited upon men and things which did not deserve it. The governor was violently attacked for things which he had no responsibility for, or others in which he had done all that forethought and intelligence could do. When everybody had to learn a new business, it would have been miraculous if grave errors had not frequently occurred. Looking back at it, the wonder is that the blunders and mishaps had not been tenfold more numerous than they were. By the middle of May the confusion had given place to reasonable system, but we were now obliged to meet the embarrassments of reorganization for three years, under the President's second call for troops. We had more than ten thousand men who had begun to know something of their duties, and it was worth a serious effort to transfer them into the permanent service; but no one who did not go through the ordeal can imagine how trying it was. In every company some discontented spirits wanted to go home, shrinking from the perils to which they had committed themselves in a moment of enthusiasm. For a few to go back, however, would be a disgrace; and every dissatisfied man, to avoid the odium of going alone, became a mischief-maker, seeking to prevent the whole company from re-enlisting. The recruiting of a majority was naturally made the condition of allowing the company organization to be preserved, and a similar rule applied to the regiment. The growing discipline was relaxed or lost in the solicitations, the electioneering, the speech-making, and the other common arts of persuasion. After a majority had re-enlisted and an organization was secure, it would have been better to have discharged the remaining three months' men and to have sent them home at once; but authority for this could not be got, for the civil officers could not see, and did not know what a nuisance these men were. Dissatisfied with themselves for not going with their comrades, they became sulky, disobedient, complaining, trying to make the others as unhappy as themselves by arguing that faith was not kept with them, and doing all the mischief it was possible to do.

In spite of all these discouragements, however, the daily drills and instruction went on with some approach to regularity, and our raw volunteers began to look more like soldiers. Captain Gordon Granger of the regular army came to muster the reenlisted regiments into the three years' service, and as he stood at the right of the Fourth Ohio, looking down the line of a thousand stalwart men, all in their Garibaldi shirts (for we had not yet received our uniforms), he turned to me and exclaimed: "My God! that such men should be food for powder!" It certainly was a display of manliness and intelligence such as had hardly ever been seen in the ranks of an army. There were in camp at that time three if not four companies, in different regiments, that were wholly made up of undergraduates of colleges who had enlisted together, their officers being their tutors and professors; and where there was not so striking evidence as this of the enlistment of the best of our youth, every company could still show that it was largely recruited from the best-nurtured and most promising young men of the community.

Granger had been in the Southwest when the secession movement began, had seen the formation of military companies everywhere, and the incessant drilling which had been going on all winter, whilst we, in a strange condition of political paralysis, had been doing nothing. His information was eagerly sought by us all, and he lost no opportunity of impressing upon us the fact that the South was nearly six months ahead of us in organization and preparation. He did not conceal his belief that we were likely to find the war a much longer and more serious piece of business than was commonly expected, and that unless we pushed hard our drilling and instruction we should find ourselves at a disadvantage in our earlier encounters. What he said had a good effect in making officers and men take more willingly to the laborious routine of the parade ground and the regimental school; for such opinions as his soon ran through the camp, and they were commented upon by the enlisted men quite as earnestly as among the officers. Still, hope kept the upper hand, and if the question had been put to vote, I believe that three-fourths of us still cherished the belief that a single campaign would end the war.

In the organization of my own brigade I had the assistance of Captain McElroy, a young man who had nearly completed the course at West Point, and who was subsequently made major of the Twentieth Ohio. He was sent to the camp by the governor as a drill officer, and I assigned him to staff duty. For commissary, I detailed Lieutenant Gibbs, who accompanied one of the regiments from Cincinnati, and who had seen a good deal of service as clerk in one of the staff departments of the regular army. I had also for a time the services of one of the picturesque adventurers who turn up in such crises. In the Seventh Ohio was a company recruited in Cleveland, of which the nucleus was an organization of Zouaves, existing for some time before the war. It was made up of young men who had been stimulated by the popularity of Ellsworth's Zouaves in Chicago to form a similar body. They had had as their drill master a Frenchman named De Villiers. His profession was that of a teacher of fencing; but he had been an officer in Ellsworth's company, and was familiar with fancy manoeuvres for street parade, and with a special skirmish drill and bayonet exercise. Small, swarthy, with angular features, and a brusque, military manner, in a showy uniform and jaunty *képi* of scarlet cloth, covered with gold lace, he created quite a sensation among us. His assumption of knowledge and experience was accepted as true. He claimed to have been a surgeon in the French army in Algiers, though we afterward learned to doubt if his rank had been higher than that of a barber-surgeon of a cavalry troop. From the testimonials he brought with him, I thought I was doing a good thing in making him my brigade-major, as the officer was then called whom we afterward knew as inspector-general. He certainly was a most indefatigable fellow, and went at his work with an enthusiasm that made him very useful for a time. It was worth something to see a man who worked with a kind of dash,—with a prompt, staccato movement that infused spirit and energy into all around him. He would drill all day, and then spend half the night trying to catch sentinels and officers of the guard at fault in their duty. My first impression was that I had got hold of a most valuable man, and others were so much of the same mind that in the reorganization of regiments he was successively elected major of the Eighth, and then colonel of the Eleventh. We shall see more of him as we go on; but it turned out that his sharp discipline was not steady or just; his knowledge was only skin-deep, and he had neither the education nor the character for so responsible a situation as he was placed in. He nearly plagued the life out of the officers of his regiment before they got rid of him, and was a most brilliant example of the way we were imposed upon by military charlatans at the beginning. He was, however, good proof also of the speed with which real service weeds out the undesirable material which seemed so splendid in the days of common inexperience and at a distance from danger. We had visits from clerical adventurers, too, for the "pay and emoluments of a captain of cavalry" which the law gave to a chaplain induced some to seek the office who were not the best representatives of their profession. One young man who had spent a morning soliciting the appointment in one of the regiments, came to me in a shamefaced sort of way before leaving camp and said, "General, before I decide this matter, I wish you would tell me just what are the pay and emoluments of a *Captain of Calvary!*" Though most of our men were native Ohioans, General Bates's brigade had in it two regiments made up of quite contrasted nationalities. The Ninth Ohio was recruited from the Germans of Cincinnati, and was commanded by Colonel "Bob" McCook. In camp, the drilling of the regiment fell almost completely into the hands of the adjutant, Lieutenant Willich (afterward a general of division), and McCook, who humorously exaggerated his own lack of military knowledge, used to say that he was only "clerk for a thousand Dutchmen," so completely did the care of equipping and providing for his regiment engross his time and labour. The Tenth was an Irish regiment, and its men used to be proud of calling themselves the "Bloody Tinth." The brilliant Lytle was its commander, and his control over them, even in the beginning of their service and near the city of their home, showed that they had fallen into competent hands. It happened, of course, that the guard-house pretty frequently contained representatives of the Tenth who, on the short furloughs that were allowed them, took a parting glass too much with their friends in the city, and came to camp boisterously drunk. But the men of the regiment got it into their heads that the Thirteenth, which lay just opposite them across the railroad, took a malicious pleasure in filling the guard-house with the Irishmen. Some threats had been made that they would go over and "clean out" the Thirteenth, and one fine evening these came to a head. I suddenly got orders from General Bates to form my brigade, and march them at once between the Tenth and Thirteenth to prevent a collision which seemed imminent. My brigade was selected because it was the one to which neither of the angry regiments belonged, the others being ordered into their quarters. My little Frenchman, De Villiers, covered himself with glory. His horse flew, under the spur, to the regimental headquarters, the long roll was beaten as if the drummers realized the full importance of the first opportunity to sound that warlike signal, and the brigade-major's somewhat theatrical energy was so contagious that many of the companies were assembled and ready to file out of the company streets before the order reached them. We marched by the moonlight into the space between the belligerent regiments; but Lytle had already got his own men under control, and the less mercurial Thirteenth were not disposed to be aggressive, so that we were soon dismissed with a compliment for our promptness. I ordered the colonels to march the regiments back to the camps separately, and with my staff rode through that of the Thirteenth, to see how matters were there. All was quiet, the men being in their quarters; so, turning, I passed along near the railway, in rear of the quartermaster's sheds. In the shadow of the buildings I had nearly ridden over some one on foot, when he addressed me, and I recognized an officer of high rank in that brigade. He was in great agitation, and exclaimed, "Oh, General, what a horrible thing that brothers should be killing each other!" I assured him the danger of that was all over, and rode on, wondering a little at his presence in that place under the circumstances.

The six weeks of our stay in Camp Dennison seem like months in the retrospect, so full were they crowded with new experiences. The change came in an unexpected way. The initiative taken by the Confederates in West Virginia had to be met by prompt action, and McClellan was forced to drop his own plans to meet the emergency. The organization and equipment of the regiments for the three years' service were still incomplete, and the brigades were broken up, to take across the Ohio the regiments best prepared to go. One by one my regiments were ordered away, till finally, when on the 3d of July I received orders to proceed to the Kanawha valley, I had but one of the four regiments to which I had been trying to give something of unity and brigade feeling, and that regiment (the Eleventh Ohio) was still incomplete. General Bates fared even worse; for he saw all his regiments ordered away, whilst he was left to organize new ones from freshly recruited companies that were sent to the camp. This was discouraging to a brigade commander, for even with veteran troops mutual acquaintance between the officer and his command is a necessary condition of confidence and a most important element of strength. My own assignment to the Great Kanawha district was one I had every reason to be content with, except that for several months I felt the disadvantage I suffered from assuming command of troops which I had never seen till we met in the field.

The period of organization, brief as it was, had been valuable to the regiments, and it had been of the utmost importance to secure the re-enlistment of those which had received some instruction. It had been, in the condition of the statute law, from necessity and not from choice that the Administration had called out the state militia for ninety days. The new term of enrolment was for "three years or the war," and the forces were now designated as United States Volunteers. It would have been well if the period of apprenticeship could have been prolonged; but events would not wait. All recognized the necessity, and thankful as we should have been for a longer preparation and more thorough instruction, we were eager to be ordered away.

McClellan had been made a major-general in the regular army, and a department had been placed under his command which included the States of Ohio, Indiana, and Illinois, to which was added a little later West Virginia north of the Great Kanawha. Rosecrans was also appointed a brigadier-general in the regulars, and there was much debate at the time whether the Administration had intended this. Many insisted that he was nominated for the volunteer service, and that the regular appointment was a clerical mistake in the bureaus at Washington. There was no solid foundation for this gossip. A considerable increase of the regular army was authorized by law, and corresponding appointments were made, from major-general downward. It was at this time that Sherman was made colonel of one of the new regiments of regulars. It would perhaps have been wiser to treat the regular commissions as prizes to be won only by conspicuous and successful service in the field, as was done later; but this policy was not then adopted, and the newly created offices were filled in all grades. They were, of course, given to men from whom great services could reasonably be expected; but when none had been tested in the great operations of war, every appointment was at the risk that the officer might not show the special talent for command which makes a general. It was something of a lottery, at best; but the system would have been improved if a method of retiring inefficient officers had been adopted at once. The ostensible reason for the different organization of volunteers and regulars was that the former, as a temporary force to meet an exigency, might be wholly disbanded when the war should end, without affecting the permanent army, which was measured in size by the needs of the country in its normal condition.

CHAPTER 3

McClellan in West Virginia

The reasons which made it important to occupy West Virginia were twofold, political and military. The people were strongly attached to the Union, and had generally voted against the Ordinance of Secession which by the action of the Richmond Convention had been submitted to a popular vote on May 23d. Comparatively few slaves were owned by them, and their interests bound them more to Ohio and Pennsylvania than to eastern Virginia. Under the influence of Mr. Lincoln's administration, strongly backed and chiefly represented by Governor Dennison of Ohio, a movement was on foot to organize a loyal Virginia government, repudiating that of Governor Letcher and the state convention as self-destroyed by the act of secession. Governor Dennison, in close correspondence with the leading loyalists, had been urging McClellan to cross the Ohio to protect and encourage the loyal men, when on the 26th of May news came that the Secessionists had taken the initiative, and that some bridges had been burned on the Baltimore and Ohio Railroad a little west of Grafton, the crossing of the Monongahela River where the two western branches of the road unite as they come from Wheeling and Parkersburg. The great line of communication between Washington and the West had thus been cut, and action on our part was necessary.

Governor Dennison had anticipated the need of more troops than the thirteen regiments which had been organized as Ohio's quota under the President's first call, and had enrolled nine other regiments, numbering them consecutively with the others. These last he had put in camps near the Ohio River, where at a moment's notice they could occupy Wheeling, Parkersburg, and the mouth of the Great Kanawha. Two Union regiments were also organizing in West Virginia itself, of which the first was commanded by Colonel B. F. Kelley of Wheeling. The left bank of the Ohio was in McClellan's department, and on the 24th General Scott, having heard that two Virginia companies had occupied Grafton, telegraphed the fact to McClellan, directing him to act promptly in counteracting the effect of this movement.

On the 27th Colonel Kelley was sent by rail from Wheeling to drive off the enemy, who withdrew at his approach, and the bridges were quickly rebuilt. Several of the Ohio regiments were ordered across the river at the same time, and an Indiana brigade under General Thomas A. Morris of that State was hurried forward from Indianapolis. As the Ohio troops at Camp Dennison which had been mustered into national service were in process of reorganizing for the three years' term, McClellan preferred not to move them till this was completed. He also adhered to his plan of making his own principal movement in the Great Kanawha valley, and desired to use there the Ohio division at our camp. The Ohio regiments first sent into West Virginia were not mustered in, and were known as State troops. General Morris reached Grafton on the 1st of June, and was entrusted with the command of all the troops in West Virginia. He found that Colonel Kelley had already planned an expedition against the enemy, who had retired southward to Philippi, about fifteen miles in a straight line, but some twenty-five by the crooked country roads. Morris approved the plan, but enlarged it by sending another column, under Colonel E. Dumont of the Seventh Indiana, to co-operate with Kelley. Both columns were directed to make a night march, starting from points on the railroad about twelve miles apart and converging on Philippi, which they were to attack at daybreak on June 3d. Each column consisted of about fifteen hundred men, and Dumont had also two smooth six-pounder cannon. The Confederate force was commanded by Colonel G. A. Porterfield, and was something less than a thousand strong, one-fourth cavalry.

The night was dark and stormy, and Porterfield's raw troops had not learned picket duty. The concerted movement against them was more successful than such marches commonly are, and Porterfield's first notice of danger was the opening of the artillery upon his sleeping troops. It had been expected that the two columns would enclose the enemy's camp and capture the whole; but, though in disorderly rout, Porterfield succeeded, by personal coolness and courage, in getting them off with but few casualties and the loss of a few arms. The camp equipage and supplies were, of course, captured. Colonel Kelley was wounded in the breast by a pistol-shot which was at first supposed to be fatal, though it did not turn out so, and this was the only casualty reported on the National side. No prisoners were taken, nor did any dead or wounded fall into our hands. Porterfield retreated to Beverly, some thirty miles further to the southeast, and the National forces occupied Philippi. The telegraphic reports had put the Confederate force at 2000, and their loss at 15 killed. This implied a considerable list of wounded and prisoners, and the newspapers gave it the air of a considerable victory. The campaign thus opened with apparent *éclat* for McClellan (who was personally at Cincinnati), and the "Philippi races," as they were locally called, greatly encouraged the Union men of West Virginia and correspondingly depressed the Secessionists.

Nearly a month elapsed, when, having received reports that large forces of the enemy were gathered at Beverly, McClellan determined to proceed in person to that region with his best prepared troops, postponing his Kanawha campaign till northwestern Virginia should be cleared of the enemy.

Military affairs in West Virginia had been complicated by the political situation, and it is necessary to recollect the dates of the swift following steps in Virginia's progress into the Confederacy. Sumter surrendered on Saturday, the 13th of April, and on Monday the 15th President Lincoln issued his first call for troops. On Wednesday the 17th the Virginia Convention passed the Ordinance of Secession in secret session. On Friday the 19th it was known in Washington, and on Saturday Lee and Johnston resigned their commissions in the United States Army, sorrowfully "going with their State." On the following Tuesday (23d) the chairman of the Virginia Convention presented to Lee his commission as Major-General and Commander of the Virginia Forces. On the same day Governor Dennison handed to McClellan his commission to command the Ohio forces in the service of the Union. Although the Confederate Congress at Montgomery admitted Virginia to the Confederacy early in May, this was not formally accepted in Virginia till after the popular vote on secession (May 23d) and the canvassing of the returns of that election. Governor Letcher issued on June 8th his proclamation announcing the result, and transferring the command of the Virginia troops to the Confederate Government. During the whole of May, therefore, Virginia's position was unsettled. Her governor, by the authority of the convention, regarded her as independent of the United States, but by an inchoate act of secession which would not become final till ratified by the popular vote. The Virginia troops were arrayed near the Potomac to resist the advance of national forces; but Confederate troops had been welcomed in eastern Virginia as early as the 10th of May, and President Davis had authorized Lee, as Commander of the Virginia forces, to assume control of them.

It was well known that the prevailing sentiment in West Virginia was loyal to the Union, and each party avoided conflict there for fear of prejudicing its cause in the election. Hence it was that as soon as the vote was cast, the aggressive was taken by the Virginia government in the burning of the bridges near Grafton. The fire of war was thus lighted. The crossing of the Ohio was with a full understanding with Colonel Kelley, who recognized McClellan at once as his military commander. The affair at Philippi was, in form, the last appearance of Virginia in the role of an independent nation, for in a very few days Lee announced by a published order that the absorption of the Virginia troops into the Confederate Army was complete. It will be well to understand the topography of the Virginia mountains and their western slope, if we would reach the reasons which determined the lines of advance chosen by the Confederates and the counter moves of McClellan. The Alleghany range passing out of Pennsylvania and running southwest through the whole length of Virginia, consists of several parallel lines of mountains enclosing narrow valleys. The Potomac River breaks through at the common boundary of Virginia and Maryland, and along its valley runs the National Road as well as the Chesapeake and Ohio Canal. The Baltimore and Ohio Railroad also follows this natural highway, which is thus indicated as the most important line of communication between Washington and the Ohio valley, though a high mountain summit must be passed, even by this route, before the tributaries of the Ohio can be reached. Half-way across the State to the southward, is a high watershed connecting the mountain ridges and separating the streams tributary to the Potomac on the north from those falling into the James and New rivers on the south. The Staunton and Parkersburg turnpike follows the line of this high "divide" looking down from among the clouds into the long and nearly straight defiles on either hand, which separate the Alleghany Mountains proper from the Blue Ridge on the east and from Cheat Mountain and other ranges on the west. Still further to the southwest the James River and the New River interlace their headwaters among the mountains, and break out on east and west, making the third natural pass through which the James River and Kanawha turnpike and canal find their way. These three routes across the mountains were the only ones on which military operations were at all feasible. The northern one was usually in the hands of the National forces, and the other two were those by which the Confederates attempted the invasion of West Virginia. Beverly, a hundred miles from Staunton, was near the gate through which the Staunton road passes on its way north-westward to Parkersburg and Wheeling, whilst Gauley Bridge was the key-point of the Kanawha route on the westerly slope of the mountains.

General Lee determined to send columns upon both these lines. General Henry A. Wise (formerly Governor of Virginia) took the Kanawha route, and General Robert S. Garnett (lately Lee's own adjutant-general) marched to Beverly. Upon Porterfield's retreat to Beverly, Garnett, who had also been an officer in the United States Army, was ordered to assume command there and to stimulate the recruiting and organization of regiments from the secession element of the population. Some Virginia regiments raised on the eastern slope of the mountains were sent with him, and to these was soon added the First Georgia. On the 1st of July he reported his force as 4500 men, but declared that his efforts to recruit had proven a complete failure, only 23 having joined. The West Virginians, he says, "are thoroughly imbued with an ignorant and bigoted Union sentiment." Other reinforcements were promised Garnett, but none reached him except the Forty-fourth Virginia Regiment, which arrived at Beverly the very day of his engagement with McClellan's troops, but did not take part in the fighting.

Tygart's valley, in which Beverly lies, is between Cheat Mountain on the east, and Rich Mountain on the west. The river, of the same name as the valley, flows northward about fifteen miles, then turns westward, breaking through the ridge, and by junction with the Buckhannon River forms the Monongahela, which passes by Philippi and afterward crosses the railroad at Grafton. The Staunton and Parkersburg turnpike divides at Beverly, the Parkersburg route passing over a saddle in Rich Mountain, and the Wheeling route following the river to Philippi. The ridge north of the river at the gap is known as Laurel Mountain, and the road passes over a spur of it. Garnett regarded the two positions at Rich Mountain and Laurel Mountain as the gates to all the region beyond and to the West. A rough mountain road, barely passable, connected the Laurel Mountain position with Cheat River on the east, and it was possible to go by this way northward through St. George to the North-western turnpike, turning the mountain ranges.

Garnett thought the pass over Rich Mountain much the stronger and more easily held, and he therefore entrenched there about 1300 of his men and four cannon, under command of Lieutenant-Colonel Pegram. The position chosen was on a spur of the mountain near its western base, and it was rudely fortified with breastworks of logs covered with an abatis of slashed timber along its front. The remainder of his force he placed in a similar fortified position on the road at Laurel Mountain, where he also had four guns, of which one was rifled. Here he commanded in person. His depot of supplies was at Beverly, which was sixteen miles from the Laurel Mountain position and five from that at Rich Mountain. He was pretty accurately informed of McClellan's forces and movements, and his preparations had barely been completed by the 9th of July, when the Union general appeared in his front.

McClellan entered West Virginia in person on the 21st of June, and on the 23d issued from Grafton a proclamation to the inhabitants. He had gradually collected his forces along the Baltimore and Ohio Railroad, and these, at the time of the affair at Rich Mountain, consisted of sixteen Ohio regiments, nine from Indiana, and two from West Virginia; in all, twenty-seven regiments with four batteries of artillery of six guns each, two troops of cavalry, and an independent company of riflemen. Of his batteries, one was of the regular army, and another, a company of regulars (Company I, Fourth U. S. Artillery), was with him awaiting mountain howitzers, which arrived a little later. The regiments varied somewhat in strength, but all were recently organized, and must have averaged at least 700 men each, making the whole force about 20,000. Of these, about 5000 were guarding the railroad and its bridges for some two hundred miles, under the command of Brigadier-General C. W. Hill, of the Ohio Militia; a strong brigade under Brigadier-General Morris of Indiana, was at Philippi, and the rest were in three brigades forming the immediate command of McClellan, the brigadiers being General W. S. Rosecrans, U. S. A., General Newton Schleich of Ohio, and Colonel Robert L. McCook of Ohio. On the date of his proclamation McClellan intended, as he informed General Scott, to move his principal column to Buckhannon on June 25th, and thence at once upon Beverly; but delays occurred, and it was not till July 2nd that he reached Buckhannon, which is twenty-four miles west of Beverly, on the Parkersburg branch of the turnpike. Before leaving Grafton the rumours he heard had made him estimate Garnett's force at 6000 or 7000 men, of which the larger part were at Laurel Mountain in front of General Morris. On the 7th of July he moved McCook with two regiments to Middle Fork bridge, about half-way to Beverly, and on the same day ordered Morris to march with his brigade from Philippi to a position one and a half miles in front of Garnett's principal camp, which was promptly done. Three days later, McClellan concentrated the three brigades of his own column at Roaring Creek, about two miles from Colonel Pegram's position at the base of Rich Mountain. The advance on both lines had been made with only a skirmishing resistance, the Confederates being aware of McClellan's great superiority in numbers, and choosing to await his attack in their fortified positions. The National commander was now convinced that his opponent was 10,000 strong, of which about 2000 were before him at Rich Mountain. A reconnaissance made on the 10th showed that Pegram's position would be difficult to assail in front, but preparations were made to attack the next day, while Morris was directed to hold firmly his position before Garnett, watching for the effect of the attack at Rich Mountain. In the evening Rosecrans took to McClellan a young man named Hart, whose father lived on the top of the mountain two miles in rear of Pegram, and who thought he could guide a column of infantry to his father's farm by a circuit around Pegram's left flank south of the turnpike. The paths were so difficult that cannon could not go by them, but Rosecrans offered to lead a column of infantry and seize the road at the Hart farm. After some discussion McClellan adopted the suggestion, and it was arranged that Rosecrans should march at daybreak of the 11th with about 2000 men, including a troop of horse, and that upon the sound of his engagement in the rear of Pegram McClellan would attack in force in front. By a blunder in one of the regimental camps, the *reveillé* and assembly were sounded at midnight, and Pegram was put on the *qui vive*. He, however, believed that the attempt to turn his position would be by a path or country road passing round his right, between him and Garnett (of which the latter had warned him), and his attention was diverted from Rosecrans's actual route, which he thought impracticable. The alert which had occurred at midnight made Rosecrans think it best to make a longer circuit than he at first intended, and it took ten hours of severe marching and mountain climbing to reach the Hart farm. The turning movement was made, but he found an enemy opposing him. Pegram had detached about 350 men from the 1300 which he had, and had ordered them to guard the road at the mountain summit. He sent with them a single cannon from the four which constituted his only battery, and they threw together a breastwork of logs. The turnpike at Hart's runs in a depression of the summit, and as Rosecrans, early in the afternoon, came out upon the road, he was warmly received by both musketry and cannon. The ground was rough, the men were for the first time under fire, and the skirmishing combat varied through two or three hours, when a charge by part of Rosecrans's line, aided by a few heavy volleys from another portion of his forces which had secured a good position, broke the enemy's line. Reinforcements from Pegram were nearly at hand, with another cannon; but they did not come into action, and the runaway team of the caisson on the hill-top, dashing into the gun that was coming up, capsized it down the mountain-side where the descending road was scarped diagonally along it. Both guns fell into Rosecrans's hands, and he was in possession of the field. The march and the assault had been made in rain and storm. Nothing was heard from McClellan; and the enemy, rallying on their reinforcements, made such show of resistance on the crest a little further on, that Rosecrans directed his men to rest upon their arms till next morning. When day broke on the 12th, the enemy had disappeared from the mountain-top, and Rosecrans, feeling his way down to the rear of Pegram's position, found it also abandoned, the two remaining cannon being spiked, and a few sick and wounded being left in charge of a surgeon. Still nothing was seen of McClellan, and Rosecrans sent word to him, in his camp beyond Roaring Creek, that he was in possession of the enemy's position. Rosecrans's loss had been 12 killed and 49 wounded. The Confederates left 20 wounded on the field, and 63 were surrendered at the lower camp, including the sick. No trustworthy report of their dead was made.

The noise of the engagement had been heard in McClellan's camp, and he formed his troops for attack, but the long continuance of the cannonade and some signs of exultation in Pegram's camp seem to have made him think Rosecrans had been repulsed. The failure to attack in accordance with the plan has never been explained. Rosecrans's messengers had failed to reach McClellan during the 11th, but the sound of the battle was sufficient notice that he had gained the summit and was engaged; and he was, in fact, left to win his own battle or to get out of his embarrassment as he could. Toward evening McClellan began to cut a road for artillery to a neighbouring height, from which he hoped his twelve guns would make Pegram's position untenable; but his lines were withdrawn again beyond Roaring Creek at nightfall, and all further action postponed to the next day.

About half of Pegram's men had succeeded in passing around Rosecrans's right flank during the night and had gained Beverly. These, with the newly arrived Confederate regiment, fled southward on the Staunton road. Garnett had learned in the evening, by messenger from Beverly, that Rich Mountain summit was carried, and evacuated his camp in front of Morris about midnight. He first marched toward Beverly, and was within five miles of that place when he received information (false at the time) that the National forces already occupied it. He then retraced his steps nearly to his camp, and, leaving the turnpike at Leadsville, he turned off upon a country road over Cheat Mountain into Cheat River valley, following the stream northward toward St. George and West Union, in the forlorn hope of turning the mountains at the north end of the ridges, and regaining his communications by a very long detour. He might have continued southward through Beverly almost at leisure, for McClellan did not enter the town till past noon on the 12th.

Morris learned of Garnett's retreat at dawn, and started in pursuit as soon as rations could be issued. He marched first to Leadsville, where he halted to communicate with McClellan at Beverly and get further orders. These reached him in the night, and at daybreak of the 13th he resumed the pursuit. His advance-guard of three regiments, accompanied by Captain H. W. Benham of the Engineers, overtook the rear of the Confederate column about noon and continued a skirmishing pursuit for some two hours. Garnett himself handled his rear-guard with skill, and at Carrick's Ford a lively encounter was had. A mile or two further, at another ford and when the skirmishing was very slight, he was killed while withdrawing his skirmishers from behind a pile of driftwood which he had used as a barricade. One of his cannon had become stalled in the ford, and with about forty wagons fell into Morris's hands. The direct pursuit was here discontinued, but McClellan had sent a dispatch to General Hill at Grafton, to collect the garrisons along the railroad and block the way of the Confederates where they must pass around the northern spurs of the mountains.

His military telegraph terminated at the Roaring Creek camp, and the dispatch written in the evening of the 12th was not forwarded to Hill till near noon of the 13th. This officer immediately ordered the collection of the greater part of his detachments at Oakland, and called upon the railway officials for special trains to hurry them to the rendezvous. About 1000 men under Colonel James Irvine of the Sixteenth Ohio were at West Union, where the St. George road reaches the Northwestern Turnpike, and Hill's information was that a detachment of these held Red House, a crossing several miles in advance, by which the retreating enemy might go. Irvine was directed to hold his positions at all hazards till he could be reinforced. Hill himself hastened with the first train from Grafton to Oakland with about 500 men and three cannon, reached his destination at nightfall, and hurried his detachment forward by a night march to Irvine, ten or twelve miles over rough roads. It turned out that Irvine did not occupy Red House, and the prevalent belief that the enemy was about 8000 in number, with the uncertainty of the road he would take, made it proper to keep the little force concentrated till reinforcements should come. The first of these reached Irvine about six o'clock on the morning of the 14th, raising his command to 1500; but a few moments after their arrival he learned that the enemy had passed Red House soon after daylight. He gave chase, but did not overtake them.

Meanwhile General Hill had spent the night in trying to hasten forward the railway trains, but none were able to reach Oakland till morning, and Garnett's forces had now more than twenty miles the start, and were on fairly good roads, moving southward on the eastern side of the mountains. McClellan still telegraphed that Hill had the one opportunity of a lifetime to capture the fleeing army, and that officer hastened in pursuit, though unprovided with wagons or extra rations. When however the Union commander learned that the enemy had fairly turned the mountains, he ordered the pursuit stopped. Hill had used both intelligence and energy in his attempt to concentrate his troops, but it proved simply impossible for the railroad to carry them to Oakland before the enemy had passed the turning-point, twenty miles to the southward.

During the 12th Pegram's situation and movements were unknown. He had intended, when he evacuated his camp, to follow the line of retreat taken by the detachment already near the mountain-top, but, in the darkness of the night and in the tangled woods and thickets of the mountain-side, his column got divided, and, with the rear portion of it, he wandered all day of the 12th, seeking to make his way to Garnett. He halted at evening at the Tygart Valley River, six miles north of Beverly, and learned from some country people of Garnett's retreat. It was still possible to reach the mountains east of the valley, but beyond lay a hundred miles of wilderness and half a dozen mountain ridges on which little, if any, food could be found for his men. He called a council of war, and, by advice of his officers, sent to McClellan, at Beverly, an offer of surrender. This was received on the 13th, and Pegram brought in 30 officers and 525 men. McClellan then moved southward himself, following the Staunton road, by which the remnant of Pegram's little force had escaped, and on the 14th occupied Huttonsville. Two regiments of Confederate troops were hastening from Staunton to reinforce Garnett. These were halted at Monterey, east of the principal ridge of the Alleghenies, and upon them the retreating forces rallied. Brigadier-General H. R. Jackson was assigned to command in Garnett's place, and both Governor Letcher and General Lee made strenuous efforts to increase this army to a force sufficient to resume aggressive operations. On McClellan's part nothing further was attempted till on the 22d he was summoned to Washington to assume command of the army which had retreated to the capital after the panic of the first Bull Run battle.

The affair at Rich Mountain and the subsequent movements were among the minor events of a great war, and would not warrant a detailed description, were it not for the momentous effect they had upon the conduct of the war, by being the occasion of McClellan's promotion to the command of the Potomac army. The narrative which has been given contains the "unvarnished tale," as nearly as official records of both sides can give it, and it is a curious task to compare it with the picture of the campaign and its results which was then given to the world in the series of proclamations and dispatches of the young general, beginning with his first occupation of the country and ending with his congratulations to his troops, in which he announced that they had "annihilated two armies, commanded by educated and experienced soldiers, entrenched in mountain fastnesses fortified at their leisure." The country was eager for good news, and took it as literally true. McClellan was the hero of the moment, and when, but a week later, his success was followed by the disaster to McDowell at Bull Run, he seemed pointed out by Providence as the ideal chieftain who could repair the misfortune and lead our armies to certain victory. His personal intercourse with those about him was so kindly, and his bearing so modest, that his dispatches, proclamations, and correspondence are a psychological study, more puzzling to those who knew him well than to strangers. Their turgid rhetoric and exaggerated pretence did not seem natural to him. In them he seemed to be composing for stage effect something to be spoken in character by a quite different person from the sensible and genial man we knew in daily life and conversation. The career of the great Napoleon had been the study and the absorbing admiration of young American soldiers, and it was perhaps not strange that when real war came they should copy his bulletins and even his personal bearing. It was, for the moment, the bent of the people to be pleased with McClellan's rendering of the role; they dubbed him the young Napoleon, and the photographers got him to stand with folded arms, in the historic pose. For two or three weeks his dispatches and letters were all on fire with enthusiastic energy. He appeared to be in a morbid condition of mental exaltation. When he came out of it, he was as genial as ever. The assumed dash and energy of his first campaign made the disappointment and the reaction more painful when the excessive caution of his conduct in command of the Army of the Potomac was seen. But the Rich Mountain affair, when analyzed, shows the same characteristics which became well known later. There was the same over-estimate of the enemy, the same tendency to interpret unfavourably the sights and sounds in front, the same hesitancy to throw in his whole force when he knew that his subordinate was engaged. If Garnett had been as strong as McClellan believed him, he had abundant time and means to overwhelm Morris, who lay four days in easy striking distance, while the National commander delayed attacking Pegram; and had Morris been beaten, Garnett would have been as near Clarksburg as his opponent, and there would have been a race for the railroad. But, happily, Garnett was less strong and less enterprising than he was credited with being. Pegram was dislodged, and the Confederates made a precipitate retreat.

Chapter 4

The Kanawha Valley

When McClellan reached Buckhannon, on the 2d of July, the rumours he heard of Garnett's strength, and the news of the presence of General Wise with a considerable force in the Great Kanawha valley, made him conclude to order a brigade to that region for the purpose of holding the lower part of the valley defensively till he might try to cut off Wise's army after Garnett should be disposed of. This duty was assigned to me. On the 22d of June I had received my appointment as Brigadier-General, U. S. Volunteers, superseding my state commission. I had seen the regiments of my brigade going one by one, as fast as they were reorganized for the three years' service, and I had hoped to be ordered to follow them to McClellan's own column. The only one left in camp was the Eleventh Ohio, of which only five companies were present, though two more companies were soon added.

McClellan's letter directed me to assume command of the First and Second Kentucky regiments with the Twelfth Ohio, and to call upon the governor for a troop of cavalry and a six-gun battery: to expedite the equipment of the whole and move them to Gallipolis *via* Hampden and Portland, stations on the Marietta Railroad, from which a march of twenty-five miles by country roads would take us to our destination. At Gallipolis was the Twenty-first Ohio, which I should add to my command and proceed at once with two regiments to Point Pleasant at the mouth of the Kanawha, five miles above. When all were assembled, one regiment was to be left at Point Pleasant, two were to be advanced up the valley to Ten-mile Creek, and the other placed at an intermediate position. "Until further orders," the letter continued, "remain on the defensive and endeavour to induce the rebels to remain at Charleston until I can cut off their retreat by a movement from Beverly."

Captain W. J. Kountz, an experienced steamboat captain, was in charge of water-transportation, and would furnish light-draught steamboats for my use.

Governor Dennison seconded our wishes with his usual earnestness, and ordered the battery of artillery and company of cavalry to meet me at Gallipolis; but the guns for the battery were not to be had, and a section of two bronze guns (six-pounder smooth-bores rifled) was the only artillery, whilst the cavalry was less than half a troop of raw recruits, useful only as messengers. I succeeded in getting the Eleventh Ohio sent with me, the lacking companies to be recruited and sent later. The Twelfth Ohio was an excellent regiment which had been somewhat delayed in its reorganization and had not gone with the rest of its brigade to McClellan. The Twenty-first was one of the regiments enlisted for the State in excess of the first quota, and was now brought into the national service under the President's second call. The two Kentucky regiments had been organized in Cincinnati, and were made up chiefly of steamboat crews and "longshoremen" thrown out of employment by the stoppage of commerce on the river. There were in them some companies of other material, but these gave the distinctive character to the regiments. The colonels and part of the field officers were Kentuckians, but the organizations were Ohio regiments in nearly everything but the name. The men were mostly of a rough and reckless class, and gave a good deal of trouble by insubordination; but they did not lack courage, and after they had been under discipline for a while, became good fighting regiments. The difficulty of getting transportation from the railway company delayed our departure. It was not till the 6th of July that a regiment could be sent, and another followed in two or three days. The two Kentucky regiments were not yet armed and equipped, but after a day or two were ready and were ordered up the river by steamboats. I myself left Camp Dennison on the evening of Sunday the 7th with the Eleventh Ohio (seven companies) and reached Gallipolis in the evening of the 9th. The three Ohio regiments were united on the 10th and carried by steamers to Point Pleasant, and we entered the theatre of war.

My movement had been made upon a telegram from General McClellan, and I found at Gallipolis his letter of instructions of the 2d, and another of the 6th which enlarged the scope of my command. A territorial district was assigned to me, including the south-western part of Virginia below Parkersburg on the Ohio, and north of the Great Kanawha, reaching back into the country as I should occupy it. The directions to restrict myself to a defensive occupation of the Lower Kanawha valley were changed to instructions to march on Charleston and Gauley Bridge, and, with a view to his resumption of the plan to make this his main line of advance, to "obtain all possible information in regard to the roads leading toward Wytheville and the adjacent region." I was also ordered to place a regiment at Ripley, on the road from Parkersburg to Charleston, and advised "to beat up Barbonsville, Guyandotte, etc, so that the entire course of the Ohio may be secured to us." Communication with Ripley was by Letart's Falls on the Ohio, some thirty miles above Gallipolis, or by Ravenswood, twenty miles further. Guyandotte was a longer distance below Gallipolis, and Barboursville was inland some miles up the Gurandotte River. As to General Wise, McClellan wrote: "Drive Wise out and catch him if you can. If you do catch him, send him to Columbus penitentiary." A regiment at Parkersburg and another at Roane Court House on the northern border of my district were ordered to report to me, but I was not authorized to move them from the stations assigned them, and they were soon united to McClellan's own column.

At Gallipolis I heard that a steamboat on the Ohio had been boarded by a rebel party near Guyandotte, and the news giving point to McClellan's suggestion to "beat up" that region, I dispatched a small steamboat down the river to meet the Kentucky regiments with orders for the leading one to land at Guyandotte and suppress any insurgents in that neighbourhood. It was hazardous to divide my little army into three columns on a base of a hundred miles, but it was thought wise to show some Union troops at various points on the border, and I purposed to unite my detachments by early convergent movements forward to the Kanawha valley as soon as I should reach Red House, thirty-two miles up the river, with my principal column.

Before I reached Charleston I added to my artillery one iron and one brass cannon, smooth six-pounders, borrowed from the civil authorities at Gallipolis; but they were without caissons or any proper equipment, and were manned by volunteers from the infantry. My total force, when assembled, would be a little over 3000 men, the regiments having the same average strength as those with McClellan. The opposing force under General Wise was 4000 by the time the campaign was fully opened, though somewhat less at the beginning.

The Great Kanawha River was navigable for small steamboats about seventy miles, to a point ten or twelve miles above Charleston, the only important town of the region, which was at the confluence of the Kanawha and Elk rivers. Steamboats were plenty, owing to the interruption of trade, and wagons were wholly lacking; so that my column was accompanied and partly carried by a fleet of stern-wheel steamers.

On Thursday the 11th of July the movement from Point Pleasant began. An advance-guard was sent out on each side of the river, marching upon the roads which were near its banks. The few horsemen were divided and sent with them to carry messages, and the boats followed, steaming slowly along in rear of the marching men. Most of two regiments were carried on the steamers, to save fatigue to the men, who were as yet unused to their work, and many of whom were footsore from their first long march of twenty-five miles to Gallipolis from Hampden station, where they had been obliged to leave the railway. The arrangement was also a good one in a military point of view, for if an enemy were met on either bank of the stream, the boats could land in a moment and the troops disembark without delay.

Our first day's sail was thirteen miles up the river, and it was the very romance of campaigning. I took my station on top of the pilot-house of the leading boat, so that I might see over the banks of the stream and across the bottom lands to the high hills which bounded the valley. The afternoon was a lovely one. Summer clouds lazily drifted across the sky, the boats were dressed in their colours and swarmed with the men like bees. The bands played national tunes, and as we passed the houses of Union citizens, the inmates would wave their handkerchiefs to us, and were answered by cheers from the troops. The scenery was picturesque, the gently winding river making beautiful reaches that opened new scenes upon us at every turn. On either side the advance-guard could be seen in the distance, the main body in the road, with skirmishers exploring the way in front, and flankers on the sides. Now and then a horseman would bring some message to the bank from the front, and a small boat would be sent to receive it, giving us the rumours with which the country was rife, and which gave just enough of excitement and of the spice of possible danger to make this our first day in an enemy's country key everybody to just such a pitch as apparently to double the vividness of every sensation. The landscape seemed more beautiful, the sunshine more bright, and the exhilaration of outdoor life more joyous than any we had ever known.

The halt for the night had been assigned at a little village on the right (northern) bank of the stream, which was nestled beneath a ridge which ran down from the hills toward the river, making an excellent position for defence against any force which might come against it from the upper valley. The sun was getting low behind us in the west, as we approached it, and the advance-guard had already halted. Captain Cotter's two bronze guns gleamed bright on the top of the ridge beyond the pretty little town, and before the sun went down, the new white tents had been carried up to the slope and pitched there. The steamers were moored to the shore, and the low slanting rays of the sunset fell upon as charming a picture as was ever painted. An outpost with pickets was set on the southern side of the river, both grand and camp guards were put out also on the side we occupied, and the men soon had their supper and went to rest. Late in the evening a panic-stricken countryman came in with the news that General Wise was moving down upon us with 4000 men. The man was evidently in earnest, and was a loyal one. He believed every word he said, but he had in fact seen only a few of the enemy's horsemen who were scouting toward us, and believed their statement that an army was at their back. It was our initiation into an experience of rumours that was to continue as long as the war. We were to get them daily and almost hourly; sometimes with a little foundation of fact, sometimes with none; rarely purposely deceptive, but always grossly exaggerated, making chimeras with which a commanding officer had to wage a more incessant warfare than with the substantial enemy in his front. I reasoned that Wise's troops were, like my own, too raw to venture a night attack with, and contented myself with sending a strong reconnoitring party out beyond my pickets, putting in command of it Major Hines of the Twelfth Ohio, an officer who subsequently became noted for his enterprise and activity in charge of scouting parties. The camp rested quietly, and toward morning Hines returned, reporting that a troop of the enemy's horse had come within a couple of miles of our position in search of information about us and our movement. They had indulged in loud bragging as to what Wise and his army would do with us, but this and nothing more was the basis of our honest friend's fright. The morning dawned bright and peaceful, the steamers were sent back for a regiment which was still at Point Pleasant, and the day was used in concentrating the little army and preparing for another advance.

On July 13th we moved again, making about ten miles, and finding the navigation becoming difficult by reason of the low water. At several shoals in the stream rough wing-dams had been built from the sides to concentrate the water in the channel, and at Knob Shoals, in one of these "chutes" as they were called, a coal barge had sometime before been sunk. In trying to pass it our leading boat grounded, and, the current being swift, it was for a time doubtful if we should get her off. We finally succeeded, however, and the procession of boats slowly steamed up the rapids. We had hardly got beyond them when we heard a distant cannon-shot from our advance-guard which had opened a long distance between them and us during our delay. We steamed rapidly ahead. Soon we saw a man pulling off from the south bank in a skiff. Nearing the steamer, he stood up and excitedly shouted that a general engagement had begun. We laughingly told him it couldn't be very general till we got in, and we moved on, keeping a sharp outlook for our parties on either bank. When we came up to them, we learned that a party of horsemen had appeared on the southern side of the river and had opened a skirmishing fire, but had scampered off as if the Old Nick were after them when a shell from the rifled gun was sent over their heads. The shell, like a good many that were made in those days, did not explode, and the simple people of the vicinity who had heard its long-continued scream told our men some days after that they thought it was "going yet."

From this time some show of resistance was made by the enemy, and the skirmishing somewhat retarded the movement. Still, about ten miles was made each day till the evening of the 16th, when we encamped at the mouth of the Pocotaligo, a large creek which enters the Kanawha from the north. The evening before, we had had one of those incidents, not unusual with new troops, which prove that nothing but habit can make men cool and confident in their duties. We had, as usual, moored our boats to the northern bank and made our camp there, placing an outpost on the left bank opposite us supporting a chain of sentinels, to prevent a surprise from that direction. A report of some force of the enemy in their front made me order another detachment to their support after nightfall. The detachment had been told off and ferried across in small boats. They were dimly seen marching in the starlight up the river after landing, when suddenly a shot was heard, and then an irregular volley was both seen and heard as the muskets flashed out in the darkness. A supporting force was quickly sent over, and, no further disturbance occurring, a search was made for an enemy, but none was found. A gun had accidentally gone off in the squad, and the rest of the men, surprised and bewildered, had fired, they neither knew why nor at what. Two men were killed, and several others were hurt. This and the chaffing the men got from their comrades was a lesson to the whole command. The soldiers were brave enough, and were thoroughly ashamed of themselves, but they were raw; that was all that could be said of it.

We were here overtaken by the Second Kentucky, which had stopped at Guyandotte on its way up the river, and had marched across the country to join us after our progress had sufficiently covered that lower region. From Guyandotte a portion of the regiment, under command of Lieutenant-Colonel Neff, had gone to Barboursville and had attacked and dispersed an encampment of Confederates which was organizing there. It was a very creditable little action, in which officers and men conducted themselves well, and which made them for the time the envy of the rest of the command.

The situation at "Poca," as it was called in the neighbourhood, was one which made the further advance of the army require some consideration. Information which came to us from loyal men showed that some force of the enemy was in position above the mouth of Scary Creek on the south side of the Kanawha, and about three miles from us. We had for two days had constant light skirmishing with the advance-guard of Wise's forces on the north bank of the river, and supposed that the principal part of his command was on our side, and not far in front of us. It turned out in fact that this was so, and that Wise had placed his principal camp at Tyler Mountain, a bold spur which reaches the river on the northern side (on which is also the turnpike road), about twelve miles above my position, while he occupied the south side with a detachment. The Pocotaligo, which entered the river from the north at our camp, covered us against an attack on that side; but we could not take our steam-boats further unless both banks of the river were cleared. We had scarcely any wagons, for those which had been promised us could not yet be forwarded, and we must either continue to keep the steamboats with us, or organize wagon transportation and cut loose from the boats. My urgent dispatches were hurrying the wagons toward us, but meanwhile I hoped the opposition on the south bank of the river would prove trifling, for artillery in position at any point on the narrow river would at once stop navigation of our light and unarmed transports. On the morning of the 17th a reconnoitring party sent forward on the south side of the river under command of Lieutenant-Colonel White of the Twelfth Ohio, reported the enemy about five hundred strong entrenched on the further side of Scary Creek, which was not fordable at its mouth, but could be crossed a little way up the stream. Colonel Lowe of the Twelfth requested the privilege of driving off this party with his regiment accompanied by our two cannon. He was ordered to do so, whilst the enemy's skirmishers should be pushed back from the front of the main column, and it should be held ready to advance rapidly up the north bank of the river as soon as the hostile force at Scary Creek should be dislodged.

The Twelfth and two companies of the Twenty-first Ohio were ferried over and moved out soon after noon. The first reports from them were encouraging and full of confidence, the enemy were retreating and they had dismounted one of his guns; but just before evening they returned, bringing the account of their repulse in the effort to cross at the mouth of the creek, and their failure to find the ford a little higher up. Their ammunition had run short, some casualties had occurred, and they had become discouraged and given it up. Their loss was 10 men killed and 35 wounded. If they had held on and asked for assistance, it would have been well enough; but, as was common with new troops, they passed from confidence to discouragement as soon as they were checked, and they retreated.

The affair was accompanied by another humiliating incident which gave me no little chagrin. During the progress of the engagement Colonel Woodruff and Lieutenant-Colonel Neff of the Second Kentucky, with Colonel De Villiers of the Eleventh Ohio, rode out in front, on the north bank of the river, till they came opposite the enemy's position, the hostile party on our side of the stream having fallen back beyond this point. They were told by a negro that the rebels were in retreat, and they got the black man to ferry them over in a skiff, that they might be the first to congratulate their friends. To their amazement they were welcomed as prisoners by the Confederates, who greatly enjoyed their discomfiture. The negro had told the truth in saying that the enemy had been in retreat; for the fact was that both sides retreated, but the Confederates, being first informed of this, resumed their position and claimed a victory. The officers who were captured had gone out without permission, and, led on by the hare-brained De Villiers, had done what they knew was foolish and unmilitary, resulting for them in a severe experience in Libby Prison at Richmond, and for us in the momentary appearance of lack of discipline and order which could not fairly be charged upon the command. I reported the facts without disguise or apology, trusting to the future to remove the bad impression the affair must naturally make upon McClellan.

The report of the strength of the position attacked and our knowledge of the increasing difficulty of the ground before us, led me to conclude that the wisest course would be to await the arrival of the wagons, now daily expected, and then, with supplies for several days in hand, move independent of the steamers, which became only an embarrassment when it was advisable to leave the river road for the purpose of turning a fortified position like that we had found before us. We therefore rested quietly in our strong camp for several days, holding both banks of the river and preparing to move the main column by a country road leading away from the stream on the north side, and returning to it at Tyler Mountain, where Wise's camp was reported to be. I ordered up the First Kentucky from Ravenswood and Ripley, but its colonel found obstacles in his way, and did not join us till we reached Charleston the following week.

On the 23d of July I had succeeded in getting wagons and teams enough to supply the most necessary uses, and renewed the advance. We marched rapidly on the 24th by the circuitous route I have mentioned, leaving a regiment to protect the steamboats. The country was very broken and the roads very rough, but the enemy had no knowledge of our movement, and toward evening we again approached the river immediately in rear of their camp at Tyler Mountain. When we drove in their pickets, the force was panic-stricken and ran off, leaving their camp in confusion, and their supper which they were cooking but did not stop to eat. A little below the point where we reached the river, and on the other side, was the steamboat *Maffet* with a party of soldiers gathering the wheat which had been cut in the neighbouring fields and was in the sheaf. I was for a moment doubtful whether it might not be one of our own boats which had ventured up the river under protection of the regiment left behind, and directed our skirmishers who were deployed along the edge of the water to hail the other side. "Who are you?" was shouted from both banks simultaneously. "United States troops," our men answered. "Hurrah for Jeff Davis!" shouted the others, and a rattling fire opened on both sides. A shell was sent from our cannon into the steamer, and the party upon her were immediately seen jumping ashore, having first set fire to her to prevent her falling into our hands. The enemy then moved away on that side, under cover of the trees which lined the river bank. Night was now falling, and, sending forward an advance-guard to follow up the force whose camp we had surprised, we bivouacked on the mountain side.

In the morning, as we were moving out at an early hour, we were met by the mayor and two or three prominent citizens of Charleston who came to surrender the town to us, Wise having hurriedly retreated during the night. He had done a very unnecessary piece of mischief before leaving, in partly cutting off the cables of a fine suspension bridge which spans the Elk River at Charleston. As this stream enters the Kanawha from the north and below the city, it may have seemed to him that it would delay our progress; but as a large number of empty coal barges were lying at the town, it took our company of mechanics, under Captain Lane of the Eleventh Ohio, but a little while to improvise a good floating bridge, and part of the command passed through the town and camped beyond it. One day was now given to the establishment of a depot of supplies at Charleston and to the organization of regular communication by water with Gallipolis, and by wagons with such positions as we might occupy further up the river. Deputations of the townspeople were informed that it was not our policy to meddle with private persons who remained quietly at home, nor would we make any inquisition as to the personal opinions of those who attended strictly to their own business; but they were warned that any communication with the enemy would be remorselessly punished.

We were now able to get more accurate information about Wise's forces than we could obtain before, and this accorded pretty well with the strength which he reported officially. His infantry was therefore more than equal to the column under my command in the valley, whilst in artillery and in cavalry he was greatly superior. Our continued advance in the face of such opposition is sufficient evidence that the Confederate force was not well handled, for as the valley contracted and the hills crowded in closer to the river, nearly every mile offered positions in which small numbers could hold at bay an army. Our success in reaching Charleston was therefore good ground for being content with our progress, though I had to blame myself for errors in the management of my part of the campaign at Pocataligo. I ought not to have assumed as confidently as I did that the enemy was only five hundred strong at Scary Creek and that a detachment could dispose of that obstacle whilst the rest of the column prepared to advance on our principal line. Wise's force at that point was in fact double the number supposed. It is true it was very inconvenient to ferry any considerable body of troops back and forth across the river; but I should nevertheless have taken the bulk of my command to the left bank, and by occupying the enemy's attention at the mouth of Scary Creek, covered the movement of a sufficient force upon his flank by means of the fords farther up that stream. This would have resulted in the complete routing of the detachment, and it is nearly certain that I could have pushed on to Charleston at once, and could have waited there for the organization of my wagon train with the prestige of victory, instead of doing so at 'Poca' with the appearance of a check.

McClellan recognized the fact that he was asking me to face the enemy with no odds in my favour, and as soon as he heard that Wise was disposed to make a stand he directed me not to risk attacking him in front, but rather to await the result of his own movement toward the Upper Kanawha. Rosecrans did the same when he assumed command; but I knew the hope had been that I would reach Gauley Bridge, and I was vexed that my movement should have the appearance of failing when I was conscious that we had not fairly measured our strength with my opponent. As soon, therefore, as the needful preparations could be made, I decided upon the turning movement which I have already described, and our resolute advance seems to have thrown Wise into a panic from which he did not recover till he got far beyond Gauley Bridge.

At Charleston I learned of the Bull Run disaster, and that McClellan had been ordered to Washington, leaving Rosecrans in command of our department. The latter sent me orders which implied that to reach Charleston was the most he could expect of me, and directing me to remain on the defensive if I should succeed in getting so far, whilst he should take up anew McClellan's plan of reaching the rear of Wise's army. His dispatches, fortunately, did not reach me till I was close to Gauley Bridge and was sure of my ability to take possession of that defile, some forty miles above Charleston. An additional reason for my prompt advance was that the Twenty-first Ohio was not yet re-enlisted for the war, was only a "three months" regiment whose time was about to expire, and Governor Dennison had telegraphed me to send it back to Ohio. I left this regiment as a post-garrison at Charleston till it could be relieved by another, or till my success in reaching Gauley Bridge should enable me to send back a detachment for that post, and, on the 26th July, pushed forward with the rest of my column, which, now that the First Kentucky had joined me, consisted of four regiments. Our first night's encampment was about eleven miles above Charleston in a lovely nook between spurs of the hills. Here I was treated to a little surprise on the part of three of my subordinates which was an unexpected enlargement of my military experience. The camp had got nicely arranged for the night and supper was over, when these gentlemen waited upon me at my tent. The one who had shown the least capacity as commander of a regiment was spokesman, and informed me that after consultation they had concluded that it was foolhardy to follow the Confederates into the gorge we were travelling, and that unless I could show them satisfactory reasons for changing their opinion they would not lead their commands further into it. I dryly asked if he was quite sure he understood the nature of his communication. There was something probably in the tone of my question which was not altogether expected, and his companions began to look a little uneasy. He then protested that none of them meant any disrespect, but that as their military experience was about as extensive as my own, they thought I ought to make no movements but on consultation with them and by their consent. The others seemed to be better pleased with this way of putting it, and signified assent. My answer was that their conduct very plainly showed their own lack both of military experience and elementary military knowledge, and that this ignorance was the only thing which could palliate their action. Whether they meant it or not, their action was mutinous. The responsibility for the movement of the army was with me, and whilst I should be inclined to confer very freely with my principal subordinates and explain my purposes, I should call no councils of war, and submit nothing to vote till I felt incompetent to decide for myself. If they apologized for their conduct and showed earnestness in military obedience to orders, what they had now said would be overlooked, but on any recurrence of cause for complaint I should enforce my power by the arrest of the offender at once. I dismissed them with this, and immediately sent out the formal orders through my adjutant-general to march early next morning. Before they slept one of the three had come to me with earnest apology for his part in the matter, and a short time made them all as subordinate as I could wish. The incident could not have occurred in the brigade which had been under my command at Camp Dennison, and was a not unnatural result of the sudden assembling of inexperienced men under a brigade commander of whom they knew nothing except that at the beginning of the war he was a civilian like themselves. These very men afterward became devoted followers, and some of them life-long friends. It was part of their military education as well as mine. If I had been noisy and blustering in my intercourse with them at the beginning, and had done what seemed to be regarded as the "regulation" amount of cursing and swearing, they would probably have given me credit for military aptitude at least; but a systematic adherence to a quiet and undemonstrative manner evidently told against me, at first, in their opinion. Through my army life I met more or less of the same conduct when assigned to a new command; but when men learned that discipline would be inevitably enforced, and that it was as necessary to obey a quiet order as one emphasized by expletives, and especially when they had been a little under fire, there was no more trouble. Indeed, I was impressed with the fact that after this acquaintance was once made, my chief embarrassment in discipline was that an intimation of dissatisfaction on my part would cause deeper chagrin and more evident pain than I intended or wished.

The same march enabled me to make the acquaintance of another army "institution,"—the newspaper correspondent. We were joined at Charleston by two men representing influential Eastern journals, who wished to know on what terms they could accompany the column. The answer was that the quartermaster would furnish them with a tent and transportation, and that their letters should be submitted to one of the staff, to protect us from the publication of facts which might aid the enemy. This seemed unsatisfactory, and they intimated that they expected to be taken into my mess and to be announced as volunteer aides with military rank. They were told that military position or rank could only be given by authority much higher than mine, and that they could be more honestly independent if free from personal obligation and from temptation to repay favours with flattery. My only purpose was to put the matter upon the foundation of public right and of mutual self-respect. The day before we reached Gauley Bridge they opened the subject again to Captain McElroy, my adjutant-general, but were informed that I had decided it upon a principle by which I meant to abide. Their reply was, "Very well; General Cox thinks he can get along without us, and we will show him. We will write him down."

They left the camp the same evening, and wrote letters to their papers describing the army as demoralized, drunken, and without discipline, in a state of insubordination, and the commander as totally incompetent. As to the troops, more baseless slander was never uttered. Their march had been orderly. No wilful injury had been done to private property, and no case of personal violence to any non-combatant, man or woman, had been even charged. Yet the printing of such communications in widely read journals was likely to be as damaging as if it all were true. My nomination as Brigadier-General of U. S. Volunteers was then before the Senate for confirmation, and "the pen" would probably have proved "mightier than the sword" but for McClellan's knowledge of the nature of the task we had accomplished, as he was then in the flood-tide of power at Washington, and expressed his satisfaction at the performance of our part of the campaign which he had planned. By good fortune also, the injurious letters were printed at the same time with the telegraphic news of our occupation of Gauley Bridge and the retreat of the enemy out of the valley. I was, however, deeply convinced that my position was the right one, and never changed my rule of conduct in the matter. The relations of newspaper correspondents to general officers of the army became one of the crying scandals and notorious causes of intrigue and demoralization. It was a subject almost impossible to settle satisfactorily; but whoever gained or lost by cultivating this means of reputation, it is a satisfaction to have adhered throughout the war to the rule I first adopted and announced.

 Wise made no resolute effort to oppose my march after I left Charleston, and contented himself with delaying us by his rear-guard, which obstructed the road by felling trees into it and by skirmishing with my head of column. We however advanced at the rate of twelve or fifteen miles a day, reaching Gauley Bridge on the morning of the 29th of July. Here we captured some fifteen hundred stands of arms and a considerable store of munitions which the Confederate general had not been able to carry away or destroy. It is safe to say that in the wild defile which we had threaded for the last twenty miles there were as many positions as there were miles in which he could easily have delayed my advance a day or two, forcing me to turn his flank by the most difficult mountain climbing, and where indeed, with forces so nearly equal, my progress should have been permanently barred. At Gauley Bridge he burned the structure which gave name to the place, and which had been a series of substantial wooden trusses resting upon heavy stone piers. My orders definitively limited me to the point we had now reached in my advance, and I therefore sent forward only a detachment to follow the enemy and keep up his precipitate retreat. Wise did not stop till he reached Greenbrier and the White Sulphur Springs, and there was abundant evidence that he regarded his movement as a final abandonment of this part of West Virginia. A few weeks later General Lee came in person with reinforcements over the mountains and began a new campaign; but until the 20th of August we were undisturbed except by a petty guerrilla warfare.

McClellan telegraphed from Washington his congratulations, and Rosecrans expressed his satisfaction also in terms which assured me that we had done more than had been expected of us. The good effect upon the command was also very apparent; for our success not only justified the policy of a determined advance, but the officers who had been timid as to results were now glad to get their share of the credit, and to make amends for their insubordination by a hearty change in bearing and conduct. My term of service as a brigadier of the Ohio forces in the three months' enrolment had now ended, and until the Senate should confirm my appointment as a United States officer there was some doubt as to my right to continue in command. My embarrassment in this regard was very pleasantly removed by a dispatch from General Rosecrans in which he conveyed the request of Lieutenant-General Scott and of himself that I should remain in charge of the Kanawha column. It was only a week, however, before notice of the confirmation was received, and dropping all thoughts of returning home, I prepared my mind for continuous active duty till the war should end.

CHAPTER 5

Gauley Bridge

The position at Gauley Bridge was an important one from a military point of view. It was where the James River and Kanawha turnpike, after following the highlands along the course of New River as it comes from the east, drops into a defile with cliffs on one side and a swift and unfordable torrent upon the other, and then crosses the Gauley River, which is a stream of very similar character. The two rivers, meeting at a right angle, there unite to form the Great Kanawha, which plunges over a ledge of rocks a mile below and winds its way among the hills, some thirty miles, before it becomes a navigable stream even for the lightest class of steamboats. From Gauley Bridge a road runs up the Gauley River to Cross Lanes and Carnifex Ferry, something over twenty miles, and continuing northward reaches Summersville, Sutton, and Weston, making almost the only line of communication between the posts then occupied by our troops in north-western Virginia and the head of the Kanawha valley. South-westward the country was extremely wild and broken, with few and small settlements and no roads worthy the name. The crossing of the Gauley was therefore the gate through which all important movements from eastern into south-western Virginia must necessarily come, and it formed an important link in any chain of posts designed to cover the Ohio valley from invasion. It was also the most advanced single post which could protect the Kanawha valley. Further to the southeast, on Flat-top Mountain, was another very strong position, where the principal road on the left bank of New River crosses a high and broad ridge; but a post could not be safely maintained there without still holding Gauley Bridge in considerable force, or establishing another post on the right bank of New River twenty miles further up. All these streams flow in rocky beds seamed and fissured to so great a degree that they had no practicable fords. You might go forty miles up New River and at least twenty up the Gauley before you could find a place where either could be passed by infantry or wagons. The little ferries which had been made in a few eddies of the rivers were destroyed in the first campaign, and the post at the Gauley became nearly impregnable in front, and could only be turned by long and difficult detours.

An interval of about a hundred miles separated this mountain fastness from the similar passes which guarded eastern Virginia along the line of the Blue Ridge. This debatable ground was sparsely settled and very poor in agricultural resources, so that it could furnish nothing for subsistence of man or beast. The necessity of transporting forage as well as subsistence and ammunition through this mountainous belt forbade any extended or continuous operations there; for actual computation showed that the wagon trains could carry no more than the food for the mule teams on the double trip, going and returning, from Gauley Bridge to the narrows of New River where the Virginia and Tennessee Railroad crossed upon an important bridge which was several times made the objective point of an expedition. This alone proved the impracticability of the plan McClellan first conceived, of making the Kanawha valley the line of an important movement into eastern Virginia. It pointed very plainly, also, to the true theory of operations in that country. Gauley Bridge should have been held with a good brigade which could have had outposts several miles forward in three directions, and, assisted by a small body of horse to scour the country fifty miles or more to the front, the garrison could have protected all the country which we ever occupied permanently. A similar post at Huttonsville with detachments at the Cheat Mountain pass and Elkwater pass north of Huntersville would have covered the only other practicable routes through the mountains south of the line of the Baltimore and Ohio Railway. These would have been small entrenched camps, defensive in character, but keeping detachments constantly active in patrolling the front, going as far as could be done without wagons. All that ever was accomplished in that region of any value would thus have been attained at the smallest expense, and the resources that were for three years wasted in those mountains might have been applied to the legitimate lines of great operations from the valley of the Potomac southward.

Nothing could be more romantically beautiful than the situation of the post at Gauley Bridge. The hamlet had, before our arrival there, consisted of a cluster of two or three dwellings, a country store, a little tavern, and a church, irregularly scattered along the base of the mountain and facing the road which turns from the Gauley valley into that of the Kanawha. The lower slope of the hillside behind the houses was cultivated, and a hedgerow separated the lower fields from the upper pasturage. Above this gentler slope the wooded steeps rose more precipitately, the sandstone rock jutting out into crags and walls, the sharp ridge above having scarcely soil enough to nourish the chestnut-trees, here, like Mrs. Browning's woods of Vallombrosa, literally "clinging by their spurs to the precipices." In the angle between the Gauley and New rivers rose Gauley Mount, the base a perpendicular wall of rocks of varying height, with high wooded slopes above. There was barely room for the road between the wall of rocks and the water on the New River side, but after going some distance up the valley, the highway gradually ascended the hillside, reaching some rolling uplands at a distance of a couple of miles. Here was Gauley Mount, the country-house of Colonel C. Q. Tompkins, formerly of the Army of the United States, but now the commandant of a Confederate regiment raised in the Kanawha valley. Across New River the heavy masses of Cotton Mountain rose rough and almost inaccessible from the very water's edge. The western side of Cotton Mountain was less steep, and buttresses formed a bench about its base, so that in looking across the Kanawha a mile below the junction of the rivers, one saw some rounded foothills which had been cleared on the top and tilled, and a gap in the mountainous wall made room on that side for a small creek which descended to the Kanawha, and whose bed served for a rude country road leading to Fayette C. H. At the base of Cotton Mountain the Kanawha equals the united width of the two tributaries, and flows foaming over broken rocks with treacherous channels between, till it dashes over the horseshoe ledge below, known far and wide as the Kanawha Falls. On either bank near the falls a small mill had been built, that on the right bank a saw-mill and the one on the left for grinding grain.

Our encampment necessarily included the saw-mill below the falls, where the First Kentucky Regiment was placed to guard the road coming from Fayette C. H. Two regiments were encamped at the bridge upon the hillside above the hedgerow, having an advanced post of half a regiment on the Lewisburg road beyond the Tompkins farm, and scouting the country to Sewell Mountain. Smaller outposts were stationed some distance up the valley of the Gauley. My headquarters tents were pitched in the door-yard of a dwelling-house facing the Gauley River, and I occupied an unfurnished room in the house for office purposes. A week was spent, without molestation, exploring the country in all directions and studying its topography. A ferry guided by a cable stretching along the piers of the burnt bridge communicated with the outposts up the New River, and a smaller ferry below the Kanawha Falls connected with the Fayette road. Systematic discipline and instruction in outpost duty were enforced, and the regiments rapidly became expert mountaineers and scouts. The population was nearly all loyal below Gauley Bridge, but above they were mostly Secessionists, a small minority of the wealthier slaveholders being the nucleus of all aggressive secession movements. These, by their wealth and social leadership, overawed or controlled a great many who did not at heart sympathize with them, and between parties thus formed a guerrilla warfare became chronic. In our scouting expeditions we found little farms in secluded nooks among the mountains, where grown men assured us that they had never before seen the American flag, and whole families had never been further from home than a church and country store a few miles away. From these mountain people several regiments of Union troops were recruited in West Virginia, two of them being organized in rear of my own lines, and becoming part of the garrison of the district in the following season.

I had been joined before reaching Gauley Bridge by Chaplain Brown of the Seventh Ohio, who had obtained permission to make an adventurous journey across the country from Sutton to bring me information as to the position and character of the outposts that were stretching from the railway southward toward our line of operations. Disguised as a mountaineer in homespun clothing, his fine features shaded by a slouched felt hat, he reported himself to me in anything but a clerical garb. Full of enterprise as a partisan leader of scouts could be, he was yet a man of high attainments in his profession, of noble character and real learning. When he reached me, I had as my guest another chaplain who had accepted a commission at my suggestion, the Rev. Mr. Dubois, son-in-law of Bishop McIlvaine of Ohio, who had been leader of the good people at Chillicothe in providing a supper for the Eleventh Ohio as we were on our way from Camp Dennison to Gallipolis. He had burned to have some part in the country's struggle, and became a model chaplain till his labours and exposure broke his health and forced him to resign. The presence of two such men gave some hours of refined social life in the intervals of rough work. One evening walk along the Kanawha has ever since remained in my memory associated with Whittier's poem "The River Path," as a wilder and more brilliant type of the scene he pictured. We had walked out beyond the camp, leaving its noise and its warlike associations behind us, for a turn of the road around a jutting cliff shut it all out as completely as if we had been transported to another land, except that the distant figure of a sentinel on post reminded us of the limit of safe sauntering for pleasure. My Presbyterian and Episcopalian friends forgot their differences of dogma, and as the sun dropped behind the mountain tops, making an early twilight in the valley, we talked of home, of patriotism, of the relation of our struggle to the world's progress, and other high themes, when:

> Sudden our pathway turned from night,
> The hills swung open to the light;
> Through their green gates the sunshine showed,
> A long, slant splendour downward flowed.
> Down glade and glen and bank it rolled;
> It bridged the shaded stream with gold;
> And borne on piers of mist, allied
> The shadowy with the sunlit side!

The surroundings, the things of which we talked, our own sentiments, all combined to make the scene stir deep emotions for which the poet's succeeding lines seem the only fit expression, and to link the poem indissolubly with the scene as if it had its birth there.

When Wise had retreated from the valley, Colonel Tompkins had been unable to remove his family, and had left a letter commending them to our courteous treatment. Mrs. Tompkins was a lady of refinement, and her position within our outposts was far from being a comfortable one. She, however, put a cheerful face upon her situation, showed great tact in avoiding controversy with the soldiers and in conciliating the good-will of the officers, and remained with her children and servants in her picturesque home on the mountain. So long as there was no fighting in the near vicinity, it was comparatively easy to save her from annoyance; but when a little later in the autumn Floyd occupied Cotton Mountain, and General Rosecrans was with us with larger forces, such a household became an object of suspicion and ill-will, which made it necessary to send her through the lines to her husband. The men fancied they saw signals conveyed from the house to the enemy, and believed that secret messages were sent, giving information of our numbers and movements. All this was highly improbable, for the lady knew that her safety depended upon her good faith and prudence; but such camp rumour becomes a power, and Rosecrans found himself compelled to end it by sending her away. He could no longer be answerable for her complete protection. This, however, was not till November, and in August it was only a pleasant variation, in going the rounds, to call at the pretty house on Gauley Mount, inquire after the welfare of the family, and have a moment's polite chat with the mistress of the mansion.

For ten days after we occupied Gauley Bridge, all our information showed that General Wise was not likely to attempt the re-conquest of the Kanawha valley voluntarily. His rapid retrograde march ended at White Sulphur Springs and he went into camp there. His destruction of bridges and abandonment of stores and munitions of war showed that he intended to take final leave of our region. The contrast between promise and performance in his case had been ludicrous. When we entered the valley, we heard of his proclamations and orders, which breathed the spirit of desperate hand-to-hand conflict. His soldiers had been told to despise long-range fire-arms, and to trust to bowie-knives, which our invading hordes would never dare to face. We found some of these knives among the arms we captured at the Gauley,—ferocious-looking weapons, made of broad files ground to a double edge, fitted with rough handles, and still bearing the cross-marking of the file on the flat sides. Such arms pointed many a sarcasm among our soldiers, who had found it hard in the latter part of our advance to get within even the longest musket-range of the enemy's column. It was not strange that ignorant men should think they might find use for weapons less serviceable than the ancient Roman short-sword; but that, in the existing condition of military science, officers could be found to share and to encourage the delusion was amusing enough! With the muskets we captured, we armed a regiment of loyal Virginians, and turned over the rest to Governor Peirpoint for similar use.

On the 5th of August Lieutenant Wagner of the Engineers arrived at Gauley Bridge with instructions from General Rosecrans to superintend the construction of such fortifications as might be proper for a post of three regiments. I had already with me Colonel Whittlesey, Governor Dennison's chief engineer, an old West Point graduate, who had for some years been devoting himself to scientific pursuits, especially to geology. In a few days these were joined by Captain Benham, who was authorized to determine definitely the plans of our defences. I was thus stronger in engineering skill than in any other department of staff assistants, though in truth there was little fortifying to be done beyond what the contour of the ground indicated to the most ordinary comprehension.

Benham stayed but two or three days, modified Wagner's plans enough to feel that he had made them his own, and then went back to Rosecrans's headquarters, where he was met with an appointment as brigadier-general, and was relieved of staff duty. He was a stout red-faced man, with a blustering air, dictatorial and assuming, an army engineer of twenty-five years' standing. He was no doubt well skilled in the routine of his profession, but broke down when burdened with the responsibility of conducting the movement of troops in the field. Wagner was a recent graduate of the Military Academy, a genial, modest, intelligent young man of great promise. He fell at the siege of Yorktown in the next year. Whittlesey was a veteran whose varied experience in and out of the army had all been turned to good account. He was already growing old, but was indefatigable, pushing about in a rather prim, precise way, advising wisely, criticising dryly but in a kindly spirit, and helping bring every department into better form. I soon lost both him and McElroy, my adjutant-general, for their three months' service was up, and they were made, the one colonel, and the other major of the Twentieth Ohio Regiment, of which my friend General Force was the lieutenant-colonel.

We fortified the post by an epaulement or two for cannon, high up on the hillside covering the ferry and the road up New River. An infantry trench, with parapet of barrels filled with earth, was run along the margin of Gauley River till it reached a creek coming down from the hills on the left. There a redoubt for a gun or two was made, commanding a stretch of road above, and the infantry trench followed the line of the creek up to a gorge in the hill. On the side of Gauley Mount facing our post, we slashed the timber from the edge of the precipice nearly to the top of the mountain, making an entanglement through which it was impossible that any body of troops should move. Down the Kanawha, below the falls, we strengthened the saw-mill with logs, till it became a block-house loopholed for musketry, commanding the road to Charleston, the ferry, and the opening of the road to Fayette C. H. A single cannon was here put in position also.

All this took time, for so small a force as ours could not make very heavy details of working parties, especially as our outpost and reconnoitring duty was also very laborious. This duty was done by infantry, for cavalry I had none, except the squad of mounted messengers, who kept carefully out of harm's way, more to save their horses than themselves, for they had been enlisted under an old law which paid them for the risk of their own horses, which risk they naturally tried to make as small as possible. My reconnoitring parties reached Big Sewell Mountain, thirty-five miles up New River, Summersville, twenty miles up the Gauley, and made excursions into the counties on the left bank of the Kanawha, thirty or forty miles away. These were not exceptional marches, but were kept up with an industry that gave the enemy an exaggerated idea of our strength as well as of our activity.

About the 10th of August we began to get rumours from the country that General Robert E. Lee had arrived at Lewisburg to assume direction of the Confederate movements into West Virginia. We heard also that Floyd with a strong brigade had joined that of Wise, whose "legion" had been reinforced, and that this division, reported to be 10,000 or 12,000 strong, would immediately operate against me at Gauley Bridge. We learned also of a general stir among the Secessionists in Fayette, Mercer, and Raleigh counties, and of the militia being ordered out under General Chapman to support the Confederate movement by operating upon my line of communications, whilst Floyd and Wise should attack in front.

The reported aggregate of the enemy's troops was, as usual, exaggerated, but we now know that it amounted to about 8000 men, a force so greatly superior to anything I could assemble to oppose it, that the situation became at once a very grave one for me. To resist this advance, I could keep but two regiments at Gauley Bridge, an advance-guard of eight companies vigorously skirmishing toward Sewell Mountain, a regiment distributed on the Kanawha to cover steamboat communications, and some companies of West Virginia recruits organizing at the mouth of the Kanawha. By extreme activity these were able to baffle the enemy, and impose upon him the belief that our numbers were more than double our actual force.

Small hostile parties began to creep in toward the navigable part of the Kanawha, and to fire upon the steamboats, which were our sole dependence for supplying our depots at Charleston and at the head of navigation. General Rosecrans informed me of his purpose to march a sufficiently strong column to meet that under Lee as soon as the purpose of the latter should be developed, and encouraged me to hold fast to my position. I resolved, therefore, to stand a siege if need be, and pushed my means of transportation to the utmost, to accumulate a store of supplies at Gauley Bridge. I succeeded in getting up rations sufficient to last a fortnight, but found it much harder to get ammunition, especially for my ill-assorted little battery of cannon.

The Twenty-sixth Ohio came into the Kanawha valley on the 8th through a mistake in their orders, and their arrival supplied for a few days the loss of the Twenty-first, which had gone home to be mustered out and reorganized. Some companies of the newly forming Fourth Virginia were those who protected the village of Point Pleasant at the mouth of the river, and part of the Twelfth and Twenty-sixth Ohio were in detachments from Charleston toward Gauley Bridge, furnishing guards for the steamboats and assisting in the landing and forwarding of supplies. The Eleventh Ohio, under Lieutenant-Colonel Frizell, which still had only eight companies, had the task of covering and reconnoitring our immediate front, and was the advance-guard already mentioned. Part of the Twelfth under Major Hines did similar work on the road to Summersville, where Rosecrans had an advanced post, consisting of the Seventh Ohio (Colonel E. B. Tyler), the Thirteenth (Colonel Wm. Sooy Smith), and the Twenty-third (Lieutenant-Colonel Stanley Matthews). On the 13th of August the Seventh Ohio, by orders from Rosecrans, marched to Cross Lanes, the intersection of the read from Summersville to Gauley Bridge, with one from Carnifex Ferry, which is on the Gauley near the mouth of Meadow River. A road called the Sunday Road is in the Meadow River valley, and joins the Lewisburg turnpike about fifteen miles in front of Gauley Bridge. To give warning against any movement of the enemy to turn my position by this route or to intervene between me and Rosecrans's posts at Summersville and beyond, was Tyler's task. He was ordered to picket all crossings of the river near his position, and to join my command if he were driven away. I was authorized to call him to me in an emergency.

On the 15th Tyler was joined at Cross Lanes by the Thirteenth and Twenty-third Ohio, in consequence of rumours that the enemy was advancing upon Summersville in force from Lewisburg. I would have been glad of such an addition to my forces, but knowing that Rosecrans had stationed them as his own outpost covering the Sutton and Weston road, I ordered Tyler to maintain his own position, and urged the others to return at once to Summersville. The road by which they had expected the enemy was the Wilderness road, which crossed the Gauley at Hughes' Ferry, six miles above Carnifex. If attacked from that direction, they should retire northward toward Rosecrans, if possible.

Rosecrans gave orders to the same effect as soon as he heard of the movement, saying that his intention had been to station Smith and Matthews at Sutton, where their retreat toward him in case of necessity would be assured. His orders for Tyler were that he should scout far toward the enemy, "striking him wherever he can," and "hold his position at the ferries as long as he can safely do it, and then fall back, as directed," toward Gauley Bridge. The incident throws important light upon the situation a week later, when Tyler was attacked by Floyd.

Floyd and Wise were now really in motion, though General Lee remained at Valley Mountain near Huntersville, whence he directed their movements. On the 17th they had passed Sewell Mountain, but made slow progress in the face of the opposition of the Eleventh Ohio, which kept up a constant skirmish with them. On the 19th Floyd's advance-guard passed the mouth of the Sunday Road on the turnpike, and on the 20th made so determined a push at my advance-guard that I believed it a serious effort of the whole Confederate column. I strengthened my own advance-guard by part of the Twelfth Ohio, which was at hand, and placed them at Pig Creek, a mile beyond the Tompkins place, where the turnpike crossed a gorge making a strongly defensible position. The advance-guard was able to withstand the enemy alone, and drove back those who assaulted them with considerable loss. It has since appeared that this movement of the enemy was by Wise's command making a direct attack upon my position, whilst Floyd was moving by the diagonal road to Dogwood Gap on the Sunday Road where it crosses the old State Road. There he encamped for the night, and next day continued his march to the mouth of Meadow River near Carnifex Ferry. It was an affair of advance guards in which Wise was satisfied as soon as he found serious resistance, and he retired during the night. On the first evidence of the enemy's presence in force, I called Tyler from Cross Lanes to Twenty-mile Creek, about six miles from Gauley Bridge, where it was important to guard a road passing to my rear, and to meet any attempt to turn my flank if the attack should be determinedly made by the whole force of the enemy. As soon as the attack was repulsed, Tyler was ordered to return to Cross Lanes and resume his watch of the roads and river crossings there. He was delayed by the issue of shoes and clothing to his men, and when he approached his former position on the 24th, he found that Floyd was reported to have crossed the Gauley at Carnifex Ferry. Without waiting to reconnoitre the enemy at all, Tyler retreated to Peters Creek, several miles. Floyd had in fact succeeded in raising two small flatboats which Tyler had sunk but had not entirely destroyed. With these for a ferry, he had crossed and was entrenching himself where he was afterward attacked by Rosecrans.

In the hope that only a small force had made the crossing, I ordered Tyler to "make a dash at them, taking care to keep your force well in hand so as to keep your retreat safe." I added: "It is important to give them such a check as to stop their crossing." Meanwhile my advance-guard up New River was ordered to demonstrate actively in front and upon the Sunday Road, so as to disquiet any force which had gone towards Tyler, and I also sent forward half a regiment to Peters Creek (six miles from Cross Lanes) to hold the pass there and secure his retreat in case of need.

But Tyler was new to responsibility, and seemed paralyzed into complete inefficiency. He took nearly the whole of the 25th to move slowly to Cross Lanes, though he met no opposition. He did nothing that evening or night, and his disposal of his troops was so improper and outpost duty so completely neglected that on the morning of the 26th, whilst his regiment was at breakfast, it was attacked by Floyd on both flanks at once, and was routed before it could be formed for action. Some companies managed to make a show of fighting, but it was wholly in vain, and they broke in confusion. About 15 were killed and 50 wounded, the latter with some 30 others falling into the enemy's hands. Tyler, with his lieutenant-colonel, Creighton, came into Gauley Bridge with a few stragglers from the regiment. Others followed until about 200 were present. His train had reached the detachment I had sent to Peters Creek, and this covered its retreat to camp, so that all his wagons came in safely. He reported all his command cut to pieces and captured except the few that were with him, and wrote an official report of the engagement, giving that result.

On the 28th, however, we heard that Major Casement had carried 400 of the regiment safely into Charleston. He had rallied them on the hills immediately after the rout, and finding the direct road to Gauley Bridge intercepted, had led them by mountain paths over the ridges to the valley of Elk River, and had then followed that stream down to Charleston without being pursued. This put a new face on the business, and Tyler in much confusion asked the return of his report that he might re-write it. I looked upon his situation as the not unnatural result of inexperience, and contented myself with informing General Rosecrans of the truth as to the affair. Tyler was allowed to substitute a new report, and his unfortunate affair was treated as a lesson from which it was expected he would profit. It made trouble in the regiment, however, where the line officers did not conceal their opinion that he had failed in his duty as a commander, and he was never afterward quite comfortable among them.

The lieutenant-colonel, Creighton, was for a time in the abyss of self-reproach. The very day they reached Gauley Bridge in their unceremonious retreat, he came to me, crying with shame, and said, "General, I have behaved like a miserable coward, I ought to be cashiered," and repeated many such expressions of remorse. I comforted him by saying that the intensity of his own feeling was the best proof that he had only yielded to a surprise and that it was clear he was no coward. He died afterward at the head of his regiment in the desperate charge up the hills at Ringgold, Georgia, in the campaign following that of Chickamauga in the autumn of 1863, having had the command for two years after Tyler became a brigadier. During those two years the Seventh had been in numberless engagements, and its list of casualties in battle, made good by recruiting, was said to have reached a thousand. Better soldiers there were none, and Creighton proved himself a lion in every fight.

Casement, who rallied and led the most of the regiment from Cross Lanes over the mountains to Charleston, became afterward colonel of the One Hundred and Third Ohio. He came again under my command in East Tennessee in the winter of 1863, and continued one of my brigade commanders to the close of the war. He was a railway builder by profession, had a natural aptitude for controlling bodies of men, was rough of speech but generous of heart, running over with fun which no dolefulness of circumstance could repress, as jolly a comrade and as loyal a subordinate as the army could show.

After the Cross Lanes affair I fully expected that the Confederate forces would follow the route which Casement had taken to Charleston. Floyd's inactivity puzzled me, for he did no more than make an entrenched camp at Carnifex Ferry, with outposts at Peters Mountain and toward Summersville. The publication of the Confederate Archives has partly solved the mystery. Floyd called on Wise to reinforce him; but the latter demurred, insistent that the duty assigned him of attacking my position in front needed all the men he had. Both appealed to Lee, and Lee decided that Floyd was the senior and entitled to command the joint forces. The letters of Wise show a capacity for keeping a command in hot water which was unique. If he had been half as troublesome to me as he was to Floyd, I should indeed have had a hot time of it. But he did me royal service by preventing anything approaching to co-operation between the two Confederate columns. I kept my advance-guards constantly feeling of both, and got through the period till Rosecrans joined me with nothing more serious than some sharp affairs of detachments.

I was not without anxiety, however, and was constantly kept on the alert. Rosecrans withdrew the Twelfth Ohio from my command, excepting two companies under Major Hines, on the 19th of August, and the imperative need of detachments to protect the river below me was such that from this time till the middle of September my garrison at Gauley Bridge, including advance-guards and outposts, was never more than two and a half regiments or 1800 men. My artillerists were also ordered back to Ohio to reorganize, leaving the guns in the hands of such infantry details as I could improvise. I was lucky enough, however, to get a very good troop of horse under command of Captain Pfau in place of the irregular squad I had before.

On the 25th my advance-guard under Lieutenant-Colonel Frizell very cleverly succeeded in drawing into an ambuscade a body of Floyd's cavalry under Colonel A. G. Jenkins. The principal body of our men lined a defile near the Hawk's Nest, and the skirmishers, retreating before the enemy, led them into the trap. Our men began firing before the enemy was quite surrounded, and putting their horses upon the run, they dashed back, running the gantlet of the fire. Wise reported that he met men with their subordinate officers flying at four miles' distance from the place of the action, and so panic-stricken that they could not be rallied or led back. Jenkins was hurt by the fall of his horse, but he succeeded in getting away; for, as we had no horsemen to pursue with, even the wounded, except one, could not be overtaken. Hats, clothing, arms, and saddles were left scattered along the road in as complete a breakneck race for life as was ever seen. The result, if not great in the list of casualties, which were only reported at 10 or 15 by the enemy, was so demoralizing in its influence upon the hostile cavalry that they never again showed any enterprise in harassing our outposts, whilst our men gained proportionally in confidence.

About the 30th of August we heard of an encampment of Confederate militia at Boone C. H. which was so situated, southwest of the Kanawha River, as to menace our communications with the Ohio. I sent Lieutenant-Colonel Enyart with half of the First Kentucky Regiment to beat up this encampment, and he did so on the 2d of September, completely routing the enemy, who left 25 dead upon the field. Enyart's march and attack had been rapid and vigorous, and the terror of the blow kept that part of the district quiet for some time afterward.

We had heard for some days the news of the assembling of a considerable force of Confederate militia at Fayette C. H. under General Chapman and Colonel Beckley. They were reported at 2500, which was a fair estimate of the numbers which answered to the call. On the 3d of September a pretty well combined attack was made by Wise and this force; Wise pushing in sharply upon the turnpike, whilst Chapman, assisted by part of Wise's cavalry, drove back our small outpost on the Fayette road. Wise was met at Pig Creek as in his former attack, the eight companies of the Eleventh Ohio being strengthened by half of the Twenty-sixth Ohio, which was brought from below for this purpose. The effort was somewhat more persistent than before, and Wise indulged in considerable noisy cannonading; but the pickets retreated to the creek without loss, and the whole advance-guard, keeping under good cover there, repelled the attack with less than half a dozen casualties on our side, none being fatal. Wise retreated again beyond Hawk's Nest. The irregular troops on the Fayette road were more boldly led, and as there was no defensible position near the river for our outposts, these fell slowly back after a very warm skirmish, inflicting a loss, as reported by prisoners, of 6 killed among the enemy. I expected Floyd to move at the same time, and was obliged to continue upon the defensive by reason of his threatening position up the Gauley River; I, however, sent Major Hines with his two companies in that direction, and Floyd appeared to be impressed with the idea that my whole force was moving to attack him and attempted nothing aggressive. As at this time Wise, in his letters to General Lee, puts Floyd's force at 5600, and his own at 2200, I had good reason, therefore, to feel satisfied with being able to keep them all at bay.

In the midst of the alarms from every side, my camp itself was greatly excited by an incident which would have been occasion for regret at any time, but which at such a juncture threatened for a moment quite serious consequences. The work of entrenching the position was going on under the direction of Lieutenant Wagner as rapidly as the small working parties available could perform it. All were overworked, but it was the rule that men should not be detailed for fatigue duty who had been on picket the preceding night. On August 28th, a detail had been called for from the Second Kentucky, which lay above the hedge behind my headquarters, and they had reported without arms under a sergeant named Joyce. A supply of entrenching tools was stacked by the gate leading into the yard where my staff tents were pitched, and my aide, Lieutenant Conine, directed the sergeant to have his men take the tools and report to Mr. Wagner, the engineer, on the line. The men began to demur in a half-mutinous way, saying they had been on picket the night before. Conine, who was a soldierly man, informed them that that should be immediately looked into, and if so, they would be soon relieved, but that they could not argue the matter there, as their company commander was responsible for the detail. He therefore repeated his order. The sergeant then became excited and said his men should not obey. Lieutenant Gibbs, the district commissary, was standing by, and drawing his pistol, said to Joyce, "That's mutiny; order your men to take the tools or I'll shoot you." The man retorted with a curse, "Shoot!" Gibbs fired, and Joyce fell dead. When the sergeant first refused to obey, Conine coolly called out, "Corporal of the guard, turn out the guard!" intending very properly to put the man in arrest, but the shot followed too quick for the guard to arrive. I was sitting within the house at my camp desk, busy, when the first thing which attracted my attention was the call for the guard and the shot. I ran out, not stopping for arms, and saw some of the men running off shouting, "Go for your guns, kill him, kill him!" I stopped part of the men, ordered them to take the sergeant quickly to the hospital, thinking he might not be dead. I then ordered Gibbs in arrest till an investigation should be made, and ran at speed to a gap in the hedge which opened into the regimental camp. It was not a moment too soon. The men with their muskets were already clustering in the path, threatening vengeance on Mr. Gibbs. I ordered them to halt and return to their quarters. Carried away by excitement, they levelled their muskets at me and bade me get out of their way or they would shoot me. I managed to keep cool, said the affair would be investigated, that Gibbs was already under arrest, but they must go back to their quarters. The parley lasted long enough to bring some of their officers near. I ordered them to come to my side, and then to take command of the men and march them away. The real danger was over as soon as the first impulse was checked. The men then began to feel some of their natural respect for their commander, and yielded probably the more readily because they noticed that I was unarmed. I thought it wise to be content with quelling the disturbance, and did not seek out for punishment the men who had met me at the gap. Their excitement had been natural under the circumstances, which were reported with exaggeration as a wilful murder. If I had been in command of a larger force, it would have been easy to turn out another regiment to enforce order and arrest any mutineers; but the Second Kentucky was itself the only regiment on the spot. The First Kentucky was a mile below, and the Eleventh Ohio was the advance-guard up New River. Surrounded as we were by so superior a force of the enemy with which we were constantly skirmishing, I could not do otherwise than meet the difficulty instantly without regard to personal risk.

The sequel of the affair was not reached till some weeks later when General Rosecrans assembled a court-martial at my request. Lieutenant Gibbs was tried and acquitted on the plain evidence that the man killed was in the act of mutiny at the time. The court was a notable one, as its judge advocate was Major R. B. Hayes of the Twenty-third Ohio, afterwards President of the United States, and one of its members was Lieutenant-Colonel Stanley Matthews of the same regiment, afterwards one of the Justices of the Supreme Court.

The constant skirmishing with the enemy on all sides continued till the 10th of September, when General Rosecrans with his column reached Cross Lanes and had the action at Carnifex Ferry which I shall describe in the next chapter. I had sent forward half a regiment from my little command to open communication with him as soon as possible. On September 9th a party from this detachment had reached Cross Lanes and learned that Floyd was keeping close within his lines on the cliffs of Gauley above Carnifex Ferry. They, however, heard nothing of Rosecrans, and the principal body of their troops heard no sound of the engagement on the 10th, though within a very few miles. On the 12th communication was opened, and I learned of Floyd's retreat across the Gauley. I immediately moved forward the Eleventh and Twenty-sixth Ohio to attack Wise, who retreated from Hawk's Nest to the mouth of the Sunday Road, and upon my closer approach retired to Sewell Mountain. At the Sunday Road I was stopped by orders from Rosecrans, who thought it unwise to advance further till he had made a ferry at the Gauley and succeeded in getting his command over; for Floyd had again sunk the flatboats within reach, and these had to be a second time raised and repaired. At his request I visited the General at Carnifex Ferry, and then got permission to move my column forward a few miles to Alderson's, or Camp Lookout as we dubbed it, where a commanding position controlled the country to the base of Sewell Mountain. I was now able to concentrate the Seventh Ohio at Gauley Bridge, and ordered forward the Second Kentucky to join me in the new camp.

The period of my separate responsibility and of struggle

against great odds was not to close without a private grief which was the more poignant because the condition of the campaign forbade my leaving the post of duty. On the day I visited General Rosecrans at Carnifex Ferry I got news of the critical illness of my youngest child, a babe of eight months old, whom I had seen but a single day after his birth, for I had been ordered into camp from the legislature without time to make another visit to my family. The warning dispatch was quickly followed by another announcing the end, and I had to swallow my sorrows as well as I could and face the public enemy before us, leaving my wife uncomforted in her bereavement and all the more burdened with care because she knew we were resuming active operations in the field.

CHAPTER 6

Carnifex Ferry—
to Sewell Mountain and Back

General Rosecrans had succeeded McClellan as ranking officer in West Virginia, but it was not until the latter part of September that the region was made a department and he was regularly assigned to command. Meanwhile the three months' enlistments were expiring, many regiments were sent home, new ones were received, and a complete reorganization of his forces took place. Besides holding the railroad, he fortified the Cheat Mountain pass looking toward Staunton, and the pass at Elkwater on the mountain summit between Huttonsville and Huntersville. My own fortifications at Gauley Bridge were part of the system of defensive works he had ordered. By the middle of August he had established a chain of posts, with a regiment or two at each, on a line upon which he afterwards marched, from Weston by way of Bulltown, Sutton, and Summersville to Gauley Bridge.

As soon as he received the news of Floyd's attack upon Tyler at Cross Lanes, he hastened his preparations and began his march southward from Clarksburg with three brigades, having left the Upper Potomac line in command of General Kelley, and the Cheat Mountain region in command of General J. J. Reynolds. His route (already indicated) was a rough one, and the portion of it between Sutton and Summersville, over Birch Mountain, was very wild and difficult. He crossed the mountain on the 9th, and left his bivouac on the morning of the 10th of September, before daybreak. Marching through Summersville, he reached Cross Lanes about two o'clock in the afternoon. Floyd's position was now about two miles distant, and, waiting only for his column to close up, he again pressed forward. General Benham's brigade was in front, and soon met the enemy's pickets. Getting the impression that Floyd was in retreat, Benham pressed forward rather rashly, deploying to the left and coming under a sharp fire from the right of the enemy's works. Floyd had entrenched a line across a bend of the Gauley River, where the road from Cross Lanes to Lewisburg finds its way down the cliffs to Carnifex Ferry. His flanks rested upon precipices rising abruptly from the water's edge, and he also entrenched some rising ground in front of his principal line. Benham's line advanced through dense and tangled woods, ignorant of the enemy's position till it was checked by the fire from his breastworks. It was too late for a proper reconnaissance, and Rosecrans could only hasten the advance and deployment of the other brigades under Colonels McCook and Scammon. Benham had sent a howitzer battery and two rifled cannon with his head of column at the left, and these soon got a position from which, in fact, they enfiladed part of Floyd's line, though it was impossible to see much of the situation. Charges were made by portions of Benham's and McCook's brigades as they came up, but they lacked unity, and Rosecrans was dissatisfied that his head of column should be engaged before he had time to plan an attack. Colonel Lowe of the Twelfth Ohio had been killed at the head of his regiment, and Colonel Lytle of the Tenth had been wounded; darkness was rapidly coming on, and Rosecrans ordered the troops withdrawn from fire till positions could be rectified, and the attack renewed in the morning. Seventeen had been killed, and 141 had been wounded in the sharp but irregular combat. Floyd, however, had learned that his position could be subjected to destructive cannonade; he was himself slightly wounded, and his officers and men were discouraged. He therefore retreated across the Gauley in the night, having great difficulty in carrying his artillery down the cliffs by a wretched road in the darkness. He had built a slight foot-bridge for infantry in the bit of smooth water known as the Ferry, though both above and below the stream is an impassable mountain torrent. The artillery crossed in the flat-boats. Once over, the bridge was broken up and the ferry-boats were sunk. He reported but twenty casualties, and threw much of the responsibility upon Wise, who had not obeyed orders to reinforce him. His hospital, containing the wounded prisoners taken from Tyler, fell into Rosecrans's hands.

General Rosecrans found the country so difficult a one that he was in no little doubt as to the plan of campaign it was now best to follow. It was out of the question to supply his column by wagon trains over the mountainous roads from Clarksburg, and the Kanawha River must therefore be made the line of communication with his base, which had to be transferred to Gallipolis. In anticipation of this, I had accumulated supplies and ordnance stores at Gauley Bridge as much as possible with my small wagon trains, and had arranged for a larger depot at the head of steamboat navigation. I was ready therefore to turn over the control of my supply lines to Rosecrans's officers of the quartermaster and commissary departments as soon as his wagon trains could be transferred. It was to consult in regard to these matters, as was as in regard to the future conduct of the campaign, that the general directed me to visit his headquarters at Carnifex Ferry. I rode over from my camp at the Sunday Road junction on the morning of the 15th, found that one of the little flatboats had been again raised and repaired at Carnifex, and passing through the field of the recent combat, reached the general's headquarters near Cross Lanes. I was able from personal observation to assure him that it was easy for his command to follow the line of the march on which Floyd had retreated, if better means of crossing the Gauley were provided; but when they should join me on the Lewisburg turnpike, that highway would be the proper line of supply, making Gauley Bridge his depot. He hesitated to commit himself to either line for decisive operations until the Gauley should be bridged, but on my description of the commodious ferry I had made at Gauley Bridge by means of a very large flatboat running along a hawser stretched from bank to bank, he determined to advance, and to have a bridge of boats made in place of my ferry. McCook's brigade was ordered to report to me as soon as it could be put over the river, and I was authorized to advance some six miles toward the enemy, to Alberson's or Spy Rock, already mentioned beyond which Big Sewell Mountain is fourteen miles further to the southwest.

At Cross Lanes I met the commanders of the other brigades who were called in by General Rosecrans of an informal consultation based upon my knowledge of the country and the enemy. I naturally scanned them with some interest, and tried to make the most of the opportunity to become acquainted with them. General Benham I knew already, from his visit to me at Gauley Bridge in his capacity of engineer officer. I had met Colonel Robert McCook at Camp Dennison, and now that it was intimated that he would be for some days under my command, I recalled a scene I had witnessed there which left many doubts in my mind whether he would prove an agreeable subordinate. I had gone, one morning, to General Bates's office, and as I entered found McCook expressing himself with more vigour than elegance in regard to some order which had been issued respecting his regiment. My presence did not seem to interfere with the fluency of his remarks or the force of his expletives, but after a moment or two he seemed to notice a look of surprise in my face, and his own broadened humorously as his manner changed from vehemence to geniality. General Bates and he were familiar acquaintances at the bar in Cincinnati, and McCook had evidently presumed upon this as a warrant for speaking his mind as he pleased. When he reported to me at this later period, I found a hearty and loyal character under his bluff exterior and rough speech, with real courage, a quick eye for topography, and no lack of earnest subordination when work was to be done. Although our service together was short, I learned to have real respect for him, and sincerely mourned his loss when, later in the war, he met his tragic death. The other brigade commander was Colonel E. P. Scammon of the Twenty-third Ohio. He had graduated from West Point in 1837, and had served in the Topographical Engineers of the regular army and as instructor in the Military Academy. In the Mexican War he had been aide-de-camp to General Scott. He had been out of the army for some years before the rebellion, and was acting as professor of mathematics in St. Xavier's College, Cincinnati, when he was appointed to the colonelcy of the Twenty-third Ohio upon Rosecrans's promotion. Like Rosecrans, he was a Roman Catholic, though himself of Puritan descent. It seems that at the time of the Puseyite movement in England and in this country there had been a good many conversions to Romanism among the students and teachers at West Point, under the influence of the chaplain of the post, and Scammon, among a number of young men who subsequently became distinguished officers, was in this number. It need hardly be said that Scammon was well instructed in his profession. He was perhaps too much wedded to the routine of the service, and was looked upon by his subordinates as a martinet who had not patience enough with the inexperience of volunteer soldiers. He was one of the older men of our army, somewhat under the average height and weight, with a precise politeness of manner which reminded one of a Frenchman, and the resemblance was increased by his free use of his snuff-box. His nervous irritability was the cause of considerable chafing in his command, but this left him under fire, and those who had been with him in action learned to admire his courage and conduct. He was with me subsequently at South Mountain and Antietam, and still later had the misfortune to be one of those prisoners in the Confederates' hands who were exposed to the fire of our batteries in front of Charleston, S. C.

But being a subordinate, I was most interested in the characteristics of our commander. Our Camp Dennison acquaintance had been a pleasant one, and he greeted me with a cordiality that was reassuring. His general appearance was attractive. He was tall but not heavy, with the rather long head and countenance that is sometimes called Norman. His aquiline nose and bright eyes gave him an incisive expression, increased by rapid utterance in his speech, which was apt to grow hurried, almost to stammering, when he was excited. His impulsiveness was plain to all who approached him; his irritation quickly flashed out in words when he was crossed, and his social geniality would show itself in smiles and in almost caressing gestures when he was pleased. In discussing military questions he made free use of his theoretic knowledge, often quoted authorities and cited maxims of war, and compared the problem before him to analogous cases in military history. This did not go far enough to be pedantic, and was full of a lively intelligence; yet it did not impress me as that highest form of military insight and knowledge which solves the question before it upon its own merits and without conscious comparison with historical examples, through a power of judgment and perception ripened and broadened by the mastery of principles which have ruled the great campaigns of the world. He was fond of conviviality, loved to banter good-humouredly his staff officers and intimates, and was altogether an attractive and companionable man, with intellectual activity enough to make his society stimulating and full of lively discussion. I could easily understand Garfield's saying, in his letter to Secretary Chase which afterward became the subject of much debate, that he "loved every bone in his body."

Rosecrans's adjutant-general was Captain George L. Hartsuff, an officer of the regular army, who was well qualified to supplement in many ways the abilities and deficiencies of his chief. He was a large man, of heavy frame; his face was broad, and his bald head, tapering high, gave a peculiar pyramidal appearance to his figure. He was systematic and accurate in administrative work, patient and insistent in bringing the young volunteer officers in his department into habits of order and good military form. His coolness tempered the impulsiveness of his chief, and as they were of similar age and had about the same standing in the army before the war, the familiarity between them was that of comrades and equals more than of commander and subordinate.

My intercourse with these officers on the occasion of my visit to Cross Lanes was only the beginning of the acquaintance on which I based the estimate of them which I have given; but it was a good beginning, for the cordial freedom of thought and speech in the conference was such as to bring out the characteristics of the men. I rode back to my camp in the evening, feeling a sense of relief at the transfer of responsibility to other shoulders. The command of my brigade under the orders of Rosecrans seemed an easy task compared with the anxieties and the difficulties of the preceding three months. And so it was. The difference between chief responsibility in military movements and the leadership even of the largest subordinate organizations of an army is heaven-wide; and I believe that no one who has tried both will hesitate to say that the subordinate knows little or nothing of the strain upon the will and the moral faculties which the chief has to bear.

McCook's brigade joined me on the 16th, and we immediately marched to Alderson's, where we made a camp afterward known as Camp Lookout. I was able to bring up the Second Kentucky Regiment from Gauley Bridge, giving me in hand three regiments of my own brigade. I sent forward Major Hines with five companies as an advance-guard, and with these he scouted the country as far as the top of Big Sewell Mountain, and was able to give us definite information that Floyd had retreated as far as Meadow Bluff, where the Wilderness road joins the turnpike. Wise halted at Big Sewell Mountain and persisted in keeping his command separate from Floyd, who ordered him to join the rest of the column at Meadow Bluff. On the 20th September my advance-guard occupied the crest of the mountain, whilst Wise withdrew to a parallel ridge a mile beyond, and loudly insisted that Floyd should join him there instead of concentrating the Confederate force at Meadow Bluff. General Lee reached the latter place in person on the 21st, but found Wise's headstrong and captious spirit hardly more amenable to his discipline than to Floyd's. He shared Floyd's opinion that it was better to await Rosecrans's advance at Meadow Bluff, throwing upon the National forces the burden of transportation over the extended line, whilst guarding against a possible turning movement by the Wilderness road. But Wise was so noisy in his assertions that his was the only position in which to fight, that Lee hesitated to order him back peremptorily, and finally yielded to his clamour and directed Floyd to advance to Wise's position. The scandal of the quarrel between the two officers had, however, become so notorious that the Richmond government had authorized Lee to send Wise elsewhere, and, probably on his advice, the Confederate War Department ordered Wise to report at Richmond in person. The last scene in the comedy was decidedly amusing. Wise appealed passionately to Lee to say whether his military honour did not require that he should disobey the order till the expected battle should be fought, and Lee, no doubt in dismay lest he should still fail to get rid of so intractable a subordinate, gravely advised him that both honour and duty would be safe in obeying promptly the order.

Whilst waiting at Camp Lookout for authority to move forward, an incident occurred which gave us a little excitement and amusement, and which shows, better than much explanation could do, the difficult and intricate character of the country in which we were operating. A wagon-master from our camp had gone out hunting for forage, which was very scarce. He soon came back in excitement, reporting that he had come upon an encampment of a regiment of the enemy between our camp and New River and somewhat in our rear. His report was very circumstantial, but was so improbable that I was confident there was some mistake about it. He was, however, so earnest in his assertions that he could not be mistaken, that McCook, in whose brigade he was, sent out an officer with some men, guided by the wagon-master, to verify the report. The story was confirmed, and the matter was brought to me for action. Puzzled but not convinced, and thinking that as McCook's command was new to the country, it would be better to send some one who was used to scouting in the mountains, I ordered a lieutenant named Bontecou, of the Second Kentucky Regiment, to take a small party and examine the case anew. Bontecou had done a good deal of successful work in this line, and was regarded as a good woodsman and an enterprising scout. He too came back at nightfall, saying that there could be no mistake about it. He had crept close to the sentinels of the camp, had counted the tents, and being challenged by the guard, had made a run for it through the thicket, losing his hat. The position of the enemy was, by all the reports, about three miles from us, diagonally in rear of our right flank. It now seemed that it must be true that some detachment had been delayed in joining the retreating column, and had found itself thus partly cut off by our advance. I therefore ordered McCook to start at earliest peep of day, upon the Chestnutburg road (on which the wagon-master had been foraging), and passing beyond the hostile detachment, attack from the other side, it being agreed by all the scouting parties that this would drive the enemy toward our camp. My own brigade would be disposed of to intercept the enemy and prevent escape. McCook moved out as ordered, and following his guides came by many devious turns to a fork in the road, following which, they told him, a few minutes would bring him upon the enemy. He halted the column, and with a small skirmishing party went carefully forward. The guides pointed to a thicket from which the Confederates could be seen. His instinct for topography had made him suspect the truth, as he had noted the courses in advancing, and crawling through the thicket, he looked out from the other side upon what he at once recognized as the rear of his own camp, and the tents of the very regiment from which he had sent an officer to test the wagon-master's report. All the scouts had been so deceived by the tangle of wooded hills and circling roads that they fully believed they were still miles from our position; and, bewildered in the labyrinth, they were sure the tents they saw were the enemy's and not ours. The march had been through rain and mist, through dripping thickets and on muddy roads, and the first impulse was wrath at the erring scouts; but the ludicrous side soon prevailed, and officers and men joined in hearty laughter over their wild-goose chase. They dubbed the expedition the "Battle of Bontecou," and it was long before the lieutenant heard the last of the chaffing at his talents as a scout.

Major Hines's reports of the strength of the position on Sewell Mountain which the enemy had occupied, and my own reconnaissance of the intervening country, satisfied me that if we meant to advance on this line, we ought not to give the enemy time to reconsider and to reoccupy the mountain top from which he had retreated. On representing this to General Rosecrans, he authorized me to advance twelve miles to the Confederate camp on Big Sewell, directing me, however, to remain upon the defensive when there, and to avoid bringing on any engagement till he could bring up the rest of the column. His means of crossing at Carnifex Ferry were so poor that what he had thought would be done in two or three days from the time McCook joined me, took a full fortnight to accomplish.

I marched with my own and McCook's brigades on the 23d September, but when I reached the Confederate camp where Hines with the advance-guard awaited me, it was evident at a glance that we must go further. The position was a very strong one for resisting an approach from our direction, but was commanded by higher ground beyond. The true crest of the mountain was two miles further on, and there alone could we successfully bar the way against a superior force coming from the east. I therefore marched rapidly forward and occupied the crest in force. It was impossible to hide the whole of our camp from view and properly hold the position, but we made use of such cover as we could find, and prepared to defend the pass against all comers, since it was vain to attempt to mystify the enemy as to our advance in force.

On the 24th we had a lively skirmish with Wise's legion in front, and forced it to retire to a ridge out of range of our artillery. We dismounted one of his howitzers in the engagement, but contented ourselves with making him yield the ground which would interfere with our easy holding of our own position and the spurs of the mountain directly connected with it. Wise had learned that Rosecrans was not with my column, and on the supposition that the advance was made by my brigade only, Lee concluded to order Floyd to Wise's camp, being now satisfied that no movement of our troops had been made by way of the Wilderness road. It was at this time that Wise was relieved of command and ordered to Richmond, and Lee found it advisable to unite his forces and take command in person.

The relations of these three distinguished Virginians had not begun with this campaign, but dated back to the capture of John Brown at Harper's Ferry. Wise was then the governor of his State, and received from Lee the prisoner whose execution at Charlestown was to become an historical event. Floyd, who himself had once been governor of Virginia, was then Buchanan's Secretary of

War, and ordered Lee with the detachment of marines to Harper's Ferry, where they stormed the engine-house which Brown had made his fort. Dealing with such men as his subordinates, and with such a history behind them, it can easily be understood that Lee would feel no ordinary delicacy in asserting his authority, and no common embarrassment at their quarrels.

Rosecrans was at first disturbed at my going further than had been expected; but he was soon satisfied that nothing better could have been done. It is true that I was thirty-five miles from the supports in the rear, whether at Carnifex Ferry or Gauley Bridge; but the position was almost impregnable in front, and by watchfulness I should know of any attempt to turn it in time to make safe my retreat to Camp Lookout. On the 26th Scammon's brigade came within easy supporting distance, and General Rosecrans came in person to my camp. He had not been able to bring up his headquarters train, and was my guest for two or three days, sharing my tent with me. Cold autumnal rains set in on the very day the general came to the front, and continued almost without intermission. In the hope of still having some favourable weather for campaigning, the other brigades were brought forward, and the whole force was concentrated at the mountain except the necessary garrisons for the posts in the rear. Brigadier-General Robert C, Schenck reported for duty in the evening of a fearfully stormy day whilst Rosecrans was still my tent-mate. He had heard rumours of fighting at the front, and had hurried forward with a couple of staff officers, but without baggage. My staff officers were sharing their shelter with the gentlemen who had accompanied Rosecrans, but the new-comers were made heartily welcome to what we had. In my own tent General Rosecrans occupied my camp cot; I had improvised a rough bunk for myself on the other side of the tent, but as General Schenck got in too late for the construction of any better resting-place, he was obliged to content himself with a bed made of three or four camp-stools set in a row. Anything was better than lying on the damp ground in such a storm; but Schenck long remembered the aching weariness of that night, as he balanced upon the narrow and unstable supports which threatened to tumble him upon the ground at the least effort to change the position of stiffened body and limbs. One could not desire better companionship than we had during our waking hours, for both my guests had had varied and interesting experience and knew how to make it the means of delightful social intercourse and discussion. The chilly temperature of the tent was pleasantly modified by a furnace which was the successful invention of the private soldiers. A square trench was dug from the middle of the tent leading out behind it; this was capped with flat stones three or four inches thick, which were abundant on the mountain. At the end of it, on the outside, a chimney of stones plastered with mud was built up, and the whole topped out by an empty cracker-barrel by way of chimney-pot. The fire built in the furnace had good draught, and the thick stones held the heat well, making, on the whole, the best means of warming a tent which I ever tried. The objection to the little sheet-iron stoves furnished with the Sibley tent is that they are cold in a minute if the fire dies out.

The rains, when once they began, continued with such violence that the streams were soon up, the common fords became impassable, and the roads became so muddy and slippery that it was with the utmost difficulty our little army was supplied. The four brigades were so reduced by sickness and by detachments that Rosecrans reported the whole as making only 5200 effective men. Every wagon was put to work hauling supplies and ammunition, even the headquarters baggage wagons and the regimental wagons of the troops, as well those stationed in the rear as those in front. We were sixty miles from the head of steamboat navigation, the wagon trains were too small for a condition of things where the teams could hardly haul half loads, and by the 1st of October we had demonstrated the fact that it was impossible to sustain our army any further from its base unless we could rely upon settled weather and good roads.

Lee had directed an effort to be made by General Loring, his subordinate, on the Staunton line, to test the strength of the posts under Reynolds at Cheat Mountain and Elkwater, and lively combats had resulted on the 12th, and 14th of September. Reynolds held firm, and as Rosecrans was not diverted from his plans and was pushing forward on the Lewisburg line, Lee ordered Loring to report to him with most of his command. Reynolds, in return, made a forced reconnaissance upon the Confederate position at Greenbrier River on October 2nd, but found it too strong to be carried. The reinforcement by Loring gave Lee a very positive advantage in numbers, but the storms and foundering roads paralyzed both armies, which lay opposite each other upon the crests of Big Sewell separated by a deep gorge. On the 5th of October the condition of the Kanawha valley had become such that Rosecrans felt compelled to withdraw his forces to the vicinity of Gauley Bridge. The freshet had been an extraordinary one. At Charleston the Kanawha River usually flows in a bed forty or fifty feet below the plateau on which the town is built; but the waters now rose above these high banks and flooded the town itself, being four or five feet deep in the first story of dwelling-houses built in what was considered a neighbourhood safe from floods. The inundation almost stopped communication, though our quartermasters tried to remedy part of the mischief by forcing light steamers up as near to the Kanawha Falls as possible. But it was very difficult to protect the supplies landed upon a muddy bank where were no warehouses, and no protection but canvas covers stretched over the piles of barrels and boxes of bread and sacks of grain. There was enormous waste and loss, but we managed to keep our men in rations, and were better off than the Confederates, in regard to whom Floyd afterward reported to his government that the eleven days of cold storms at Sewell Mountain had "cost more men, sick and dead, than the battle of Manassas Plains."

It has been asserted by Confederate writers that Lee was executing a movement to turn Rosecrans's left flank when the latter marched back from Sewell Mountain. If so, it certainly had not gone far enough to attract our attention, and from my own knowledge of the situation, I do not believe it had passed beyond the form of discussion of a possible movement when the weather should become settled. Such plans were discussed on both sides, but the physical condition of the country was an imperative veto upon aggressive action.

During the 5th of October our sick and spare baggage were sent back to Camp Lookout. Tents were struck at ten o'clock in the evening, and the trains sent on their way under escort at eleven. The column moved as soon as the trains were out of the way, except my own brigade, to which was assigned the duty of rear-guard. We remained upon the crest of the hill till half-past one, the men being formed in line of battle and directed to lie down till the time for them to march. Our sentinels had been posted with extra precaution, so that they might be withdrawn an hour or two after the brigade should move. Extra reserves were assigned to them, and Major Hines put in command of the whole detachment, with orders to keep in communication with me at the extreme rear of the marching column. It was interesting to observe the effect of this night movement upon the men. Their imagination was excited by the novelty of the situation, and they furnished abundant evidence that the unknown is always, in such cases, the wonderful. The night had cleared off and the stars were out. The Confederate position was eastward from us, and as a bright star rose above the ridge on which the enemy was, we could hear soldiers saying in a low tone to each other, "There goes a fire balloon—it must be a signal—they must have discovered what we are doing!" The exaggerated parallax at the horizon made the rising star seem to move rapidly for the first few minutes, and men, ignorant of this, naturally mistook its character. In a similar way an occasional shot on the picket line would be the cause of a subdued excitement. I doubt if soldiers ever make a night movement in an enemy's presence without being under a nervous strain which exaggerates the importance of everything they see and hear, and this gives uncertainty and increases the difficulty of such duty. It is no small part of the duty of officers, in such cases, to allay this tendency to excitement, to explain the situation, and by a wise mixture of information and discipline to keep the men intelligently cool and in full command of their faculties.

General Rosecrans had gone with the head of the column, and had left with me Major Slemmer, his inspector-general, to bring him word when the rear of the column should be in march. Slemmer was the officer who, as a lieutenant, had distinguished himself by holding Fort Pickens in Pensacola harbour at the outbreak of the rebellion. He was a man of marked character, and in view of his experience it may easily be understood that we had no lack of interesting matter for conversation as we paced in rear of the reclining men during the midnight hours. His failing health prevented his taking the prominent part in the war that his abilities warranted, but I have retained, from that evening's work together, a pleasing impression of his character and a respect for his military knowledge and talents. In impressing on me the fact that my position was the one of special honour in this movement, he expressed the wish that Rosecrans had himself remained there; but the result showed that hardly less than the commanding general's own authority and energy could have got the column forward in the mud and darkness. The troops had marched but a mile or two when they overtook part of the wagon train toiling slowly over the steep and slippery hills. Here and there a team would be "stalled" in the mud, and it looked as if daylight would overtake us before even a tolerably defensive position would be reached. Rosecrans now gave his personal supervision to the moving of the wagons and artillery—wagon-master's work, it maybe said, but it was work which had to be done if the little army was not to be found in the morning strung out and exposed to the blows of the enemy if he should prove enterprising.

We who were at the rear did not know of the difficulty the column was having, and when my messenger reported the rear of the preceding brigade a mile or more from the camp, I gave the order to march, and my men filed into the road. Slemmer went forward to inform the general that we were in movement, and I remained with Major Hines till all was quiet, when he was directed to call in his pickets and sentinels and follow. I had gone hardly a mile when we were brought to a halt by the head of the brigade overtaking those who had preceded us. Word was brought back that the artillery was finding great difficulty in getting over the first considerable hill west of the mountain. We ourselves were upon the downward road from the mountain crest, but our way led along the side of a spur of the mountain which towered above us on our left. We were in a dense wood that shut out the stars, and in darkness that could almost be felt. I rode back a little to meet Hines and to keep some distance between the column and his little rear-guard. We sent a chain of sentinels over the hill commanding the road, and waited, listening for any evidence that the enemy had discovered our movement and followed. An hour passed in this way, and the column moved on a short distance. Again there was a halt, and again a deployment of our sentries. When at last day broke, we were only three or four miles from our camp of the evening before; but we had reached a position which was easily defensible, and where I could halt the brigade and wait for the others to get entirely out of our way. The men boiled their coffee, cooked their breakfast, and rested. Early in the forenoon a small body of the enemy's cavalry followed us, but were contented with very slight skirmishing, and we marched leisurely to Camp Lookout before evening. Such night marches from the presence of an enemy are among the most wearing and trying in the soldier's experience, yet, in spite of the temptation to invest them with extraordinary peril, they are rarely interfered with. It is the uncertainty, the darkness, and the effect of these upon men and officers that make the duty a delicate one. The risk is more from panic than from the foe, and the loss is more likely to be in baggage and in wagons than in men. I have several times been in command of rear-guards on such occasions, and I believe that I would generally prefer an open withdrawal by day. It is not hard to hold even a bold enemy at bay by a determined brigade or division, and a whole army may be saved from the exhaustion and exposure which rapidly fill the hospitals, and may cost more than several combats between rear and advance guards.

    My brigade remained two or three days at Camp Lookout, where we were put upon the alert on the 7th by a reported advance of the enemy, but it amounted to nothing more than a lively skirmish of some cavalry with our outposts. Lee was glad to move back to Meadow Bluff to be nearer his supplies, and Rosecrans encamped his troops between Hawk's Nest and the Tompkins farm, all of them being now within a few miles of Gauley Bridge. Part of my brigade garrisoned the post at the bridge, but by Rosecrans's direction my own headquarters tents were pitched near his own upon the Tompkins farm. Both parties now remained in observation till near the end of October. Floyd, more enterprising in plans than resolute or skilful in carrying them out, had obtained Lee's consent to make an attempt to render our position untenable by operations on the opposite side of New River. Lee had intended to co-operate by moving against us with the rest of his force, but on the 20th of October the reports from the Staunton region were so threatening that he determined to send Loring back there, and this, of course, settled it that Lewisburg would be covered in front only by Wise's Legion, commanded by Colonel Davis. Although Floyd complained of this change of plan, he did not abandon his purpose, but ordering the militia on that side of the river to reassemble, he marched to Fayette C. H.

Rosecrans had distributed his brigades in *echelon* along the turnpike—Schenck's, the most advanced, being ten miles from Gauley Bridge; McCook's eight miles, where the road from Fayette C. H. by way of Miller's Ferry comes in across New River; Benham's six miles, whilst of my own one regiment at the Tompkins farm guarded headquarters, and the rest were at Gauley Bridge and lower posts where they could protect the navigation of the Kanawha. McCook by Rosecrans's direction marched to Fayette C. H. about the 20th of October, and on his return reported that only guerrilla parties were abroad in that vicinity. Rosecrans seems to have expected that at least a foothold would be kept on the other side of New River at Miller's Ferry, but McCook left nothing there, and when he tried to place a detachment on that side about the 25th, the shore and cliffs were found to be held by a force of sharpshooters. This marked the advance of Floyd, who established his camp in front of Fayette C. H. at the forking of the roads to Miller's Ferry and to Gauley Bridge. For a few days he made no serious demonstration, and Rosecrans hastened forward the work of clothing and paying his men, recruiting his teams and bringing back to the ranks the soldiers whom exposure had sent to the hospital. He had heard in a trustworthy way of Lee's intention to move against us by the turnpike whilst Floyd advanced on the other side of the river, but Tie had not yet learned of the withdrawal of Lee with Loring's troops. He therefore remained quiet and expectant, awaiting the definite development of events.

As this had been my first service in the field as part of a larger command, I was keenly alive to the opportunity of comparing the progress we had made in discipline and instruction with that of other brigades, so that I might cure defects in my own methods and improve the soldierly character as well as the administration of my own command. I was gratified to see in my troops evidence of a pride in their own organization and a wholesome emulation, which made them take kindly to the drill and discipline which were necessary to improvement. I was particularly interested in observing Rosecrans's methods with the men. His standard of soldierly excellence was high, and he was earnest in insisting that his brigadiers and his staff officers should co-operate vigorously in trying to attain it. His impulsiveness, however, led him sometimes into personal efforts at discipline where the results were at least doubtful. He would sometimes go out through the camps in the evening, and if he saw a tent lighted after "taps," or heard men singing or talking, he would strike loudly on the canvas with the flat of his sword and command silence or the extinguishment of the light. The men, in good-humoured mischief, would try different ways of "getting even" with him. One that gave much amusement to the camp was this: the men in a tent thus attacked pretended to believe that their regimental wagon-master was playing a practical joke on them, and shouted back to him all sorts of rough camp chaff. When the exasperated general appeared at the door of the tent, they were, of course, overwhelmed with the most innocent astonishment, and explained that that wagon-master was in the habit of annoying them, and that they really had not heard the "taps." I have been with the general in approaching a picket, when he would hotly lecture a sentinel who showed ignorance of some of his duties or inattention to them. I thought I could see in all such cases that it would have been wiser to avoid any unnecessary collision with the privates, but to take the responsible officer aside and make him privately understand that he must answer for such lack of instruction or of discipline among his men. An impulsive man is too apt to meddle with details, and so to weaken the sense of responsibility in the intermediate officers, who hate to be ignored or belittled before the soldiers. But if Rosecrans's method was not an ideal one, it was at least vigorous, and every week showed that the little army was improving in discipline and in knowledge of duty.

Chapter 7

Cotton Mountain

On the 1st of November the early morning was fair but misty, and a fog lay in the gorge of New River nearly a thousand feet below the little plateau at the Tompkins farm, on which the headquarters tents were pitched. General Rosecrans's tents were not more than a hundred yards above mine, between the turnpike and the steep descent to the river, though both our little camps were secluded by thickets of young trees and laurel bushes. Breakfast was over, the fog was lifting out of the valley, and I was attending to the usual morning routine of clerical work, when the report and echo of a cannon-shot, down the gorge in the direction of Gauley Bridge, was heard. It was unusual, enough so to set me thinking what it could mean, but the natural explanation suggested itself that it was one of our own guns, perhaps fired at a target. In a few moments an orderly came in some haste, saying the general desired to see me at his tent. As I walked over to his quarters, another shot was heard. As I approached, I saw him standing in front of his tent door, evidently much excited, and when I came up to him, he said in the rapid, half-stammering way peculiar to him at such times: "The enemy has got a battery on Cotton Mountain opposite our post, and is shelling it! What d' ye think of that?" The post at the bridge and his headquarters were connected by telegraph, and the operator below had reported the fact of the opening of the cannonade from the mountain side above him, and added that his office was so directly under fire that he must move out of it. Indeed he was gone and communication broken before orders could be sent to him or to the post. The fact of the cannonade did not disturb me so much as the way in which it affected Rosecrans. He had been expecting to be attacked by Lee in front, and knew that McCook was exchanging shots across the river with some force of the enemy at Miller's Ferry; but that the attack should come two miles or more in our rear, from a point where artillery had a plunging fire directly into our depot of supplies and commanded our only road for a half-mile where it ran on a narrow bench along New River under Gauley Mountain cliffs, had been so startling as to throw him decidedly off his balance. The error in not occupying Cotton Mountain himself was now not only made plain, but the consequences were not pleasant to contemplate. I saw that the best service I could render him for the moment was to help him back into a frame of mind in which cool reasoning on the situation would be possible. I have already stated the contrast between my own sense of care when in sole command and the comparative freedom from it when a senior officer came upon the field; and I now realized how much easier it was for a subordinate to take things coolly. I therefore purposely entered into a discussion of the probabilities of the situation, and drew it out at length enough to assist the general in recovering full control of himself and of his own faculties. We could not, from where we stood, see the post at Gauley Bridge nor even the place on Cotton Mountain where the enemy's battery was placed, and we walked a little way apart from our staff officers to a position from which we could see the occasional puffs of white smoke from the hostile guns. From our camp the road descended sharply along the shoulders of steep hills covered with wood for a mile and a half, till it reached the bottom of the New River gorge, and then it followed the open bench I have mentioned till it reached the crossing of the Gauley. On the opposite side of New River there was no road, the mass of Cotton Mountain crowding close upon the stream with its picturesque face of steep inclines and perpendicular walls of rock. The bridge of boats which Rosecrans had planned at Gauley Bridge had not been built, because it had been found impossible to collect or to construct boats enough to make it. We were therefore still dependent on the ferry. Whilst the general and I were talking, Colonel De Villiers galloped up, having crossed at the ferry and run the gantlet of skirmishers whom he reported as lining the other side of New River opposite the unsheltered part of our road. He had recently reported for duty, having, as he asserted, escaped in a wonderful way from captivity in Libby Prison at Richmond. His regiment was at the bridge and he was the senior officer there; but, in his characteristic light-headed way, instead of taking steps to protect his post and re-establish the telegraph communications, he had dashed off to report in person at headquarters. As he was willing to take the risks of the race back again, he was allowed to go, after being fully instructed to set up a new telegraph office in a ravine out of range of fire, to put the ferry-boat out of danger as soon as he should be over, and prepare the ordnance stores to be moved into the valley of Scrabble Creek at night. I begged the general to be allowed to go back with De Villiers, as the thing I most feared was some panic at the post which might result in the destruction of our stores in depot there. He, however, insisted on my staying at headquarters for a time at least.

Information of the attack was sent to the brigades up the river, and Schenck, who was farthest up, was directed to push out scouting parties and learn if there was any advance of the enemy from Sewell Mountain. Benham, who was nearest, was ordered to send down part of his brigade to meet the efforts of the enemy to stop our communication with Gauley Bridge. The battery of mountain howitzers under Captain Mack of the regular army was also ordered to report at headquarters, with the intention of placing it high up on Gauley cliffs, where it could drop shells among the enemy's skirmishers on the opposite bank of the river. An hour or two passed and the detachment from Benham's brigade approached. It was the Thirteenth Ohio, led by one of its field officers, who halted the column and rode up to General Rosecrans for orders. The general's manner was still an excited one, and in the rapidity with which his directions were given the officer did not seem to get a clear idea of what was required of him. He made some effort to get the orders explained, but his failure to comprehend seemed to irritate Rosecrans, and he therefore bowed and rode back to his men with a blank look which did not promise well for intelligent action. Noticing this, I quietly walked aside among the bushes, and when out of sight hurried a little in advance and waited at the roadside for the column. I beckoned the officer to me, and said to him, "Colonel, I thought you looked as if you did not fully understand the general's wishes." He replied that he did not, but was unwilling to question him as it seemed to irritate him. I said that was a wrong principle to act on, as a commanding officer has the greatest possible interest in being clearly understood. I then explained at large what I knew to be Rosecrans's purposes. The officer thanked me cordially and rode away. I have ventured to give this incident with such fullness, because subsequent events in Rosecrans's career strengthened the impression I formed at the time, that the excitability of his temperament was such that an unexpected occurrence might upset his judgment so that it would be uncertain how he would act—whether it would rouse him to a heroism of which he was quite capable, or make him for the time unfit for real leadership by suspending his self-command.

Soon after noon I obtained permission to go to Gauley Bridge and assume command there; but as the road along New River was now impracticable by reason of the increased fire of the enemy upon it, I took the route over the top of Gauley Mountain, intending to reach the Gauley River as near the post as practicable. I took with me only my aide, Captain Christie, and an orderly. We rode a little beyond the top of the mountain, and sending the orderly back with the horses, proceeded on foot down the northern slope. We soon came to the slashing which I had made in August to prevent the enemy's easy approach to the river near the post. The mist of the morning had changed to a drizzling rain. We had on our heavy horsemen's overcoats with large capes, cavalry boots and spurs, swords and pistols. This made it toilsome work for us. The trees had been felled so that they crossed each other in utmost confusion on the steep declivity. Many of them were very large, and we slid over the great wet trunks, climbed through and under branches, let ourselves down walls of natural rock, tripped and hampered by our accoutrements, till we came to the end of the entanglement at what we supposed was the edge of the river. To our dismay we found that we had not kept up stream far enough, and that at this point was a sheer precipice some thirty feet high. We could find no crevices to help us climb down it. We tried to work along the edge till we should reach a lower place, but this utterly failed. We were obliged to retrace our steps to the open wood above the slashing. But if the downward climbing had been hard, this attempt to pull ourselves up again—... *superasque evadere ad auras*...—was labour indeed. We stopped several times from sheer exhaustion, so blown that it seemed almost impossible to get breath again. Our clothes were heavy from the rain on the outside and wet with perspiration on the inside. At last, however, we accomplished it, and resting for a while at the foot of a great tree till we gained a little strength, we followed the upper line of the slashing till we passed beyond it, and then turned toward the river, choosing to reach its banks high up above the camp rather than attempt again to climb through the fallen timber. Once at the water's edge we followed the stream down till we were opposite the guard post above the camp, when we hailed for a skiff and were ferried over.

It was now almost dark, but the arrangements were soon made to have wagons ready at the building on the Kanawha front used as a magazine, and to move all our ammunition during the night to the place I had indicated in the ravine of Scrabble Creek, which runs into the Gauley. The telegraph station was moved there and connection of wires made. We also prepared to run the ferry industriously during the night and to put over the necessary trainloads of supplies for the troops above. A place was selected high up on the hill behind us, where I hoped to get up a couple of Parrott guns which might silence the cannon of the enemy on Cotton Mountain. I was naturally gratified at the expressions of relief and satisfaction of the officers of the post to have me in person among them. They had already found that the plunging fire from the heights across the river was not a formidable thing, and that little mischief would happen if the men were kept from assembling in bodies or large groups within range of the enemy's cannon.

The fatigues of the day made sleep welcome as soon as the most pressing duties had been done, and I went early to rest, giving orders to the guard at my quarters to call me at peep of day. The weather cleared during the night, and when I went out in the morning to see what progress had been made in transferring the ammunition to a safe place, I was surprised to find the train of wagons stopped in the road along the Gauley in front of the camp. General Rosecrans's ordnance officer was of the regular army, but unfortunately was intemperate. He had neglected his duty during the night, leaving his sergeant to get on without guidance or direction. The result was that the ordnance stores had not been loaded upon the waiting wagons till nearly daylight, and soon after turning out of the Kanawha road into that of the Gauley, the mules of a team near the head of the train balked, and the whole had been brought to a standstill. There was a little rise in the road on the hither side of Scrabble Creek, where the track, cutting through the crest of a hillock, was only wide enough for a single team, and this rise was of course the place where the balky animals stopped. The line of the road was enfiladed by the enemy's cannon, the morning fog in the valley was beginning to lift under the influence of the rising sun, and as soon as the situation was discovered we might reckon upon receiving the fire of the Cotton Mountain battery. The wagon-drivers realized the danger of handling an ammunition train under such circumstances and began to be nervous, whilst the onlookers not connected with the duty made haste to get out of harm's way. My presence strengthened the authority of the quartermaster in charge, Captain E. P. Fitch, helped in steadying the men, and enabled him to enforce promptly his orders. He stopped the noisy efforts to make the refractory mules move, and sent in haste for a fresh team. As soon as it came, this was put in place of the balky animals, and at the word of command the train started quickly forward. The fog had thinned enough, however, to give the enemy an inkling of what was going on, and the rattling of the wagons on the road completed the exposure. Without warning, a ball struck in the road near us and bounded over the rear of the train, the report of the cannon following instantly. The drivers involuntarily crouched over their mules and cracked their whips. Another shot followed, but it was also short, and the last wagon turned the shoulder of the hill into the gorge of the creek as the ball bounded along up the Gauley valley. It was perhaps fortunate for us that solid shot instead of shrapnel were used, but it is not improbable that the need of haste in firing made the battery officer feel that he had no time to cut and adjust fuses to the estimated distance to our train; or it is possible that shells were used but did not explode. It was my first acquaintance with Captain Fitch, who had accompanied Rosecrans's column, and his cool efficiency was so marked that I applied for him as quartermaster upon my staff. He remained with me till I finally left West Virginia in 1863, and I never saw his superior in handling trains in the field. He was a West Virginian, volunteering from civil life, whose outfit was a good business education and an indomitable rough energy that nothing could tire.

During the evening of the 1st of November General Benham's brigade came to the post at Gauley Bridge to strengthen the garrison, and was encamped on the Kanawha side near the falls, where the widening of the valley put them out of range of the enemy's fire. The ferry below the falls was called Montgomery's and was at the mouth of Big Falls Creek, up which ran the road to Fayette C. H. A detachment of the enemy had pushed back our outposts on this road, and had fired upon our lower camp with cannon, but the position was not a favourable one for them and they did not try to stay long. After a day or two we were able to keep pickets on that side with a flatboat and hawser to bring them back, covered by artillery on our side of the Kanawha.

During November 2nd Rosecrans matured a plan of operations against Floyd, who was now definitely found to be in command of the hostile force on Cotton Mountain. It was also learned through scouting parties and the country people that Lee had left the region, with most of the force that had been at Sewell Mountain. It seemed possible therefore to entrap Floyd, and this was what Rosecrans determined to attempt. Benham was ordered to take his brigade down the Kanawha and cross to the other side at the mouth of Loup Creek, five miles below. Schenck was ordered to prepare wagon bodies as temporary boats, to make such flatboats as he could, and get ready to cross the New River at Townsend's Ferry, about fifteen miles above Gauley Bridge. McCook was ordered to watch Miller's Ferry near his camp, and be prepared to make a dash on the short road to Fayette C. H. I was ordered to hold the post at Gauley Bridge, forward supplies by night, keep down the enemy's fire as far as possible, and watch for an opportunity to co-operate with Benham by way of Montgomery's Ferry. Benham's brigade was temporarily increased by 1500 picked men from the posts between Kanawha Falls and Charleston. He was expected to march up Loup Creek and cut off Floyd's retreat by way of Raleigh C. H., whilst Schenck should co-operate from Townsend's Ferry. On the 5th the preparations had been made, and Benham was ordered to cross the Kanawha. He did so on the night of the 6th, but except sending scouting parties up Loup Creek, he did nothing, as a sudden rise in New River made Rosecrans suspend the concerted movement, and matters remained as they were, awaiting the fall of the river, till the 10th.

For a week after the 1st, Floyd's battery on Cotton Mountain fired on very slight provocation, and caution was necessary in riding or moving about the camp. The houses of the hamlet were not purposely injured, for Floyd would naturally be unwilling to destroy the property of West Virginians, and it was a safe presumption that we had removed the government property from buildings within range of fire, as we had in fact done. Our method of forwarding supplies was to assemble the wagon trains near my lower camp during the day, and push them forward to Gauley Mount and Tompkins farm during the night. The ferry-boat at Gauley Bridge was kept out of harm's way in the Gauley, behind the projection of Gauley Mount, but the hawser on which it ran was not removed. At nightfall the boat would be manned, dropped down to its place, made fast to the hawser by a snatch-block, and commence its regular trips, passing over the wagons. The ferries, both at the bridge and at Montgomery's, were under the management of Captain Lane of the Eleventh Ohio and his company of mechanics. We had found at points along the Kanawha the gunwales of flatboats, gotten out by lumbermen in the woods and brought to the river bank ready to be put into boats for the coal trade, which had already much importance in the valley. These gunwales were single sticks of timber, sixty or eighty feet long, two or three feet wide, and say six inches thick. Each formed the side of a boat, which was built by tying two gunwales together with cross timbers, the whole being then planked. Such boats were three or four times as large as those used for the country ferries upon the Gauley and New rivers, and enabled us to make these larger ferries very commodious. Of course the enemy knew that we used them at night, and would fire an occasional random shot at them, but did us no harm.

The enemy's guns on the mountain were so masked by the forest that we did not waste ammunition in firing at them, except as they opened, when our guns so quickly returned their fire that they never ventured upon continuous action, and after the first week we had only occasional shots from them. We had planted our sharpshooters also in protected spots along the narrower part of New River near the post, and made the enemy abandon the other margin of the stream, except with scattered sentinels. In a short time matters thus assumed a shape in which our work went on regularly, and the only advantage Floyd had attained was to make us move our supply trains at night. His presence on the mountain overlooking our post was an irritation under which we chafed, and from Rosecrans down, everybody was disgusted with the enforced delay of Benham at Loup Creek. Floyd kept his principal camp behind Cotton Mountain, in the position I have already indicated, in an inaction which seemed to invite enterprise on our part. His courage had oozed out when he had carried his little army into an exposed position, and here as at Carnifex Ferry he seemed to be waiting for his adversary to take the initiative.

To prepare for my own part in the contemplated movement, I had ordered Captain Lane to build a couple of flatboats of a smaller size than our large ferry-boats, and to rig these with sweeps or large oars, so that they could be used to throw detachments across the New River to the base of Cotton Mountain, at a point selected a little way up the river, where the stream was not so swift and broken as in most places. Many of our men had become expert in managing such boats, and a careful computation showed that we could put over 500 men an hour with these small scows.

From the 5th to the both Rosecrans had been waiting for the waters to subside, and pressing Benham to examine the roads up Loup Creek so thoroughly that he could plant himself in Floyd's rear as soon as orders should be given. Schenck would make the simultaneous movement when Benham was known to be in march, and McCook's and my own brigade would at least make demonstrations from our several positions. From my picket post at Montgomery's Ferry I had sent scouts up the Fayette road, and by the 9th had discovered such symptoms of weakness in the enemy that I thought the time had come to make an effort to dislodge the battery and get command of the crest of Cotton Mountain overlooking my camp. On the both I made a combined movement from both my upper and lower camps. Colonel De Villiers was ordered to take all of the Eleventh Ohio fit for duty (being only 200 men), and crossing by the small boats, make a vigorous reconnaissance over the New River face of Cotton Mountain, reaching the crest if possible. Lieutenant-Colonel Enyart of the First Kentucky was directed to cross below the falls with a similar force, and push a reconnaissance out on the Fayette road, whilst he also should try to co-operate with De Villiers in clearing the enemy from the heights opposite Gauley Bridge. The place at which De Villiers crossed was out of sight and range from the enemy's battery. His first boat-load of forty men reached the opposite shore safely, and dividing into two parties, one pushed up the New River to a ravine making a somewhat easy ascent toward the crest, whilst the others skirmished up the almost perpendicular face of the rocks where they landed. The remainder of the men of the Eleventh were put over as fast as possible, and joined their colonel in the ravine mentioned, up which they marched to a little clearing high up the hill, known as Blake's farm, where the advanced party had found the enemy. The battery was withdrawn as soon as De Villiers' approach at the Blake farm was known, supports being sent to the outpost there to check our advance. The men of the Eleventh, led by Major Coleman, attacked sharply, drove back the enemy, and succeeded in extending their right to the crest above the recent position of the battery. They were of course stretched out into a mere skirmish line, and I directed them to hold the crest without advancing further till Enyart should be heard from. He also found the enemy indisposed to be stubborn, and skirmished up the opposite side of the mountain till he joined hands with De Villiers on the top. The enemy seemed to be increasing before them, and our men held their position as directed, having relieved us from the hostile occupation of ground commanding our camps. Enyart's reconnoitring party sent toward Fayette advanced a mile on that road and remained in observation, finding no enemy. I reported our success to Rosecrans, and doubtful whether he wished to press the enemy in front till Benham and Schenck should be in his rear, I asked for further instructions. General Rosecrans authorized me to take over the rest of my available force and press the enemy next day, as he was very confident that Benham would by that time be in position to attack him in rear. Accordingly I passed the Second Kentucky regiment over the river during the night and joined them in person on the crest at daybreak. The remainder of the First Kentucky, under Major Lieper, was ordered to cross at Montgomery's Ferry later in the day, and advance upon the Fayette road as far as possible. My climb to the crest of Cotton Mountain was a repetition of the exhausting sort of work I had tried on Gauley Mount on the 1st. I took the short route straight up the face of the hill, clambering over rocks, pulling myself up by clinging to the laurel bushes, and often literally lifting myself from one great rocky step to another. This work was harder upon officers who were usually mounted than upon the men in the line, as we were not used to it, and the labour of the whole day was thus increased, for of course we could take no horses. Resuming the advance along the mountain crest, the enemy made no serious resistance, but fell back skirmishing briskly, till we came to more open ground where the mountain breaks down toward some open farms where detachments of Floyd's forces had been encamped. Their baggage train was seen in the distance, moving off upon the Fayette turnpike. As we were now in the close neighbourhood of the whole force of the enemy, and those in our presence were quite as numerous as we, I halted the command on the wooded heights commanding the open ground below, till we should hear some sound from Benham's column. Toward evening Major Lieper came up on our right to the place where the Fayette road passes over a long spur of the mountain which is known in the neighbourhood as Cotton Hill. Here he was halted, and nothing being heard from co-operating columns, the troops bivouacked for the night.

Rosecrans had informed Benham of my advance and ordered him to push forward; but he spent the day in discussing the topography which he was supposed to have learned before, and did not move. Schenck had not been put across New River at Townsend's Ferry, because Rosecrans thought it hazardous to do this whilst Floyd was near that point in force, and he intended that when Floyd should be forced to attack Benham (whose command was now equal to two brigades), it would withdraw the enemy so far that Schenck would have room to operate after crossing. But as Benham had not advanced, toward evening of the 11th Rosecrans sent him orders to march immediately up the Kanawha to my position and follow Major Lieper on the road that officer had opened to the top of Cotton Hill, and as much further toward Fayette C. H. as possible, taking Lieper's detachment with him; meanwhile I was ordered to keep the remainder of my troops on the mountain in the position already occupied. Benham was expected to reach Lieper's position by ten o'clock that evening, but he did not reach there in fact till three o'clock in the following afternoon (12th). After some skirmishing with an outpost of the enemy at Laurel Creek behind which Major Lieper had been posted, nothing more was done till the evening of the 13th. Floyd's report shows that he retired beyond Fayette C. H. on the 12th, having conceived the mistaken idea that Benham's column was a new reinforcement of 5000 men from Ohio. Abandoning the hope of using Schenck's brigade in a movement from Townsend's Ferry, Rosecrans now ordered him to march to Gauley Bridge on the 13th, and joining Benham by a night march, assume command of the moving column. Schenck did so, but Floyd was now retreating upon Raleigh C. H. and a slight affair with his rear-guard was the only result. Fayette C. H. was occupied and the campaign ended. It would appear from official documents that Floyd did not learn of Benham's presence at the mouth of Loup Creek till the 12th, when he began his retreat, and that at any time during the preceding week a single rapid march would have placed Benham's brigade without resistance upon the line of the enemy's communications. Rosecrans was indignant at the balking of his elaborate plans, and ordered Benham before a court-martial for misconduct; but I believe that McClellan caused the proceedings to be quashed to avoid scandal, and Benham was transferred to another department. It is very improbable that Schenck's contemplated movement across New River at Townsend's Ferry could have been made successfully; for his boats were few and small, and the ferrying would have been slow and tedious. Floyd would pretty surely learn of it soon after it began, and would hasten his retreat instead of waiting to be surrounded. It would have been better to join Schenck to Benham by a forced march as soon as the latter was at the mouth of Loup Creek, and then to push the whole to the Fayette and Raleigh road, Rosecrans leading the column in person. As Floyd seems to have been ignorant of what was going on in Loup Creek valley, decisive results might have followed from anticipating him on his line of retreat. Capturing such a force, or, as the phrase then went, "bagging it," is easier talked of than done; but it is quite probable that it might have been so scattered and demoralized as to be of little further value as an army, and considerable parts of it might have been taken prisoners.

Rosecrans had begun the campaign in August with the announced purpose of marching to Wytheville and Abingdon in the Holston valley, and thence into East Tennessee. McClellan had cherished the idea of making the Kanawha line the base of operations into the same region; still later Fremont, and after him Halleck did the same. Looking only at the map, it seemed an easy thing to do; but the almost wilderness character of the intervening country with its poor and sparsely scattered people, the weary miles of steep mountain-roads becoming impassable in rainy weather, and the total absence of forage for animals, were elements of the problem which they all ignored or greatly underestimated. It was easy, sitting at one's office table, to sweep the hand over a few inches of chart showing next to nothing of the topography, and to say, "We will march from here to here;" but when the march was undertaken, the natural obstacles began to assert themselves, and one general after another had to find apologies for failing to accomplish what ought never to have been undertaken. After a year or two, the military advisers of the War Department began to realize how closely the movements of great bodies of soldiers were tied to rivers and railways; but they seemed to learn it only as the merest civilian could learn it, by the experience of repeated failures of plans based on long lines of communication over forest-clad mountains, dependent upon wagons to carry everything for man and beast.

Instead of reaching Wytheville or Abingdon, Rosecrans found that he could not supply his little army even at Big Sewell Mountain; and except for a few days, he occupied no part of the country in advance of my positions in August, then held by a single brigade in the presence of the same enemy. It was not

Floyd's army, but the physical obstacles presented by the country that chained him to Gauley Bridge. I shall have occasion hereafter to note how the same ignoring of nature's laws came near starving Burnside's command in East Tennessee, where the attempt to supply it by wagon trains from Lexington in Kentucky or from Nashville failed so utterly as to disappear from the calculation of our problem of existence through the winter of 1863-64.

Chapter 8
Winter-Quarters

Floyd's retreat was continued to the vicinity of Newberne and Dublin Depot, where the Virginia and East Tennessee Railway crosses the upper waters of New River. He reported the country absolutely destitute of everything and the roads so broken up that he could not supply his troops at any distance from the railroad. Rosecrans was of a similar opinion, and on the 19th of November signified to General McClellan his purpose to hold Gauley Bridge, Cheat Mountain, and Romney as the frontier of his department, and to devote the winter to the instruction and discipline of his troops, and the sifting out of incompetent officers. About the 1st of December he fixed his headquarters at Wheeling, assigning the District of the Kanawha to my command, with headquarters at Charleston. This gave me substantially the same territorial jurisdiction I had in the summer, but with a larger body of troops.

Before we left Gauley Bridge, however, I received orders direct from army headquarters at Washington to take my three oldest Ohio regiments and report to General Buell in Kentucky. This was exactly in accordance with my own strong desire to join a large army on one of the principal lines of operation. I therefore went joyfully to Rosecrans, supposing, of course, that he also had received orders to send me away. To my intense chagrin I found that he not only was without such orders, but that he was, naturally enough, disposed to take umbrage at the sending of orders direct to me. He protested against the irregularity, and insisted that if his forces were to be reduced, he should himself indicate those which were to go. He carried his point on the matter, and was directed to send eight regiments to Buell. He insisted that I should stay, and whilst the reasons he gave were sufficiently complimentary, it was none the less a great disappointment to have to abandon the hope of service in a more important field. There was nothing to be done but to summon philosophy to my aid, and to hope that all would turn out for the best. Before Rosecrans left Gauley Bridge four more regiments were added to the eight already ordered away, together with four batteries of artillery. Some new regiments had joined us, and the aggregate of troops remaining was perhaps not much below the number present when Rosecrans reached Carnifex Ferry in September; but most of them were freshly organized regiments, with whom the work of drill and discipline had to begin at first lessons. Three of the batteries taken away were regulars, and the other was Loomis's Michigan battery, one of the oldest and best instructed of our volunteer batteries. The places of these were not supplied. The good policy of these reductions is not to be questioned; for it was agreed that nothing aggressive could be done in the mountains during the winter, and it was wise to use part of the forces elsewhere.—Yet for those of us who had hoped to go with the troops, and now found ourselves condemned to the apparently insignificant duty of garrisoning West Virginia, the effect was, for the time, a very depressing one.

General Schenck had left us on account of sickness, and did not return. His brigade was again commanded by Colonel Scammon, as it had been at Carnifex Ferry, and was stationed at Fayette C. H. One regiment was at Tompkins farm, another at Gauley Bridge, two others at intervals between that post and Charleston, where were three regiments out of what had been my own brigade. Three partially organized West Virginia regiments of infantry and one of cavalry were placed at recruiting stations in the rear, and one Ohio regiment was posted at Barboursville. The chain of posts which had been established in the summer between Weston and Cross Lanes was not kept up; but the Thirty-sixth Ohio, Colonel George Crook, was stationed at Cross Lanes, reporting to me, as did all the other troops enumerated above.

The Cheat Mountain district continued in command of General Milroy, his principal posts being at Beverly and Huttonsville, with small garrisons holding the mountain passes. General Kelley remained also in command of the railroad district covering the communication with Washington by the Baltimore and Ohio Railroad. General J. J. Reynolds was assigned to command a new division organizing at Romney, but was soon transferred to another department.

Such was the general organization of the department for the winter, and we soon settled down to regular work in fitting the troops for the next campaign. Courtsmartial were organized to try offenders of all grades, and under charges of conduct prejudicial to good order and military discipline, worthless officers were driven from the service and negligent ones disciplined. Regimental schools were opened, and strenuous efforts were made to increase the military knowledge and skill of the whole command. Careful drill was enforced, and picket and outpost duty systematically taught. Each post became a busy camp of instruction, and the regiments repeated under more favourable circumstances the work of the original camp in Ohio.

The work of the military courts gave me one very unpleasant duty to perform, which, happily, was of rare occurrence and never again fell to my lot except on a single occasion in North Carolina near the close of the war. A soldier of the First Kentucky Volunteers was condemned to death for desertion, mutiny, and a murderous assault upon another soldier. The circumstances were a little peculiar, and gave rise to fears that his regiment might resist the execution. I have already mentioned the affair of Captain Gibbs who had shot down a mutinous man of the Second Kentucky at Gauley Bridge in the summer, and who had been acquitted by a court-martial. The camp is very like a city in which popular impressions and rumours have quick circulation and large influence. The two Kentucky regiments were so closely related as to be almost one, and were subject to the same influences. A bitter feeling toward Captain Gibbs prevailed in them both, and camp demagogues busied themselves in trying to make mischief by commenting on the fact that the officer was acquitted whilst the private was condemned. There was not a particle of justice in this, for the one had simply suppressed a mutiny, whereas the other was inciting one. But it is not necessary for complaints to be just among those who are very imperfectly informed in regard to the facts, and very unpleasant reports were received as to the condition of things in the regiment to which the condemned man belonged.

It is the military custom, in executions by shooting, to select the firing party from the regiment to which the condemned man belongs. To have changed the rule would have looked like timidity, and I determined that it must not be done, but resolved upon an order of procedure which would provide, as far as possible, against the chances of interference. On such occasions the troops are usually paraded upon three sides of a hollow square, without arms, the place of execution being in the middle of the open side, where the prisoner kneels upon his coffin. The place chosen was in the meadows on the lower side of the Elk River, opposite Charleston, a short distance from the regimental camp. The camps of two other regiments at the post were half a mile from the place of execution. These regiments were, therefore, marched to the field with their arms. That to which the prisoner belonged was marched without arms to its position as the centre of the parade, and the others were formed on their right and left at right angles, thus forming the three sides of the enclosure. The arms of these last regiments were stacked immediately behind them where they could be seized in a moment, but the parade was formed without muskets. Captain Gibbs was on duty as commissary at my headquarters, and his appearance with the staff would have been unpleasant to himself as well as a possible cause of excitement in the Kentucky regiment. To solve the difficulty without making a significant exception, I ordered only the personal staff and the adjutant-general with the chief surgeon to accompany me, leaving out the administrative officers of both quartermaster's and commissary's departments.

When the parade was formed, I took my place with my staff at the right of the line, and, as upon a review, rode slowly down the whole line, on the inside of the square. In going along the front of the First Kentucky, I took especial pains to meet the eyes of the men as they were turned to me in passing, desirous of impressing them with my own feeling that it was a solemn but inevitable duty. Immediately after we returned to our places, the music of the dead-march was heard, and an ambulance was seen approaching from the camp, escorted by the provost-marshal and the execution party with the music. The solemn strains, the slow funereal step of the soldiers, the closed ambulance, the statue-like stillness of the paraded troops made an impression deeper and more awful than a battle scene, because the excitement was hushed and repressed. The ambulance stopped, the man was helped out at the back, and led by the provost-marshal to his place upon the coffin, where he was blindfolded. The firing party silently took its place. The muskets were cocked and aimed, while the noise of the retiring ambulance covered the sound. The provost-marshal, with a merciful deception, told the prisoner he must wait a moment and he would return to him before the final order, but stepping quickly out of the range of the muskets, he gave the signal with his handkerchief, and the man fell dead at the volley, which sounded like a single discharge. The detail of soldiers for the firing had been carefully instructed that steadiness and accuracy made the most merciful way of doing their unwelcome duty. The surgeon made his official inspection of the body, which was placed in the coffin and removed in the ambulance. The drums and fifes broke the spell with quick marching music, the regiments took their arms, sharp words of command rattled along the lines, which broke by platoons into column and moved rapidly off the field.

I confess it was a relief to have the painful task ended, and especially to have it ended in the most perfect order and discipline. The moral effect was very great, for our men were so intelligent that they fully appreciated the judicial character of the act, and the imposing solemnity of the parade and execution made the impression all the more profound. As it was accompanied and followed by a searching test of the capacity and character of their officers, of which they daily saw the effects in the retirement of some from the service and in the increased industry and studious devotion to duty of all, it gave a new tone to the whole command. I spared no effort to make the feeling pervade every regiment and company, that the cause of the country, their own success and honour, and even their own personal safety depended upon their entering the next campaign with such improved discipline and instruction as should make them always superior to an equal number of the enemy. Leaves of absence and furloughs were limited as closely as possible, and I set the example of remaining without interruption on duty, though there were many reasons why a visit home was very desirable. My wife made me a visit at Charleston in mid-winter, and this naturally brought me into more frequent social relations to the people, and led me to observe more closely their attitude to the government and its cause.

Before the secession of Virginia a very large majority of the inhabitants of the Kanawha valley were Unionists; but the attachment to the state organization had become so exaggerated in all slave-holding communities, that most of the well-to-do people yielded to the plea that they must "go with their State." The same state pride led this class of people to oppose the division of Virginia and the forming of the new State on the west of the mountains. The better class of society in Charleston, therefore, as in other towns, was found to be disloyal, and in sympathy with the rebellion. The young men were very generally in the Confederate army; the young women were full of the most romantic devotion to their absent brothers and friends, and made it a point of honour to avow their sentiments. The older people were less demonstrative, and the men who had a stake in the country generally professed acquiescence in the position of West Virginia within the Union, and a desire to bring back their sons from the Confederate service. The necessity of strict watch upon the communications sent through the lines brought to my notice a great deal of family history full of suffering and anxiety, and showed that that was indeed a fearful situation for a family when its young men were not only separated from them by military service in the field, but could only be heard from by the infrequent chances of communication under flags of truce, and with all the restrictions and reserves necessary to the method. The rule I adopted in dealing personally with non-combatants of either sex was to avoid all controversy or discussion, to state with perfect frankness but courteously my own attitude and sense of duty, and to apply all such stringent rules as a state of war compels with an evenness of temper and tone of dispassionate government which should make as little chafing as possible. Most intelligent people, when they are not excited, are disposed to recognize the obligations imposed upon a military officer in such circumstances, and it was rarely the case that any unpleasant collisions occurred.

The following incident will illustrate some of the embarrassments likely to occur. When I reached Charleston in July previous, I was visited by the wife of a gentleman named Parks, who told me that her husband had left the valley with General Wise, but not in any military capacity, being fearful that he might suffer arrest at our hands on account of his sympathy with the Confederates. I told her, what I had told to a formal deputation of citizens, that I did not propose to meddle with non-combatants if they in good faith remained at home, minding their own business, and carefully abstaining from giving aid or information to the enemy. I had, on general principles, a dislike for test oaths, and preferred to make conduct the test, and to base my treatment of people on that, rather than on oaths which the most unscrupulous would be first to take. Had her husband known this, she said, he would not have left home, and begged that she might be allowed to send an open letter through the lines to him to bring him back. I allowed her to do so at the first proper opportunity, and Mr. Parks at once returned. In the latter part of September, however, Governor Peirpoint of West Virginia thought it necessary to arrest some prominent citizens, known as Secessionists, and hold them as hostages for Union men that the Confederate troops had seized and sent to Richmond. It happened that Mr. Parks was arrested as one of these hostages, without any knowledge on the part of the civil authorities of the circumstances under which he had returned home. I was ignorant of his arrest till I received a letter from the lady, complaining bitterly of what seemed to her a breach of faith. I was at Sewell Mountain at the time, but lost no time in writing her a careful explanation of the complete disconnection between his arrest by the civil authorities as a hostage, and a promise of non-interference with him on my part as an officer of the United States army. I also showed her that the arrest of non-combatant Union men by the Confederate forces was the real cause of her husband's unpleasant predicament. In view of the circumstances, however, I thought it right to request the Governor to substitute some other hostage for Mr. Parks, so that there might not be the least question whether the letter or the spirit of my military safeguard had been broken, and the result was that the gentleman was very soon at home again.

The most prominent citizen of the valley was the Hon. George Summers, who had represented it in the Congress of the United States, and had opposed secession in the Virginia Convention with a vigour that had brought him into personal peril. When, however, secession was an accomplished fact, his ideas of allegiance to his State so far influenced him that he was unwilling to take active part in public affairs, and sought absolute retirement at his pleasant home a little below Charleston on the Kanawha. His house was on a hill overlooking the beautiful valley, broad enough at this point to give room for ample fields in the rich bottom lands. I had called upon him, as I passed with my troops when I went up the valley. He was a dignified and able man, just past middle life, but in full physical and mental force, and capable of exerting a very great influence if he could have thrown himself heartily into public activity. But he was utterly saddened and depressed by the outbreak of civil war, and deliberately chose the part of suffering in seclusion whatever it might bring, unable to rouse himself to a combative part. As a slave-holder, he was bitter against the anti-slavery movement, and as a Unionist he condemned the Secessionists. He was very glad to have the Kanawha valley in the possession of the National troops, now that Wise had made the effort to occupy it for the Confederacy; though he had tried to procure the adoption of a policy which should leave it neutral ground—a policy as impossible here as in Kentucky. The result was that he was distrusted by both sides, for in civil war each acts upon the maxim that "he that is not for us is against us." I renewed my acquaintance with him in the winter, making his house the limit of an occasional ride for exercise. I appreciated his feelings, and respected his desire to set an example of obedient private citizenship with renunciation of all other or more active influence.

There were other men of social prominence who had less hesitation in throwing themselves actively upon the National side. Mr. Patrick was an elderly man, of considerable wealth, whose home was a very similar one to Mr. Summers', a little nearer to Charleston upon the same road. His wife was of old Virginia stock, a relative of Chief Justice Marshall, and a pronounced Southern woman, though too good a wife to make her sympathies give annoyance to her husband or his guests. Lewis Ruffner was also a prominent Union man, and among the leaders of the movement to make West Virginia a separate State. Mr. Doddridge, long the cashier and manager of the Bank at Charleston, whose family was an old and well-known one, was an outspoken Unionist, and in the next year, when the war put an end for the time to banking in the valley, he became a paymaster in the National army. Colonel Benjamin F. Smith was a noteworthy character also. He was a leading lawyer, a man of vigorous and aggressive character, and of tough fibre both physically and mentally. He shared the wish of Summers to keep West Virginia out of the conflict if possible, but when we had driven Wise out of the valley, he took a pronounced position in favour of the new state movement. A little afterward he was appointed District Attorney for the United States. Although the loyal people had such competent leaders, the majority of the men of wealth and of the families recognized as socially eminent were avowed Secessionists. They were a small minority of the whole people, but in all slave-holding communities social rank is so powerful that their influence was out of proportion to their numbers. Even the leaders of the Unionists found their own "house divided against itself," for scarce one of them but had a son in Wise's legion, and the Twenty-second Virginia Regiment was largely composed of the young men of Charleston and the vicinity. I have already referred to the journal of Major Smith which fell into my hands as "captured rebel mail," and its pages are full of pathetic evidence of the conflicting emotions which such a situation excited. He was the son of B. F. Smith, whom I have just mentioned, and whilst in Floyd's camp in front of us at Sewell Mountain he wrote: "My source of constant trouble is that my father will be in danger. Wicked and unscrupulous men, with whom he has lived in friendship for years, absolutely thirst for his blood, as I truly believe. He and Summers, as one of their friends remarked to me to-day, are especial objects of hatred and aversion to men here. I am actually leading a set of men one of whose avowed objects is the arrest and the judicial or lynch murder of my father!" In the next month he heard "the startling news" that his father had fully identified himself with the new state movement, and writes: "Those with whom I was connected, call and curse him as a traitor—and he knew it would be so! Why my dear father has chosen to place me in this terrible situation is beyond my comprehension. I have been shocked beyond description in contemplating the awful consequences to the peace, safety, and happiness of both of us!" The family distress and grief revealed by accident in this case is only an example of what was common in all the families of prominent Union men. In some cases, as in that of Major Smith, the young men resigned their commissions and made their way home, finding the mental and moral strain too great to bear; but in many more, pride and the influence of comrades kept them in the Confederate service with the enlisted men who could not resign, and with hearts sorely torn by conflicting duties, they fought it out to the end.

The slavery question was the vexed one which troubled the relations of the army and the people in all the border States. My own position was that of the party which had elected Mr. Lincoln. We disclaimed any purpose of meddling with the institution in the States which remained loyal to the Union, whilst we held it to be within the war powers of the government to abolish it in the rebellious States. We also took satisfaction in enforcing the law which freed the "contrabands" who were employed by their masters in any service within the Confederate armies. These principles were generally understood and acquiesced in by the West Virginians; but it was impossible to come to any agreement in regard to fugitive slaves who took refuge in our camps. The soldiers and many of the officers would encourage the negroes to assert their freedom, and would resist attempts to recapture them. The owners, if Union men, would insist that the fugitives should be apprehended and restored to them by military authority. This was simply impossible, for the public sentiment of the army as a whole was so completely with the slaves that any such order would have been evaded and made a farcical dead letter. The commanders who made such orders uniformly suffered from doing it; for the temper of the volunteer army was such that the orders were looked upon as evidence of sympathy with the rebellion, and destroyed the usefulness of the general by creating an incurable distrust of him among his own men. Yet nearly all the department commanders felt obliged at first, by what they regarded as the letter of the law, to order that fugitive slaves claimed by loyal citizens should be arrested, if within the camps, and delivered up.

Within the district of the Kanawha I tried to avoid the difficulty by stringent orders that slaves should be kept out of the camps; but I declined to order the troops to arrest and return them. I had two little controversies on the subject, and in both of them I had to come in collision with Colonel Benjamin Smith. After they were over we became good friends, but the facts are too important an illustration of the war-time and its troubles to be omitted.

The first raised the question of "contraband." A negro man was brought into my camp by my advance-guard as we were following Floyd to Sewell Mountain in September. He was the body-servant of Major Smith, and had deserted the major, with the intention of getting back to his family at Charleston. In our camp he soon learned that he was free, under the Act of Congress, and he remained with us, the servants about headquarters giving him food. When I returned to Gauley Bridge, Mr. Smith appeared and demanded the return of the man to him, claiming him as his slave. He, however, admitted that he had been servant to Major Smith in the rebel army with his consent. The man refused to go with him, and I refused to use compulsion, informing Mr. Smith that the Act of Congress made him free. The claimant then went to General Rosecrans, and I was surprised by the receipt, shortly after, of a note from headquarters directing the giving up of the man. On my stating the facts the matter was dropped, and I heard no more of it for a month, the man meanwhile disappearing. Soon after my headquarters were moved to Charleston, in December, I received another note from headquarters, again directing the delivery of the fugitive. Again I gave a temperate and clear statement of the facts, adding that I had reason to believe the man had now taken advantage of his liberty to go to Ohio. Mr. Smith's case thus ended, but it left him with a good deal of irritation at what he thought a wrong done to him as well as insubordination on my part.

In March following, another case arose, and I received a paper from headquarters containing an alleged statement of the facts, and referred to me in usual course for report. I had been absent from Charleston when the incidents occurred, but made careful inquiry satisfying myself of the truth, and perhaps cannot give an intelligent explanation better than by quoting the report itself, for its tone shows the sort of annoyance I felt, and it exhibits some of the conditions of an army command involving administrative duties that were far from pleasant.

I said: "The document is in the handwriting of B. F. Smith, Esq., U. S. District Attorney, residing here, though signed only by John Slack, Jr., and William Kelly; the former an acting deputy U. S. marshal, the latter the jailer at the county jail. Its composition is so peculiar that it is difficult to tell what part of the statement is Slack's or Kelly's and what is Colonel Smith's, and therefore I do not know whom to hold responsible for the misstatements contained in it.

"Mr. Slack is a respectable young man, who I believe would do his duty as far as he understands it, but who has not energy enough to keep him from being the tool of others. Mr. Kelly, the jailer, is sufficiently described when I state the fact that he has attempted to add to his profits as turnkey by selling bad whisky to soldiers put in his calaboose, at the rate of five dollars per pint bottle. Mr. Smith, the District Attorney, has lost no opportunity of being annoying to the military officers here, since the controversy about the negro man captured from his son, Major Isaac Smith of the rebel army. This reference to the parties concerned is necessary to enable the commanding general to understand the *animus* of their complaints.

"The facts are substantially as follows: Henry H. Hopkins is a notorious Secessionist living near Coal River, and a man of considerable property. Some time before his arrest he sent the negro man mentioned in the complaint *South*, in charge of some Logan County 'bushwhackers.' On his way and in McDowell County the man managed to escape and returned into Hopkins's neighbourhood, near Boone C. H., where he took his wife and three children alleged to have been the property of a woman named Smoot, and brought them to this post. Upon his representation that he had escaped from armed rebels in McDowell County, and without further knowledge of the facts, the Post Quartermaster set him at work. About the 19th of February Hopkins came to town with Mrs. Smoot, and without notice to the quartermaster or any colour of authority by any civil process, procured the aid of Kelly, the jailer, seized the negro and took him to Wright's hotel. The provost-marshal, knowing that Hopkins was an active Secessionist and that he had been personally engaged in the combat at Boone C. H. last fall, ordered his arrest. Shortly after, he was waited upon by B. F. Smith, Esq., U. S. District Attorney, who stated that he had known Mr. Hopkins for a good many years and was confident he was a good Union man, although in fact the deputy-marshal at the very time held a warrant for the arrest of Hopkins for treason and conspiracy, under an indictment found in the U. S. Court, of which, to say the least of it, it is very strange Mr. Smith should have been ignorant. At the request of the provost-marshal, the warrant was served on Hopkins, who was admitted to bail in the sum of $2000, which is most inadequate security for the appearance of a man of Hopkins's wealth and influence, accused of such a crime. After the arrest of Hopkins, the negro being left to himself returned to his quarters, but sometime during the night stole a skiff and attempted to escape with his family down the Kanawha River. The circumstances of his accident in the river, the drowning of his family and his subsequent capture, I have not been able to investigate fully.

"The only matter of controversy now is in regard to the horse. The bar-keeper at the tavern denies that he has said it was taken by Wagon-master West (a man who has since been discharged by the Post Quartermaster), and I have been unable to trace it, although every effort has been made in perfect good faith to do so. The man West was put under arrest, to see if that would make him admit anything with regard to it, but without effect. I advised Slack to procure some one who knew the horse to pass through the government stables and teams, and if he recognized the animal to let me know at once, and I would give an order to him to obtain it. The statement that 'Slack says he told Cox he could not find him, that a soldier or employee in his command got him, and if proper measures were taken he could be had,' is both impudent and false, and I respectfully submit that it is not, in matter or manner, such a complaint as the Commanding General should call upon me to reply to.

"The statement of these civil officials at once gives me the opportunity and makes it my duty to state to the Commanding General that the only occasions on which these gentlemen show any vitality, is when some Secessionist's runaway negroes are to be caught. For any purpose of ordinary municipal magistracy they seem utterly incompetent. I have urged the organization of the county and of the town, but to no effect. Every street that is mended, every bridge that is repaired, or wharf that is put in order, must be done by the army at the expense of the U. S. government. They will not elect officers to look after the poor, but leave us to feed the starving near our camps. They will establish no police, and by force of public opinion keep suitors out of the courts ordered to be held by Governor Peirpoint. Yet a U. S. Commissioner, without any warrant or even pretended jurisdiction, will stop any vagrant negro, drive him through the streets in person, and say that he does it as a U. S. officer! Of course we simply look on and have had no controversy with them, unless driven to it by direct efforts on their part to interfere with our necessary regulations.

"The simple fact is that a few men of property who are avowed Secessionists control the town and make its public sentiment. By this means they practically control these officers also. Many of the negroes employed at the salt-works, and under hire in other capacities in the vicinity, are the slaves of rebels who are either in the rebel army or fled with it from the valley. The great problem upon which the Secessionists remaining here are exercising their ingenuity is to find the means of using the U. S. Commissioner and Marshal to secure to them the services of these persons without cost or legitimate contract of hiring, for the present profit of these gentlemen here, and the future advantage of their compatriots across the lines.

"Colonel Smith and Mr. Slack say that they made the statement at the express request of Major Darr of the Commanding General's staff. A simple inquiry by the Major would have saved me the necessity of writing this long letter."

It is due to General Rosecrans to say that although he had been anything but an anti-slavery man before the war, he made no pressure upon me to violate my own sense of right in these or similar cases, and they ended with my reports of the facts and of my reasons for the course I pursued. The side lights thrown upon the situation by the letter last quoted will be more instructive than any analysis I could now give, and the spice of flavour which my evident annoyance gave it only helps to revive more perfectly the local colour of the time. In the case of Mr. Smith's "negro boy Mike," I had the satisfaction of finding in the intercepted correspondence of his son the major, the express recognition of the man's right to liberty by reason of his use in the enemy's service, and could not deny myself the pleasure of calling attention to it in my letters to headquarters.

My experience during the winter begot in me a rooted dislike for the military administration of the border districts, and strengthened my wish to be in the most active work at the front, where the problems were the strictly military ones of attack and defence in the presence of the armed enemy. Not that the winter was without compensating pleasures, for we were recipients of much social attention of a very kindly and agreeable sort, and carried away cherished memories of refined family circles in which the collision of opinions and the chafing of official relations were forgotten in hearty efforts to please. With the unconditionally loyal people our sympathies were very deep, for we found them greatly torn and disturbed in the conflict of duties and divided affections, where scarce a single household stood as a unit in devotion to the cause, and where the triumph of either side must necessarily bring affliction to some of them.

CHAPTER 9

Volunteers And Regulars

The work of sifting the material for an army which went on through the winter of 1861-62, naturally suggests an analysis of the classes of men who composed both parts of the military force of the nation—the volunteers and the regulars. I need add nothing to what I have already said of the unexampled excellence of the rank and file in the regiments raised by the first volunteering. Later in the war, when "bounty jumping" and substitution for conscripts came into play, the character of the material, especially that recruited in the great cities and seaports, was much lower. I think, however, that the volunteers were always better men, man for man, than the average of those recruited for the regular army. The rigidity of discipline did not differ so much between good volunteer regiments and regulars, as the mode of enforcing it. There were plenty of volunteer regiments that could not be excelled in drill, in the performance of camp duty, or in the finish and exactness of all the forms of parades and of routine. But it was generally brought about by much milder methods of discipline. A captain of volunteers was usually followed by his neighbours and relatives. The patriotic zeal of the men of the company as well as their self-respect made them easily amenable to military rule so far as it tended to fit them better to do the noble work they had volunteered for, and on which their hearts were as fully set as the hearts of their colonels or generals. In the regular army, officers and men belonged to different castes, and a practically impassable barrier was between them. Most of the men who had enlisted in the long years of domestic peace were, for one cause or another, outcasts, to whom life had been a failure and who followed the recruiting sergeant as a last desperate resource when every other door to a livelihood was shut. The war made some change in this, but the habits and methods of the officers had been formed before that time and under the old surroundings. The rule was arbitrary, despotic, often tyrannical, and it was notorious that the official bearing and the language used toward the regular soldiers was out of the question in a volunteer organization. Exceptions could be found in both parts of the service, but there could be no doubt as to the custom and the rule. To know how to command volunteers was explicitly recognized by our leading generals as a quality not found in many regular officers, and worth noting when found. A volunteer regiment might have a "free and easy" look to the eye of a regular drill sergeant, but in every essential for good conduct and ready manoeuvre on the field of battle, or for heroic efforts in the crisis of a desperate engagement, it could not be excelled if its officers had been reasonably competent and faithful. There was inevitable loss of time in the organization and instruction of a new army of volunteers; but after the first year in the field, in every quality which tends to give victory in battle to a popular cause, the volunteer regiment was, in my judgment, unquestionably superior. It is necessary to say this, because there has been a fashion of speaking of regular regiments or brigades in the civil war as though they were capable of accomplishing more in proportion to their numbers or on some occasion of peculiar peril than the volunteers. I did not find it so.

The material in the line, then, was as good as could be; the weakness was in the officers, and it was here that the sifting was necessary. Most of these officers had themselves enlisted as privates, and their patriotic zeal was not to be questioned. They had been chosen to be lieutenants, captains, and even colonels by their men because of faith in their ability to lead, or to recognize their influence in raising the troops. Yet a considerable part of them proved incompetent to command. The disqualifications were various. Some lacked physical strength and stamina. Some had or quickly developed intemperate habits. Some lacked the education and intelligence needful for official responsibility. Some were too indolent to apply themselves to the work of disciplining themselves or their men. Fitness for command is a very general term, yet it implies a set of qualities which intelligent people easily understand and attach to the phrase. Self-command is proverbially one of the chief. Courage and presence of mind are indispensable. Ability to decide and firmness to stick to a decision are necessary. Intelligence enough to understand the duties demanded of him and to instruct his subordinates in theirs is another requisite. But beside all these, there is a constitution of body and mind for which we can find no better name than military aptitude. For lack of it many estimable, intelligent, and brave men failed as officers. Again, not every good captain made a good colonel, and not every good brigade commander was fit for a division or a larger command. There was a constantly widening test of capacity, and a rapid thinning of the numbers found fit for great responsibilities until the command of great armies was reached, when two or three names are all that we can enumerate as having been proven during the four years of our civil strife to be fully equal to the task.

Besides the indications of unfitness for the subordinate commands which I have mentioned, another classification may be made. In an agricultural community (and the greater part of our population was and is agricultural), a middle-aged farmer who had been thrifty in business and had been a country magistrate or a representative in the legislature, would be the natural leader in his town or county, and if his patriotism prompted him to set the example of enlisting, he would probably be chosen to a company office, and perhaps to a field office in the regiment. Absolutely ignorant of tactics, he would find that his habits of mind and body were too fixed, and that he could not learn the new business into which he had plunged. He would be abashed at the very thought of standing before a company and shouting the word of command. The tactical lessons conned in his tent would vanish in a sort of stage-fright when he tried to practise them in public. Some would overcome the difficulty by perseverance, others would give it up in despair and resign, still others would hold on from pride or shame, until some pressure from above or below would force them to retire. Some men of this stamp had personal fighting qualities which kept them in the service in spite of their tactical ignorance, like brave old Wolford of Kentucky, of whom it used to be jocosely said, that the command by which he rallied his cavalry regiment was "Huddle on the Hill, boys!"

A man wholly without business training would always be in embarrassment, though his other qualifications for military life were good. Even a company has a good deal of administrative business to do. Accounts are to be kept, rations, clothing, arms, accoutrements, and ammunition are to be receipted and accounted for. Returns of various kinds are to be made, applications for furlough, musters, rolls, and the like make a good deal of clerical work, and though most of it may fall on the first sergeant, the captain and commissioned officers must know how it should be done and when it is well done, or they are sure to get into trouble. It was a very rare thing for a man of middle age to make a good company officer. A good many who tried it at the beginning had to be eliminated from the service in one way or another. In a less degree the same was found to hold true of the regimental field officers. Some men retain flexibility of mind and body longer than others, and could more easily adapt themselves to new circumstances and a new occupation. Of course such would succeed best. But it is also true that in the larger and broader commands solidity of judgment and weight of character were more essential than in the company, and the experience of older men was a more valuable quality. Such reasons will account for the fact that youth seemed to be an almost essential requisite for a company officer, whilst it was not so in the same degree in the higher positions.

It was astonishing to see the rapidity with which well-educated and earnest young men progressed as officers. They were alert in both mind and body. They quickly grasped the principles of their new profession, and with very little instruction made themselves masters of tactics and of administrative routine.

Add to this, bravery of the highest type and a burning zeal in the cause they were fighting for, and a campaign or two made them the peers of any officers of their grade in our own or any other army.

Another class which cannot be omitted and which is yet very hard to define accurately, is that of the "political appointments."

Of the learned professions, the lawyers were of course most strongly represented among officers of the line. The medical men were so greatly needed in their own professional department that it was hard to find a sufficient number of suitable age and proper skill to supply the regiments with surgeons and the hospitals with a proper staff. The clergy were non-combatants by profession, and a few only were found in other than chaplain's duty. Civil engineers, railroad contractors, architects, and manufacturers were well represented and were valuable men. Scarce any single qualification was more useful in organizing the army than that of using and handling considerable bodies of men such as mechanics and railway employees.

The profession of the law is in our country so closely allied to political activity that the lawyers who put on the uniform were most likely to be classed among political appointments. The term was first applied to men like Banks, Butler, Baker, Logan, and Blair, most of whom left seats in Congress to serve in the army. If they had not done so, it would have been easy for critics to say that the prominent politicians took care to keep their own bodies out of harm's way. Most of them won hard-earned and well-deserved fame as able soldiers before the war was over. In an armed struggle which grew out of a great political contest, it was inevitable that eager political partisans should be among the most active in the new volunteer organizations. They called meetings, addressed the people to rouse their enthusiasm, urged enlistments, and often set the example by enrolling their own names first. It must be kept constantly in mind that we had no militia organization that bore any appreciable proportion to the greatness of the country's need, and that at any rate the policy of relying upon volunteering at the beginning was adopted by the government. It was a foregone conclusion that popular leaders of all grades must largely officer the new troops. Such men might be national leaders or leaders of country neighbourhoods; but big or little, they were the necessity of the time. It was the application of the old Yankee story, "If the Lord *will* have a church in Paxton, he must take *sech as ther' be* for deacons."

I have, in a former chapter, given my opinion that the government made a mistake in following General Scott's advice to keep its regular army intact and forbid its officers from joining volunteer regiments; but good or bad, that advice was followed at the beginning, and the only possible thing to do next was to let popular selection and natural leadership of any sort determine the company organizations. The governors of States generally followed a similar rule in the choice of field officers, and selected the general officers from those in the state militia, or from former officers of the army retired to civil life. In one sense, therefore, the whole organization of the volunteer force might be said to be political, though we heard more of "political generals" than we did of political captains or lieutenants. When the organization of the United States Volunteers took the place of the state contingents which formed the "three months' service," the appointments by the President were usually selections from those acting already under state appointment. The National Government was more conservative than the Confederacy in this respect. Our service was always full of colonels doing duty as brigadiers and brigadiers doing duty as major-generals, whilst the Southern army usually had a brigadier for every brigade and a major-general for every division, with lieutenant-generals and generals for the highest commands. If some rigid method had been adopted for mustering out all officers whom the government, after a fair trial, was unwilling to trust with the command appropriate to their grade, there would have been little to complain of; but an evil which grew very great was that men in high rank were kept upon the roster after it was proven that they were incompetent, and when no army commander would willingly receive them as his subordinates. Nominal commands at the rear or of a merely administrative kind were multiplied, and still many passed no small part of the war "waiting orders."

As the total number of general officers was limited by law, it followed, of course, that promotion had to be withheld from many who had won it by service in the field. This evil, however, was not peculiar to the class of appointments from civil life. The faults in the first appointments were such as were almost necessarily connected with the sudden creation of a vast army. The failure to provide for a thorough test and sifting of the material was a governmental error. It was palliated by the necessity of conciliating influential men, and of avoiding antagonisms when the fate of the nation trembled in the balance; but this was a political motive, and the evil was probably endured in spite of its well-known tendency to weaken the military service.

A few months' campaigning in the field got us rid of most of the "town-meeting style" of conducting military affairs in the army itself, though nothing could cure the practice on the part of unscrupulous men of seeking reputation with the general public by dishonest means. The newspapers were used to give fictitious credit to some and to injure others. If the regular correspondents of the press had been excluded from the camps, there would no doubt have been surreptitious correspondence which would have found its way into print through private and roundabout channels. But this again was not a vice peculiar to officers appointed from civil life. It should be always remembered that honourable conduct and devoted patriotism was the rule, and self-seeking vanity and ambition the exception; yet a few exceptions would be enough to disturb the comfort of a large command. To sum up, the only fair way to estimate the volunteer army is by its work and its fitness for work after the formative period was passed, and when the inevitable mistakes and the necessary faults of its first organization had been measurably cured. My settled judgment is that it took the field in the spring of 1862 as well fitted for its work as any army in the world, its superior excellences in the most essential points fully balancing the defects which were incident to its composition.

This opinion is not the offspring of partiality toward the volunteer army on the part of one himself a volunteer. It was shared by the most active officers in the field who came from the regular service. In their testimony given in various ways during the war, in their Official Records, and in their practical conduct in the field which showed best of all where their reliance was placed, these officers showed their full faith in and admiration for the volunteer regiments. Such an opinion was called out by the Committee on the Conduct of the War in its examination of General Gibbon in regard to the Gettysburg campaign, and his judgment may fairly be taken as that of the better class of the regular officers. He declared of some of these regiments in his division, that they were as well disciplined as any men he ever wished to see; that their officers had shown practical military talent; that a young captain from civil life, whom he instanced, was worthy to be made a general. He named regiments of volunteers which he said were among the finest regiments that ever fought on any field, and in which every officer was appointed from civil life. He added the criticism which I have above made, that no proper method of getting rid of incompetent officers and of securing the promotion of the meritorious had been adopted; but this in no way diminishes the force of his testimony that every kind of military ability was abundantly found in our volunteer forces and needed only recognition and encouragement. It would be easy to multiply evidence on this subject. General Grant is a witness whose opinion alone may be treated as conclusive. In his Personal Memoirs he explicitly and unqualifiedly says that at the close of the Vicksburg campaign his troops fulfilled every requirement of an army, and his volunteer officers were equal to any duty, some of them being in his judgment competent to command an independent army in the field. Sherman fully shared this opinion.

In trying to form a just estimate of the officers of the regular army in 1861, we have to consider not only their education, but the character of their military life and experience up to that time. It is, on the whole, a salutary popular notion that "professionals" in any department of work are more likely to succeed than amateurs. At the beginning of the Civil War our only professional soldiers were the officers of our little regular army, nearly all of whom were graduates of the West Point Military

Academy. Since the Mexican War of 1848, petty conflicts with Indians on the frontier had been their only warlike experience. The army was hardly larger than a single division, and its posts along the front of the advancing wave of civilization from the mouth of the Rio Grande to the Canada border were so numerous that it was a rare thing to see more than two or three companies of soldiers together. To most of the officers their parade of the battalion of cadets at West Point was the largest military assemblage they had ever seen. Promotion had been so slow that the field officers were generally superannuated, and very few who had a rank higher than that of captain at the close of 1860 did any active field work on either side during the Civil War. The total number of captains and lieutenants of the line would hardly have furnished colonels for the volunteer regiments of the single State of New York as they were finally mustered into the National service during the war; and they would have fallen far short of it when their own numbers were divided by the rebellion itself.

Our available professional soldiers, then, were captains and subalterns whose experience was confined to company duty at frontier posts hundreds of miles from civilization, except in the case of the engineers, the staff corps, and some of the artillery in sea-coast forts. With the same exceptions, the opportunities for enlarging their theoretic knowledge had been small. It was before the days of post libraries, and books of any sort were a rarity at the garrisons. In the first year of the war, I expressed to General Gordon Granger my surprise at finding how little most line officers had added to the theoretic reading they got at the academy. "What could you expect," he said in his sweeping way, "of men who have had to spend their lives at a two-company post, where there was nothing to do when off duty but play draw-poker and drink whiskey at the sutler's shop?" This was, of course, meant to be picturesquely extravagant, but it hit the nail on the head, after all. Some of the officers of the old regime did not conceal their contempt for books. It was a stock story in the army that when the Utah expedition was fitting out in 1856, General Henry Hunt, chief of artillery of the army of the Potomac, then a young artillery officer, applied to General Twiggs, from whose command part of the expedition was making up, for leave to take a little box of military books. "No, sir," was the peremptory response; "no room in the train for such nonsense." Hunt retired chop-fallen; but soon after another officer came in, with "General, our mess has a keg of very nice whiskey we don't want to lose; won't you direct the quartermaster to let it go in the wagons?" "Oh yes, sir. Oh yes, anything in reason!" If not true, the story is good enough to be true, as its currency attests; but whether true or no, the "fable teaches" that post-graduate study in the old army was done under difficulties.

The course of study at West Point had narrower limitations than most people think, and it would be easy to be unfair by demanding too much of the graduates of that military college. The course of study was of four years, but the law forbade any entrance examinations on subjects outside of the usual work done in the rural common schools. The biographies of Grant, of Sherman, of Sheridan, of Ormsby Mitchell, and of others show that they in fact had little or no other preparatory education than that of the common country school. The course of study and amount of education given must necessarily be limited, therefore, to what boys of average ability and such preparation could accomplish in the four years. They were no further advanced, on entering, than they would have to be to enter any ordinary fitting school for one of our first-class colleges, or the high schools in the graded systems of public schools in our cities. Three years of study would put them abreast of students entering college elsewhere, and four years would carry them about as far as the end of the Freshman year in Yale, Harvard, or Princeton. The corps of professors and teachers at West Point has always deservedly ranked high as instructors, but there is no "royal road" to knowledge, and it cannot be claimed that three or four years at the Military Academy would count for more, as general education, than the same period spent in any other good school. A very few men of high standing in the classes supplemented their education by obtaining appointments as temporary instructors in the academy after graduating, but most of them left their books behind them and began at once the subaltern's life at the distant frontier post.

If we analyze the course of study they pursued, we find that it covered two years' work in mathematics, one in physics and chemistry, and one in construction of fortifications. This was the scientific part, and was the heaviest part of the curriculum. Then, besides a little English, mental philosophy, moral philosophy, and elementary law, there were two years' study of the French and one of Spanish. This was the only linguistic study, and began with the simplest elements. At the close of the war there was no instruction in strategy or grand tactics, in military history, or in what is called the Art of War. The little book by Mahan on Outpost Duty was the only text-book in Theory, outside the engineering proper. At an earlier day they had used Jomini's introduction to his "Grandes Opérations Militaires," and I am unable to say when its use was dropped. It is not my wish to criticise the course of study; on the other hand, I doubt if it could be much improved for boys who had only the preparation required by the law. But since we are trying to estimate its completeness as professional education fitting men to command armies in the field, it is absolutely necessary to note the fact that it did not pretend to include the military art in that sense. Its scientific side was in the line of engineering and that only. Its prize-men became engineers, and success at the academy was gauged by the student's approach to that coveted result.

That the French which was learned was not enough to open easily to the young lieutenant the military literature which was then found most abundantly in that language, would seem to be indicated by the following incident. In my first campaign I was talking with a regular officer doing staff duty though belonging in the line, and the conversation turned on his West Point studies. The little work of Jomini's mentioned above being casually referred to as having been in his course, I asked him if he had continued his reading into the History of the Seven Years' War of Frederick the Great, to which it was the introduction. He said no, and added frankly that he had not read even the Introduction in the French, which he had found unpleasantly hard reading, but in the English translation published under the title of the Art of War. This officer was a thoroughly estimable, modest, and intelligent man, and seemed in no way inferior to other line officers of his age and grade. It would of course be true that some men would build industriously upon the foundation laid at the academy, and perfect themselves in those things of which they had only acquired the elements; but the surroundings of frontier life at a post were so unfavourable that I believe few in fact did so. The officers of the engineer corps and the ordnance were specifically devoted to scientific careers, and could go steadily forward to expertness in their specialties. Those who were permanently attached to the staff corps or to bureaus at Washington had also opportunity to enlarge their professional knowledge by study if they were so inclined. But all these were exceptionally situated, and do not help us answer the question What kind and amount of military education was implied in the fact that a man had graduated at West Point and been sent to serve in the line? I have purposely omitted for the present to consider the physical training and the practical instruction in tactics by means of drill, because the question is in terms one of science, not of practice; that will come later. The conclusion is that the intellectual education at the Military Academy was essentially the same, as far as it went, as that of any polytechnic school, the peculiarly military part of it being in the line of engineering. In actual warfare, the laying out and construction of regular forts or the conduct of a regular siege is committed to professional engineers. For field work with an army, therefore, the mental furnishing of the West Point man was not superior to that of any other liberally educated man. In some of our volunteer regiments we had whole companies of private soldiers who would not have shunned a competitive examination with West Point classes on the studies of the Military Academy, excepting the technical engineering of fortifications.

Let us look now at the physical and practical training of the cadet. The whole period of his student life at West Point had more or less of this. He was taken as a raw recruit would be, taught the school of the soldier in marching, in the manual of arms, and in personal carriage. He passed on to the drill of the squad, the platoon, the company. The tactics of the battalion came last, and the cadet might become a corporal, sergeant, lieutenant, or captain in the corps if he showed aptitude for drill and tactics. It is noticeable, however, that Grant and Sheridan remained privates during their whole cadetship, and Sherman, though once he became sergeant, was put back in the ranks. The fair conclusion is that this part of the cadet discipline is not very closely connected with generalship, though it is important as preparation for the ready handling of a company or a battalion. Sherman tells us, in his Memoirs, that he studied evolutions of the line out of the books, as a new subject, when he was in camp in front of Washington, after the first battle of Bull Run. The tactical education of the cadet stopped at the evolutions of the battalion, and for nearly all of them it was, even in that respect, the education of the soldier in the ranks and not of the officer, since a very small proportion became officers in the cadet corps.

This practical drill was, of course, the same as that which was used in organized militia regiments, and the famous Ellsworth Zouaves of Chicago, the New York Seventh Regiment, with a number of other militia regiments in different States, were sufficient proof that this training could be made as exact outside of the cadet corps as in it. It certainly was enough for the practical handling of the company and the regiment under the simplified tactics which not only prevailed during the war itself, but, with Upton's Manual as a basis, has been authoritatively adopted as an improvement upon the older and more complicated methods. It must not be forgotten that although our militia system had fallen into scandalous neglect, the voluntary efforts of citizen soldiers had kept many good independent companies organized everywhere, as well as full regiments in most of the older States; so that there were in fact more well-drilled regiments in the militia than there were in the little regular army. It was the small ratio all these, of both classes, bore to the demands of the gigantic war that was upon us, which made the problem so troublesome. The officers of the organized militia regiments, before the end of the three months' service, did what I have said it was desirable that those of the regular regiments should have done—they scattered from their original commands and were active in organizing the new volunteer regiments. General De Trobriand, who went out as Colonel of the Fifty-fifth New York, says that the New York Seventh Regiment furnished three hundred officers to volunteer regiments. In a similar way, though not to the same extent, the other organized and disciplined militia, in both Eastern and Western States, furnished the skeletons of numerous new regiments.

The really distinguishing feature in the experience of the regular officers of the line was their life in garrison at their posts, and their active work in guarding the frontier. Here they had become familiar with duty of the limited kind which such posts would afford. This in time became a second nature to them, and to the extent it reached, was, as other men's employments are, their business. They necessarily had to learn pretty thoroughly the army regulations, with the methods and forms of making returns and conducting business with the adjutant-general's office, with the ordnance office, the quartermaster's and subsistence departments, etc. In this ready knowledge of the army organization and its methods their advantage over the new volunteer officers was more marked, as it seemed to me, than in any and all other things. The routine of army business and the routine of drill had to be learned by every army officer. The regular officer of some years' standing already knew, as a matter of course, what a new volunteer officer must spend some time in learning. There is something of value also in the habit of mind formed in actual service, even if the service is in subaltern grades and on a petty scale. Familiarity with danger and with the expectation of danger is acquired, both by the Indian wars of the frontier and by the hunting and field sports which fill more or less of the leisure of garrison life.

But there were some drawbacks upon the value of the preparation for war which these officers possessed. There was a marked conservatism as to military methods and arms, and an almost slavish reverence for things which were sanctioned by European authority, especially that of the second French Empire. American invention was never more fruitful than when applied to military weapons. Repeating and magazine small arms, breach-loading cannon, and Gatling guns with other repeating artillery, were brought out or improved with wonderful variety of form and of demonstrable excellence. The regular army influence was generally against such innovations. Not once, but frequently, regular army officers argued to me that the old smooth-bore musket with "buck and ball" cartridge was the best weapon our troops could desire. We went through the war with a muzzle-loading musket, the utmost that any commander could do being to secure repeating rifles for two or three infantry regiments in a whole army. Even to the end the "regular" chiefs of artillery insisted that the Napoleon gun, a light smooth-bore twelve-pounder cannon, was our best field-piece, and at a time when a great campaign had reduced our forces so that a reduction of artillery was advisable, I received an order to send to the rear my three-inch rifled ordnance guns and retain my Napoleons. The order was issued by a regular officer of much experience, but I procured its suspension in my own command by a direct appeal to the army commander. There was no more doubt then than there is to-day of the superiority of rifled guns, either for long-range practice with shells or in close work with canister. They were so much lighter that we could jump them across a rough country where the teams could hardly move a Napoleon. We could subdue our adversaries' fire with them, when their smooth-bores could not reach us. Yet we were ordered to throw away our advantages and reduce ourselves to our enemy's condition upon the obstinate prejudice of a worthy man who had had all flexibility drilled out of him by routine. Models of automatic rapid-fire and repeating field-pieces were familiar objects "at the rear," but I saw none of them in action in any army in which I served. The conservatism of the old army must be held responsible for this.

The question of zeal and devotion to the cause for which we fought cannot be ignored in such a war as ours was. It is notorious that comparatively few of the regular officers were political friends of Mr. Lincoln's administration at the beginning. Of those who did not "go with the South" but remained true to the National flag, some were full of earnest patriotism, like the young officers whom I have mentioned as volunteering to assist the governors of States in organizing their contingents and as seeking places in volunteer regiments. There were others who meant to do their duty, but began with little hopefulness or zeal. There were still others who did not hesitate to predict defeat and to avow that it was only for professional honour or advancement that they continued to serve under the National flag. These last were confessedly soldiers of fortune. The war was an education for all who were in it, and many a man began with reluctance and half-heartedness who was abundantly radical before the conflict was over. There was, however, a considerable class who practised on Talleyrand's diplomatic motto, *point de zèle*, and limited their efforts to the strict requirement of duty. Such men would see disaster occur for lack of a little spontaneity on their part, and yet be able to show that they literally obeyed every order received. I was once ordered to support with my command a movement to be made by another. It was an important juncture in a campaign. Wondering at delay, I rode forward and found the general officer I was to support. I told him I was ordered to support him in doing what we both saw was needing to be done; but he had no explicit orders to begin the movement. I said that my orders to support him were sufficient to authorize his action, and it was plain that it would be unfortunate if the thing were not done at once. He answered cynically, "If you had been in the army as long as I have, you would be content to do the things that are ordered, without hunting up others." The English regulars, also, have a saying, "Volunteering brings bad luck."

There was altogether too much of this spirit in the army, and one who can read between the lines will see it in the history of many a campaign. It did not necessarily mean wavering loyalty. It was sometimes the mental indecision or timidity which shrinks from responsibility. It was sometimes also the result of education in an army on the peace establishment, where any spontaneity was snubbed as an impertinence or tyrannically crushed as a breach of discipline. I would not be understood to make more of these things than is necessary to a just estimate of the situation, but it seems to me an entirely fair conclusion that with us in 1861 as with the first French republic, the infusion of the patriotic enthusiasm of a volunteer organization was a necessity, and that this fully made up for lack of instruction at the start. This hasty analysis of what the actual preparation for war was in the case of the average line officer of the regular army will show, to some extent, the basis of my judgment that there was nothing in it which a new volunteer officer, having what I have called military aptitude, should not learn in his first campaign.

How far the officers of the engineers and of the staff corps applied themselves to general military study, would depend upon their taste and their leisure. Their opportunities for doing so were much better than those of line officers, but there was also a tendency to immerse themselves in the studies of their special department of work. Very eminent officers of engineers have told me since the war that the pressure of their special professional work was such that they had found no time to read even the more noteworthy publications concerning the history of our own great struggle. The surveys of the great lakes and the coast, the engineering problems of our great rivers, etc., have both formerly and in recent years absorbed their time and their strength. The ordnance and the staff corps, also, had abundant special duties. Still it may reasonably be assumed that officers of the classes mentioned have usually made themselves somewhat familiar with the best writings on military art. If we had in the country in 1861 a class of men who could be called educated soldiers in the scientific sense, we certainly should find them in the several corps just referred to.

Here, however, we have to meet the question What is military art as applied to the problem of winning battles or campaigns? We are obliged to answer that outside of the business administration and supply of an army, and apart from the technical knowledge of engineering and the construction of fire-arms and ammunition, it consists in the tactical handling of bodies of men in accordance with very few and very simple principles of strategy. The literature of the subject is found in the history of wars analyzed by competent men like Napoleon, Jomini, the Archduke Charles, Sir William Napier, Clausewitz, Moltke, Hamley, and others; but it may be broadly said that the principles of this criticism and analysis may be so briefly stated as to be printed on the back of a visiting-card. To trace the campaigns of great soldiers under the guidance of such a critic as Jomini is full of interest to any intelligent person, and there is nothing in the subject of the slightest difficulty of comprehension if full and authentic topographical maps are before the reader. To make much instructive use of military history in this way demands a good deal of voluminous reading and the command of charts and maps extensive enough to allow the presentation of the face of a country on a large scale. With these advantages all wars, both ancient and modern, are full of instructive examples of the application of the simple principles of strategy under innumerable varying circumstances and situations; and this union of simple theory in ever-changing practical application is what constitutes the theoretic knowledge of the general as distinguished from the tactical and administrative duties of the subordinate. It was the very simplicity of the principles that made many successful generals question whether there was any art in the matter, except to use courage and natural sagacity in the actual situation in which the commander found himself and the enemy. Marshal Saxe asserted in his *Rêveries* that down to his time there had been no formulation of principles, and that if any had been recognized as such in the minds of commanders of armies, they had not made it known.

It was precisely in this department of military history *raisonnée* that frontier garrison life shut the young army officer out from the opportunities of profiting by his leisure. The valuable books were all foreign publications in costly form with folio atlases, and were neither easy to procure nor easily carried about with the limited means and the rigid economy of transportation which marked army life in the far West. That this was true even in the artillery is indicated by General Gibbon before the Committee on the Conduct of the War when questioned in reference to the relative amount of artillery used at Gettysburg as compared with great European battles; that distinguished officer having himself been in the artillery when the Civil War began.

If then the officers of the regular army, as a body, were not in fact deeply read in what, as we have seen, Jomini calls "the science of generals," their advantage over equally well-educated civilians is reduced to a practical knowledge of the duties of the company and the petty post, and in comparison with the officers of well-drilled militia companies it amounted to little more than a better knowledge of the army regulations and the administrative processes. It is no reproach to them that this was so, for it resulted from the operation of law in the course of education at the Military Academy and the insignificant size of our army in times of peace. It had been the peculiar blessing of our country that a great standing army was unnecessary, and it would be foolish to regret that our little army could not have the experience with great bodies of troops and the advantages of theoretical instruction which are part of the life of officers in the immense establishments of Continental Europe. My only purpose is to make an approximately true balance sheet of the actual advantages of the two parts of our National army in 1861. Whilst on the subject, however, I will go a little further and say that prior to our Civil War, the history of European conflicts proves that there also the theoretic preparation of military men had not, up to that time, saved them from the necessity of learning both generalship and army administration in the terrible school of experience, during their first year in the field when a new war broke out after a long interval of peace.

The first volume of Kinglake's *Crimean War* appeared in 1863, and I immediately and eagerly devoured it for the purpose of learning the lesson it could teach. It was one of the memorable sensations of a lifetime, to find that the regular armies of England, of France, and of Russia had had to learn their lesson anew when they faced each other on the shore of the Euxine, and that, whether in matters of transportation, of subsistence, of the hospital, of grand tactics, or of generalship, they had no advantage over our army of volunteers fresh from their peaceful pursuits. The photographic fidelity to detail on the part of the historian, and his apparent unconsciousness of the sweeping conclusions to be drawn from his pictures, made the lesson all the more telling. I drew a long breath of relief, and nothing which happened to me in the whole war so encouraged me to hopeful confidence in the outcome of it, as the evidence I saw that our blunders at the beginning had been no greater than those of old standing armies, and that our capacity to learn was at least as quick as theirs. Their experience, like ours, showed that the personal qualities of a commanding officer counted for much more than his theoretic equipment, and that a bold heart, a cool head, and practical common-sense were of much more importance than anything taught at school. With these, a brief experience would enable an intelligent man to fill nearly any subordinate position with fair success; without them any responsibility of a warlike kind would prove too heavy for him. The supreme qualification of a general-in-chief is the power to estimate truly and grasp clearly the situation on a field of operations too large to be seen by the physical eye at once, and the undaunted temper of will which enables him to execute with persistent vigour the plan which his intellect approves. To act upon uncertainties as if they were sure, and to do it in the midst of carnage and death when immeasurable results hang upon it—this is the supreme presence of mind which marks a great commander, and which is among the rarest gifts even of men who are physically brave. The problem itself is usually simple. It is the confusing and overwhelming situation under which it must be solved that causes timidity or dismay. It is the thought of the fearful consequences of the action that begets a nervous state of hesitation and mental timidity in most men, and paralyzes the will. No education will ensure this greatest and most essential quality. It is born in a man, not communicated. With it his acquired knowledge will be doubly useful, but without it an illiterate slave-trader like Forrest may far outshine him as a soldier. Nor does success as a subordinate give any certain assurance of fitness for supreme command. Napoleon's marshals generally failed when trusted with an independent command, as Hooker did with us; and I do not doubt that many men, like McClellan, who failed as generals-in-chief, would have made brave and good subordinates. The test of quality is different in kind, and, as I have said, the only proof of its possession is in the actual trial. It is safe to say that a timid subordinate will not be a good commander, but it cannot be affirmed that a bold one will, though there are more chances in his favour.

The education of peril is so powerful in bringing out the qualities that can master it, and for any one who has true military courage the acquirement of skill in the more mechanical part of his duty in war is so rapid, that my experience has led me to reckon low, in the comparison, the value of the knowledge a soldier gains in times of peace. I say "in the comparison." Tactics are essential to the handling of large bodies of men, and must be learned. But the zealous young soldier with aptitude for his work will learn this part of his duty so fast that a single campaign will find him abreast of any. At the beginning of a great war and in the organization of a great army, the knowledge of routine and of details undoubtedly saves time and saves cost both of treasure and of life. I am therefore far from arguing that the knowledge which was found in the regular army should not be made the most of. I have already said that it should have been scattered through the whole volunteer organization. So I also say that it was quite right to look for the higher qualities for command in those who had the technical information and skill. But I reckon patriotic zeal and devotion so high that I have no hesitation in adding, that our army as a whole would have been improved if the distinction between regular and volunteer had been abolished, and, after the first beginnings, a freer competition for even the highest commands had been open to all. To keep up the regular army organization was practically to say that a captaincy in it was equivalent to a brigade command in the volunteers, and to be a brigadier in it was a reward which regular officers looked forward to as a result of the successful conduct of a great campaign as general-in-chief of an army. The actual command in war was thus ridiculously belittled in the official scale in comparison with grades of a petty peace establishment, and the climax of absurdity was reached when, at the close of hostilities, men who had worthily commanded divisions and corps found themselves reduced to subordinate places in regiments, whilst others who had vegetated without important activity in the great struggle were outranking them by virtue of seniority in the little army which had existed before the Rebellion!

CHAPTER 10

The Mountain Department— Spring Campaign

As the spring of 1862 approached, the discussion of plans for the opening of a new campaign was resumed. Rosecrans had suggested, early in February, that he would prefer to attempt reaching the Virginia and East Tennessee Railroad by two columns moving simultaneously upon Abingdon in the Holston valley. One of these would start from Gauley Bridge and go by way of Fayette, Raleigh, and Princeton; the other would leave some point in the Big-Sandy valley on the common boundary of Kentucky and Virginia, and march by most direct route to Abingdon. If this plan were approved, he asked that the west side of the Big-Sandy valley be added to his department. He proposed to depend largely upon pack-mule trains in place of wagons, to substitute the French shelter tent for the larger tents still in use, and to carry hand-mills by which the soldiers might grind into meal the Indian corn to be found in the country. McClellan, as general-in-chief, gave his approval, suggesting a modification in regard to the column to move from the Big-Sandy valley. His information led him to believe that the Big-Sandy River could be relied upon as navigable to Prestonburg, which was seventy miles from Abingdon by what was supposed to be a good road. He thought, therefore, that it would be easier to make Prestonburg the base and to use wagons. On investigation Rosecrans reported that the most feasible route in that region was by steamboat transportation to Pikeville, twenty-five miles above Prestonburg, in the Big-Sandy valley, and thence up the Louisa Fork of the Big-Sandy by way of Pound Gap to the Holston valley; but there would still be eighty-eight miles of marching after leaving the steamboats, and navigation on the Big-Sandy was limited to brief and infrequent periods of high water.

On the 12th of March he submitted his modified plan to the adjutant-general of the army. It had grown more complex with the passage of time. The eastern line of the department had been moved forward so as to bring the South Branch of the Potomac and the Cow-pasture branch of the James River under Rosecrans's command. He now planned four separate columns. The first was to move up the south branch of the Potomac with a view to turn and to capture the enemy's position at Alleghany Summit or Monterey on the Staunton turnpike. The second and third were to be in my district, and to move toward the Virginia and Tennessee Railroad on the two sides of New River. The fourth should march from the Big-Sandy valley on the line indicated above. Rosecrans seems to have limited his plan to the occupation of the mountain valleys as far east as the Blue Ridge, and did not submit any scheme for uniting his columns for further work. He asked for reinforcements to the extent of six regiments of infantry, one of cavalry, and two field batteries to enable him to perform his task. The use of pack trains was given up, as they required a greater number of animals than could be procured. In fact, it was never found to be an economical use of mule power, and important movements were always confined to lines upon which wheel vehicles could be used. A rapid cavalry raid could be thus supplied, but heavy columns of infantry and artillery demanded wagon trains.

The weakness of Rosecrans's scheme is found in the wide separation of parallel columns, which could never have co-operated with success, and which had no common object had success been possible. To be sure, it was presumed that McClellan with the Army of the Potomac, and Banks in the Shenandoah valley, would be operating in eastern Virginia; but as McClellan was already bent on making Chesapeake Bay his base, and keeping as far as possible from the mountains, there was no real connection or correlation between his purposed campaign and that of the others. Indeed, had he succeeded in driving Lee from Richmond toward the west, as Grant did three years later, the feeble columns of National troops coming from West Virginia would necessarily have fallen back again before the enemy. If the general scheme had been planned by Lee himself, it could not have secured for him more perfectly the advantage of interior lines. Yet it was in substance that which was tried when the spring opened.

When Rosecrans's letter, enclosing his final plan, reached Washington, McClellan had taken the field, and President Lincoln had made use of the occasion to relieve him from the direction of all other forces, so that he might give undivided attention to his campaign with the Potomac army. This was done by an executive order on March 11, which assigned General Halleck to the command of everything west of a line drawn north and south through Knoxville, Tennessee, and formed the Mountain Department from the territory between Halleck and McClellan. This last department was put under the command of Major-General John C. Frémont. General Banks was commanding in the Shenandoah valley, but he was at this time subordinate to McClellan. These changes were unexpected to both McClellan and Rosecrans. The change in McClellan's relations to the whole army was the natural result of his inactivity during the autumn of 1861, and the consequent loss of confidence in him. The union of Buell's and Halleck's commands in the west was the natural counterpart to the concentration of Confederate armies under A. S. Johnston at Corinth, Miss., and was a step in the right direction. There was, however, a little too much sentiment and too little practical war in the construction of the Mountain Department out of five hundred miles of mountain ranges, and the appointment of the "pathfinder" to command it was consistent with the romantic character of the whole. The mountains formed a natural and admirable barrier, at which comparatively small bodies of troops could cover and protect the Ohio valley behind them; but, for reasons which I have already pointed out, extensive military operations across and beyond the Alleghenies from west or east were impracticable, because a wilderness a hundred miles wide, crossed by few and most difficult roads, rendered it impossible to supply troops from depots on either side.

Such assurances of other satisfactory employment seem to have been given Rosecrans that he acquiesced without open complaint, and prepared to turn over his command to Frémont when the latter should arrive in West Virginia. Political motives had, no doubt, much to do with Frémont's appointment. The President had lost faith in his military capacity as well as in his administrative ability, but the party which elected Mr. Lincoln had not. The Republicans of the Northern States had a warm side for the man they had nominated for the Presidency in 1856, and there was a general feeling among them that Frémont should have at least another opportunity to show what he could do in the field. I myself shared that feeling, and reported to him as my immediate superior with earnest cordiality.

In my own district, preparations had been made during the winter for the expected advance in the spring. I had visited Rosecrans at Wheeling, and he had conversed freely upon his plans for the new campaign. Under his directions the old piers of the turnpike bridge across the Gauley had been used for a new superstructure. This was a wire suspension bridge, hung from framed towers of timber built upon the piers. Instead of suspending the roadway from the wire cables by the ordinary connecting rods, and giving stiffness to it by a trussed railing, a latticed framing of wood hung directly from the cables, and the timbers of the roadway being fastened to this by stirrups, the wooden lattice served both to suspend and to stiffen the road. It was a serviceable and cheap structure, built in two weeks, and answered our purposes well till it was burned in the next autumn, when Colonel Lightburn retreated before a Confederate invasion.

The variable position of the head of steamboat navigation on the Kanawha made it impossible to fix a permanent depot as a terminus for our wagon trains in the upper valley. My own judgment was in favour of placing it at Kanawha Falls, a mile below Gauley Bridge, and within the limits of that post. To connect this with the steamboats wherever the shoaling water might force them to stop, I recommended the use of *batteaux* or keelboats, a craft which a natural evolution had brought into use in the changeable mountain rivers. They were a canoe-shaped open boat, sixty feet long by eight wide, and were pushed up the stream by *quants* or poles. They required a crew of five men—four to do the poling, and a steersman. In the swiftest "chutes" they carried a line ashore and made fast to a tree, then warped the boat up to quieter water and resumed the poling. Each boat would carry eight tons, and, compared with teaming over roads of which the "bottom had dropped out," it proved a most economical mode of transport. The *batteaux* dropped alongside the steamer wherever she had to stop, the freight was transferred to them directly, covered with tarpaulins, and the boats pushed off. The number of hands was no greater than for teaming, and the whole cost of the teams and their forage was saved. I had built two of these early in the winter and they were in successful operation. Two more were partly done when Frémont assumed command, and I urgently recommended a fleet of fifteen or twenty as an auxiliary to our transportation when active operations should be resumed. By their use Gauley Bridge could be made the practical depot of supply, and from ten to twenty miles of wretched and costly wagonning be saved.

I became satisfied, also, that the regulation army wagon was too heavy for the difficult mountain roads, and recommended a strong but much lighter farm wagon, in which four mules could draw nearly or quite as much as six usually drew in the heavier wagon. This became a matter of great consequence in a country where forage could not be found, and where the wagon had to be loaded with the food for the team as well as the rations and ordnance stores for the men.

It had already been determined to substitute the shelter tent for other forms in the principal armies, and the change soon became general. We, however, had to wait our turn after more important columns were supplied, and our turn did not come till the campaign was over. Even our requisitions for ammunition were not filled, our artillery was not reduced to uniformity, and we could not secure muskets enough of any one calibre for a single regiment. We made the best of the situation, and whilst keeping "headquarters" informed of our lack, were ready to do our best with the means we had. No attention was paid, perhaps none could be paid, to our recommendations for any special supplies or means adapted to the peculiar character of our work. We received, in driblets, small supplies of the regulation wagons, some droves of unbroken mules, some ordnance stores, and a fair amount of clothing. Subsistence stores had never been lacking, and the energy of the district quartermaster and commissary kept our little army always well fed.

The formal change in department commanders took place on the 29th of March, Frémont having reached Wheeling the day before. Mr. Lincoln's desire by some means to free the loyal people of East Tennessee from the oppressive sway of the Confederates showed itself in the instructions given to all the military officers in the West. He had been pressing the point from the beginning. It had entered into McClellan's and Rosecrans's plans of the last campaign. It had been the object of General George H. Thomas's organization of troops at Camp Dick Robinson in Kentucky. For it General Ormsby Mitchell had laboured to prepare a column at Cincinnati. It was not accomplished till the autumn of 1863, when Rosecrans occupied Chattanooga and Burnside reached Knoxville; but there had never been a day's cessation of the President's urgency to have it accomplished. It was prominent in his mind when he organized the Mountain Department, and Frémont was called upon to suggest a plan to this end as soon as he was appointed. His choice was to assemble the forces of his department in Kentucky at the southern terminus of the Central Kentucky Railroad, at Nicholasville, and to march southward directly to Knoxville, upon what was substantially the line taken by Burnside a year and a half later. Frémont was mistaken, however, in saying that from Nicholasville to Knoxville supplies could be "transported over level and good roads." General Buell had, on the 1st of February, reported that line to be some two hundred miles long from the end of the railway to Knoxville, the whole of it mountainous, and the roads bad. He estimated a train of a thousand wagons, constantly going and returning, as needful to supply ten thousand men at Knoxville after allowance was made for what could be gathered from the country. General Buell was unquestionably correct in his view of the matter, but the strong political reasons for liberating East Tennessee made the President unwilling to be convinced that it was then impracticable. He, however, could not furnish the transportation required for the movement proposed by Frémont, and hesitated to interfere further with the conduct of military affairs within Buell's territorial limits. Besides this, Rosecrans's plan had found such favour with the Secretary of War that it was laid before Frémont with official approval. The stripping of West Virginia of troops to make a column in Kentucky seemed too hazardous to the government, and Frémont changed his plan so as to adopt that of Rosecrans with some modifications.

He proposed to leave General Kelley with sufficient troops to protect the line of the Baltimore and Ohio Railroad, and with Blenker's division (which was taken from the Army of the Potomac and given to him) to advance from Romney in the valley of the South Branch of the Potomac, ascending this valley toward the south, picking up Schenck's and Milroy's brigades in turn, the latter joining the column at Monterey on the great watershed by way of the Cheat Mountain pass. From Monterey Frémont purposed to move upon Staunton, and thence, following the south-western trend of the valleys, to the New River near Christiansburg. Here he would come into communication with me, whose task it would have been to advance from Gauley Bridge on two lines, the principal one by Fayette and Raleigh C. H. over Flat-top Mountain to Princeton and the Narrows of New River, and a subordinate one on the turnpike to Lewisburg. His plan looked to continuing the march with the whole column to the southwest, down the Holston valley, till Knoxville should be reached, the last additions to the force to be from the troops in the Big-Sandy valley.

General Garfield (then colonel of the Forty-second Ohio) had already been sent by General Buell with a brigade into the

Big-Sandy valley, and General George W. Morgan was soon to be sent with a division to Cumberland Gap. Although these were in Frémont's department, the War Department issued an order that they should continue under General Buell's command at least until Frémont should by his operations come into their vicinity and field of work. They would, of course, co-operate with him actively if he should reach the Holston valley. When he should form his junction with me, he expected to supply the whole column from my depots in the Kanawha valley, and when he reached Knoxville he would make his base on the Ohio River, using the line of supply he first suggested, by way of central Kentucky.

The plan was an improvement upon Rosecrans's in arranging for a progressive concentration of his forces into one column led by himself; but it would probably have failed, first, from the impossibility of supplying the army on the route, and second, because the railroads east of the mountains ran on routes specially well adapted to enable the enemy quickly to concentrate any needed force at Staunton, at Lynchburg, at Christiansburg, or at Wytheville, to overpower the column. The Union army would be committed to a whole season of marching in the mountains, while the Confederates could concentrate the needed force and quickly return it to Richmond when its work was done, making but a brief episode in a larger campaign. But the plan was not destined to be thoroughly tried. Stonewall Jackson, after his defeat by Kimball at Kernstown, March 23d, had retired to the Upper Shenandoah valley with his division, numbering about 10,000 men; Ewell, with his division, was waiting to co-operate with him at the gaps of the Blue Ridge on the east, and Edward Johnson was near Staunton with a similar force facing Milroy. In April General N. P. Banks, commanding the National forces in the Shenandoah valley, had ascended it as far as Harrisonburg, and Jackson observed him from Swift-Run Gap in the Blue Ridge, on the road from Harrisonburg to Gordonsville. Milroy also pushed eastward from Cheat Mountain summit, in which high region winter still lingered, and had made his way through snows and rains to McDowell, ten miles east of Monterey, at the crossing of Bull-Pasture River, where he threatened Staunton. But Banks was thought to be in too exposed a position, and was directed by the War Department to fall back to Strasburg. On the 5th of May he had retired in that direction as far as New-Market. Blenker's division had not yet reached Frémont, who was waiting for it in Hardy County at Petersburg. Jackson saw his opportunity and determined to join General Johnson by a rapid march to Staunton, to overwhelm Milroy first, and then return to his own operations in the Shenandoah. Moving with great celerity, he attacked Milroy at McDowell on the 8th, the latter calling upon Frémont for help. Schenck was sent forward to support him, and reached McDowell after marching thirty-four miles in twenty-four hours. Jackson had not fully concentrated his forces, and the Union generals held their ground and delivered a sharp combat in which their casualties of all kinds numbered 256, while the Confederate loss was 498, General Johnson being among the wounded. Schenck, as senior, assumed the command, and on the 9th began his retreat to Franklin, abandoning the Cheat Mountain road. Franklin was reached on the 11th, but Jackson approached cautiously, and did not reach there till the 12th, when, finding that Frémont had united his forces, he did not attack, but returned to McDowell, whence he took the direct road to Harrisonburg, and then marched to attack Banks at Strasburg, Ewell meeting and joining him in this movement.

Frémont resumed preparations for his original campaign, but Banks's defeat deranged all plans, and those of the Mountain Department were abandoned. A month passed in efforts to destroy Jackson by concentration of McDowell's, Banks's, and Frémont's troops; but it was too late to remedy the ill effects of the division of commands at the beginning of the campaign. On the 26th of June General John Pope was assigned to command all the troops in northern Virginia, Frémont was relieved at his own request, and the Mountain Department ceased to exist.

My own operations in the Kanawha valley had kept pace with those in the northern portion of the department. The early days of April were spent by Frémont in obtaining reports of the condition of the several parts of his command. My report of the condition of affairs in the Kanawha valley was made on the 5th of April. In it I called attention to the necessities of my troops and to the equipment necessary for any extended campaigning. Requisitions for supplies and transportation had been sent to the proper staff departments during the winter, but had not yet been filled. My forces consisted of eleven regiments of Ohio infantry, three new and incomplete regiments of West Virginia infantry, one regiment of cavalry (the Second West Virginia) with three separate cavalry troops from other commands, and, nominally, three batteries of artillery. One of the batteries was of mountain howitzers, and the other two of mixed smooth-bore and rifled guns of different calibres. My force at the opening of the campaign numbered 8500 present for duty. Detachments were at the mouth of the Big-Sandy River, at Guyandotte, at the mouth of the Kanawha on the Ohio River, at several points in the Kanawha valley below Gauley Bridge, at Summersville on the upper Gauley, at Gauley Bridge, at Gauley Mount or Tompkins farm on New River, and at Fayette C. H. The last-named post had the only brigade organization which had been retained in winter quarters, and was commanded by Colonel Scammon of the Twenty-third Ohio. The post at Summersville had been brought into my command for the winter, and was garrisoned by the Thirty-sixth Ohio under Colonel George Crook. At Gauley Bridge was the Twenty-eighth Ohio (a German regiment), under Colonel August Moor.

When the decision of General Fremont to have my command advance on both sides of the New River was received, I immediately submitted my plan of organization to that end. I proposed to leave the West Virginia Infantry regiments with half the Second West Virginia Cavalry to guard the Kanawha valley and our depots of supply, with Colonel J. A. J. Lightburn of the Fourth West Virginia in command. The Ohio regiments were to be moved forward so that the Eleventh, Forty-fourth, and Forty-seventh could be quickly concentrated on the Lewisburg turnpike in front of Gauley Bridge, where Colonel Crook could join them with the Thirty-sixth by a diagonal road and take command of this column. I assigned to him a mixed battery of fieldpieces and mountain howitzers. Colonel Scammon's brigade was to advance from Fayette C. H. to Flat-top Mountain as soon as the weather would permit, and thus secure the barrier covering our further movement southward. The brigade consisted of the Twelfth, Twenty-third, arid Thirtieth Ohio, with McMullin's battery, and one half the Second Virginia Cavalry. When Scammon advanced, the remaining Ohio regiments (Twenty-eighth, Thirty-fourth, and Thirty-seventh), with Simmonds's battery should concentrate at Fayette C. H. and form a new brigade under Colonel Moor. This organization was approved by Fremont, and the preliminary steps were quietly taken. By the 20th of April Scammon's brigade was at Raleigh, only awaiting the settling of the roads to advance to Flat-top. A week later he held the passes of the mountain, with a detachment on the New River at the mouth of the Blue-stone, where he communicated with the right of Crook's brigade. The front was thus covered from Summersville to Flat-top Mountain, and the regiments in rear were moving into their assigned positions.

My brigade commanders were all men of marked character. Colonel Moor was a German of portly presence and grave demeanour, a gentleman of dignity of character as well as of bearing, and a brave, resolute man. He had been long a citizen of the United States, and had, as a young man, seen some military service, as was reported, in the Seminole War in Florida. He was a rigid disciplinarian, and his own regiment was a model of accuracy in drill and neatness in the performance of all camp duties. He was greatly respected by his brother officers, and his square head, with dark, smooth-shaven face, and rather stern expression, inspired his troops with something very like awe, insuring prompt obedience to his commands. At home, in Cincinnati, he was a man of influence among the German residents, and his daughter was the wife of General Godfrey Weitzel of the regular army. My association with him was every way agreeable and satisfactory.

Colonel Crook was an officer of the regular army who had taken early advantage of the relaxation of the rule preventing such from accepting a volunteer appointment. A man of medium size, with light hair and sandy beard, his manner was rather diffident and shy, and his whole style quiet and reticent. His voice was light rather than heavy, and he was so laconic of speech that this, with his other characteristics, caused it to be commonly said of him that he had been so long fighting Indians on the frontier that he had acquired some of their traits and habits. His system of discipline was based on these peculiarities. He aimed at a stoical command of himself as the means of commanding others, and avoided noisy bluster of every sort, going, perhaps, to an excess in brevity of speech and in enforcing his orders by the consequences of any disobedience. His subordinates recognized his purpose to be just, and soon learned to have the greatest confidence in him as a military officer. Unless common fame did him injustice, he was one of those officers who had, at the beginning, no deep sympathy with the National cause, and had no personal objection to the success of the Rebellion. But he was a Northern man, and an ambitious professional soldier who did not mean to let political opinions stand in the way of military success. In his case, as in many others, I believe this attitude was modified by his service under the flag, and that in 1864 he voted for Mr. Lincoln's re-election; he, with General Sheridan, casting at the improvised army ballot-box, what was understood to be their first vote ever cast in a civil election.

Colonel Lightburn was one of the loyal West Virginians whose standing and intelligence made him naturally prominent among his people. He was a worthy man and an honourable officer, whose knowledge of the country and of the people made him a fit selection to preserve the peace and protect our communications in the valley during our forward movement. As his duties thus separated him from the principal columns, I saw less of him than of the other brigade commanders. The two West Virginia regiments which remained in the district were freshly organized, and were distributed in camps where they could practise company drill and instruction whilst they kept the country in order. Of Colonel Scammon, my senior brigade commander, I have already spoken in a former chapter.

Frémont limited our advance to the line of Flat-top Mountain until he should himself be ready to open the campaign in the north. Blenker's division had been given to him from the Potomac army when McClellan began his movement to the peninsula, but on the 12th of April it had only reached Salem, a station on the Manassas Gap Railway between the Bull-Run Mountains and the Blue Ridge. The War Department now sent General Rosecrans to conduct the division with speed to Frémont, but extraordinary delays still occurred, and the command did not reach Frémont at Petersburg till the 11th of May, when he immediately moved forward with it to the support of Schenck and Milroy at Franklin. This delay was one of a series of misfortunes; for could Frémont have been at McDowell with this strong reinforcement added to Schenck's and Milroy's brigades, there can be no reasonable doubt that Jackson's attack, if delivered at all, would have proven a disaster for the Confederates. This, however, would not have ensured success for the general campaign, for Banks might still have been driven back in the Shenandoah valley, and Frémont's position would have been compromised. Nothing but a union of the two columns would have met the situation.

At the beginning of May, the additional transportation necessary for my advance beyond Flat-top had not arrived, but we did not wait for it. The regiments were ordered to leave tents behind, and to bivouac without shelter except such as they could make with "brush," for the expected shelter tents also were lacking. The whole distance from the head of navigation to the railroad at Newberne was one hundred and forty miles. Flat-top Mountain and Lewisburg were, respectively, about halfway on the two routes assigned to us. Some two thousand of the enemy's militia were holding the mountain passes in front of us, and a concentration of the regular Confederate troops was going on behind them. These last consisted of two brigades under General Henry Heth, as well as J. S. Williams's and Marshall's brigades, under General Humphrey Marshall, with the Eighth Virginia Cavalry. General Marshall appears to have been senior when the commands were united. Looking south from Flat-top Mountain we see the basin of the Blue-stone River, which flows north-eastward into New River. This basin, with that of the Greenbrier on the other side of New River, forms the broadest stretch of cultivated land found between the mountain ranges, though the whole country is rough and broken even here. The crest of Flat-top Mountain curves southward around the headwaters of the Blue-stone, and joins the more regular ranges in Tazewell County. The straight ridge of East-River Mountain forms a barrier on the southern side of the basin, more than thirty miles away from the summit of Flat-top where Scammon's camp was placed on the road from Raleigh C. H. to Princeton, the county-seat of Mercer. The Narrows of New River were where that stream breaks through the mountain barrier I have described, and the road from Princeton to Giles C. H. passes through the defile. Only one other outlet from the basin goes southward, and that is where the road from Princeton to Wytheville passes through Rocky Gap, a gorge of the wildest character, some thirty miles south-westward from the Narrows. These passes were held by Confederate forces, whilst their cavalry, under Colonel W. H. Jenifer, occupied Princeton and presented a skirmishing resistance to our advance-guard.

On the 1st of May a small party of the Twenty-third Ohio met the enemy's horse at Camp Creek, a branch of the Blue-stone, six miles from the crest of Flat-top, and had a lively engagement, repulsing greatly superior numbers. On hearing of this, Lieutenant-Colonel R. B. Hayes marched with part of the Twenty-third Ohio and part of the West Virginia cavalry, and followed up the enemy with such vigour that Jenifer was driven through Princeton too rapidly to permit him to remove the stores collected there. To avoid their falling into our hands, Jenifer set fire to the town. Hayes succeeded in saving six or eight houses, but the rest were destroyed. Jenifer retreated on the Wytheville road, expecting us to follow by that route; but Hayes, learning that the Narrows were not strongly held, and being now reinforced by the rest of his regiment (the Twenty-third), marched on the 6th to the Narrows which he held, whilst he sent Major Comly with a detachment into Pearisburg, the county-seat of Giles. The affair at Camp Creek had cost Jenifer some twenty in killed and wounded, and an equal number were captured in the advance on Giles C. H. Our casualties were 1 killed and 20 wounded. Our line, however, was getting too extended, and the utmost exertions were needed to supply the troops in their present positions. Princeton, being at the forking of the roads to Pearisburg and Wytheville, was too important a point to be left unguarded, and I at once sent forward Colonel Scammon with the Thirtieth Ohio to hold it. On the 9th of May the Twelfth Ohio was put in march from Raleigh to join him, and Moor's brigade was approaching the last-named place where my headquarters were, that being the terminus, for the time, of the telegraph line which kept me in communication with Frémont. The same day the department commander informed me of the attack by Jackson on Milroy on the 7th, and ordered me to suspend movements in advance until my forces should be concentrated. The weather was rainy, and the roads suffered badly from cutting up by the wagons, but I had hoped to push forward a strong advanced guard to the great railway bridge near Newberne, and destroy it before the enemy had time to concentrate there. This made it necessary to take some risk, for it was not possible to move the whole command till some supplies could be accumulated at Raleigh and at Flat-top Mountain.

As fast as the supplies would permit, Moor went forward, taking no tents beyond Raleigh, and all of the troops on this line now faced the continuing rains without shelter. Guerrilla parties were set actively at work by the Confederates in the region of the Guyandotte and at other points in our rear. Colonel Lightburn was directed to keep his forces actively moving to suppress these outbreaks, and the forward movement was pressed. On the 10th of May Heth's two brigades of the enemy attacked our advance-guard at Pearisburg, and these, after destroying the enemy's stores, which they had captured there, retired skirmishing, till they joined Scammon, who had advanced from Princeton to their support. Scammon's brigade was now together, a mile below the Narrows of New River, with the East River in front of him, making a strong, defensible position. The telegraph reached

Flat-top Mountain on the 13th, even this being delayed because wagons to carry the wire could not be spared from the task of supplying the troops with food. I moved my headquarters to Princeton on this day, and pressed forward Moor's brigade in the hope of being able to push again beyond the barrier at the Narrows of New River, where Heth's brigades had now taken position. Neither Scammon nor Moor was able to take with him ammunition enough for more than a slight engagement, nor was any accumulation of food possible. We were living "from hand to mouth," no additional transportation had reached us, and every wagon and pack-mule was doing its best. As fast as Moor's regiments reached Princeton they were hurried forward to French's Mill, five miles in rear of Scammon, on the road running up East River, and intersecting the Wytheville road so as to form a triangle with the two going from Princeton. During the 14th and 15th Moor's regiments arrived, and were pushed on to their position, except one half regiment (detachments of the Thirty-fourth and Thirty-seventh Ohio), under Major F. E. Franklin, and one troop of cavalry, which were kept at Princeton as a guard against any effort on the enemy's part to interrupt our communications. Moor was ordered to send a detachment up the East River to the crossing of the Wytheville road, so as to give early warning of any attempt of the enemy to come in upon our flank from that direction. My purpose was to attack Heth with Scammon's and Moor's brigades, drive him away from the Narrows of New River, and prevent him, if possible, from uniting with Marshall's command, which was understood to be somewhere between Jeffersonville (Tazewell C. H.) and Wytheville. If we succeeded in beating Heth, we could then turn upon Marshall.

On the afternoon of the 15th Moor threw a detachment of two companies over East River Mountain as a reconnaissance to learn whether the roads in that direction were practicable for a movement to turn the left of Heth. It attacked and handsomely routed a post of the enemy on Wolf Creek. The few wagons and pack-mules were hurrying forward some rations and ammunition; but the 17th would be the earliest possible moment at which I could lead a general advance. The telegraph wire would reach Princeton by the evening of that day, and I waited there for the purpose of exchanging messages with Frémont before pushing toward Newberne, the expected rendezvous with the other troops of the department. But all our efforts could not give us the needed time to anticipate the enemy. They had railway communication behind a mountain wall which had few and difficult passes. Marshall and Williams were already marching from Tazewell C. H. to strike our line of communications at Princeton, and were far on the way.

About noon of the 16th Colonel Moor reported that his detachment on the Wytheville road was attacked by a force of the enemy estimated at 1500. This seems to have been the command of Colonel Wharton, marching to join Marshall, who was coming from the west by a road down the head-waters of East River. Of this, however, we were ignorant. I ordered Moor to take the remainder of his command (leaving half a regiment only at French's) to drive off the force at the cross-roads, and if he were overpowered to retreat directly upon Princeton by the western side of the triangle of roads, of which each side was twelve or fifteen miles long. Colonel Scammon reported no change in Heth's positions or force in front of him. Patrols were sent out on all the roads west and south of Princeton, our little force of horsemen being limited to Smith's troop of Ohio cavalry which was acting as headquarters escort. About two o'clock the patrol on the Wyoming road, five miles out of Princeton, was fired upon by the enemy's cavalry, and came rapidly in with the report. The four companies of infantry under Majors Franklin and Ankele were moved out on that road, and soon developed the infantry of Marshall's command. He and Williams had marched across from the Tazewell to the Wyoming road, and were coming in upon our flank and rear. I reconnoitred them personally with care, and satisfied myself of their overwhelming superiority to the little detachment I had in hand. Franklin and Ankele were ordered to deploy their whole force as skirmishers and to hold the enemy back as long as possible. Some of our troopers were shown on the flanks, and so imposing a show was made that Marshall advanced cautiously. Our men behaved beautifully, holding every tree and rock, delaying the enemy for more than three hours from reaching the crests of the hills looking down upon the town. I had sent orderlies to stop and turn back our wagon trains on the way from Flat-top, and had directed headquarters baggage and the few stores in Princeton to be loaded and sent on the road toward Moor and Scammon. Our only tents were three or four wall tents for headquarters (the adjutant-general's, quartermaster's, and commissary's offices), and these I ordered to be left standing to impose upon the enemy the idea that we did not mean to retire. As evening approached, the hostile force occupied the summits of surrounding hills, and directing the infantry slowly to fall back and follow me, I galloped with my staff to bring back Scammon and restore our broken communications. At French's, twelve miles from Princeton, I found that Moor had not had time to execute the orders of the afternoon, and that ten companies from the Twenty-eighth and Thirty-seventh Ohio were all that he had been able to send to Wytheville road crossing. These, we learned later in the night, had succeeded in re-occupying the cross-roads. They were ordered to hold fast till morning, and if the enemy still appeared to be mainly at Princeton, to march in that direction and attack them from the rear. Scammon was ordered to send half a regiment to occupy Moor's position at French's during the night, and to march his whole command at daybreak toward Princeton. There was but one and a half regiments now with Moor, and these were roused and ordered to accompany me at once on our return to Princeton. It was a dark and muddy march, and as we approached the town we deployed skirmishers in front, though they were obliged to move slowly in the darkness. Day was just breaking as we came out of the forest upon the clearing, line of battle was formed, and the troops went forward cheering. The enemy made no stubborn resistance, but retired gradually to a strong position on rough wooded hills about a mile from the village, where they covered both the Wytheville and the Wyoming road. They had artillery on both flanks, and could only be reached over open and exposed ground. We recovered our headquarters tents, standing as we had left them. We had captured a few prisoners and learned that Marshall and Williams were both before us. Whilst pushing them back, Lieutenant-Colonel Von Blessingh with the ten companies of Moor's brigade approached on the Wytheville road and attacked; but the enemy was aware of their approach and repulsed them, having placed a detachment in a very strong position to meet them. Von Blessingh withdrew his men, and later joined the command by a considerable detour. With less than two regiments in hand, and with the certainty of the enemy's great superiority, there was nothing for it but to take the best position we could and await Scammon's arrival. We made as strong a show of force as possible, and by skirmishing advances tempted the enemy to come down to attack; but he also was expecting reinforcements, and a little artillery firing was the only response we provoked. As some evidence of the physical exhaustion from the continuous exertions of the preceding day and night, I may mention the fact that during the artillery firing I threw myself for a little rest on the ground, close beside the guns; and though these were firing at frequent intervals, I fell asleep and had a short but refreshing nap almost within arm's length of the wheels of a gun-carriage.

Toward evening Scammon arrived with his brigade, reporting that Heth's force had followed his retiring movement as far as French's, and confirming the information that four brigades of the enemy were before us. Shortly after dark the officer of the day, on the right, reported the noise of artillery marching around that flank. Our last day's rations had been issued, and our animals were without forage. Small parties of the enemy had gone far to our rear and cut the telegraph, so that we had had no news from the Kanawha valley for two days. The interruption was likely to create disturbance there and derange all our plans for supply. It was plain that we should have to be content with having foiled the enemy's plan to inflict a severe blow upon us, and that we might congratulate ourselves that with two brigades against four we had regained our line without serious loss. I therefore ordered that the troops be allowed to rest till three o'clock in the morning of the 18th, and that the column then retire behind the Bluestone River. The movement was made without interruption, and a camp on Flat-top Mountain was selected, from which the roads on every side were well guarded, and which was almost impregnable in itself. Our casualties of all kinds in the affairs about Princeton had been only 113, as the enemy had not delivered any serious attack, and the contest on our side had been one of manoeuvre in which our only chance of important results was in attacking either Heth or Marshall when they were so far separated that they could not unite against us on the field of battle. After the 15th this chance did not exist, and wisdom dictated that we should retire to a safe point from which we could watch for contingencies which might give us a better opportunity. Our experience proved what I have before stated, that the facility for railway concentration of the enemy in our front made this line a useless one for aggressive movements, as they could always concentrate a superior force after they received the news of our being in motion. It also showed the error of dividing my forces on two lines, for had Crook's brigade been with me, or my two brigades with him, we should have felt strong enough to cope with the force which was actually in our front, and would at least have made it necessary for the enemy to detach still more troops from other movements to meet us. Our campaign, though a little one, very well illustrates the character of the subordinate movements so often attempted during the war, and shows that the same principles of strategy are found operating as in great movements. The scale is a reduced one, but cause and effect are linked by the same necessity as on a broader theatre of warfare.

CHAPTER 11

Pope in Command—Transfer to Washington

Our retreat to Flat-top Mountain had been made without loss of material, except one baggage-wagon, which broke down irreparably, and was burned by my order. At the crossing of Blue-stone River we were beyond the junction of roads by which our flank could be turned, and we halted there as the end of the first march. As the men forded the stream, the sun broke through the clouds, which had been pretty steadily raining upon us, the brass band with the leading brigade struck up the popular tune, "Aren't you glad to get out of the wilderness?" and the soldiers, quick to see the humorous application of any such incident, greeted it with cheers and laughter. All felt that we were again masters of the situation. Next day we moved leisurely to the mountain summit, a broad undulating table-land with some cultivated farms, where our camp was perfectly hidden from sight, whilst we commanded a most extensive view of the country in front. Outposts at the crossing of the Blue-stone and at Pack's Ferry on New River, with active scouting-parties and patrols scouring the country far and wide, kept me fully informed of everything occurring near us. We had time to organize the new wagon-trains which were beginning to reach us, and, while waiting till Frémont could plan new co-operative movements, to prepare for our part in such work.

The camp on Flat-top Mountain deserved the name of a "key point" to the country in front as well, perhaps, as that much abused phrase ever is deserved. The name of the mountain indicates its character. The northern slope is gentle, so that the approach from Raleigh C. H. is not difficult, whilst the southern declivity falls off rapidly to the Blue-stone valley. The broad ridge at the summit is broken into rounded hills which covered the camp from view, whilst they still permitted manoeuvre to meet any hostile approach. The mountain abutted on the gorge of the New River on the northeast, and stretched also southwestward into the impracticable wilderness about the headwaters of the Guyandotte and the Tug Fork of Sandy. The position was practically unassailable in front by any force less than double our own, and whilst we occupied it the enemy never ventured in force beyond the passes of East River Mountain. We built a flying-bridge ferry at Pack's, on New River, near the mouth of the Blue-stone, where a passable road up the valley of the Greenbrier connected us with Colonel Crook's position at Lewisburg. The post at Pack's Ferry was held by a detachment from Scammon's brigade in command of Major Comly of the Twenty-third Ohio. On the 6th of August a detachment of the enemy consisting of three regiments and a section of artillery under Colonel Wharton made an effort to break up the ferry by an attack from the east side, but they accomplished nothing. Major Comly was quickly supported by reinforcements from Scammon's brigade, and drove off his assailants.

I have not yet spoken of the movements of Colonel Crook's brigade on the Lewisburg route, because circumstances so delayed his advance that it had no immediate relation to our movements upon Pearisburg and Princeton. As the march of my own column was beginning, General Frémont, upon information of guerrilla raids north of Summersville, directed that Crook be sent into Webster County to co-operate with troops sent southward from Weston to destroy the lawless parties. This involved a march of more than seventy miles each way, and unforeseen delays of various kinds. Two of the guerrillas captured were tried and convicted of murder, and Colonel Crook was obliged to remain in that region to protect the administration of justice till the execution of the murderers and the dispersion of the guerrilla bands. The organization and movement of his brigade upon Lewisburg was by this means put back so far that his column could not get within supporting distance of mine. He reached Lewisburg on the day of our affair at Princeton. He had been energetic in all his movements, but the diversion of parts of his command to so distant an enterprise as that into Webster County had been fatal to co-operation. The Confederate General Heth had been able to neglect the Lewisburg route and to carry his brigade to the assistance of Marshall in his opposition to my advance. As it turned out, I should have done better to have waited at Flat-top Mountain till I knew that Crook was at Lewisburg, and then to have made a fresh combination of movements. Our experience only added another to the numerous proofs the whole campaign furnished, of the futility of such combined operations from distant bases,

Major-General Loring took command of all the Confederate forces in south-western Virginia on the 19th or 20th of May, and Heth was already in march to oppose Crook's forward movement. On the 23rd Heth, with some 3000 men, including three batteries of artillery, attacked Crook at Lewisburg, soon after daybreak in the morning. Crook met him in front of the town, and after a sharp engagement routed him, capturing four cannon, some 200 stand of arms and 100 prisoners. His own loss was 13 killed and 53 wounded, with 7 missing. He did not think it wise to follow up the retreating enemy, but held a strong position near Lewisburg, where his communications were well covered, and where he was upon the same range of highlands on which we were at Flat-top, though fifty miles of broken country intervened. Meanwhile Frémont had been ordered to Banks's relief, and had been obliged to telegraph me that we must be left to ourselves till the results of the Shenandoah campaign were tested. Rumours were rife that after Jackson retired from Frémont's front at Franklin, Johnson's division was ordered to march into our part of West Virginia. We were thus thrown, necessarily, into an expectant attitude, awaiting the outcome of Frémont's eastward movement and the resumption of his plans. Our men were kept busy in marching and scouting by detachments, putting down guerrilla bands and punishing disorders. They thus acquired a power of sustained exertion on foot which proved afterward of great value.

There was, in a way, a resemblance in our situation and in our work to that of feudal chiefs in the middle ages. We held a lofty and almost impregnable position, overlooking the country in every direction. The distant ridges of the Alleghenies rose before us, the higher peaks standing out in the blue distance, so that we seemed to watch the mountain passes fifty miles away without stirring from our post. The loyal people about us formed relations to us not unlike those of the feudal retainers of old. They worked their farms, but every man had his rifle hung upon his chimney-piece, and by day or by night was ready to shoulder it and thread his way by paths known only to the natives, to bring us news of open movement or of secret plots among the Secessionists. They were organized, also, in their own fashion, and every neighbourhood could muster its company or its squad of home-guards to join in quelling seditious outbreaks or in strengthening a little column sent against any of the enemy's outposts. No considerable hostile movement was possible within a range of thirty miles without our having timely notice of it. The smoke from the camp-fires of a single troop of horse could be seen rising from the ravines, and detachments of our regiments guided by the native scouts would be on the way to reconnoitre within an hour. Officers as well as men went on foot, for they followed ridges where there was not even a bridle-path, and depended for safety, in no small degree, on their ability to take to the thickets of the forest-clad hillside if they found themselves in the presence of a body of the Confederate cavalry. Thirty miles a day was an easy march for them after they had become hardened to their work, and taking several days together they could outmarch any cavalry, especially when they could take "short cuts" over hills and away from travelled roads. They knew at what farms they could find "rations," and where were the hostile neighbourhoods from which equally enterprising scouts would glide away to carry news of their movements to the enemy. At headquarters there was a constant going and coming. Groups of home-guards were nearly always about, as picturesque in their homely costume as Leather-stocking himself, and many of our officers and men were hardly less expert as woodsmen. Constant activity was the order of the day, and the whole command grew hardy and self-reliant with great rapidity.

General Pope was, on the 26th of June, assigned to command the Army of Virginia, including the forces under McDowell and Banks as well as those in the Mountain Department. Fremont was relieved from command at his own request, and the Mountain Department ceased to exist. Pope very wisely determined to unite in one army under his own command as many as possible of the troops reporting to him, and meanwhile directed us to remain on the defensive. I ventured on the 3d of July to suggest by telegraph that my division would make a useful reinforcement to his active army in the field, and reiterated it on the 5th, with some explanation of my views. I indicated Fayetteville and Hawk's Nest as points in front of Gauley Bridge where moderate garrisons could cover the valley defensively, as I had done in the preceding year. Getting no answer, I returned to the subject on the 13th. Pope, however, did not issue his address upon assuming active command till the 14th, when his much ridiculed manifesto to the army appeared. Since the war General Pope has himself told me that this, as well as the other orders issued at that time and which were much criticised, were drafted under the dictation, in substance, of Mr. Stanton, the Secretary of War. He admitted that some things in them were not quite in good taste; but the feeling was that it was desirable to infuse vigour into the army by stirring words, which would by implication condemn McClellan's policy of over-caution in military matters, and over-tenderness toward rebel sympathizers and their property. The Secretary, as he said, urged such public declarations so strongly that he did not feel at liberty to resist. They were unfairly criticised, and were made the occasion of a bitter and lasting enmity toward Pope on the part of most of the officers and men of the Potomac Army. It seems that Mr. Lincoln hesitated to approve the one relating to the arrest of disloyal persons within the lines of the army, and it was not till Pope repeated his sense of the need of it that the President yielded, on condition that it should be applied in exceptional cases only. It was probably intended more to terrify citizens from playing the part of spies than to be literally enforced, which would, indeed, have been hardly possible. No real severity was used under it, but the Confederate government made it the occasion of a sort of outlawry against Pope and his army.

On the 5th of August Pope suggested to Halleck that I should be ordered to leave about 2500 men entrenched near Gauley Bridge, and march with the remainder of my command (say nine regiments) by way of Lewisburg, Covington, Staunton, and Harrisonburg to join him. Halleck replied that it was too much exposed, and directed him to select one more in the rear. Pope very rightly answered that there was no other route which would not make a great circuit to the rear. Halleck saw that Jackson's army near Charlottesville with a probable purpose of turning Pope's right flank might make a junction impossible for me, and stated the objection, but concluded with authority to Pope to order as he deemed best, "but with caution."

On the 8th of August Pope telegraphed me, accordingly, to march by way of Lewisburg, Covington, Warm Springs, and Augusta Springs to Harrisonburg, and there join him by shortest route. He indicated Winchester or Romney as my secondary aim if I should find the junction with him barred. This route avoided Staunton, but by so short a distance that it was scarcely safer, and the roads to be travelled were much harder and longer. At this time several detachments of considerable size were out, chasing guerrilla parties and small bodies of Confederate troops, and assisting in the organization or enlistment of Union men. The movement ordered could not begin for several days, and I took advantage of the interval to lay before General Pope, by telegraph, the proof that the march would take fifteen days of uninterrupted travel through a mountainous region, most of it a wilderness destitute of supplies, and with the enemy upon the flank. Besides this there was the very serious question whether the Army of Virginia would be at Charlottesville when I should approach that place. On the other hand, my calculation was that we could reach Washington in ten days or less, by way of the Kanawha and Ohio rivers to Parkersburg, and thence by the Baltimore and Ohio Railroad to the capital. My dispatches were submitted to General Halleck, and on the 11th of August General Pope telegraphed a modified assent to my suggestions. He directed that 5000 men should remain in West Virginia under my command, and the remainder proceed to Washington by river and rail. An incursion of the enemy's cavalry into Logan County on my right and rear was at the moment in progress, and we used great activity in disposing of it, so that the change in our dispositions might not be too quickly known to our adversaries nor have the appearance of retreat.

It is a natural wish of every soldier to serve with the largest army in the most important campaign. The order to remain with a diminished command in West Virginia was a great disappointment to me, against which I made haste to protest. On the 13th I was rejoiced by permission to accompany my command to the East. Preliminary orders had already been given for making Fayetteville and Hawk's Nest the principal advanced posts in the contracted operations of the district, with Gauley Bridge for their common depot of supply and point of concentration in case of an advance of the enemy in force. I organized two small brigades and two batteries of artillery for the movement to Washington. Colonels Scammon and Moor, who were my senior colonels, were already in command of brigades, and Colonel Lightburn was in command of the lower valley. The arrangement already existing practically controlled. Scammon's brigade was unchanged, and in Moor's the Thirty-sixth Ohio under Crook and the Eleventh were substituted for the Thirty-seventh and Thirty-fourth. The organization therefore was as follows; namely, First Brigade, Colonel Scammon commanding, consisted of the Twelfth, Twenty-third, and Thirtieth Ohio and McMullin's Ohio Battery; Second Brigade, Colonel Moor commanding, consisted of the Eleventh, Twenty-eighth, and Thirty-sixth Ohio and Simmonds's Kentucky Battery. One troop of horse for orderlies and headquarters escort, and another for similar service, with the brigades, also accompanied us. The regiments left in the Kanawha district were the Thirty-fourth, Thirty-seventh, Forty-fourth, and Forty-seventh Ohio, the Fourth and Ninth West Virginia Infantry, the Second West Virginia Cavalry, a battery, and some incomplete local organizations. Colonel J. A. J. Lightburn of the Fourth West Virginia was in command as senior officer within the district.

Portions of the troops were put in motion on the 14th of August, and a systematic itinerary was prepared for them in advance. They marched fifty minutes, and then rested the remaining ten minutes of each hour. The day's work was divided into two stages of fifteen miles each, with a long rest at noon, and with a half day's interval between the brigades. The weather was warm, but by starting at three o'clock in the morning the heat of the day was reserved for rest, and they made their prescribed distance without distress and without straggling. They went by Raleigh C. H. and Fayetteville to Gauley Bridge, thence down the right bank of the Kanawha to Camp Piatt, thirteen miles above Charleston. The whole distance was ninety miles, and was covered easily in the three days and a half allotted to it. The fleet of light-draft steamboats which supplied the district with military stores was at my command, and I gave them rendezvous at Camp Piatt, where they were in readiness to meet the troops when the detachments began to arrive on the 17th. In the evening of the 14th I left the camp at Flat-top with my staff and rode to Raleigh C. H. On the 15th we completed the rest of the sixty miles to Gauley Bridge. From that point I was able to telegraph General Meigs, the Quartermaster-General at Washington, that I should reach Parkersburg, the Ohio River terminus of the Baltimore and Ohio Railroad, on the evening of the 20th, and should need railway transportation for 5000 men, two batteries of six guns each, 1100 horses, 270 wagons, with camp equipage and regimental trains complete, according to the army regulations then in force.

At Gauley Bridge I met Colonel Lightburn, to whom I turned over the command of the district, and spent the time, whilst the troops were on the march, in completing the arrangements both for our transportation and for the best disposition of the troops which were to remain. The movement of the division was the first in which there had been a carefully prepared effort to move a considerable body of troops with wagons and animals over a long distance within a definitely fixed time, and it was made the basis of the calculations for the movement of General Hooker and his two corps from Washington to Tennessee in the next year. It thus obtained some importance in the logistics of the war. The president of the railway put the matter unreservedly into the hands of W. P. Smith, the master of transportation; Mr. P. H. Watson, Assistant Secretary of War, represented the army in the management of the transfer, and by thus concentrating responsibility and power, the business was simplified, and what was then regarded as a noteworthy success was secured. The command could have moved more rapidly, perhaps, without its wagons and animals, but a constant supply of these was needed for the eastern army, and it was wise to take them, for they were organized into trains with drivers used to their teams and feeling a personal interest in them. It turned out that our having them was a most fortunate thing, for not only were the troops of the Army of the Potomac greatly crippled for lack of transportation on their return from the peninsula, but we were able to give rations to the Ninth Army Corps after the battle of Antietam, when the transportation of the other divisions proved entirely insufficient to keep up the supply of food.

From the head of navigation on the Kanawha to Parkersburg on the Ohio was about one hundred and fifty miles; but the rivers were so low that the steamboats proceeded slowly, delayed by various obstacles and impediments, At Letart's Falls, on the Ohio, the water was a broken rapid, up which the boats had to be warped one at a time, by means of a heavy warp-line made fast to the bank and carried to the steam-capstan on the steamer. At the foot of Blennerhassett's Island there was only two feet of water in the channel, and the boats dragged themselves over the bottom by "sparring," a process somewhat like an invalid's pushing his wheel-chair along by a pair of crutches. But everybody worked with a will, and on the 21st the advanced regiments were transferred to the railway cars at Parkersburg, according to programme, and pulled out for Washington. These were the Thirty-sixth Ohio, Colonel Crook, and the Thirtieth Ohio, Colonel Ewing. They passed through Washington to Alexandria, and thence, without stopping, to Warrenton, Virginia, where they reported at General Pope's headquarters. The Eleventh Ohio (Lieutenant-Colonel Coleman) and Twelfth (Colonel White), with Colonel Scammon commanding brigade, left Parkersburg on the 22d, reaching Washington on the 24th. One of them passed on to Alexandria, but the other (Eleventh Ohio) was stopped in Washington by reason of a break in Long Bridge across the Potomac, and marched to Alexandria the next day. The last of the regiments (Twenty-eighth Ohio, Colonel Moor, and Twenty-third, Lieutenant-Colonel Hayes), with the artillery and cavalry followed, and on the 26th all the men had reached Washington, though the wagons and animals were a day or two later in arriving.

In Washington I reported to the Secretary of War, and was received with a cordiality that went far to remove from my mind the impression I had got from others, that Mr. Stanton was abrupt and unpleasant to approach. Both on this occasion and later, he was as affable as could be expected of a man driven with incessant and importunate duties of state. In the intervals of my constant visits to the railway offices (for getting my troops and my wagons together was the absorbing duty) I found time for a hurried visit to Secretary Chase, and found also my friend Governor Dennison in the city, mediating between the President and General McClellan with the good-will and diplomatic wisdom which peculiarly marked his character. I had expected to go forward with three regiments to join General Pope on the evening of the 26th; but Colonel Haupt, the military superintendent of railways at Alexandria, was unable to furnish the transportation by reason of the detention of trains at the front. Lee's flank movement against Pope's army had begun, and as the latter retreated all the railway cars which could be procured were needed to move his stores back toward Washington. On the afternoon of the 26th, however, arrangements had been made for moving the regiments at Alexandria early next morning. The wagons and animals were near at hand, and I ordered Colonel Moor with the Twenty-eighth Ohio to march with them to Manassas as soon as they should be unloaded from the railway trains. But during the night occurred a startling change in the character of the campaign which upset all our plans and gave a wholly unexpected turn to my own part in it.

About nine o'clock in the evening Colonel Haupt received at Alexandria the information that the enemy's cavalry had attacked our great depot of supplies at Manassas Junction. The telegrapher had barely time to send a message, break the connection of the wires, and hurry away to escape capture. It was naturally supposed to be only a cavalry raid, but the interruption of communication with Pope in that crisis was in itself a serious mishap. The first thing to be done was to push forward any troops at hand to protect the railway bridge over Bull Run, and by authority of the War Department Colonel Haupt was authorized to send forward, under Colonel Scammon, the Eleventh and Twelfth Ohio without waiting to communicate with me. They were started very early in the morning of the 27th, going to support a New Jersey brigade under General George W. Taylor which had been ordered to protect the Bull Run bridge. Ignorant of all this, I was busy on Wednesday morning (27th), trying to learn the whereabouts of the trains with my wagon teams, which had not yet reached Washington, and reported the situation as to my command to the Assistant Secretary of War, Mr. Watson. I then learned of Scammon's sudden movement to the front, and of the serious character of the enemy's movement upon Manassas. I marched at once with the two regiments still in Washington, expecting to follow the rest of the command by rail as soon as we should reach Alexandria. Arriving there, I hastened to the telegraph office at the railway station, where I found not only Colonel Haupt, but General McClellan, who had come from Fortress Monroe the night before. Of the Army of the Potomac, Heintzelman's and Porter's corps were already with Pope, Franklin's was at Alexandria, and Sumner's was beginning to arrive. As soon as it was known at the War Department that McClellan was present, General Halleck's correspondence was of course with him, and we passed under his orders. It had already been learned that 'Stonewall' Jackson was with infantry as well as cavalry at Manassas, and that the Bull Run bridge had been burned, our troops being driven back three or four miles from it. McClellan thought it necessary to organize the two corps at Alexandria and such other troops as were there, including mine, first to cover that place and Washington in the possible contingency that Lee's whole army had interposed between General Pope and the capital, and, second, to open communication with Pope as soon as the situation of the latter could be learned. Couch's division was still at Yorktown, and orders had been issued by Halleck to ship 5000 new troops there to relieve Couch and allow his veteran division to join the Potomac Army.

McClellan directed me to take the two regiments with me into camp with Franklin's corps at Annandale, three miles in front of Alexandria, and to obey Franklin's orders if any emergency should occur. I found, at the post-quartermaster's office, an officer who had served in West Virginia a year before, and by his hearty and efficient good-will secured some supplies for the regiments with me during the days that were yet to pass before we got our own trains and could feel that we had an assured means of living and moving in an independent way. We bivouacked by the roadside without shelter of any sort, enveloped in dense clouds of dust from the marching columns of the Army of the Potomac, their artillery and wagons, as they passed and went into camp just in front of us. About noon, on Thursday (28th), Colonel Scammon joined me with the two regiments he had taken toward Manassas, and we learned the particulars of the sharp engagement he had at the railway bridge.

The train carrying the troops approached the bridge over Bull Run about eight o'clock in the morning on Wednesday, and Colonel Scammon immediately pushed forward the Twelfth Ohio (Colonel White) to the bridge itself and the bank of the stream. He met the New Jersey brigade of four regiments coming back in confusion and panic. The commander, General Taylor, had taken position on the west side of the creek, covering the bridge; but he had no artillery, and though his advance was made with great spirit (as Jackson recognized in his report, his lines had been subjected to a heavy artillery fire from the batteries of A. P. Hill's and Jackson's own divisions, and broke, retreating in disorder to the eastern side of the stream. General Taylor himself fell severely wounded whilst trying to rally them. It was at this moment that Scammon reached the field with the Twelfth Ohio. He had heard the artillery fire, but little or no musketry, and was astonished at seeing the retreat. He sent his adjutant-general, Lieutenant Robert P. Kennedy, to communicate with General Taylor and to try to rally the fugitives. Meanwhile he ordered Colonel White to line the bank of the creek with his men and try to protect the bridge structure. Kennedy found General Taylor in a litter being carried to the rear, and the general, though in anguish from his wound, was in great mental distress at the rout of his men. He begged every one to rally the flying troops if possible, and sent his own adjutant-general, Captain Dunham, to turn over the general command to Scammon. All efforts to rally the panic-stricken brigade were fruitless, and Scammon resisted the advance of Hill's division through nearly a whole day with the two regiments alone. A Lieutenant Wright of the Fourth New Jersey, with ten men, reported to Colonel Scammon and begged assignment in the line. Their names are honourably enrolled in Scammon's report, and these, with Captain Dunham, did heroic service, but were all of the brigade that took any further part in the fight. Dunham succeeded in rallying a portion of the brigade later in the day, but too late to enter the engagement.

Taking advantage of the bridges near the stream, Scammon kept his men covered from the artillery fire as well as possible, driving back with his volleys every effort to pass by the bridge or to ford the stream in his front. Hill moved brigades considerably to right and left, and attempted to surround White and the Twelfth Ohio. But Coleman, with the Eleventh, had come up in support, and Scammon ordered him to charge on the enemy's right, which was passing White's left flank. Coleman did so in splendid style, driving his foe before him, and crossing the bridge to the west side. The odds, however, were far too great where a brigade could attack each regiment of ours and others pass beyond them, so that Scammon, having fully developed the enemy's force, had to limit himself to delaying their advance, retiring his little command in echelon from one ridge to another, as his wings were threatened. This he did with perfect coolness and order, maintaining the unequal struggle without assistance till about half-past three in the afternoon. The enemy's efforts now relaxed, and Scammon withdrew at leisure to a position some three miles from the bridge. Hill still showed a disposition to surround the detachment by manoeuvres, and Scammon retired toward Annandale in the night. He himself underestimated the enemy's force in infantry, which Jackson's report puts at "several brigades." His loss in the two Ohio regiments was 106 in killed, wounded, and missing. Those of the New Jersey brigade are not reported. The combat was a most instructive military lesson, teaching what audacity and skill may do with a very small force in delaying and mystifying a much larger one, which was imposed upon by its firm front and its able handling.

Some of Scammon's wounded being too badly hurt to be removed, he detailed a surgeon to remain with them and care for them till they should be exchanged or otherwise brought within our lines. This surgeon was taken to Jackson's headquarters, where he was questioned as to the troops which had held the Confederates at bay. General J. E. B. Stuart was with Jackson, and on the surgeon's stating that the fighting during most of the day had been by the two Ohio regiments alone, Stuart's racy expressions of admiration were doubly complimentary as coming from such an adversary, and, when repeated, were more prized by the officers and men than any praise from their own people.

Toward evening on Thursday, a thunderstorm and gale of wind came up, adding greatly to the wretched discomfort of the troops for the moment, but making the air clearer and laying the dust for a day or two. I found partial shelter with my staff, on the veranda of a small house which was occupied by ladies of the families of some general officers of the Potomac Army, who had seized the passing opportunity to see their husbands in the interval of the campaign. We thought ourselves fortunate in getting even the shelter of the veranda roof for the night. On Friday morning (29th), Captain Fitch, my quartermaster, was able to report his train and baggage safe at Alexandria, and we were ready for any service. Orders came from General McClellan during the forenoon to move the four regiments now with me into Forts Ramsey and Buffalo, on Upton's and Munson's hills, covering Washington on the direct road to Centreville by Aqueduct Bridge, Ball's Cross-Roads, and Fairfax C. H. General McClellan had established his headquarters on Seminary Ridge beyond the northern outskirts of Alexandria, and after putting my command in motion I rode there to get fuller instructions from him as to the duty assigned me. His tents were pitched in a high airy situation looking toward the Potomac on the east; indeed he had found them a little too airy in the thunder-squall of the previous evening which had demolished part of the canvas village. It must have been about noon when I dismounted at his tent. The distant pounding of artillery had been in our ears as we rode. It was Pope's battle with Jackson along the turnpike between Bull Run and Gainesville and on the heights above Groveton, thirty miles away.

General Franklin had ridden over from Annandale and was with McClellan receiving his parting directions under the imperative orders which Halleck had sent to push that corps out to Pope. McClellan's words I was not likely to forget. "Go," he said, "and whatever may happen, don't allow it to be said that the Army of the Potomac failed to do its utmost for the country." McClellan then explained to me the importance of the position to which I was ordered. The heights were the outer line of defence of Washington on the west, which had been held at one time, a year before, by the Confederates, who had an earthwork there, notorious for a while under the camp name of "Fort Skedaddle." From them the unfinished dome of the Capitol was to be seen, and the rebel flag had flaunted there, easily distinguishable by the telescopes which were daily pointed at it from the city. McClellan had little expectation that Pope would escape defeat, and impressed upon me the necessity of being prepared to cover a perhaps disorderly retreat within the lines.

Some heavy artillery troops (Fourth New York Heavy Artillery) were in garrison at one of the forts, and these with the forces at Falls Church were ordered to report to me. Assuring me that he would soon visit me in my new quarters, McClellan dismissed me, and I galloped forward to overtake my troops.

I found the position of the forts a most commanding one, overlooking the country in every direction. Westward the ground sloped away from us toward Fairfax Court House and Centreville. Northward, in a pretty valley, lay the village of Falls Church, and beyond it a wooded ridge over which a turnpike road ran to Vienna and on to Leesburg. Behind us was the rolling country skirting the Potomac, and from Ball's Cross-Roads, a mile or two in rear, a northward road led to the chain bridge above Georgetown, whilst the principal way went directly to the city by the Aqueduct Bridge. Three knolls grouped so as to command these different directions had been crowned with forts of strong profile. The largest of these, Fort Ramsey, on Upton's Hill was armed with twenty-pounder Parrott rifles, and the heavy-artillery troops occupied this work. I had a pair of guns of the same kind and calibre in my mixed battery, and these with my other field artillery were put in the other forts. Lines of infantry trench connected the works and extended right and left, and my four regiments occupied these.

We pitched our headquarters tents on Upton's Hill, just in rear of Fort Ramsey, and had a sense of luxury in "setting our house in order" after the uncomfortable experience of our long journey from West Virginia. The hurry of startling events in the past few days made our late campaign in the mountains seem as far away in time as it was in space. We were now in the very centre of excitement, and had become a very small part of a great army. The isolation and the separate responsibility of the past few months seemed like another existence indefinitely far away. I lost no time in making a rapid ride about my position, studying its approaches in the gathering twilight and trying to fix in mind the leading features of the topography with their relation to the possible retreat of our army and advance of the enemy. And all the while the rapid though muffled thumping of the distant cannon was in our ears, coming from the field in front of Groveton, where Lee, having now united his whole army against Pope, was sending part of Longstreet's divisions against McDowell's corps along the Warrenton turnpike.

On Saturday the 30th ambulances began coming through our lines with wounded men, and some on foot with an arm in a sling or bandages upon the head were wearily finding their way into the city. All such were systematically questioned, their information was collated and corrected, and reports were made to General Halleck and General McClellan. The general impression of all undoubtedly was that the engagement of Friday had been victorious for our army, and that the enemy was probably retreating at dark. During the day the cannonade continued with occasional lulls. It seemed more distant and fainter, requiring attentive listening to hear it. This was no doubt due to some change in the condition of the atmosphere; but we naturally interpreted it according to our wishes, and believed that the success of Friday was followed by the pursuit of the enemy. About four o'clock in the afternoon the distant firing became much more rapid; at times the separate shots could not be counted. I telegraphed to McClellan the fact which indicated a crisis in the battle. It was the fierce artillery duel which preceded the decisive advance of Longstreet against Pope's left wing. This was the decisive turning-point in the engagement, and Pope was forced to retreat upon Centreville.

Early in the evening all doubt was removed about the result of the battle. Ill news travels fast, and the retreat toward us shortened the distance to be travelled. But as Sumner's and Franklin's corps had gone forward and would report to Pope at Centreville, we were assured that Pope was "out of his scrape" (to use the words of McClellan's too famous dispatch to the President), and that the worst that could now happen would be the continuance of the retreat within our lines. The combat at Chantilly on the evening of September 1st was the last of Pope's long series of bloody engagements, and though the enemy was repulsed, the loss of Generals Kearny and Stevens made it seem to us like another disaster.

Chapter 12
Retreat Within the Lines

On Sunday, the 31st, McClellan rode over to Upton's Hill and spent most of the day with me. He brought me a copy of the McDowell map of the country about Washington, the compilation of which had been that officer's first work at the beginning of hostilities. It covered the region to and beyond the Bull Run battlefield, and although not wholly accurate, it was approximately so, and was the only authority relied upon for topographical details of the region. McClellan's primary purpose was to instruct me as to the responsibilities that might fall upon me if the army should be driven in. A day or two later I received formal orders to prepare to destroy buildings in front within my lines of artillery fire, and to be ready to cover the retreat of our army should any part be driven back near my position. All this, however, had been discussed with McClellan himself. We rode together over all the principal points in the neighbourhood, and he pointed out their relation to each other and to positions on the map which we did not visit. The discussion of the topography led to reminiscences of the preceding year—of the manner in which the enemy had originally occupied these hills, and of their withdrawal from them—of the subsequent construction of the forts and connecting lines, who occupied them all, and the system of mutual support, of telegraphic communication, and of plans for defence in case of attack.

McClellan had received me at Alexandria on the 27th with all his old cordiality, and had put me at once upon our accustomed footing of personal friendship. On my part, there was naturally a little watchfulness not to overstep the proper line of subordination or to be inquisitive about things he did not choose to confide to me; but, this being assumed, I found myself in a circle where he seemed to unbosom himself with freedom. I saw no interruption in this while I remained in the Potomac Army. He was, at this time, a little depressed in manner, feeling keenly his loss of power and command, but maintaining a quiet dignity that became him better than any show of carelessness would have done. He used no bitter or harsh language in criticising others. Pope and McDowell he plainly disliked, and rated them low as to capacity for command; but he spoke of them without discourtesy or vilification. I think it necessary to say this because of the curious sidelight thrown on his character by the private letters to his wife which have since been published in his "Own Story," and of which I shall have more to say. Their inconsistency with his expressions and manner in conversation, or at least their great exaggeration of what he conveyed in familiar talk, has struck me very forcibly and unpleasantly.

He discussed his campaign of the peninsula with apparent unreserve. He condemned the decision to recall him from Harrison's Landing, arguing that the one thing to do in that emergency was to reinforce his army there and make it strong enough to go on with its work and capture Richmond. He said that if the government had lost confidence in his ability to conduct the campaign to a successful end, still it was unwise to think of anything else except to strengthen that army and give it to some one they could trust. He added explicitly, "If Pope was the man they had faith in then Pope should have been sent to Harrison's Landing to take command, and however bitter it would have been, I should have had no just reason to complain." He predicted that they would yet be put to the cost of much life and treasure to get back to the position left by him.

On Monday, September 1st, he visited me again, and we renewed our riding and our conversation. The road from his headquarters encampment near Alexandria to Upton's Hill was a pleasant one for his "constitutional" ride, and my position was nearest the army in front where news from it would most likely be first found. The Army of the Potomac had all passed to the front from Alexandria, and according to the letter of the orders issued, he was wholly without command; though Halleck personally directed him to exercise supervision over all detachments about the works and lines. He came almost alone on these visits, an aide and an orderly or two being his only escort. Colonel Colburn of his staff was usually his companion. He wore a blue flannel hunting-shirt quite different from the common army blouse. It was made with a broad yoke at the neck, and belt at the waist, the body in plaits. He was without sash or side arms, or any insignia of rank except inconspicuous shoulder-straps. On this day he was going into Washington, and I rode down with him to the bridge. Bodies of troops of the new levies were encamped at different points near the river. In these there seemed to be always some veterans or officers who knew the general, and the men quickly gathered in groups and cheered him. He had a taking way of returning such salutations. He went beyond the formal military salute, and gave his cap a little twirl, which with his bow and smile seemed to carry a little of personal good fellowship even to the humblest private soldier. If the cheer was repeated, he would turn in his saddle and repeat the salute. It was very plain that these little attentions to the troops took well, and had no doubt some influence in establishing a sort of comradeship between him and them. They were part of an attractive and winning deportment which adapted itself to all sorts and ranks of men.

On Tuesday he came a little later in the day, and I noticed at once a change in his appearance. He wore his yellow sash with sword and belt buckled over it, and his face was animated as he greeted me with "Well, General, I am in command again!" I congratulated him with hearty earnestness, for I was personally rejoiced at it. I was really attached to him, believed him to be, on the whole, the most accomplished officer I knew, and was warmly disposed to give him loyal friendship and service. He told me of his cordial interview with President Lincoln, and that the latter had said he believed him to be the only man who could bring organized shape out of the chaos in which everything seemed then to be. The form of his new assignment to duty was that he was to "have command of the fortifications of Washington, and of all the troops for the defence of the capital." The order was made by the personal direction of the President, and McClellan knew that Secretary Stanton did not approve of it. General Halleck seemed glad to be rid of a great responsibility, and accepted the President's action with entire cordiality. Still, he was no doubt accurate in writing to Pope later that the action was that of the President alone without any advice from him. McClellan was evidently and entirely happy in his personal relation to things. He had not been relieved from the command of the Army of the Potomac, though the troops had passed temporarily to Pope's army. As commandant of all within the defences, his own army reported to him directly when they came within our lines. Pope's army of northern Virginia would, of course, report through its commander, and Burnside's in a similar way. The first thing to be done was to get the army in good condition, to strengthen its corps by the new regiments which were swarming toward the capital, and to prepare it for a new campaign. McClellan seemed quite willing to postpone the question who would command when it took the field. Of the present he was sure. It was in his own hands, and the work of reorganization was that in which his prestige was almost sure to increase. This attitude was plainly shown in all he said and in all he hinted at without fully saying it.

Halleck had already directed Pope to bring the army within the fortifications, though the latter had vainly tried to induce him to ride out toward Centreville, to see the troops and have a consultation there before determining what to do. We were therefore expecting the head of column to approach my lines, and I arranged that we should be notified when they came near. McClellan had already determined to put the corps and divisions of the Army of the Potomac in the works, at positions substantially the same as they had occupied a year before—Porter near Chain Bridge, Sumner next, Franklin near Alexandria, etc. I was directed to continue in the position I already occupied, to be supported by part of McDowell's corps.

About four o'clock McClellan rode forward, and I accompanied him. We halted at the brow of the hill looking down the Fairfax road. The head of the column was in sight, and rising dust showed its position far beyond. Pope and McDowell, with the staff, rode at the head. Their uniform and that of all the party was covered with dust, their beards were powdered with it; they looked worn and serious, but alert and self-possessed. When we met, after brief salutations, McClellan announced that he had been ordered to assume command within the fortifications, and named to General Pope the positions the several corps would occupy. This done, both parties bowed, and the cavalcade moved on. King's division of McDowell's corps was the leading one, General Hatch, the senior brigadier, being in command by reason of King's illness. Hatch was present, near Pope, when McClellan assumed command, and instantly turning rode a few paces to the head of his column and shouted, "Boys, McClellan is in command again; three cheers!" The cheers were given with wild delight, and were taken up and passed toward the rear of the column. Warm friend of McClellan as I was, I felt my flesh cringe at the unnecessary affront to the unfortunate commander of that army. But no word was spoken. Pope lifted his hat in a parting salute to McClellan and rode quietly on with his escort.

McClellan remained for a time, warmly greeted by the passing troops. He then left me, and rode off toward Vienna, northward. According to my recollection, Colonel Colburn was the only member of his staff with him; they had a small cavalry escort. My understanding also was that they proposed to return by Chain Bridge, avoiding the crowding of the road on which they had come out, and on which McDowell's corps was now moving. In his "Own Story" McClellan speaks of going in that direction to see the situation of Sumner's troops, supposed to be attacked, and intimates a neglect on Pope's part of a duty in that direction. I am confident he is mistaken as to this, and that I have given the whole interview between him and Pope. The telegraphic connection with my headquarters was such that he could learn the situation in front of any part of the line much more promptly there than by riding in person. Lee did not pursue, in fact, beyond Fairfax C. H. and Centreville, and nothing more than small bodies of cavalry were in our vicinity. I had kept scouting-parties of our own cavalry active in our front, and had also collected news from other sources. On the 1st of September I had been able to send to army headquarters authentic information of the expectation of the Confederate army to move into Maryland, and every day thereafter added to the evidence of that purpose, until they actually crossed the Potomac on the 5th.

Hatch's division was put into the lines on my left with orders to report to me in case of attack. Patrick's brigade of that division was next day placed near Falls Church in support of my cavalry, reporting directly to me. My two regiments which had been with Pope rejoined the division, and made it complete again. The night of the 2d was one in which I was on the alert all night, as it was probable the enemy would disturb us then if ever; but it passed quietly. A skirmish in our front on the Vienna road on the 4th was the only enlivening event till we began the campaign of South Mountain and Antietam on the 6th.

Pope's proposed reorganization of his army, which would have put me with most of Sigel's corps under Hooker, was prevented by a larger change which relieved him of command and consolidated his army with that of the Potomac on September 5th. I had a very slight acquaintance with Pope at the beginning of the war, but no opportunity of increasing it till he assumed command in Virginia and I reported to him as a subordinate. The events just sketched had once more interfered with my expected association with him, and I did not meet him again till long afterward. Then I came to know him well. His wife and the wife of my intimate friend General Force were sisters, and in Force's house we often met. He was then broken in health and softened by personal afflictions. His reputation in 1861 was that of an able and energetic man, vehement and positive in character, apt to be choleric and even violent toward those who displeased him. I remember well that I shrunk a little from coming under his immediate orders through fear of some chafing, though I learned in the army that choleric commanders, if they have ability, are often warmly appreciative of those who serve them with soldierly spirit and faithfulness. No one who had any right to judge questioned Pope's ability or his zeal in the National cause. His military career in the West had been a brilliant one. The necessity for uniting the columns in northern Virginia into one army was palpable; but it was a delicate question to decide who should command them. It seems to have been assumed by Mr. Lincoln that the commander must be a new man—neither Frémont, McDowell, nor Banks. The reasons were probably much the same as those which later brought Grant and Sheridan from the West.

Pope's introduction to the Eastern army, which I have already mentioned, was an unfortunate one; but neither he nor any one else could have imagined the heat of partisan spirit or the lengths it would run. No personal vilification was too absurd to be credited, and no characterization was too ridiculous to be received as true to the life. It was assumed that he had pledged himself to take Richmond with an army of 40,000 men when McClellan had failed to do so with 100,000. His defeat by Lee was taken to prove him contemptible as a commander, by the very men who lauded McClellan for having escaped destruction from the same army. There was neither intelligence nor consistency in the vituperation with which he was covered; but there was abundant proof that the wounded *amour propre* of the officers and men of the Potomac Army made them practically a unit in intense dislike and distrust of him. It may be that this condition of things destroyed his possibility of usefulness at the East; but it would be asking too much of human nature (certainly too much of Pope's impetuous nature) to ask him to take meekly the office of scapegoat for the disastrous result of the whole campaign. His demand on Halleck that he should publish the approval he had personally given to the several steps of the movements and combats from Cedar Mountain to Chantilly was just, but it was imprudent. Halleck was irritated, and made more ready to sacrifice his subordinate. Mr. Lincoln was saddened and embarrassed; but being persuaded that Pope's usefulness was spoiled, he swallowed his own pride and sense of justice, and turned again to McClellan as the resource in the emergency of the moment.

Pope seems to me entirely right in claiming that Jackson's raid to Manassas was a thing which should have resulted in the destruction of that column. He seems to have kept his head, and to have prepared his combinations skilfully for making Jackson pay the penalty of his audacity. There were a few hours of apparent hesitation on August 28th, but champions of McClellan should be the last to urge that against him. His plans were deranged on that day by the accident of McDowell's absence from his own command. This happened through an excess of zeal on McDowell's part to find his commander and give him the benefit of his knowledge of the topography of the country; yet it proved a serious misfortune, and shows how perilous it is for any officer to be away from his troops, no matter for what reason. Many still think Porter's inaction on the 29th prevented the advantage over Jackson from becoming a victory. But after all, when the army was united within our lines, the injuries it had inflicted on the enemy so nearly balanced those it had received that if Grant or Sherman had been in Halleck's place, Lee would never have crossed the Potomac into Maryland. McClellan, Pope, and Burnside would have commanded the centre and wings of the united and reinforced army, and under a competent head it would have marched back to the Rappahannock with scarcely a halt.

That Halleck was in command was, in no small measure, Pope's own work. He reminded Halleck of this in his letter of September 30th, written when he was chafing under the first effects of his removal. "If you desire," said he, "to know the personal obligation to which I refer, I commend you to the President, the Secretary of War, or any other member of the administration. Any of these can satisfy your inquiries." This means that he had, before the President and the cabinet, advocated putting Halleck in supreme command over himself and McClellan to give unity to a campaign that would else be hopelessly broken down. McClellan was then at Harrison's Landing, believing Lee's army to be 200,000 strong, and refusing to listen to any suggestion except that enormous reinforcements should be sent to him there. He had taught the Army of the Potomac to believe implicitly that the Confederate army was more than twice as numerous as it was in fact. With this conviction it was natural that they should admire the generalship which had saved them from annihilation. They accepted with equal faith the lessons which came to them from headquarters teaching that the "radicals" at Washington were trying for political ends to destroy their general and them. In regard to the facts there were varying degrees of intelligence among officers and men; but there was a common opinion that they and he were willingly sacrificed, and that Pope, the radical, was to succeed him. This made them hate Pope, for the time, with holy hatred. If the army could at that time have compared authentic tables of strength of Lee's army and their own, the whole theory would have collapsed at once, and McClellan's reputation and popularity with it. They did not have the authentic tables, and fought for a year under the awful cloud created by a blundering spy-system.

The fiction as to Lee's forces is the most remarkable in the history of modern wars. Whether McClellan was the victim or the accomplice of the inventions of his "secret service," we cannot tell. It is almost incredible that he should be deceived, except willingly. I confess to a contempt for all organizations of spies and detectives, which is the result of my military experience. The only spies who long escape are those who work for both sides. They sell to each what it wants, and suit their wares to the demand. Pinkerton's man in the rebel commissariat at Yorktown who reported 119,000 rations issued daily, laughed well in his sleeve as he pocketed the secret service money.

A great deal of valuable information may be got from a hostile population, for few men or women know how to hold their tongues, though they try never so honestly. A friendly population overdoes its information, as a rule. I had an excellent example of this in the Kanawha valley. After I had first advanced to Gauley Bridge, the Secessionists behind me were busy sending to the enemy all they could learn of my force. We intercepted, among others, a letter from an intelligent woman who had tried hard to keep her attention upon the organization of my command as it passed her house. In counting my cannon, she had evidently taken the teams as the easiest units to count, and had set down every caisson as a gun, with the battery-forge thrown in for an extra one. In a similar way, every accidental break in the marching column was counted as the head of a new regiment. She thus, in perfect good faith, doubled my force, and taught me that such information to the enemy did them more harm than good.

As to the enemy's organization and numbers, the only information I ever found trustworthy is that got by contact with him. No day should pass without having some prisoners got by "feeling the lines." These, to secure treatment as regular prisoners of war, must always tell the company and regiment to which they belong. Rightly questioned, they rarely stop there, and it is not difficult to get the brigade, division, etc. The reaction from the dangers with which the imagination had invested capture, to the commonly good-humoured hospitality of the captors, makes men garrulous of whom one would not expect it. General Pope's chief quartermaster, of the rank of colonel, was captured by Stuart's cavalry in this very campaign; and since the war I have read with amazement General Lee's letters to President Davis, to the Secretary of War at Richmond, and to General Loring in West Virginia, dated August 23d, in which he says: "General Stuart reports that General Pope's chief quartermaster, who was captured last night, positively asserts that Cox's troops are being withdrawn by the way of Wheeling." Of course Lee suggests the importance of "pushing things" in the Kanawha valley. Stuart thus knew my movement on the day I left Parkersburg.

Even when the captured person tells nothing he is bound to conceal, enough is necessarily known to enable a diligent provost-marshal to construct a reasonably complete roster of the enemy in a short time. In the Atlanta campaign I always carried a memorandum book in which I noted and corrected all the information of this sort which came to me, and by comparing this with others and with the lists at General Sherman's headquarters, there was no difficulty in keeping well up in the enemy's organization. It may therefore be said that every commanding officer ought to know the divisions and brigades of his enemy. The strength of a brigade is fairly estimated from the average of our own, for in people of similar race and education, the models of organization are essentially the same, and subject to the same causes of diminution during a campaign. Such considerations as these leave no escape from the conclusion that McClellan's estimates of Lee's army were absolutely destructive of all chances of success, and made it impossible for the President or for General Halleck to deal with the military problem before them. That he had continued this erroneous counting for more than a year, and through an active campaign in the field, destroyed every hope of correcting it. The reports of the peninsular campaign reveal, at times, the difficulty there was in keeping up the illusion. The known divisions in the Confederate army would not account for the numbers attributed to them, and so these divisions occasionally figure in our reports as "grand divisions." That the false estimate was unnecessary is proven by the fact that General Meigs, in Washington, on July 28th, made up an estimate from the regiments, brigades, etc., mentioned in the newspapers that got through the lines, which was reasonably accurate. But McClellan held Meigs for an enemy. When I joined McClellan at Washington, I had no personal knowledge of either army except as I had learned it from the newspapers. My predilections in favour of McClellan made me assume that his facts were well based, as they ought to have been. I therefore accepted the general judgment of himself and his intimate friends as to his late campaign and Pope's, and believed that his restoration to command was an act of justice to him and of advantage to the country. I did not stay long enough with that army to apply any test of my own to the question of relative numbers, and have had to correct my opinions of the men and the campaigns by knowledge gained long afterward. I however used whatever influence I had to combat the ideas in McClellan's mind that the administration meant to do him any wrong, or had any end but the restoration of National unity in view.

Whether Halleck was appointed on Pope's urgent recommendation or no, his campaign in the West was the ground of his promotion. The advance from the Ohio to Fort Donelson, to Nashville, to Shiloh, and to Corinth had been under his command, and he deservedly had credit for movements which had brought Kentucky and Tennessee within the Union lines. He had gone in person to the front after the battle of Shiloh, and though much just criticism had been made of his slow digging the way to Corinth by a species of siege operations, he had at any rate got there. Mr. Lincoln was willing to compromise upon a slow advance upon Richmond, provided it were sure and steady. Halleck's age and standing in the army were such that McClellan himself could find no fault with his appointment, if any one were to be put over him.

Everything points to the expectation, at the time of his appointment, that Halleck would assume the personal command in the field. He visited McClellan at Harrison's Landing on July 25th, however, and promised him that if the armies should be promptly reunited, he (McClellan) should command the whole, with Burnside and Pope as his subordinates. That he did not inform Pope of this abdication of his generalship in the field is plain from Pope's correspondence during the campaign. It is made indisputably clear by Pope's letter to him of the 25th of August. He probably did not tell the President or Mr. Stanton of it. He seems to have waited for the union of the parts of the army, and when that came his prestige was forever gone, and he had become, what he remained to the close of the war, a bureau officer in Washington. He had ordered the transfer of the Potomac Army from the James to Acquia Creek, intending to unite it with Burnside's at Falmouth, opposite Fredericksburg, and thus begin a fresh advance from the line of the Rappahannock. He believed, and apparently with reason, that ten days was sufficient to complete this transfer with the means at McClellan's disposal, but at the end of ten days the movement had not yet begun. He was right in thinking that the whole army should be united. McClellan thought the same. The question was where and how. McClellan said, "Send Pope's men to me." Halleck replied that it would not do to thus uncover Washington. McClellan had said that vigorous advance upon the enemy by his army and a victory would best protect the capital. Again he was right, but he seemed incapable of a vigorous advance. Had he made it when he knew (on July 30) that Jackson had gone northward with thirty thousand men to resist Pope's advance, his army would not have been withdrawn. He was then nearly twice as strong as Lee, but he did not venture even upon a forced reconnaissance. The situation of the previous year was repeated. He was allowing himself to be besieged by a fraction of his own force. Grant would have put himself into the relation to McClellan which he sustained to Meade in 1864, and would have infused his own energy into the army. Halleck did not do this. It would seem that he had become conscious of his own lack of nerve in the actual presence of an enemy, and looked back upon his work at St. Louis in administering his department, whilst Grant and Buell took the field, with more satisfaction than upon his own advance from Shiloh to Corinth. He seemed already determined to manage the armies from his office in Washington and assume no responsibility for their actual leadership.

When the Army of the Potomac was arriving at Alexandria, another crisis occurred in which a single responsible head in the field was a necessity. McClellan had been giving a continuous demonstration, since August 4th, how easy it is to thwart and hinder any movement whilst professing to be accomplishing everything that is possible. No maxim in war is better founded in experience than that a man who believes that a plan is sure to fail should never be set to conduct it. McClellan had written that Pope would be beaten before the Army of the Potomac could be transferred to him, and Pope was beaten. The only chance for any other result was for Halleck himself to conduct the transfer. If Halleck meant that Franklin should have pushed out to Manassas on the 27th of August, he should have taken the field and gone with the corps. He did not know and could not know how good or bad McClellan's excuses were, and nothing but his own presence, with supreme power, could certainly remove the causes for delay. He wrote to Pope that he could not leave Washington, when he ought not to have been in Washington. He worked and worried himself ill trying to make McClellan do what he should have done himself, and then, overwhelmed with details he should never have burdened himself with, besought his subordinate to relieve him of the strain by practically taking command.

As soon as McClellan began the movement down the James, Lee took Longstreet's corps to Jackson, leaving only D. H. Hill's at Richmond. From that moment McClellan could have marched anywhere. He could have marched to Fredericksburg and joined Pope, and Halleck could have met them with Burnside's troops. But the vast imaginary army of the Confederacy paralyzed everything, and the ponderous task of moving the Army of the Potomac and its enormous material by water to Washington went on. The lifeless and deliberate way in which it went on made it the 1st of September when Sumner and Franklin reached Centreville, and the second battle of Bull Run had ended in defeat on the evening before.

But the army was at last reunited, within the fortifications of Washington, it is true, and not on the James or on the line of the Rappahannock. There was another opportunity given to Halleck to put himself at its head, with McClellan, Pope, and Burnside for his three lieutenants. Again he was unequal to his responsibility. Mr. Lincoln saw his feebleness, and does not seem to have urged him. Halleck was definitely judged in the President's mind, though the latter seems to have clung to the idea that he might be useful by allowing him to assume the role he chose, and confine himself to mere suggestions and to purely routine work. Pope's unpopularity with the army was adopted by popular clamour, which always finds a defeated general in the wrong. The President, in real perplexity, compromised by assigning McClellan to command for the purpose of organizing, a work in which he was admitted by all to be able. The command in the field was a second time offered to Burnside, who declined it, warmly advocating McClellan's claims and proving his most efficient friend. Within three days from the time I had ridden with McClellan to meet the retreating army, the enemy had crossed the Potomac, and decision could not be postponed. The President met McClellan, and told him in person that he was assigned to command in the field.

On the 5th of September Halleck had sent to McClellan a confidential note, telling of the President's action relieving Pope, and anticipating the issue of formal orders: "The President has directed that General Pope be relieved and report to the War Department; that Hooker be assigned to command of Porter's corps, and that Franklin's corps be temporarily attached to Heintzelman's. The orders will be issued this afternoon. Generals Porter and Franklin are to be relieved from duty till the charges against them are examined. I give you this memorandum in advance of orders, so that you may act accordingly in putting forces in the field." Later in the same day Halleck sent to McClellan the opinion that the enemy was without doubt crossing the Potomac, and said, "If you agree with me, let our troops move immediately." The formal order to Pope was: "The armies of the Potomac and Virginia being consolidated, you will report for orders to the Secretary of War." Pope had caused charges to be preferred against Porter and Franklin, and had accused McClellan of wilfully delaying reinforcements and so causing his defeat. His indignation that the interpretation of affairs given by McClellan and his friends should be made into public opinion by the apparent acquiescence of Halleck and the administration overcame his prudence. Had he controlled his feelings and schooled himself into patience, he would hardly have been relieved from active service, and his turn would probably have come again. As it stood, the President saw that McClellan and Pope could not work together, and the natural outcome was that he retired Pope, so that McClellan should not have it to say that he was thwarted by a hostile subordinate. McClellan himself was so manifestly responsible for Franklin's movements from the 27th to the 30th of August, that it was a matter of course that when the chief was assigned to command the condonation should cover the subordinate, and at McClellan's request Franklin was allowed to take the field at once. A few days later he urged the same action in Porter's case, and it was done. Porter joined the army at South Mountain on the 14th of September. The same principle demanded that McDowell, who was obnoxious to McClellan, should be relieved, and this was also done. As an ostensible reason for the public, McDowell's request for a Court of Inquiry upon his own conduct was assumed to imply a desire to be relieved from the command of his corps. But the court was not assembled till the next winter. McDowell had been maligned almost as unscrupulously as Pope. A total abstainer from intoxicating drinks, he was persistently described as a drunkard, drunken upon the field of battle. One of the most loyal and self-forgetting of subordinates, he was treated as if a persistent intriguer for command. A brave and competent soldier, he was believed to be worthless and untrustworthy. As between Halleck, McClellan, and Pope, the only one who had fought like a soldier and manoeuvred like a general was sent to the north-western frontier to watch the petty Indian tribes, carrying the burden of others' sins into the wilderness. Mr. Lincoln's sacrifice of his sense of justice to what seemed the only expedient in the terrible crisis, was sublime. McClellan commanded the army, and Porter and Franklin each commanded a corps. If the country was to be saved, confidence and power could not be bestowed by halves.

In his "Own Story" McClellan speaks of the campaign in Maryland as made "with a halter round his neck," meaning that he had no real command except of the defences of Washington, and that he marched after Lee without authority, so that, if unsuccessful, he might have been condemned for usurpation of command. It would be incredible that he adopted such a mere illusion, if he had not himself said it. It proves that some at least of the strange additions to history which he thus published had their birth in his own imagination brooding over the past, and are completely contradicted by the official records. The consolidation of the armies under him was, in fact, a promotion, since it enlarged his authority and committed to him the task that properly belonged to Halleck as general-in-chief. For a few days, beginning September 1st, McClellan's orders and correspondence were dated "Headquarters, Washington," because no formal designation had been given to the assembled forces at the capital. When he took the field at Rockville on the 8th of September, he assumed, as he had the right to do in the absence of other direction from the War Department, that Burnside's and Pope's smaller armies were lost in the larger Army of the Potomac by the consolidation, and resumed the custom of dating his orders and dispatches from "Headquarters, Army of the Potomac," from the command of which he had never been removed, even when its divisions were temporarily separated from him. The defences of Washington were now entrusted to Major-General Banks, strictly in subordination, however, to himself. The official record of authority and command is consistent and perfect, and his notion in his later years, that there was anything informal about it, is proven to be imaginary. Halleck's direction, which I have quoted, to "let our troops move immediately," would be absurd as addressed to the commandant of the Army of the Potomac into which the Army of Virginia was consolidated, unless that commandant was to take the field, or a formal order relieved him of command as Pope was relieved. Certainly no other commander was designated, and I saw enough of him in those days to say with confidence that he betrayed no doubt that the order to "move immediately" included himself. McClellan's popularity with the Army of the Potomac had seemed to Mr. Lincoln the only power sufficient to ensure its prompt and earnest action against the Confederate invasion. His leadership of it, to be successful, had to be accompanied with plenary powers, even if the stultification of the government itself were the consequence. When the patriotism of the President yielded to this, the suggestion of McClellan twenty years afterward, that it had all been a pitfall prepared for him, would be revolting if, in view of the records, the absurdity of it did not prove that its origin was in a morbid imagination. It is far more difficult to deal leniently with the exhibition of character in his private letters, which were injudiciously added to his "Own Story" by his literary executor. In them his vanity and his ill-will toward rivals and superiors are shockingly naked; and since no historian can doubt that at every moment from September, 1861, to September, 1862, his army greatly outnumbered his enemy, whilst in equipment and supply there was no comparison, his persistent outcry that he was sacrificed by his government destroys even that character for dignity and that reputation for military intelligence which we fondly attributed to him.

The general arrangement of the campaign seems to have been settled between Halleck and McClellan on the 5th of September. General Sumner with the Second and Twelfth corps moved up the Potomac by way of Tenallytown, Burnside with the First and Ninth corps moved to Leesboro with a view to covering Baltimore, the front was explored by the cavalry under Pleasonton, and the Sixth Corps, under Franklin, constituted a reserve. The preliminary movements occupied the 5th and 6th, but on the 7th the positions were as I have stated them. The principal bodies were designated, respectively, as right and left wings instead of armies. The two corps from the Army of Virginia were separated, one being assigned to the right wing under Burnside, and the other to the left under Sumner.

Chapter 13

South Mountain

Late in the night of the 5th I received orders from McClellan's headquarters to march from my position on Upton's Hill through Washington toward Leesboro, as soon as my pickets could be relieved by troops of McDowell's corps. My route was designated as by the road which was a continuation northward of Seventh Street, and I was directed to report to General Ambrose E. Burnside, commanding right wing, whose headquarters were in the suburbs of the city on that road. This was in accordance with my wish, expressed to McClellan that I might have active field work. For two or three days we were not attached to a corps, but as the organization of the army became settled we were temporarily assigned to the Ninth, which had been Burnside's, and had been with him in North Carolina. During this campaign it was commanded by Major-General Jesse L. Reno, who had long had a division in it, and had led the corps in the recent battle. We marched from Upton's Hill at daybreak of the 6th, taking the road to Georgetown by Ball's Cross-Roads. In Georgetown we turned eastward through Washington to Seventh Street, and thence northward to the Leesboro road. As we passed General Burnside's quarters, I sent a staff officer to report our progress. It was about ten o'clock, and Burnside had gone to the White House to meet the President and cabinet by invitation. His chief of staff, General J. G. Parke, sent a polite note, saying we had not been expected so soon, and directed us to halt and bivouac for the present in some fields by the roadside, near where the Howard University now is. In the afternoon I met Burnside for the first time, and was warmly attracted by him, as everybody was. He was pre-eminently a manly man, as I expressed it in writing home. His large, fine eyes, his winning smile and cordial manners, bespoke a frank, sincere, and honourable character, and these indications were never belied by more intimate acquaintance. The friendship then begun lasted as long as he lived. I learned to understand the limitations of his powers and the points in which he fell short of being a great commander; but as I knew him better I estimated more and more highly his sincerity and truthfulness, his unselfish generosity, and his devoted patriotism. In everything which makes up an honourable and lovable personal character he had no superior. I shall have occasion to speak frequently of his peculiarities and his special traits, but shall never have need to say a word in derogation of the solid virtues I have attributed to him. His chief-of-staff, General Parke, was an officer of the Engineers, and one of the best instructed of that corps. He had served with distinction under Burnside in North Carolina, in command of a brigade and division. I always thought that he preferred staff duty, especially with Burnside, whose confidence in him was complete, and who would leave to him almost untrammelled control of the administrative work of the command.

On September 7th I was ordered to take the advance of the Ninth Corps in the march to Leesboro, following Hooker's corps. It was my first march with troops of this army, and I was shocked at the straggling I witnessed. The "roadside brigade," as we called it, was often as numerous, by careful estimate, as our own column moving in the middle of the road. I could say of the men of the Kanawha division, as Richard Taylor said of his Louisiana brigade with Stonewall Jackson, that they had not yet *learned* to straggle. I tried to prevent their learning it. We had a roll-call immediately upon halting after the march, and another half an hour later, with prompt reports of the result. I also assigned a field officer and medical officer to duty at the rear of the column, with ambulances for those who became ill and with punishments for the rest. The result was that, in spite of the example of others, the division had no stragglers, the first roll-call rarely showing more than twenty or thirty not answering to their names, and the second often proving every man to be present. In both the Army of the Potomac and the Army of Northern Virginia the evil had become a most serious one. After the battle of Antietam, for the express purpose of remedying it, McClellan appointed General Patrick Provost-Marshal with a strong provost-guard, giving him very extended powers, and permitting nobody, of whatever rank, to interfere with him. Patrick was a man of vigour, of conscience, and of system, and though he was greatly desirous of keeping a field command, proved so useful, indeed so necessary a part of the organization, that he was retained in it against his wishes, to the end of the war, each commander of the Army of the Potomac in turn finding that he was indispensable.

The Confederate army suffered from straggling quite as much, perhaps, as ours, but in a somewhat different way. At the close of the Antietam campaign General Lee made bitter complaints in regard to it, and asked the Confederate government for legislation which would authorize him to apply the severest punishments. As the Confederate stragglers were generally in the midst of friends, where they could sleep under shelter and get food of better quality than the army ration, this grew to be the regular mode of life with many even of those who would join their comrades in an engagement. They were not reported in the return of "effectives" made by their officers, but that they often made part of the killed, wounded, and captured I have little doubt. In this way a rational explanation may be found of the larger discrepancies between the Confederate reports of casualties and ours of their dead buried and prisoners taken.

The weather during this brief campaign was as lovely as possible, and the contrast between the rich farming country in which we now were, and the forest-covered mountains of West Virginia to which we had been accustomed, was very striking. An evening march, under a brilliant moon, over a park-like landscape with alternations of groves and meadows which could not have been more beautifully composed by a master artist, remains in my memory as a page out of a lovely romance. On the day that we marched to Leesboro, Lee's army was concentrated near Frederick, behind the Monocacy River, having begun the crossing of the Potomac on the 4th. There was a singular dearth of trustworthy information on the subject at our army headquarters. We moved forward by very short marches of six or eight miles, feeling our way so cautiously that Lee's reports speak of it as an unexpectedly slow approach. The Comte de Paris excuses it on the ground of the disorganized condition of McClellan's army after the recent battle. It must be remembered, however, that Sumner's corps and Franklin's had not been at the second Bull Run, and were veterans of the Potomac Army. The Twelfth Corps had been Banks's, and it too had not been engaged at the second Bull Run, its work having been to cover the trains of Pope's army on the retrograde movement from Warrenton Junction. Although new regiments had been added to these corps, it is hardly proper to say that the army as a whole was not one which could be rapidly manoeuvred. I see no good reason why it might not have advanced at once to the left bank of the Monocacy, covering thus both Washington and Baltimore, and hastening by some days Lee's movement across the Blue Ridge. We should at least have known where the enemy was by being in contact with him, instead of being the sport of all sorts of vague rumours and wild reports.

The Kanawha division took the advance of the right wing when we left Leesboro on the 8th, and marched to Brookville. On the 9th it reached Goshen, where it lay on the 10th, and on the 11th reached Ridgeville on the railroad. The rest of the Ninth Corps was an easy march behind us. Hooker had been ordered further to the right on the strength of rumours that Lee was making a circuit towards Baltimore, and his corps reached Cooksville and the railroad some ten miles east of my position. The extreme left of the army was at Poolesville, near the Potomac, making a spread of thirty miles across the whole front. The cavalry did not succeed in getting far in advance of the infantry, and very little valuable information was obtained. At Ridgeville, however, we got reliable evidence that Lee had evacuated Frederick the day before, and that only cavalry was east of the Catoctin Mountains. Hooker got similar information at about the same time. It was now determined to move more rapidly, and early in the morning of the 12th I was ordered to march to New Market and thence to Frederick. At New Market I was overtaken by General Reno, with several officers of rank from the other divisions of the corps, and they dismounted at a little tavern by the roadside to see the Kanawha division go by. Up to this time they had seen nothing of us whatever. The men had been so long in the West Virginia mountains at hard service, involving long and rapid marches, that they had much the same strength of legs and ease in marching which was afterward so much talked of when seen in Sherman's army at the review in Washington at the close of the war. I stood a little behind Reno and the rest, and had the pleasure of hearing their involuntary exclamations of admiration at the marching of the men. The easy swinging step, the graceful poise of the musket on the shoulder, as if it were a toy and not a burden, and the compactness of the column were all noticed and praised with a heartiness which was very grateful to my ears. I no longer felt any doubt that the division stood well in the opinion of my associates.

I enjoyed this the more because, the evening before, a little incident had occurred which had threatened to result in some ill-feeling. It had been thought that we were likely to be attacked at Ridgeville, and on reaching the village I disposed the division so as to cover the place and to be ready for an engagement. I ordered the brigades to bivouac in line of battle, covering the front with outposts and with cavalry vedettes from the Sixth New York Cavalry (Colonel Devin), which had been attached to the division during the advance. The men were without tents, and to make beds had helped themselves to some straw from stacks in the vicinity. Toward evening General Reno rode up, and happening first to meet Lieutenant-Colonel Rutherford B. Hayes, commanding the Twenty third Ohio, he rather sharply inquired why the troops were not bivouacking "closed in mass," and also blamed the taking of the straw. Colonel Hayes referred him to me as the proper person to account for the disposition of the troops, and quietly said he thought the quartermaster's department could settle for the straw if the owner was loyal. A few minutes later the general came to my own position, but was now quite over his irritation. I, of course, knew nothing of his interview with Hayes, and when he said that it was the policy in Maryland to make the troops bivouac in compact mass, so as to do as little damage to property as possible, I cordially assented, but urged that such a rule would not apply to the advance-guard when supposed to be in presence of the enemy; we needed to have the men already in line if an alarm should be given in the night. To this he agreed, and a pleasant conversation followed. Nothing was said to me about the straw taken for bedding, and when I heard of the little passage-at-arms with Colonel Hayes, I saw that it was a momentary disturbance which had no real significance. Camp gossip, however, is as bad as village gossip, and in a fine volume of the *History of the Twenty-first Massachusetts Regiment*, I find it stated that the Kanawha division coming fresh from the West was disposed to plunder and pillage, giving an exaggerated version of the foregoing story as evidence of it. This makes it a duty to tell what was the small foundation for the charge, and to say that I believe no regiments in the army were less obnoxious to any just accusation of such a sort. The gossip would never have survived the war at all but for the fact that Colonel Hayes became President of the United States, and the supposed incident of his army life thus acquired a new interest.

From New Market we sent the regiment of cavalry off to the right to cover our flank, and to investigate reports that heavy bodies of the enemy's cavalry were north of us. The infantry pushed rapidly toward Frederick. The opposition was very slight till we reached the Monocacy River, which is perhaps half a mile from the town. Here General Wade Hampton, with his brigade as rear-guard of Lee's army, attempted to resist the crossing. The highway crosses the river by a substantial stone bridge, and the ground upon our bank was considerably higher than that on the other side. We engaged the artillery of the enemy with a battery of our own, which had the advantage of position, whilst the infantry forced the crossing both by the bridge and by a ford a quarter of a mile to the right. As soon as Moor's brigade was over, it was deployed on the right and left of the turnpike, which was bordered on either side by a high and strong post-and-rail fence. Scammon's was soon over, and similarly deployed as a second line, with the Eleventh Ohio in column in the road. Moor had with him a troop of horse and a single cannon, and went forward with the first line, allowing it to keep abreast of him on right and left. I also rode on the turnpike between the two lines, and only a few rods behind Moor, having with me my staff and a few orderlies. Reno was upon the other bank of the river, overlooking the movement, which made a fine military display as the lines advanced at quick-step toward the city. Hampton's horsemen had passed out of our sight, for the straight causeway turned sharply to the left just as it entered the town, and we could not see beyond the turn. We were perhaps a quarter of a mile from the city, when a young staff officer from corps headquarters rode up beside me and exclaimed in a boisterous way:

"Why don't they go in faster? There's nothing there!"

I said to the young man, "Did General Reno send you with any order to me?"

"No," he replied.

"Then," said I, "when I want your advice I will ask it."

He moved off abashed, and I did not notice what had become of him, but, in fact, he rode up to Colonel Moor, and repeated a similar speech. Moor was stung by the impertinence which he assumed to be a criticism upon him from corps headquarters, and, to my amazement, I saw him suddenly dash ahead at a gallop with his escort and the gun. He soon came to the turn of the road where it loses itself among the houses; there was a quick, sharp rattling of carbines, and Hampton's cavalry was atop of the little party. There was one discharge of the cannon, and some of the brigade staff and escort came back in disorder. I ordered up at "double quick" the Eleventh Ohio, which, as I have said, was in column in the road, and these, with bayonets fixed, dashed into the town. The enemy had not waited for them, but retreated out of the place by the Hagerstown road. Moor had been ridden down, unhorsed, and captured. The artillery-men had unlimbered the gun, pointed it, and the gunner stood with the lanyard in his hand, when he was struck by a charging horse; the gun was fired by the concussion, but at the same moment it was capsized into the ditch by the impact of the cavalry column. The enemy had no time to right the gun or carry it off, nor to stop for prisoners. They forced Moor on another horse, and turned tail as the charging lines of infantry came up on right and left as well as the column in the road, for there had not been a moment's pause in the advance. It had all happened, and the gun with a few dead and wounded of both sides were in our hands, in less time than it has taken to describe it. Those who may have a fancy for learning how Munchausen would tell this story, may find it in the narrative of Major Heros von Borke of J. E. B. Stuart's staff. Moor's capture, however, had consequences, as we shall see. The command of his brigade passed to Colonel George Crook of the Thirty-sixth Ohio.

Frederick was a loyal city, and as Hampton's cavalry went out at one end of the street and our infantry came in at the other, and whilst the carbine smoke and the smell of powder still lingered, the closed window-shutters of the houses flew open, the sashes went up, the windows were filled with ladies waving their handkerchiefs and national flags, whilst the men came to the column with fruits and refreshments for the marching soldiers as they went by in the hot sunshine of the September afternoon. Pleasonton's cavalry came in soon after by the Urbana road, and during the evening a large part of the army drew near the place. Next morning (13th) the cavalry went forward to reconnoitre the passes of Catoctin Mountain, Rodman's division of our corps being ordered to support them and to proceed toward Middletown in the Catoctin valley. Through some misunderstanding Rodman took the road to Jefferson, leading to the left, where Franklin's corps was moving, and did not get upon the Hagerstown road. About noon I was ordered to march upon the latter road to Middletown. McClellan himself met me as my column moved out of town, and told me of the misunderstanding in Rodman's orders, adding that if I found him on the march I should take his division also along with me. I did not meet him, but the other two divisions of the corps crossed Catoctin Mountain that night, whilst Rodman returned to Frederick. The Kanawha division made an easy march, and as the cavalry was now ahead of us, met no opposition in crossing Catoctin Mountain or in the valley beyond. On the way we passed a house belonging to a branch of the Washington family, and a few officers of the division accompanied me, at the invitation of the occupant, to look at some relics of the Father of his Country which were preserved there. We stood for some minutes with uncovered heads before a case containing a uniform he had worn, and other articles of personal use hallowed by their association with him, and went on our way with our zeal strengthened by closer contact with souvenirs of the great patriot. Willcox's division followed us, and encamped a mile and a half east of Middletown. Sturgis's halted not far from the western foot of the mountain, with corps headquarters near by. My own camp for the night was pitched in front (west) of the village of Middletown along Catoctin Creek. Pleasonton's cavalry was a little in advance of us, at the forks of the road where the old Sharpsburg road turns off to the left from the turnpike. The rest of the army was camped about Frederick, except Franklin's corps (Sixth), which was near Jefferson, ten miles further south but also east of Catoctin Mountain.

The Catoctin or Middletown valley is beautifully included between Catoctin Mountain and South Mountain, two ranges of the Blue Ridge, running northeast and southwest. It is six or eight miles wide, watered by Catoctin Creek, which winds southward among rich farms and enters the Potomac near Point of Rocks. The National road leaving Frederick passes through Middletown and crosses South Mountain, as it goes north-westward, at a depression called Turner's Gap. The old Sharpsburg road crosses the summit at another gap, known as Fox's, about a mile south of Turner's. Still another, the old Hagerstown road, finds a passage over the ridge at about an equal distance north. The National road, being of easier grades and better engineering, was now the principal route, the others having degenerated to rough country roads. The mountain crests are from ten to thirteen hundred feet above the Catoctin valley, and the "gaps" are from two to three hundred feet lower than the summits near them. These summits are like scattered and irregular hills upon the high rounded surface of the mountain top. They are wooded, but along the south-easterly slopes, quite near the top of the mountain, are small farms, with meadows and cultivated fields.

The military situation had been cleared up by the knowledge of Lee's movements which McClellan got from a copy of Lee's order of the day for the both. This had been found at Frederick on the 13th, and it tallied so well with what was otherwise known that no doubt was left as to its authenticity. It showed that Jackson's corps with Walker's division were besieging Harper's Ferry on the Virginia side of the Potomac, whilst McLaws's division supported by Anderson's was co-operating on Maryland Heights. Longstreet, with the remainder of his corps, was at Boonsboro or near Hagerstown. D. H. Hill's division was the rear-guard, and the cavalry under Stuart covered the whole, a detached squadron being with Longstreet, Jackson, and McLaws each. The order did not name the three separate divisions in Jackson's command proper (exclusive of Walker), nor those remaining with Longstreet except D. H. Hill's; but it is hardly conceivable that these were not known to McClellan after his own and Pope's contact with them during the campaigns of the spring and summer. At any rate, the order showed that Lee's army was in two parts, separated by the Potomac and thirty or forty miles of road. As soon as Jackson should reduce Harper's Ferry they would reunite. Friday the 12th was the day fixed for the concentration of Jackson's force for his attack, and it was Saturday when the order fell into McClellan's hands. Three days had already been lost in the slow advance since Lee had crossed Catoctin Mountain, and Jackson's artillery was now heard pounding at the camp and earthworks of Harper's Ferry. McLaws had already driven our forces from Maryland Heights, and had opened upon the ferry with his guns in commanding position on the north of the Potomac. McClellan telegraphed to the President that he would catch the rebels "in their own trap if my men are equal to the emergency." There was certainly no time to lose. The information was in his hands before noon, for he refers to it in a dispatch to Mr. Lincoln at twelve. If his men had been ordered to be at the top of South Mountain before dark, they could have been there; but less than one full corps passed Catoctin Mountain that day or night, and when the leisurely movement of the 14th began, he himself, instead of being with the advance, was in Frederick till after 2 P.M., at which hour he sent a dispatch to Washington, and then rode to the front ten or twelve miles away. The failure to be "equal to the emergency" was not in his men. Twenty-four hours, as it turned out, was the whole difference between saving and losing Harper's Ferry with its ten or twelve thousand men and its unestimated munitions and stores. It may be that the commanders of the garrison were in fault, and that a more stubborn resistance should have been made. It may be that Halleck ought to have ordered the place to be evacuated earlier, as McClellan suggested. Nevertheless, at noon of the 13th McClellan had it in his power to save the place and interpose his army between the two wings, of the Confederates with decisive effect on the campaign. He saw that it was an "emergency," but did not call upon his men for any extraordinary exertion. Harper's. Ferry surrendered, and Lee united the wings of his army beyond the Antietam before the final and general engagement was forced upon him.

At my camp in front of Middletown, I received no orders looking to a general advance on the 14th; but only to support, by a detachment, Pleasonton's cavalry in a reconnaissance toward Turner's Gap. Pleasonton himself came to my tent in the evening, and asked that one brigade might report to him in the morning for the purpose. Six o'clock was the hour at which he wished them to march. He said further that he and Colonel Crook were old army acquaintances and that he would like Crook to have the detail. I wished to please him, and not thinking that it would make any difference to my brigade commanders, intimated that I would do so. But Colonel Scammon, learning what was intended, protested that under our custom his brigade was entitled to the advance next day, as the brigades had taken it in turn. I explained that it was only as a courtesy to Pleasonton and at his request that the change was proposed. This did not better the matter in Scammon's opinion. He had been himself a regular officer, and the point of professional honour touched him. I recognized the justice of his demand, and said he should have the duty if he insisted upon it. Pleasonton was still in the camp visiting with Colonel Crook, and I explained to him the reasons why I could not yield to his wish, but must assign Scammon's brigade to the duty in conformity with the usual course. There was in fact no reason except the personal one for choosing one brigade more than the other, for they were equally good. Crook took the decision in good part, though it was natural that he should wish for an opportunity of distinguished service, as he had not been the regular commandant of the brigade. Pleasonton was a little chafed, and even intimated that he claimed some right to name the officer and command to be detailed. This, of course, I could not admit, and issued the formal orders at once. The little controversy had put Scammon and his whole brigade upon their mettle, and was a case in which a generous emulation did no harm. What happened in the morning only increased their spirit and prepared them the better to perform what I have always regarded as a very brilliant exploit.

The morning of Sunday the 14th of September was a bright one. I had my breakfast very early and was in the saddle before it was time for Scammon to move. He was prompt, and I rode on with him to see in what way his support was likely to be used. Two of the Ninth Corps batteries (Gibson's and Benjamin's) had accompanied the cavalry, and one of these was a heavy one of twenty-pounder Parrotts. They were placed upon a knoll a little in front of the cavalry camp, about half a mile beyond the forks of the old Sharpsburg road with the turnpike. They were exchanging shots with a battery of the enemy well up in the gap. Just as Scammon and I crossed Catoctin Creek I was surprised to see Colonel Moor standing at the roadside. With astonishment I rode to him and asked how he came there. He said that he had been taken beyond the mountain after his capture, but had been paroled the evening before, and was now finding his way back to us on foot. "But where are *you* going?" said he. I answered that Scammon was going to support Pleasonton in a reconnaissance into the gap. Moor made an involuntary start, saying, "My God! be careful!" then checking himself, added, "But I am paroled!" and turned away. I galloped to Scammon and told him that I should follow him in close support with Crook's brigade, and as I went back along the column I spoke to each regimental commander, warning them to be prepared for anything, big or little—it might be a skirmish, it might be a battle. Hurrying to camp, I ordered Crook to turn out his brigade and march at once. I then wrote a dispatch to General Reno, saying I suspected we should find the enemy in force on the mountain top, and should go forward with both brigades instead of sending one. Starting a courier with this, I rode forward again and found Pleasonton. Scammon had given him an inkling of our suspicions, and in the personal interview they had reached a mutual good understanding. I found that he was convinced that it would be unwise to make an attack in front, and had determined that his horsemen should merely demonstrate upon the main road and support the batteries, whilst Scammon should march by the old Sharpsburg road and try to reach the flank of the force on the summit. I told him that in view of my fear that the force of the enemy might be too great for Scammon, I had determined to bring forward Crook's brigade in support. If it became necessary to fight with the whole division, I should do so, and in that case I should assume the responsibility myself as his senior officer. To this he cordially assented.

One section of McMullin's six-gun battery was all that went forward with Scammon (and even these not till the infantry reached the summit), four guns being left behind, as the road was rough and steep. There were in Simmonds's battery two twenty-pounder Parrott guns, and I ordered these also to remain on the turnpike and to go into action with Benjamin's battery of the same calibre. It was about half-past seven when Crook's head of column filed off from the turnpike upon the old Sharpsburg road, and Scammon had perhaps half an hour's start. We had fully two miles to go before we should reach the place where our attack was actually made, and as it was a pretty sharp ascent the men marched slowly with frequent rests. On our way up we were overtaken by my courier who had returned from General Reno with approval of my action and the assurance that the rest of the Ninth Corps would come forward to my support.

When Scammon had got within half a mile of Fox's Gap (the summit of the old Sharpsburg road), the enemy opened upon him with case-shot from the edge of the timber above the open fields, and he had judiciously turned off upon a country road leading still further to the left, and nearly parallel to the ridge above. His movement had been made under cover of the forest, and he had reached the extreme southern limit of the open fields south of the gap on this face of the mountain. Here I overtook him, his brigade being formed in line under cover of the timber, facing open pasture fields having a stone wall along the upper side, with the forest again beyond this. On his left was the Twenty-third Ohio under Lieutenant-Colonel R. B. Hayes, who had been directed to keep in the woods beyond the open, and to strike if possible the flank of the enemy. His centre was the Twelfth Ohio under Colonel Carr B. White, whose duty was to attack the stone wall in front, charging over the broad open fields. On the right was the Thirtieth Ohio, Colonel Hugh Ewing, who was ordered to advance against a battery on the crest which kept up a rapid and annoying fire. It was now about nine o'clock, and Crook's column had come into close support. Bayonets were fixed, and at the word the line rushed forward with loud hurrahs. Hayes, being in the woods, was not seen till he had passed over the crest and turned upon the enemy's flank and rear. Here was a sharp combat, but our men established themselves upon the summit and drove the enemy before them. White and Ewing charged over the open under a destructive fire of musketry and shrapnel. As Ewing approached the enemy's battery (Bondurant's), it gave him a parting salvo, and limbered rapidly toward the right along a road in the edge of the woods which follows the summit to the turnpike near the Mountain House at Turner's Gap. White's men never flinched, and the North Carolinians of Garland's brigade (for it was they who held the ridge at this point) poured in their fire till the advancing line of bayonets was in their faces when they broke away from the wall. Our men fell fast, but they kept up their pace, and the enemy's centre was broken by a heroic charge. Garland strove hard to rally his men, but his brigade was hopelessly broken in two. He rallied his right wing on the second ridge a little in rear of that part of his line, but Hayes's regiment was here pushing forward from our left. Colonel Ruffin of the Thirteenth North Carolina held on to the ridge road beyond our right, near Fox's Gap. The fighting was now wholly in the woods, and though the enemy's centre was routed there was stubborn resistance on both flanks. His cavalry dismounted (said to be under Colonel Rosser) was found to extend beyond Hayes's line, and supported the Stuart artillery, which poured canister into our advancing troops. I now ordered Crook to send the Eleventh Ohio (under Lieutenant-Colonel Coleman) beyond Hayes's left to extend our line in that direction, and to direct the Thirty-sixth Ohio (Lieutenant-Colonel Clark) to fill a gap between the Twelfth and Thirtieth caused by diverging lines of advance. The only remaining regiment (the Twenty-eighth, Lieutenant-Colonel Becker) was held in reserve on the right. The Thirty-sixth aided by the Twelfth repulsed a stout effort of the enemy to re-establish their centre. The whole line again sprung forward. A high knoll on our left was carried. The dismounted cavalry was forced to retreat with their battery across the ravine in which the Sharpsburg road descends on the west of the mountain, and took a new position on a separate hill in rear of the heights at the Mountain House. There was considerable open ground at this new position, from which their battery had full play at a range of about twelve hundred yards upon the ridge held by us. But the Eleventh and Twenty-third stuck stoutly to the hill which Hayes had first carried, and their line was nearly parallel to the Sharpsburg road, facing north. Garland had rushed to the right of his brigade to rally them when they had broken before the onset of the Twenty-third Ohio upon the flank, and in the desperate contest there he had been killed and the disaster to his command made irreparable. On our side Colonel Hayes had also been disabled by a severe wound as he gallantly led the Ohio regiment.

I now directed the centre and right to push forward toward Fox's Gap. Lieutenant Croome with a section of McMullin's battery had come up, and he put his guns in action in the most gallant manner in the open ground near Wise's house. The Thirtieth and Thirty-sixth changed front to the right and attacked the remnant of Garland's brigade, now commanded by Colonel McRae, and drove it and two regiments from G. B. Anderson's brigade back upon the wooded hill beyond Wise's farm at Fox's Gap. The whole of Anderson's brigade retreated further along the crest toward the Mountain House. Meanwhile the Twelfth Ohio, also changing front, had threaded its way in the same direction through laurel thickets on the reverse slope of the mountain, and attacking suddenly the force at Wise's as the other two regiments charged it in front, completed the rout and brought off two hundred prisoners. Bondurant's battery was again driven hurriedly off to the north. But the hollow at the gap about Wise's was no place to stay. It was open ground and was swept by the batteries of the cavalry on the open hill to the northwest, and by those of Hill's division about the Mountain House and upon the highlands north of the National road; for those hills run forward like a bastion and give a perfect flanking fire along our part of the mountain. The gallant Croome with a number of his gunners had been killed, and his guns were brought back into the shelter of the woods, on the hither side of Wise's fields. The infantry of the right wing was brought to the same position, and our lines were reformed along the curving crests from that point which looks down into the gap and the Sharpsburg road, toward the left. The extreme right with Croome's two guns was held by the Thirtieth, with the Twenty-eighth in second line. Next came the Twelfth, with the Thirty-sixth in second line, the front curving toward the west with the form of the mountain summit. The left of the Twelfth dipped a little into a hollow, beyond which the Twenty-third and Eleventh occupied the next hill facing toward the Sharpsburg road. Our front was hollow, for the two wings were nearly at right angles to each other; but the flanks were strongly placed, the right, which was most exposed, having open ground in front which it could sweep with its fire and having the reserve regiments closely supporting it. Part of Simmonds's battery which had also come up had done good service in the last combats, and was now disposed so as to check the fire of the enemy.

It was time to rest. Three hours of up-hill marching and climbing had been followed by as long a period of bloody battle, and it was almost noon. The troops began to feel the exhaustion of such labour and struggle. We had several hundred prisoners in our hands, and the field was thickly strewn with dead, in grey and in blue, while our field hospital a little down the mountain side was encumbered with hundreds of wounded. We learned from our prisoners that the summit was held by D. H. Hill's division of five brigades with Stuart's cavalry, and that Longstreet's corps was in close support. I was momentarily expecting to hear from the supporting divisions of the Ninth Corps, and thought it the part of wisdom to hold fast to our strong position astride of the mountain top commanding the Sharpsburg road till our force should be increased. The two Kanawha brigades had certainly won a glorious victory, and had made so assured a success of the day's work that it would be folly to imperil it.

General Hill has since argued that only part of his division could oppose us; but his brigades were all on the mountain summit within easy support of each other, and they had the day before them. It was five hours from the time of our first charge to the arrival of our first supports, and it was not till three o'clock in the afternoon that Hooker's corps reached the eastern base of the mountain and began its deployment north of the National road. Our effort was to attack the weak end of his line, and we succeeded in putting a stronger force there than that which opposed us. It is for our opponent to explain how we were permitted to do it. The two brigades of the Kanawha division numbered less than 3000 men. Hill's division was 5000 strong, even by the Confederate method of counting their effectives, which should be increased nearly one-fifth to compare properly with our reports. In addition to these Stuart had the principal part of the Confederate cavalry on this line, and they were not idle spectators. Parts of Lee's and Hampton's brigades were certainly there, and probably the whole of Lee's. With less than half the numerical strength which was opposed to it, therefore, the Kanawha division had carried the summit, advancing to the charge for the most part over open ground in the storm of musketry and artillery fire, and held the crests they had gained through the livelong day, in spite of all efforts to retake them.

In our mountain camps of West Virginia I had felt discontented that our native Ohio regiments did not take as kindly to the labours of drill and camp police as some of German birth, and I had warned them that they would feel the need of accuracy and mechanical precision when the day of battle came. They had done reasonably well, but suffered in comparison with some of the others on dress parade and in the form and neatness of the camp. When, however, on the slopes of South Mountain I saw the lines go forward steadier and more even under fire than they ever had done at drill, their intelligence making them perfectly comprehend the advantage of unity in their effort and in the shock when they met the foe—when their bodies seemed to dilate, their step to have better cadence and a tread as of giants as they went cheering up the hill—I took back all my criticisms and felt a pride and glory in them as soldiers and comrades that words cannot express.

It was about noon that the lull in the battle occurred, and it lasted a couple of hours, while reinforcements were approaching the mountain top from both sides. The enemy's artillery kept up a pretty steady fire, answered occasionally by our few cannon; but the infantry rested on their arms, the front covered by a watchful line of skirmishers, every man at his tree. The Confederate guns had so perfectly the range of the sloping fields about and behind us, that their canister shot made long furrows in the sod with a noise like the cutting of a melon rind, and the shells which skimmed the crest and burst in the tree-tops at the lower side of the fields made a sound like the crashing and falling of some brittle substance, instead of the tough fibre of oak and pine. We had time to notice these things as we paced the lines waiting for the renewal of the battle.

Willcox's division reported to me about two o'clock, and would have been up earlier, but for a mistake in the delivery of a message to him. He had sent from Middletown to ask me where I desired him to come, and finding that the messenger had no clear idea of the roads by which he had travelled, I directed him to say that General Pleasonton would point out the road I had followed, if inquired of. Willcox understood the messenger that I wished him to inquire of Pleasonton where he had better put his division in, and on doing so, the latter suggested that he move against the crests on the north of the National road. He was preparing to do this when Burnside and Reno came up and corrected the movement, recalling him from the north and sending him by the old Sharpsburg road to my position. As his head of column came up, Longstreet's corps was already forming with its right outflanking my left. I sent two regiments o extend my left, and requested Willcox to form the rest of the division on my right facing the summit. He was doing this when he received an order from General Reno to take position overlooking the National road facing northward. I can hardly think the order could have been intended to effect this, as the turnpike is deep between the hills there, and the enemy quite distant on the other side of the gorge. But Willcox, obeying the order as he received it, formed along the Sharpsburg road, his left next to my right, but his line drawn back nearly at right angles to it. He placed Cook's battery in the angle, and this opened a rapid fire on one of the enemy's which was on the bastion-like hill north of the gorge already mentioned. Longstreet's men were now pretty well up, and pushed a battery forward to the edge of the timber beyond Wise's farm, and opened upon Willcox's line, enfilading it badly. There was a momentary break there, but Willcox was able to check the confusion, and to reform his lines facing westward as I had originally directed; Welch's brigade was on my right, closely supporting Cook's battery and Christ's beyond it. The general line of Willcox's division was at the eastern edge of the wood looking into the open ground at Fox's Gap, on the north side of the Sharpsburg road. A warm skirmishing fight was continued along the whole of our line, our purpose being to hold fast my extreme left which was well advanced upon and over the mountain crest, and to swing the right up to the continuation of the same line of hills near the Mountain House.

At nearly four o'clock the head of Sturgis's column approached. McClellan had arrived on the field, and he with Burnside and Reno was at Pleasonton's position at the knoll in the valley, and from that point, a central one in the midst of the curving hills, they issued their orders. They could see the firing of the enemy's battery from the woods beyond the open ground in front of Willcox, and sent orders to him to take or silence those guns at all hazards. He was preparing to advance, when the Confederates anticipated him (for their formation had now been completed) and came charging out of the woods across the open fields. It was part of their general advance and their most determined effort to drive us from the summit we had gained in the morning. The brigades of Hood, Whiting, Drayton, and D. R. Jones in addition to Hill's division (eight brigades in all) joined in the attack on our side of the National road, batteries being put in every available position. The fight raged fiercely along the whole front, but the bloodiest struggle was around Wise's house, where Drayton's brigade assaulted my right and Willcox's left, coming across the open ground. Here the Sharpsburg road curves around the hill held by us so that for a little way it was parallel to our position. As the enemy came down the hill forming the other side of the gap, across the road and up again to our line, they were met by so withering a fire that they were checked quickly, and even drifted more to the right where their descent was continuous. Here Willcox's line volleyed into them a destructive fire, followed by a charge that swept them in confusion back along the road, where the men of the Kanawha division took up the attack and completed their rout. Willcox succeeded in getting a foothold on the further side of the open ground and driving off the artillery which was there. Along our centre and left where the forest was thick, the enemy was equally repulsed, but the cover of the timber enabled them to keep a footing near by, whilst they continually tried to extend so as to outflank us, moving their troops along a road which goes diagonally down that side of the mountain from Turner's Gap to Rohrersville. The batteries on the north of the National road had been annoying to Willcox's men as they advanced, but Sturgis sent forward Durell's battery from his division as soon as he came up, and this gave special attention to these hostile guns, diverting their fire from the infantry. Hooker's men, of the First Corps, were also by this time pushing up the mountain on that side of the turnpike, and we were not again troubled by artillery on our right flank.

It was nearly five o'clock when the enemy had disappeared in the woods beyond Fox's Gap and Willcox could reform his shattered lines. As the easiest mode of getting Sturgis's fresh men into position, Willcox made room on his left for Ferrero's brigade supported by Nagle's, doubling also his lines at the extreme right. Rodman's division, the last of the corps, now began to reach the summit, and as the report came from the extreme left that the enemy was stretching beyond our flank, I sent Fairchild's brigade to assist our men there, whilst Rodman took Harland's to the support of Willcox. A staff officer now brought word that McClellan directed the whole line to advance. At the left this could only mean to clear our front decisively of the enemy there, for the slopes went steadily down to the Rohrersville road. At the centre and right, whilst we held Fox's Gap, the high and rocky summit at the Mountain House was still in the enemy's possession. The order came to me as senior officer upon the line, and the signal was given. On the left Longstreet's men were pushed down the mountain side beyond the Rohrersville and Sharpsburg roads, and the contest there was ended. The two hills between the latter road and the turnpike were still held by the enemy, and the further one could not be reached till the Mountain House should be in our hands. Sturgis and Willcox, supported by Rodman, again pushed forward, but whilst they made progress they were baffled by a stubborn and concentrated resistance.

Reno had followed Rodman's division up the mountain, and came to me a little before sunset, anxious to know why the right could not get forward quite to the summit. I explained that the ground there was very rough and rocky, a fortress in itself and evidently very strongly held. He passed on to Sturgis, and it seemed to me he was hardly gone before he was brought back upon a stretcher, dead. He had gone to the skirmish line to examine for himself the situation, and had been shot down by the enemy posted among the rocks and trees. There was more or less firing on that part of the field till late in the evening, but when morning dawned the Confederates had abandoned the last foothold above Turner's Gap and retreated by way of Boonsboro to Sharpsburg. The casualties in the Ninth Corps had been 889, of which 356 were in the Kanawha division. Some 600 of the enemy were captured by my division and sent to the rear under guard.

On the north of the National road the First Corps under Hooker had been opposed by one of Hill's brigades and four of Longstreet's, and had gradually worked its way along the old Hagerstown road, crowning the heights in that direction after dark in the evening. Gibbon's brigade had also advanced in the National road, crowding up quite close to Turner's Gap and engaging the enemy in a lively combat. It is not my purpose to give a detailed history of events which did not come under my own eye. It is due to General Burnside, however, to note Hooker's conduct toward his immediate superior and his characteristic efforts to grasp all the glory of the battle at the expense of truth and of honourable dealing with his commander and his comrades. Hooker's official report for the battle of South Mountain was dated at Washington, November 17th, when Burnside was in command of the Army of the Potomac, and when the intrigues of the former to obtain the command for himself were notorious and near their final success. In it he studiously avoided any recognition of orders or directions received from Burnside, and ignores his staff, whilst he assumes that his orders came directly from McClellan and compliments the staff officers of the latter, as if they had been the only means of communication. This was not only insolent but a military offence, had Burnside chosen to prosecute it. He also asserts that the troops on our part of the line had been defeated and were at the turnpike at the base of the mountain in retreat when he went forward. At the close of his report, after declaring that "the forcing of the passage of South Mountain will be classed among the most brilliant and satisfactory achievements of this army," he adds, "its principal glory will be awarded to the First Corps."

Nothing is more justly odious in military conduct than embodying slanders against other commands in an official report. It puts into the official records misrepresentations which cannot be met because they are unknown, and it is a mere accident if those who know the truth are able to neutralize their effect. In most cases it will be too late to counteract the mischief when those most interested learn of the slanders. All this is well illustrated in the present case. Hooker's report got on file months after the battle, and it was not till the January following that Burnside gave it his attention. I believe that none of the division commanders of the Ninth Corps learned of it till long afterward. I certainly did not till 1887, a quarter of a century after the battle, when the volume of the official records containing it was published. Burnside had asked to be relieved of the command of the Army of the Potomac after the battle of Fredericksburg unless Hooker among others was punished for insubordination. As in the preceding August, the popular sentiment of that army as an organization was again, in Mr. Lincoln's estimation, too potent a factor to be opposed, and the result was the superseding of Burnside by Hooker himself, though the President declared in the letter accompanying the appointment that the latter's conduct had been blameworthy. It was under these circumstances that Burnside learned of the false statements in Hooker's report of South Mountain, and put upon file his stinging response to it. His explicit statement of the facts will settle that question among all who know the reputation of the men, and though unprincipled ambition was for a time successful, that time was so short and things were "set even" so soon that the ultimate result is one that lovers of justice may find comfort in. The men of the First Corps and its officers did their duty nobly on that as on many another field, and the only spot on the honour of the day is made by the personal unscrupulousness and vainglory of its commander.

Franklin's corps had attacked and carried the ridge about five miles further south, at Crampton's Gap, where the pass had been so stubbornly defended by Mahone's and Cobb's brigades with artillery and a detachment of Hampton's cavalry as to cause considerable loss to our troops. The principal fighting was at a stone wall near the eastern base of the mountain, and when the enemy was routed from this position, he made no successful rally and the summit was gained without much more fighting. The attack at the stone wall not far from Burkettsville was made at about three o'clock in the afternoon. The Sixth Corps rested upon the summit at night.

Chapter 14

Antietam: Preliminary Movements

Before morning on the 15th of September it became evident that Lee had used the night in withdrawing his army. An advance of the pickets at daybreak confirmed this, and Pleasonton's cavalry was pushed forward to Boonsboro, where they had a brisk skirmish with the enemy's rear-guard. At Boonsboro a turnpike to Sharpsburg leaves the National road, and the retreat of the Confederate cavalry, as well as other indications, pointed out the Sharpsburg road as the line of Lee's retreat. He had abandoned his plan of moving further northward, and had chosen a line bringing him into surer communication with Jackson. His movements before the battle of South Mountain revealed a purpose of invasion identical with that which he tried to carry out in 1863 in the Gettysburg campaign. Longstreet, with two divisions and a brigade (D. R. Jones, Hood, and Evans), had advanced to Hagerstown, and it seems that a large part of the Confederate trains reached there also. D. H. Hill's division held Boonsboro and the passes of South Mountain at Turner's and Fox's Gaps. McLaws invested our fortifications on Maryland Heights, supported by R. H. Anderson's division. Jackson, with four divisions (A. P. Hill, Ewell, and Starke of his own corps, with Walker temporarily reporting to him), was besieging Harper's Ferry.

On Saturday, the 13th, Lee determined to draw back Longstreet from his advanced position, in view of the fact that Jackson had not yet reduced Harper's Ferry and that McClellan was marching to its relief. Longstreet's divisions therefore approached Boonsboro so as to support D. H. Hill, and thus it happened that they took part in the battle of South Mountain. Hill again occupied the summit where we found him on the 14th. From all this it is very plain that if McClellan had hastened his advance on the 13th, the passes of South Mountain at Turner's and Fox's gaps would not have been occupied in force by the enemy, and the condition of things would have been what he believed it was on the morning of the 14th, when a single brigade had been thought enough to support Pleasonton's reconnaissance. Twenty-four hours had changed all that.

The turnpike from Boonsboro to Sharpsburg continues southward a couple of miles, crossing the Potomac to Shepherdstown, which lies on the Virginia side of the river. A bridge which formerly carried the road over the stream had been burned; but not far below the ruined piers was a ford, which was a pretty good one in the present stage of water. Shepherdstown was the natural place of junction for Lee and Jackson; but for Lee to have marched there at once would have exposed Jackson to attack from the northern side of the Potomac. The precious stores and supplies captured at Harper's Ferry must be got to a place of safety, and this was likely to delay Jackson a day or two. Lee therefore ordered McLaws to obstruct Franklin's movement as much as he could, whilst he himself concentrated the rest of Longstreet's corps at Sharpsburg, behind the Antietam. If McClellan's force should prove overwhelming, the past experience of the Confederate general encouraged him to believe that our advance would not be so enterprising that he could not make a safe retreat into Virginia. He resolved therefore to halt at Sharpsburg, which offered an excellent field for a defensive battle, leaving himself free to resume his aggressive campaign or to retreat into Virginia according to the result.

McClellan had ordered Richardson's division of the Second Corps to support the cavalry in the advance, and Hooker's corps followed Richardson. It would seem most natural that the whole of Sumner's wing should take the advance on the 15th, though the breaking up of organizations was so much a habit with McClellan that perhaps it should not be surprising that one of Sumner's divisions was thus separated from the rest, and that Burnside's right wing was also divided. The Ninth Corps was ordered to follow the old Sharpsburg road through Fox's Gap, our line of march being thus parallel to the others till we should reach the road from Boonsboro to Sharpsburg.

But we were not put in motion early in the day. We were ordered first to bury the dead, and to send the wounded and prisoners to Middletown It was nearly noon when we got orders to march, and when the head of column filed into the road, the way was blocked by Porter's corps, which was moving to the front by the same road. As soon as the way was clear, we followed, leaving a small detachment to complete the other tasks which had been assigned us. In the wooded slope of the mountain west of the gap, a good many of the Confederate dead still lay where they had fallen in the fierce combats for the possession of the crest near Wise's house. Our road led through a little hamlet called Springvale, and thence to another, Porterstown, near the left bank of the Antietam, where it runs into the Boonsboro and Sharpsburg turnpike. Sumner's two corps had taken temporary position on either side of the turnpike, behind the line of hills which there borders the stream. Porter's corps was massed in rear of Sumner, and Hooker's had been moved off to the right, around Keedysville. I was with the Kanawha division, assuming that my temporary command of the corps ended with the battle on the mountain. As we came up in rear of the troops already assembled, we received orders to turn off the road to the left, and halted our battalions closed in mass. It was now about three o'clock in the afternoon. McClellan, as it seemed, had just reached the field, and was surrounded by a group of his principal officers, most of whom I had never seen before. I rode up with General Burnside, dismounted, and was very cordially greeted by General McClellan. He and Burnside were evidently on terms of most intimate friendship and familiarity. He introduced me to the officers I had not known before, referring pleasantly to my service with him in Ohio and West Virginia, putting me upon an easy footing with them in a very agreeable and genial way.

We walked up the slope of the ridge before us, and looking westward from its crest, the whole field of the coming battle was before us. Immediately in front the Antietam wound through the hollow, the hills rising gently on both sides. In the background, on our left, was the village of Sharpsburg, with fields enclosed by stone fences in front of it. At its right was a bit of wood (since known as the West Wood), with the little Dunker Church standing out white and sharp against it. Farther to the right and left, the scene was closed in by wooded ridges with open farm lands between, the whole making as pleasing and prosperous a landscape as can easily be imagined.

We made a large group as we stood upon the hill, and it was not long before we attracted the enemy's attention. A puff of white smoke from a knoll on the right of the Sharpsburg road was followed by the screaming of a shell over our heads. McClellan directed that all but one or two should retire behind the ridge, while he continued the reconnaissance, walking slowly to the right. I think Fitz-John Porter was the only general officer who was retained as a companion in this walk. I noted with satisfaction the cool and business-like air with which McClellan made his examination under fire. The Confederate artillery was answered by a battery of ours, and a lively cannonade ensued on both sides, though without any noticeable effect. The enemy's position was revealed, and he was evidently in force on both sides of the turnpike in front of Sharpsburg, covered by the undulations of the rolling ground which hid his infantry from our sight.

The examination of the enemy's position and the discussion of it continued till near the close of the day. Orders were then given for the Ninth Corps to move to the left, keeping off the road, which was occupied by other troops. We moved through fields and farm lands, an hour's march in the dusk of evening, going into bivouac about a mile south of the Sharpsburg bridge, and in rear of the hills bordering the Antietam.

The village of Sharpsburg is in the midst of a plateau which is almost enclosed by the Potomac River and the Antietam. The Potomac bounds it on the south and west, and the Antietam on the east. The plateau in general outline may be considered a parallelogram, four miles in length from north to south, and two and a half miles in width inside the bends of the river. The northern side of this terrain appears the narrowest, for here the river curves sharply away to the west, nearly doubling the width of the field above and below the bend. From the village the ground descends in all directions, though a continuous ridge runs northward, on which is the Hagerstown turnpike. The Boonsboro turnpike enters the village from the northeast, crossing the Antietam on a stone bridge, and continuing through Sharpsburg to the southwest, reaches Shepherdstown by the ford of the Potomac already mentioned. The Hagerstown turnpike enters the town from the north, passing the Dunker Church a mile out, and goes nearly due south, crossing the Antietam at its mouth, and continuing down the Potomac toward Harper's Ferry.

The Antietam is a deep creek, with few fords at an ordinary stage of water, and the principal roads cross it upon stone bridges. Of these there were three within the field of battle; the upper one in front of Keedysville, the middle one upon the Boonsboro turnpike, and the lower one on the Sharpsburg and Rohrersville road, since known as Burnside's bridge. McClellan's staff was better supplied with officers of engineers than the staff of most of our separate armies, and Captain Duane, his chief engineer, systematized the work of gathering topographical information. This was communicated to the general officers in connection with the orders which were given them. In this way we were instructed that the only fords of the Antietam passable at that time were one between the two upper bridges named, and another about half a mile below Burnside's bridge, in a deep bend of the stream. We found, however, during the engagement of the 17th, another practicable crossing for infantry a short distance above the bridge. This was not a ford in common use, but in the low stage of water at the time it was made available for a small force.

It was about noon of the 15th of September that Lee placed the forces which he had in hand across the turnpike in front of Sharpsburg. D. H. Hill's division was on the north of the road, and on the south of it Longstreet's own old division (now under General D. R. Jones), Hood's division, and Evans's independent brigade. Stuart's cavalry and the reserve artillery were also present. The rest of the army was with Jackson at Harper's Ferry, or co-operating with him in the neighbourhood of Maryland Heights. Out of forty-four brigades, Lee could put but fourteen or fifteen in line that day to oppose McClellan. He was very strong in artillery, however, and his cannon looked grimly over the hill-crests behind which his infantry were lying. Cutts's and Jones's battalions of the reserve artillery were ordered to report to Hill for the protection of the left of the Confederate line, and gave him in all the sixty or seventy guns which he speaks of in his report, and which have puzzled several writers who have described the battle. Whenever our troops showed themselves as they marched into position, they were saluted from shotted cannon, and the numerous batteries that were developed on the long line of hills before us no doubt did much to impress McClellan with the belief that he had the great bulk of Lee's army before him.

The value of time was one of the things McClellan never understood. He should have been among the first in the saddle at every step in the campaign after he was in possession of Lee's order of the 9th, and should have infused energy into every unit in his army. Instead of making his reconnaissance at three in the afternoon of Monday, it might have been made at ten in the morning, and the battle could have been fought before night, if, indeed, Lee had not promptly retreated when support from Jackson would thus have become impossible. Or if McClellan had pushed boldly for the bridge at the mouth of the Antietam, nothing but a precipitate retreat by Lee could have prevented the interposition of the whole National army between the separated wings of the Confederates. The opportunity was still supremely favourable for McClellan, but prompt decision was not easy for him. Nothing but reconnoitring was done on Monday afternoon or on Tuesday, whilst Lee was straining every nerve to concentrate his forces and to correct what would have proven a fatal blunder in scattering them, had his opponent acted with vigour. The strongest defence the eulogists of the Confederate general have made for him is that he perfectly understood McClellan's caution and calculated with confidence upon it; that he would have been at liberty to perfect his combinations still more at leisure, but for the accident by which the copy of his plan had fallen into our hands at Frederick City.

During the 16th we confidently expected a battle, and I kept with my division. In the afternoon I saw General Burnside, and learned from him that McClellan had determined to let Hooker make a movement on our extreme right to turn Lee's position. Burnside's manner in speaking of this implied that he thought it was done at Hooker's solicitation, and through his desire, openly evinced, to be independent in command. I urged Burnside to assume the immediate command of the corps and allow me to lead my own division. He objected that as he had been announced as commander of the right wing of the army, composed of the two corps, he was unwilling to waive his precedence or to assume that Hooker was detached for anything more than a temporary purpose. I pointed out that Reno's staff had been granted leave of absence to take the body of their chief to Washington, and that my division staff was too small for corps duty; but he met this by saying that he would use his staff for this purpose, and help me in every way he could till the crisis of the campaign should be over. Sympathizing with his very natural feeling, I ceased objecting, and accepted with as good grace as I could the unsatisfactory position of nominal commander of the corps to which I was a comparative stranger, and which, under the circumstances, naturally looked to him as its accustomed and real commander. Burnside's intentions in respect to myself were thoroughly friendly, as he afterward proved, and I had no ground for complaint on this score; but the position of second in command is always an awkward and anomalous one, and such I felt it.

The 16th passed without serious fighting, though we had desultory cannonading and picket firing. It was hard to restrain our men from showing themselves on the crest of the long ridge in front of us, and whenever they did so they drew the fire from some of the enemy's batteries, to which ours would respond. McClellan reconnoitred the line of the Antietam near us, and the country immediately on our left, down the valley. As the result of this we were ordered to change our positions at nightfall, staff officers being sent to guide each division to its new camp. The selected positions were marked by McClellan's engineers, who then took members of Burnside's staff to identify the locations, and these in turn conducted our divisions. There was far more routine of this sort in that army than I ever saw elsewhere. Corps and division commanders should have the responsibility of protecting their own flanks and in choosing ordinary camps. To depend upon the general staff for this is to take away the vigour and spontaneity of the subordinate and make him perform his duty in a mechanical way. He should be told what is known of the enemy and his movements so as to be put upon his guard, and should then have freedom of judgment as to details. The changes made were as follows: Rodman's division went half a mile further to the left, where a country road led to the Antietam ford, half a mile below the Burnside bridge. Sturgis's division was placed on the sides of the road leading to the stone bridge just mentioned. Willcox's was put in reserve in rear of Sturgis. My own was divided, Scammon's brigade going with Rodman, and Crook's going with Sturgis. Crook was ordered to take the advance in crossing the bridge in case we should be ordered to attack. This selection was made by Burnside himself as a compliment to the division for the vigour of its assault at South Mountain. While we were moving we heard Hooker's guns far off on the right and front, and the cannonade continued an hour or more after it became dark.

What, then, was the plan of battle of which the first step was this movement of Hooker's? McClellan's dispositions on the 15th were made whilst Franklin's corps was still absent, and, under the orders he received, was likely to be so for a day at least. Sumner's two corps had been treated as the centre of the army in hand, Burnside's had been divided by putting Hooker on the extreme right and the Ninth Corps on the extreme left, and Porter's corps was in reserve. This looked as if a general attack in front with this organization of the army were intended. But the more McClellan examined the enemy's position the less inclined he was to attack the centre. He could cross the bridge there and on the right, and deploy; but the gentle slopes rising toward Sharpsburg were swept by formidable batteries and offered no cover to advancing troops. The enemy's infantry was behind stone fences and in sunken roads, whilst ours must advance over the open. Lee's right rested upon the wooded bluffs above the Burnside bridge, where it could only be approached by a small head of column charging along the narrow roadway under a concentrated fire of cannon and small arms. No point of attack on the whole field was so unpromising as this. Then, as Jackson was still at Harper's Ferry, there was the contingency of an attack in rear if anything less than the mass of our army were pushed beyond Lee's right.

On our right, in front of Hooker, it was easy to turn the Confederate line. The road from Keedysville through Smoketown to the Hagerstown turnpike crossed the Antietam in a hollow, out of the line of fire, and a march around Lee's left flank could be made almost wholly under cover. The topography of the field therefore suggested a flank attack from our right, if the National commander rejected the better strategy of interposing his army between Lee and Jackson as too daring a movement. This flank attack McClellan determined to make, and some time after noon of the 16th issued his orders accordingly. In his preliminary report of the battle, made before he was relieved from command, McClellan says:

> The design was to make the main attack upon the enemy's left—at least to create a diversion in favour of the main attack, with the hope of something more, by assailing the enemy's right—and as soon as one or both of the flank movements were fully successful, to attack their centre with any reserve I might then have in hand.

His report covering his whole career in the war, dated August 4, 1863 (and published February, 1864, after warm controversies had arisen, and he had become a political character), modifies the above statement in some important particulars. It says:

My plan for the impending general engagement was to attack the enemy's left with the corps of Hooker and Mansfield supported by Sumner's and if necessary by Franklin's, and as soon as matters looked favourably there, to move the corps of Burnside against the enemy's extreme right upon the ridge running to the south and rear of Sharpsburg, and having carried their position to press along the crest toward our right, and whenever either of these flank movements should be successful, to advance our centre with all the forces then disposable.

The opinion I got from Burnside at the time, as to the part the Ninth Corps was to take, was fairly consistent with the design first quoted, namely, that when the attack by Sumner, Hooker, and Franklin should be progressing favourably, we were "to create a diversion in favour of the main attack, with the hope of something more." It is also probable that Hooker's movement was at first intended to be made by his corps alone, the attack to be taken up by Sumner's two corps as soon as Hooker began, and to be shared in by Franklin if he reached the field in time, thus making a simultaneous oblique attack from our right by the whole army except Porter's corps, which was in reserve, and the Ninth Corps, which was to create the "diversion" on our left and prevent the enemy from stripping his right to reinforce his left. It is hardly disputable that this would have been a better plan than the one actually carried out. Certainly the assumption that the Ninth Corps could cross the Antietam alone at the only place on the field where the Confederates had their line immediately upon the stream which must be crossed under fire by two narrow heads of column, and could then turn to the right along the high ground occupied by the hostile army before that army had been broken or seriously shaken elsewhere, is one which would hardly be made till time had dimmed the remembrance of the actual position of Lee's divisions upon the field. It is also noticeable that the plan as given in the final report leaves no "centre" with which to "advance" when either of the flank movements should be successful, Porter's corps in reserve being the only one not included in the movement as described.

Further evidence that the plan did not originally include the wide separation of two corps to the right to make the extended turning movement is found in Hooker's incomplete report, and in the wide interval in time between the marching of his corps and that of Mansfield. Hooker was ordered to cross the Antietam at about two o'clock in the afternoon of the 16th by the bridge in front of Keedysville and the ford below it. He says that after his troops were over and in march, he rode back to McClellan, who told him that he might call for reinforcements, and that when they came they should be under his command. Somewhat later McClellan rode forward with his staff to observe the progress making, and Hooker again urged the necessity of reinforcements. Yet Sumner did not receive orders to send Mansfield's corps to his support till evening, and it marched only half an hour before midnight, reaching its bivouac, about a mile and a half in rear of that of Hooker, at 2 A.M. of the 17th.

After crossing the Antietam, Hooker had shaped his course to the westward, aiming to reach the ridge on which the Hagerstown turnpike runs, and which is the dominant feature in the landscape. This ridge is about two miles distant from the Antietam, and for the first mile of the way no resistance was met. However, his progress had been observed by the enemy, and Hood's two brigades were taken from the centre and passed to the left of D. H. Hill. Here they occupied an open wood (since known as the East Wood) northeast of the Dunker Church. Hooker was now trying to approach the Confederate positions, Meade's division of the Pennsylvania Reserves being in the advance. A sharp skirmishing combat ensued, and artillery was brought into action on both sides. I have mentioned our hearing the noise of this engagement from the other extremity of the field in the fading light of evening. On our side Seymour's brigade had been chiefly engaged, and had felt the enemy so vigorously that Hood supposed he had repulsed a serious effort to take the wood. Hooker was, however, aiming to pass quite beyond the flank, and kept his other divisions north of the hollow beyond the wood, and upon the ridge which reaches the turnpike near the largest re-entrant bend of the Potomac, which is only half a mile distant. Here he bivouacked upon the slopes of the ridge, Doubleday's division resting with its right upon the turnpike, Ricketts's division upon the left of Doubleday, and Meade covering the front of both with the skirmishers of Seymour's brigade. Between Meade's skirmishers and the ridge were the farmhouse and barn of J. Poffenberger, on the east side of the road, where Hooker made his own quarters for the night. Half a mile further in front was the farm of D. R. Miller, the dwelling on the east, and the barn surrounded by stacks on the west of the road. Mansfield's corps (the Twelfth), marching as it did late in the night, kept further to the right than Hooker's, but moved on a nearly parallel course, and bivouacked on the farm of another J. Poffenberger, near the road which, branching from the Hagerstown turnpike at the Dunker Church, intersects the one running from Keedysville through Smoketown to the same turnpike about a mile north of Hooker's position.

On the Confederate side, Hood's division had been so roughly handled that it was replaced by two brigades of Ewell's division (commanded by Lawton), which with Jackson's own (commanded by J. R. Jones) had been led to the field from Harper's Ferry by Jackson, reaching Sharpsburg in the afternoon of the 16th. These divisions were formed on the left of D. H. Hill, and in continuation of his line along the turnpike, but with a brigade advanced to the East Wood, which was held as a salient. Hood's division, on being relieved, was placed in reserve near the Dunker Church, and spent part of the night in cooking rations, of which its supply had been short for a day or two. The combatants on both sides slept upon their arms, well knowing that the dawn would bring bloody work.

During the evening McClellan issued orders looking toward the joining of a general engagement at daybreak. McLaws's Confederate division, which had been opposing Franklin, crossed the Potomac at Maryland Heights, and marched by way of Shepherdstown, reaching Sharpsburg on the morning of the 17th. Walker's division, which had come from Harper's

Ferry on the 16th, extended Lee's right down the Antietam, covering the ford at which Rodman, on our side, was expected to cross. A. P. Hill's division was the only force of the enemy completing the work at Harper's Ferry, and Franklin was ordered to leave Couch's division to observe Hill's movements from our side of the Potomac, and to bring the remainder of his corps on the field early in the morning. In the respite given him since Sunday, Lee had therefore concentrated all his army but one division, and was better ready for the battle than McClellan, for Franklin's corps could come upon the field only after a considerable march, and he did not, in fact, reach it till ten o'clock or later. Sumner was ordered to have the Second Corps ready to march an hour before day, but he had no authority to move till explicit orders to that effect should reach him. I have said that Hooker claims in his report that the promise was made him that Mansfield's corps, when it came to reinforce him, should be under his orders. If this were so, it would unite all the troops now present which had fought in Pope's Army of Virginia. I find no trace, however, in the reports of the battle, that Hooker exercised any such command. He seems to have confined his work to the independent action of his own corps until Mansfield's death, and was himself disabled almost immediately afterward. As there were commanders of wings of the army duly designated, and two corps were now separated by a long interval from the rest in an independent turning movement, it can hardly be debated that that was the place of all others where one of them should have been, unless McClellan were there in person. Had Burnside's two corps been kept together as the right wing, the right attack could have been made a unit. If Sumner had then been directed to keep in communication with Burnside, and to advance when the latter did, nobody will doubt that Sumner would have been prompt in sustaining his comrades. But both Sumner and Burnside were made to feel that they were reduced from their proper rank, and however conscientious they might be in carrying out such orders as reached them, it was not in human nature that they should volunteer suggestions or anticipate commands. McClellan had thus thrown away the advantages, if there were any, in holding only two or three men directly responsible for the co-ordination of his movements, and had assumed the full personal responsibility of watching each phase of the battle and suiting the proper orders to each conjuncture as it should arise.

Chapter 15
Antietam:
the Fight on the Right

Before the break of day on Wednesday the 17th, it was discovered that Doubleday's division of Hooker's corps lay exposed to artillery fire from batteries of the enemy supposed to be in position on their front and right. In rousing the men and changing their place, the stillness of the night was so far broken that the Confederates believed they were advancing to attack, and a lively cannonade and picket firing anticipated the dawn. The chance for getting their breakfast was thus destroyed, and Hooker prepared his whole command for action as soon as it should be light enough to move. Looking south from the Poffenberger farm along the turnpike, he then saw a gently rolling landscape of which the commanding point was the Dunker Church, whose white brick walls appeared on the right of the road, backed by the foliage of the West Wood, which came toward him filling a hollow that ran parallel to the turnpike, with a single row of fields between. On the east side of the turnpike was the Miller house, with its barn and stack-yard across the road to the right, and beyond these the ground dipped into a little depression. Still further on was seen a large cornfield between the East Wood and the turnpike, rising again to the higher level, and Hooker noticed the glint from a long line of bayonets beyond the corn, struck by the first rays of the rising sun. There was, however, another little hollow at the further side of the cornfield, which could not be seen from Hooker's position; and on the farthest ridge, near the church and extending across the turnpike toward the East Wood, were the Confederate lines, partly sheltered by piles of rails taken from the fences. They looked to Hooker as if they were deployed along the edge of the corn, but an open sloping field lay between the corn and them, after passing the second hollow. It was plain that the high ground about the little white church was the key of the enemy's position, and if that could be carried, Hooker's task would be well done.

The enemy's artillery had opened early from a high hill nearly east of the Miller house in a position to strike our forces in flank and rear as they should go forward, and Hooker placed batteries on the equally commanding height above Poffenberger's and detached Hofmann's brigade from Doubleday's division to support it and to prevent the enemy from turning our extreme right.

Doubleday's division (except Hofmann), was in two lines, Gibbon's and Phelps's in front, supported by Patrick's. Of Meade's division Seymour's brigade, which had sustained the combat of the evening before, had continued to cover the front with skirmishers during the night, and remained on the northeast side of the East Wood. The other brigades (Anderson and Magilton) were placed in reserve behind Doubleday. The Tenth Regiment Pennsylvania Reserves was sent from Anderson's to a strong position west of the turnpike near the extremity of the strip of wood northwest of the Miller house. It was among ledges of rock looking into the ravine beyond which were Stuart and Early. The ravine was the continuation northward to the Potomac of a little watercourse which headed near the Dunker Church and along one side of which the West Wood lay, the outcrop of rock making broken ledges along its whole length. Indeed, all the pieces of wood in the neighbourhood seemed to be full of such rocks, and for that reason had been allowed to remain in forest. The regiment was ordered to cover its front with skirmishers and to hold its position at all hazards. Ricketts's division had bivouacked in a wood east of Doubleday's. Its three brigades (Duryea's, Hartsuff's, and Christian's) were deployed on the left of Doubleday, and were to march toward the Dunker Church through the East Wood, passing the line of Seymour's brigade, which was then to become its support.

The Confederates opened a rapid artillery fire from the open ground in front of the Dunker Church as well as from Stuart's position, and Hooker answered the challenge by an immediate order for his line to advance. Doubleday directed Gibbon, who was on the right, to guide upon the turnpike. Patrick remained for a time in the wood north of the Miller house, till he should be needed at the front. Doubleday and his brigade commanders seem to have supposed that Meade's men occupied part at least of the West Wood, and that they would cover Gibbon's flank as he advanced. This belief was based on the stationing of the Tenth Pennsylvania Reserves; but that regiment was fifteen or twenty rods north of the northern end of the West Wood, and Gibbon's right flank, as he advanced, was soon exposed to attack from Ewell's division (Lawton in command), which held the wood, hidden from view and perfectly protected by the slope of the ground and the forest, as they looked over the rim into the undulating open fields in front. Part of Battery B, Fourth United States Artillery (Gibbon's own battery), was run forward to Miller's barn and stack-yard on the right of the road, and fired over the heads of the advancing regiments. Other batteries were similarly placed, more to the left, and our cannon roared from all the hill crests encircling the field. The line moved swiftly forward through Miller's orchard and kitchen garden, breaking through a stout picket fence on the near side, down into the moist ground of the hollow, and up through the corn which was higher than their heads and shut out everything from view. At the southern side of the field they came to a low fence, beyond which was the open field already mentioned, and the enemy's line at the further side of it. But the cornfield only covered part of the line, and Gibbon's right had out marched the left, which had been exposed to a terrible fire. The direction taken had been a little oblique, so that the right wing of the Sixth Wisconsin (the flanking regiment) had crossed the turnpike and was suddenly assailed by a sharp fire from the West Wood on its flank. They swung back into the road, lying down along the high, stout post-and-rail fence, keeping up their fire by shooting between the rails.

Leaving this little band to protect their right, the main line, which had come up on the left, leaped the fence at the south edge of the cornfield, and charged up hill across the open at the enemy in front. But the concentrated fire of artillery and musketry was more than they could bear. Men fell by scores and hundreds, and the thinned lines gave way and ran for the shelter of the corn. They were rallied in the hollow on the north side of the field. The enemy had rapidly extended his left under cover of the West Wood, and now made a dash at the right flank and at Gibbon's exposed guns. His men on the right faced by that flank and followed him bravely, though with little order, in a dash at the Confederates who were swarming out of the wood. The gunners double-charged the cannon with canister, and under a terrible fire of artillery and rifles Lawton's division broke and sought shelter.

Patrick's brigade had now come up in support of Gibbon, and was sent across the turnpike into the West Wood to cover that flank, two regiments of Gibbon's going with him. His men pushed forward, the enemy retiring, until they were in advance of the principal line in the cornfield upon which the Confederates of Jackson's division were now marching to attack. Patrick faced his brigade to the left, parallel to the edge of the wood and to the turnpike, and poured his fire into the flank of the enemy, following it by a charge through the field and up to the fence along the road. Again the Confederates were driven back, but their left came forward in the wood again, attacking Patrick's right, forcing him to resume his original direction of front and to retire to the cover of a rocky ledge in the open at right angles to the turnpike not far from the northern end of the timber. Phelps's brigade had gone forward with Gibbon's, pushing nearly to the Confederate lines, and being driven back with great loss when they charged over open ground against the enemy.

Ricketts's division advanced from the wood in which it had spent the night, passed through Seymour's skirmishers and entered the East Wood, swinging his left forward as he went. This grove was open, but the rocks made perfect cover for Jackson's men, and every stone and tree blazed with deadly fire. Hartsuff endeavoured to reconnoitre the ground, but was wounded and disabled immediately. Ricketts pushed on, suffering fearfully from an enemy which in open order could fall back from rock to rock and from tree to tree with little comparative loss. He succeeded at last in reaching the west edge of this wood, forming along the road and fences that were just within its margin. Here he kept up a rapid fire till his ammunition was exhausted.

When Doubleday's men had been finally repulsed, our line on the right curved from the ledge where Patrick took refuge, forward in front of Miller's orchard and garden, part of Gibbon's men lying down along the turnpike fence facing to the west. Meade's two brigades in reserve were sent forward, but when they reached Gibbon and Phelps, Ricketts was calling for assistance in the East Wood and Magilton's brigade was sent to him, leaving a gap on the left of Anderson. Another gallant effort was now made, Seymour's depleted brigade striving to cover the opening, but the enemy dashed at it as Anderson came up the slope, and the left being taken in flank, the whole broke again to the rear. Ricketts's right was also imperilled, and he withdrew his exhausted lines to reorganize and to fill their empty cartridge-boxes. There was a lull in the battle, and the combatants on both sides were making desperate efforts to reform their broken regiments.

Mansfield had called the Twelfth Corps to arms at the first sound of Hooker's battle and marched to his aid. It consisted of two divisions, Williams's and Greene's, the first of two and the other of three brigades. There were a number of new and undrilled regiments in the command, and in hastening to the front in columns of battalions in mass, proper intervals for deployment had not been preserved, and time was necessarily lost before the troops could be put in line. Indeed, some of them were not regularly deployed at all. They had left their bivouac at sunrise which, as it was about the equinox, was not far from six o'clock. They had marched across the country without reference to roads, always a very slow mode of advancing, and doubly so with undrilled men. The untrained regiments must, in the nature of things, have been very much like a mob when their so-called columns-in-mass approached the field of battle. It is impossible to reconcile the statements of the reports as to the time they became engaged. General Williams says they were engaged before seven o'clock. General Meade says they relieved his men not earlier than ten or eleven. It seems to be guesswork in both cases, and we are forced to judge from circumstantial evidence. Ricketts thinks he had been fighting four hours when he retired for lack of ammunition, and the Twelfth Corps men had not yet reached him. Patrick, on the extreme right, says that his men had made their coffee in the lull after his retreat to the sheltering ledge of rocks, and had completed their breakfast before the first of Mansfield's men joined him there. The circumstantial details given by several officers make the interval between the attack by the Twelfth Corps and the arrival of Sumner a very short one. It may be regarded as probable, therefore, that Hooker's battle covered the larger part of the time between six o'clock and the arrival of Sumner at about ten.

On reaching the field, Mansfield had a brief consultation with Hooker, resulting in his ordering Williams to form his division nearly as Doubleday's had been, and to advance with his right upon the turnpike. He himself led forward the left of Crawford's brigade, which was the first to arrive, and pushed toward the East Wood. The regiments were still in columns of companies, and though Williams had ordered them deployed, the corps commander himself, as Crawford says, countermanded this order and led them under fire in column. He evidently believed Ricketts's men to be still holding the East Wood, and tried to keep his own from opening fire upon the troops that were seen there. At this moment he was mortally wounded, before the deployment was made.

General Alpheus S. Williams, on whom the command devolved, was a cool and experienced officer. He hastened the deployment of Crawford's and Gordon's brigades of his own division, sending one of the new and large regiments to assist the Pennsylvania regiment in holding the important position covering the right beyond the turnpike. As Greene's division came up, he ordered him to form beyond Gordon's left, and when deployed to move on the Dunker Church through the East Wood, guiding his left by the cloud of smoke from the Mumma house, which had been set on fire by D. H. Hill's men. At Doubleday's request, he detached Goodrich's brigade from Greene, and sent it to Patrick on the right with orders to advance into the West Wood from its northern extremity. Patrick says the regiments came separately and at considerable intervals, and it is not unlikely that the older regiments were sent in to relieve Hooker's men as fast as they were ready, and the more disorganized ones were obliged to delay till they could be got into some sort of shape. Williams made his first disposition of his troops according to Hooker's suggestion, but the latter received a serious wound in the foot, as it would seem, before the attack by the Twelfth Corps had begun. Hooker turned over the command to Meade, and a formal order confirming this was issued from McClellan's head-quarters later in the day.

So many of the regiments were carried under fire while still in column that not only was the formation of the line an irregular one, but the deployment when made was more diagonal to the turnpike than Hooker's had been, and the whole line faced more to the westward. But they advanced with a courage equal to the heroism already shown on that field. The Confederates who now held the open space at the Dunker Church were Hood's two brigades, and the rest of Jackson's corps extended into the West Wood. Stuart had found his artillery position on the hill too far from Jackson's line, and the fighting was so near the church that he could not fire upon our men without hurting his own. He therefore moved further to the south and west, and Early carried his brigade (except the Thirteenth Virginia) back toward Ewell's division, which now came under his command by the disabling of General Lawton in the fight.

Williams's first line was a good deal shortened, and the divisions, guiding as well as they could upon Greene, crowded so far to the south that even Crawford's brigade, which was on the right of all, went partly through the East Wood advancing on a line nearly at right angles to the turnpike. The enemy had followed Ricketts's retiring battalions and were again in occupation of the East Wood. His work was to be done over again, though the stubborn courage of Hood's depleted brigades could not make up for the numbers which the National officers now led against him. But the rocks, the ledges, and the trees still gave him such cover that it was at a fearful cost that the Twelfth Corps men pushed him steadily back and then by a final rush drove him from the roads which skirted the grove on west and south. What was left of Jackson's corps except Early's brigade had come out of the West Wood to meet Crawford's division, and the stout high fences along the turnpike were the scene of frightful slaughter. The Confederates tried to climb them, but the level fire of our troops swept over the field so that the top of the fence seemed in the most deadly line of the leaden storm, and the men in grey fell in windrows along its panels. Our own men were checked by the same obstacle, and lay along the ground shooting between the rails and over the fallen bodies of the Confederate soldiers which made a sort of rampart.

In obedience to his original orders, Greene took ground a little more to his left, occupying a line along a fence from the burning Mumma house to the road leading from the East Wood directly to the Dunker Church. The two brigades with thinned ranks barely filled this space, and Crawford's division connected with them as well as it could. Batteries came forward on Greene's left and right, and helped to sweep the grove around the church. Hill attempted to hold him back, and a bold dash was made at Greene, probably by Hill's left brigades which were ordered forward to support Hood. Greene's men lay on the ground just under the ridge above the burning house till the enemy were within a few rods of them, then rose and delivered a volley which an eyewitness (Major Crane, Seventh Ohio) says cut them down "like grass before the mower." Those who escaped sought refuge in the wood behind the church, where the crowning ridge is some distance back from the road. Greene now dashed forward and gained the grove immediately about the church, where he held on for an hour or two. Crawford's division, after several ebbs and flows in the tide of battle, was holding the western skirt of the East wood with one or two of its regiments still close to the turnpike fence on his right.

Meanwhile Goodrich had been trying to advance from the north end of the West Wood to attack the flank of the enemy there; but Early with his own brigade held the ledges along the ravine so stubbornly that he was making little progress.

Greene was calling for support about the Dunker Church, for he was close under the ridge on which Hill and Jackson were forming such line as they could, and he was considerably in advance of our other troops. Williams withdrew one regiment from Goodrich's brigade and sent it to Greene, and directed Crawford to send also to him the Thirteenth New Jersey, a new and strong regiment which had been left in reserve, as we have seen, in a bit of wood northeast of the field of battle. Gordon's brigade was withdrawn by Crawford to enable it to reorganize in rear of the East Wood, and Crawford's own brigade held the further margin of it. It will thus be seen that the Twelfth Corps was now divided into three portions—Greene's division at the church, Crawford's in the East Wood, and Goodrich's brigade near the north end of the West Wood.

Meade had withdrawn the First Corps to the ridge at Poffenberger's, where it had bivouacked the night before, except that Patrick's brigade remained in support of Goodrich. The corps had suffered severely, having lost 2470 in killed and wounded, but it was still further depleted by straggling, so that Meade reported less than 7000 men with the colours that evening. Its organization had been preserved, however, and the story that it was utterly dispersed was a mistake. The Twelfth Corps also had its large list of casualties, increased a little later by its efforts to support Sumner, and aggregating, before the day was over, 1746.

But the fighting of Hooker's and Mansfield's men, though lacking unity of force and of purpose, had also cost the enemy dear. J. R. Jones, who commanded Jackson's division, had been wounded; Starke, who succeeded Jones, was killed; Lawton, who commanded Ewell's division, was wounded. Lawton's and Trimble's brigades had been fearfully crippled in the first fight against Hooker on the plateau between the Dunker Church and the East Wood, and Hood was sent back to relieve them. He, in turn, had been reinforced by the brigades of Ripley, Colquitt, and McRae (Garland's) from D. H. Hill's division. When Greene reached the Dunker Church, therefore, the Confederates on that wing were more nearly disorganized than our own troops. Nearly half their numbers were killed and wounded, and Jackson's famous "Stonewall" division was so completely broken up that only a handful of men under Colonels Grigsby and Stafford remained, and attached themselves to Early's command. Of the division now under Early, his own brigade was all that retained much strength, and this, posted among the rocks in the West Wood and vigorously supported by Stuart and the artillery on that flank, was all that covered the left of Lee's army. Could Hooker and Mansfield have attacked together, or, still better, could Sumner's Second Corps have marched before day and united with the first onset, Lee's left must inevitably have been crushed long before the Confederate divisions of McLaws, Walker, and A. P. Hill could have reached the field. It is this failure to carry out any intelligible plan which the historian must regard as the unpardonable military fault on the National side. To account for the hours between daybreak and eight o'clock on that morning, is the most serious responsibility of the National commander.

Sumner's Second Corps was now approaching the scene of action, or rather two divisions of it, Sedgwick's and French's, for Richardson's was still delayed till his place could be filled by Porter's troops. Although ordered to be ready to move at daybreak, Sumner emphasizes in his report the fact that whilst his command was prepared to move at the time ordered, he "did not receive from headquarters the order to march till 7.20 A. M." By the time he could reach the field, Hooker had fought his battle and had been repulsed. The same strange tardiness in sending orders is noticeable in regard to every part of the army, and Richardson was not relieved so that he could follow French till an hour or two later.

Sumner advanced, after crossing the Antietam, in a triple column, Sedgwick's division in front, the three brigades marching by the right flank and parallel to each other. French followed in the same formation. They crossed the Antietam by Hooker's route, but did not march so far to the northwest as Hooker had done. On the way Sumner met Hooker, who was being carried from the field, and the few words he could exchange with the wounded general were enough to make him feel the need of haste, but not enough to give him any clear idea of the situation. When the centre of the corps was opposite the Dunker Church, and nearly east of it, the change of direction was given; the troops faced to their proper front, and advanced in line of battle in three lines, fully deployed and sixty or seventy yards apart, Sumner himself being in rear of Sedgwick's first line and near its left. As they approached the position held by Greene's division at the church, French kept on so as to form on Greene's left, but Sedgwick, under Sumner's immediate leading, diverged somewhat to the right, passing through the East Wood, crossing the turnpike on the right of Greene and of the Dunker Church, and plunged into the West Wood. The fences there had been destroyed by the Confederates before the battle began, for the purpose of making room for their own manoeuvres as well as to make barricades in front of the cornfield. Sedgwick's right did not extend far enough north to be obstructed by the fences where the Twelfth Corps men had lain along them in repulsing Jackson. When he entered the wood, there were absolutely no Confederate troops in front of him. The remnants of Jackson's men, except Early's brigade, were clustered at the top of the ridge immediately in front of Greene, and Early was further to the right, opposing Goodrich and Patrick; Early, however, made haste under cover of the woods to pass around Sedgwick's right and to get in front of him to oppose his progress. This led to a lively skirmishing fight in which Early was making as great a demonstration as possible, but with no chance of solid success.

Sedgwick pushed him back, and his left was coming obliquely into the open at the bottom of the hollow beyond the wood, when, at the very moment, McLaws's and Walker's Confederate divisions came upon the field. The former had only just arrived by rapid marching from Shepherdstown beyond the Potomac; the latter had been hastily called away by Lee from his position on the lower Antietam opposite the left wing of Burnside's Ninth Corps.

Walker charged headlong upon the left flank of Sedgwick's lines, and McLaws, passing by Walker's left, also threw his division diagonally upon the already broken and retreating brigades. Taken at such a disadvantage, these had never a chance; and in spite of the heroic bravery of Sumner and Sedgwick with most of their officers (Sedgwick being severely wounded), the division was driven off to the north with terrible losses, carrying along in their rout Goodrich's brigade of the Twelfth Corps which had been holding Early at bay. Goodrich was killed, and his brigade suffered hardly less than the others. Patrick's brigade of Hooker's corps was in good order at the rocky ledges north of the West Wood which are at right angles to the turnpike, and he held on stubbornly till the disorganized troops drifted past his left, and then made an orderly retreat in line toward the Poffenberger hill. Meade was already there with the remnants of Hooker's men. Here some thirty cannon of both corps were quickly concentrated, and, supported by everything which retained organization, easily checked the pursuers and repulsed all efforts of Jackson and Stuart to resume the offensive or to pass between them and the Potomac.

Sumner did not accompany the routed troops to this position, but as soon as it was plain that the division could not be rallied, he galloped off to put himself in communication with French and with headquarters of the army and to try to retrieve the situation. From the flag station east of the East Wood he signalled to McClellan, "Reinforcements are badly wanted; our troops are giving way." Williams was in that part of the field, and Sumner sent a staff officer to him ordering that he should push forward to Sedgwick's support anything he could. Williams in person ordered Gordon's brigade to advance, for this, as we have seen, had been reorganized behind the East Wood. He sent the same order to Crawford for the rest of that division. Crawford had withdrawn his men in the East Wood to let Sedgwick pass diagonally along his front, and now advanced again to the west margin of the grove. Gordon was ahead of him in time and further to the right, and again charged up to the turnpike fences. But the routed troops were already swarming from the wood across his front, and their pursuers were charging after them. Again the turnpike was made the scene of a bloody conflict, and the bodies of many more of the slain of both armies were added to those which already lined those fences. Gordon's men were overpowered and fell back in the direction they had come. The enemy's attack spread out toward Greene and toward Crawford, who was now at the edge of the East Wood again; but both of these held firm, and a couple of batteries on the rise of ground in front poured canister into the enemy till he took refuge again in the wood beyond the church. It was between nine and ten o'clock, probably about ten, when Sumner entered the West Wood, and in fifteen minutes or a little more the one-sided combat was over.

Sumner's principal attack was made, as I have already indicated, at right angles to that of Hooker. He had thus crossed the line of Hooker's movement in both the advance and the retreat of the latter. This led to some misconceptions on Sumner's part. Crawford's division had retired to the right and rear to make way for Sedgwick as he came up. It thus happened that Greene's division was the only part of the Twelfth Corps troops Sumner saw, and he led Sedgwick's men to the right of these. Ignorant as he necessarily was of what had occurred before, he assumed that he formed on the extreme right of the Twelfth Corps, and that he fronted in the same direction as Hooker had done. This misconception of the situation led him into another error. He had seen only stragglers and wounded men on the line of his own advance, and hence concluded that Hooker's Corps was completely dispersed and its division and brigade organizations broken up. He not only gave this report to McClellan at the time, but reiterated it later in his statement before the Committee on the Conduct of the War. The truth was that he had marched westward more than a mile south of the Poffenberger hill where Meade was with the sadly diminished but still organized First Corps, and half that distance south of the Miller farm buildings, near which Goodrich's brigade had entered the north end of the West Wood, and in front of which part of Williams's men had held the ground along the turnpike till they were relieved by Sedgwick's advance. Sedgwick had gone in, therefore, between Greene and Crawford, and the four divisions of the two corps alternated in their order from left to right, thus: French, Greene, Sedgwick, Crawford, the last being Williams's, of which Crawford was in command.

It was not Sumner's fault that he was so ill-informed of the actual situation on our right; but it is plain that in the absence of McClellan from that part of the field he should have left the personal leadership of the men to the division commanders, and should himself have found out by rapid examination the positions of all the troops operating there. It was his part to combine and give intelligent direction to the whole, instead of charging forward at haphazard with Sedgwick's division. Both Meade and Williams had men enough in hand to have joined in a concerted movement with him; and had he found either of those officers before plunging into the West Wood, he would not have taken a direction which left his flank wholly exposed, with the terrible but natural results which followed. The original cause of the mischief, however, was McClellan's failure to send Sumner to his position before daybreak, so that the three corps could have acted together from the beginning of Hooker's attack.

But we must return to Sumner's divisions, which were advancing nearer the centre. The battle on the extreme right was ended by ten o'clock in the morning, and there was no more serious fighting north of the Dunker Church. The batteries on the Poffenberger hill and those about the East Wood swept the open ground and the cornfield over which Hooker and Mansfield had fought, and for some time Greene was able to make good his position at the church. The Confederates were content to hold the line of the West Wood and the high ground back of the church, and French's attack upon D. H. Hill was now attracting their attention. French advanced toward Greene's left, over the open farm lands, and after a fierce combat about the Rullett and Clipp farm buildings, drove Hill's division from them. At what time the Confederates made a rush at Greene and drove him back to the edge of the East Wood is uncertain; but it must have been soon after the disaster to Sedgwick. It seems to have been an incident of the aggressive movement against Sedgwick, though not coincident with it. It must certainly have been before French's advance reached the Rullett and Clipp houses, for the enemy's men holding them would have been far in rear of Greene at the church, and he must by that time have been back near the burnt house of Mumma and the angle of the East Wood.

Richardson's division followed French after an hour or two, and then, foot by foot, field by field, from fence to fence, and from hill to hill, the enemy was pressed back, till the sunken road, since known as "Bloody Lane," was in our hands, piled full of the Confederate dead who had defended it with their lives. Richardson had been mortally wounded, and Hancock had been sent from Franklin's corps to command the division. Colonel Barlow had been conspicuous in the thickest of the fight, and after a series of brilliant actions had been carried off desperately wounded. On the Confederate side equal courage and a magnificent tenacity had been exhibited. Men who had fought heroically in one position no sooner found themselves free from the struggle of an assault than they were hurried away to repeat their exertions, without even a breathing-spell, on another part of the field. They exhausted their ammunition, and still grimly held crests, as Longstreet tells us, with their bayonets, but without a single cartridge in their boxes. The story of the fight at this part of the field is simpler than that of the early morning, for there was no such variety in the character of the ground or in the tactics of the opposing forces. It was a sustained advance with continuous struggle, sometimes ebbing a moment, then gaining, but with the organization pretty well preserved and the lines kept fairly continuous on both sides. Our men fought their way up to the Piper house, near the turnpike, and that position marks the advance made by our centre. The crest of the ridge on which the Hagerstown turnpike runs had been secured from Piper's north to Miller's, and it was held until the Confederate retreat on the 19th.

The head of Franklin's Corps (the Sixth) had arrived about ten o'clock, and had taken the position near the Sharpsburg bridge, which Sumner had occupied in the night. Before noon Smith's and Slocum's divisions were both ordered to Sumner's assistance. As they passed by the farm buildings in front of the East Wood, the enemy made a dash at Greene and French. Smith ordered forward Irwin's brigade to their support, and Irwin charged gallantly, driving the assailants back to the cover of the woods about the church. Franklin's men then formed under the crest already mentioned, from "Bloody Lane" by the Clipp, Rullett, and Mumma houses to the East Wood and the ridge in front. The aggressive energy of both sides seemed exhausted. French and Richardson's battle may be considered as ended at one or two o'clock. There was no fighting later but that on the extreme left, where Burnside's Ninth Corps was engaged, and we must turn our attention to that part of the field.

Chapter 16
Antietam:
The Fight on the Left

We have seen that the divisions of the Ninth Corps were conducted by staff officers of Burnside's staff to positions that had been indicated by McClellan and marked by members of his staff. The morning of Wednesday the 17th broke fresh and fair. The men were astir at dawn, getting breakfast and preparing for a day of battle. The artillery fire which opened Hooker's battle on the right spread along the whole line, and the positions which had been assigned us in the dusk of evening were found to be exposed, in some places, to the direct fire of the Confederate guns. Rodman's division suffered more than the others, Fairchild's brigade alone reporting thirty-six casualties before they could find cover. My own tents had been pitched at the edge of a little grove of forest trees, and the headquarters mess was at breakfast at sunrise when the cannonade began. The rapid explosion of shrapnel about us hastened our morning meal; the tents were struck and loaded upon the wagons, horses were saddled, and everything made ready for the contingencies of the day. It was not till seven o'clock that orders came to advance toward the creek as far as could be done without exposing the men to unnecessary loss. Rodman was directed to acquaint himself with the situation of the ford in front of him, and Sturgis to seek the best means of approach to the stone bridge. All were then to remain in readiness to obey further orders.

When these arrangements had been made, I rode to the position Burnside had selected for himself, which was upon a high knoll northeast of the Burnside bridge, near a haystack which was a prominent landmark. Near by was Benjamin's battery of twenty-pounder Parrotts, and a little further still to the right, on the same ridge, General Sturgis had sent in Durell's battery. These were exchanging shots with the enemy's guns opposite, and had the advantage in range and weight of metal. At this point I remained until the order for our attack came, later in the day. We anxiously watched what we could see at the right, and noted the effect of the fire of the heavy guns of Benjamin's battery. We could see nothing distinctly that occurred beyond the Dunker Church, for the East and West Woods with farm-houses and orchards between made an impenetrable screen. A column of smoke stood over the burning Mumma house, marking plainly its situation.

As the morning wore on, we saw lines of troops advancing from our right upon the other side of the Antietam, and engaging the enemy between us and the East Wood. The Confederate lines facing them now also rose into view. From our position we looked, as it were, down between the opposing lines as if they had been the sides of a street, and as the fire opened we saw wounded men carried to the rear and stragglers making off. Our lines halted, and we were tortured with anxiety as we speculated whether our men would charge or retreat. The enemy occupied lines of fences and stone walls, and their batteries made gaps in the National ranks. Our long-range guns were immediately turned in that direction, and we cheered every well-aimed shot. One of our shells blew up a caisson close to the Confederate line. This contest was going on, and it was yet uncertain which would succeed, when one of McClellan's staff rode up with an order to Burnside. The latter turned to me, saying we were ordered to make our attack. I left the hill-top at once to give personal supervision to the movement ordered, and did not return to it. My knowledge by actual vision of what occurred on the right ceased.

The question at what hour Burnside received this order, has been warmly disputed. The manner in which we had waited, the free discussion of what was occurring under our eyes and of our relation to it, the public receipt of the order by Burnside in the usual and business-like form, all forbid the supposition that this was any reiteration of a former order. If then we can determine whose troops we saw engaged, we shall know something of the time of day; for there has been a general agreement reached as to the hours of movement of Sumner's divisions during the forenoon on the right and right centre. The official map settles this. No lines of our troops were engaged in the direction of Bloody Lane and the Rullett farm-house, and between the latter and our station on the hill, till French's division made its attack. We saw them distinctly on the hither side of the farm buildings, upon the open ground, considerably nearer to us than the Dunker Church or the East Wood. In number we took them to be a corps. The place, the circumstances, all fix it beyond controversy that they were French's men or French's and Richardson's. No others fought on that part of the field until Franklin went to their assistance at noon or later. The incident of their advance and the explosion of the caisson was illustrated by the pencil of Mr. Forbes on the spot, and was placed by him at the time Franklin's head of column was approaching from the direction of Rohrersville, which was about ten o'clock.

It seems now very clear that about ten o'clock in the morning was the great crisis in this battle. The sudden and complete rout of Sedgwick's division was not easily accounted for, and, with McClellan's theory of the enormous superiority of Lee's numbers, it looked as if the Confederate general had massed overwhelming forces on our right. Sumner's notion that Hooker's corps was utterly dispersed was naturally accepted, and McClellan limited his hopes to holding on at the East Wood and the Poffenberger hill, where Hooker's batteries were massed and supported by the troops that had been rallied there. Franklin's corps, as it came on the field, was detained to support the threatened right centre, and McClellan determined to help it further by a demonstration upon the extreme left by the Ninth Corps. At this time, therefore, he gave his order to Burnside to cross the Antietam and attack the enemy, thus creating a diversion in favour of our hard-pressed right. His preliminary report of the battle (dated October 16, 1862) explicitly states that the order to Burnside to attack was "communicated to him at ten o'clock A.M." This exactly agrees with the time stated by Burnside in his official report, and would ordinarily be quite conclusive.

In the book published in 1864 as his official report of his whole military career, McClellan says he ordered Burnside to make this attack at eight o'clock. The circumstances under which his final published statements were made take away from them the character of a calm and judicial correction of his first report. He was then a general set aside from active service and a political aspirant to the Presidency. His book was a controversial one, issued as an argument to the public, and the earlier report must be regarded in a military point of view as the more authoritative unless good grounds are given for the changes. When he wrote his preliminary report he certainly knew the hour and the condition of affairs on the field when he gave the order to Burnside. To do so at eight o'clock would not accord with his plan of battle. His purpose had been to move the Ninth Corps against the enemy "when matters looked favourably" on our right, after an attack by Hooker, Mansfield, and Sumner, supported, if necessary, by Franklin. But Sumner's attack was not made till after nine, and Franklin's head of column did not reach the field till ten. McClellan's book, indeed, erroneously postpones Franklin's arrival till past noon, which, if true, would tend to explain why the day wore away without any further activity on the right; but the preliminary report better agrees with Franklin's when it says that officer reached the field about an hour after Sedgwick's disaster.

Still further, matters had at no time "looked favourably" on the right up to ten o'clock. The condition, therefore, which was assumed as precedent to Burnside's movement, never existed; and this was better known to McClellan than to any one else, for he received the first discouraging reports after Mansfield fell, and the subsequent alarming ones when Sedgwick was routed. Burnside's report was dated on the 30th of September, within two weeks of the battle, and at a time when public discussion of the incomplete results of the battle was animated. It was made after he had in his hands my own report as his immediate subordinate, in which I had given about nine o'clock as my remembrance of the time. As I directed the details of the action at the bridge in obedience to this order, it would have been easy for him to have accepted the hour named by me, for I should have been answerable for any delay in execution after that time. But he then had in his possession the order which came to him upon the hill-top overlooking the field, and no officer in the whole army has a better established reputation for candour and freedom from any wish to avoid full personal responsibility for his acts. It was not till his report was published in the Official Records (1887) that I saw it or learned its contents, although I enjoyed his personal friendship down to his death. He was content to have stated the fact as he knew it, and did not feel the need of debating it. The circumstances have satisfied me that his accuracy in giving the hour was greater than my own.

It will not be wondered at, therefore, if to my mind the story of the eight o'clock order is an instance of the way in which an erroneous recollection is based upon the desire to make the facts accord with a theory. The actual time must have been as much later than nine o'clock as the period during which, with absorbed attention, we had been watching the battle on the right—a period, it is safe to say, much longer than it seemed to us. The judgment of the hour which I gave in my report was merely my impression from passing events, for I hastened at once to my own duties without thinking to look at my watch; whilst the cumulative evidence seems to prove, conclusively, that the time stated by Burnside, and by McClellan himself in his original report, is correct. The order, then, to Burnside to attack was not sent at eight o'clock, but reached him at ten; it was not sent to follow up an advantage gained by Hooker and Sumner, but to create, if possible, a strong diversion in favour of the imperilled right wing when the general outlook was far from reassuring.

McClellan truly said, in his original report, that the task of carrying the bridge in front of Burnside was a difficult one. The hill on which I have placed the station of General Burnside was the bolder and more prominent crest of the line of hills which skirted the Antietam on the east, and was broken by depressions here and there, through which the country roads ran down to the stream. Such a hollow was just at the south of Burnside's position at the haystack on the Rohrback farm. In rear of him and a little lower down were the farm buildings, and from these a road ran down the winding hollow to the Antietam, but reached the stream several hundred yards below the bridge. Following the road, therefore, it was necessary to turn up stream upon the narrow space between the hills and the water, without any cover from the fire of the enemy on the opposite side. The bluffs on that side were wooded to the water's edge, and were so steep that the road from the bridge could not go up at right angles to the bank, but forked both ways and sought the upper land by a more gradual ascent to right and left. The fork to the right ran around a shoulder of the hill into a ravine which there reaches the Antietam, and thence ascends by an easy grade toward Sharpsburg. The left branch of the road rises by a similar but less marked depression.

These roads were faced by stone fences, and the depth of the valley and its course made it impossible to reach the enemy's position at the bridge by artillery fire from the hill-tops on our side. Not so from the enemy's position, for the curve of the valley was such that it was perfectly enfiladed near the bridge by the Confederate batteries at the position now occupied by the National Cemetery. The bridge itself was a stone structure of three arches with stone parapets on the sides. These curved outward at the end of the bridge to allow for the turn of the roadway. On the enemy's side, the stone fences came down close to the bridge.

The Confederate defence of the passage was entrusted to D. R. Jones's division of six brigades, which was the one Longstreet himself had disciplined and led till he was assigned to a larger command. Toombs's brigade was placed in advance, occupying the defences of the bridge itself and the wooded slopes above, while the other brigades supported him, covered by the ridges which looked down upon the valley. The division batteries were supplemented by others from the enemy's reserve, and the valley, the bridge, and the ford below were under the direct and powerful fire of shot and shell from the Confederate cannon. Toombs's force, thus strongly supported, was as large as could be disposed of at the head of the bridge, and abundantly large for resistance to any that could be brought against it. Our advance upon the bridge could only be made by a narrow column, showing a front of eight men at most; but the front which Toombs deployed behind his defences was three or four hundred yards both above and below the bridge. He himself says in his report: "From the nature of the ground on the other side, the enemy were compelled to approach mainly by the road which led up the river near three hundred paces parallel with my line of battle and distant therefrom from fifty to a hundred and fifty feet, thus exposing his flank to a destructive fire the most of that distance." Under such circumstances the Confederate position was nearly impregnable against a direct attack over the bridge; for the column approaching it was not only exposed at almost pistol-range to the perfectly covered infantry of the enemy and to two batteries which were assigned to the special duty of supporting Toombs, having the exact range of the little valley with their shrapnel; but, if it should succeed in reaching the bridge, its charge across it must be made under a fire ploughing through its length, the head of the column melting away as it advanced, so that, as every soldier knows, it could show no front strong enough to make an impression upon the enemy's breastworks, even if it should reach the other side. As a desperate sort of diversion in favour of the right wing, it might be justifiable; but I believe that no officer or man who knew the actual situation at that bridge thinks that a serious attack upon it was any part of McClellan's original plan. Yet, in his detailed report of 1863, instead of speaking of it as the difficult task the original report had called it, he treats it as little different from a parade or march across which might have been done in half an hour.

Burnside's view of the matter was that the front attack at the bridge was so difficult that the passage by the ford below must be an important factor in the task; for if Rodman's division should succeed in getting across there, at the bend of the Antietam, he would come up in rear of Toombs, and either the whole of D. R. Jones's division would have to advance to meet Rodman, or Toombs must abandon the bridge. In this I certainly concurred, and Rodman was ordered to push rapidly for the ford. It is important to remember, however, that Walker's Confederate division had been posted during the earlier morning to hold that part of the Antietam line, supporting Toombs as well, and it was probably from him that Rodman suffered the first casualties that occurred in his ranks. But, as we have seen, Walker had been called away by Lee only an hour before, and had made the hasty march by the rear of Sharpsburg to fall upon Sedgwick. If therefore Rodman had been sent to cross at eight o'clock, it is safe to say that his column, fording the stream in the face of Walker's deployed division, would never have reached the further bank—a contingency that McClellan did not consider when arguing, long afterward, the favourable results that might have followed an earlier attack. As Rodman died upon the field, no full report for his division was made, and we only know that he met with some resistance from both infantry and artillery; that the winding of the stream made his march longer than he anticipated, and that, in fact, he only approached the rear of Toombs's position from that direction about the time when our last and successful charge upon the bridge was made, between noon and one o'clock.

The attacks at the Burnside bridge were made under my own eye. Sturgis's division occupied the centre of our line, with Crook's brigade of the Kanawha division on his right front, and Willcox's division in reserve, as I have already stated. Crook's position was somewhat above the bridge, but it was thought that by advancing part of Sturgis's men to the brow of the hill, they could cover the advance of Crook, and that the latter could make a straight dash down the hill to our end of the bridge. The orders were accordingly given, and Crook advanced, covered by the Eleventh Connecticut (of Rodman's) under Colonel Kingsbury, deployed as skirmishers. In passing over the spurs of the hills, Crook came out on the bank of the stream above the bridge and found himself under a heavy fire at short range. He faced the enemy and returned the fire, getting such cover for his men as he could and trying to drive off or silence his opponents. The engagement was one in which the Antietam prevented the combatants from coming to close quarters, but it was none the less vigorously continued with musketry fire. Crook reported that his hands were full and that he could not approach closer to the bridge. Later in the contest, his men, lining the stream, made experiments in trying to get over, and found a fordable place a little way above, by which he got over five companies of the Twenty-eighth Ohio at about the same time as the final and successful charge. But on the failure of Crook's first effort, Sturgis ordered forward an attacking column from Nagle's brigade, supported and covered by Ferrero's brigade, which took position in a field of corn on one of the lower slopes of the hill opposite the head of the bridge. The whole front was carefully covered with skirmishers, and our batteries on the heights overhead were ordered to keep down the fire of the enemy's artillery. Nagle's effort was gallantly made, but it failed, and his men were forced to seek cover behind the spur of the hill from which they had advanced. We were constantly hoping to hear something from Rodman's advance by the ford, and would gladly have waited for some more certain knowledge of his progress, but at this time McClellan's sense of the necessity of relieving the right was such that he was sending reiterated orders to push the assault. Not only were these forwarded to me, but to give added weight to my instructions, Burnside sent direct to Sturgis urgent messages to carry the bridge at all hazards.

I directed Sturgis to take two regiments from Ferrero's brigade, which had not been engaged, and make a column by moving them together by the flank, the one left in front and the other right in front, side by side, so that when they passed the bridge they could turn to left and right, forming line as they advanced on the run. He chose the Fifty-first New York, Colonel Robert B. Potter, and the Fifty-first Pennsylvania, Colonel John F. Hartranft (both names afterward greatly distinguished), and both officers and men were made to feel the necessity of success. At the same time Crook succeeded in bringing a light howitzer of Simmonds's mixed battery down from the hilltops, and placed it where it had a point-blank fire on the further end of the bridge. The howitzer was one we had captured in West Virginia, and had been added to the battery, which was partly made up of heavy rifled Parrott guns. When everything was ready, a heavy skirmishing fire was opened all along the bank, the howitzer threw in double charges of canister, and in scarcely more time than it takes to tell it, the bridge was passed and Toombs's brigade fled through the woods and over the top of the hill. The charging regiments were advanced in line to the crest above the bridge as soon as they were deployed, and the rest of Sturgis's division, with Crook's brigade, were immediately brought over to strengthen the line. These were soon joined by Rodman's division, with Scammon's brigade, which had crossed at the ford, and whose presence on that side of the stream had no doubt made the final struggle of Toombs's men less obstinate than it would otherwise have been, the fear of being taken in rear having always a strong moral effect upon even the best of troops.

It was now about one o'clock, and nearly three hours had been spent in a bitter and bloody contest across the narrow stream. The successive efforts to carry the bridge had been as closely following each other as possible. Each had been a fierce combat, in which the men with wonderful courage had not easily accepted defeat, and even, when not able to cross the bridge, had made use of the walls at the end, the fences, and every tree and stone as cover, while they strove to reach with their fire their well-protected and nearly concealed opponents. The lulls in the fighting had been short, and only to prepare new efforts. The severity of the work was attested by our losses, which, before the crossing was won, exceeded 500 men, and included some of our best officers, such as Colonel Kingsbury of the Eleventh Connecticut, Lieutenant-Colonel Bell of the Fifty-first Pennsylvania, and Lieutenant-Colonel Coleman of the Eleventh Ohio, two of them commanding regiments. The proportion of casualties to the number engaged was much greater than common; for the nature of the combat required that comparatively few troops should be exposed at once, the others remaining under cover.

Our next task was to prepare to hold the heights we had gained against the return assault of the enemy which we expected, and to reply to the destructive fire from the enemy's abundant artillery. Light batteries were brought over and distributed in the line. The men were made to lie down behind the crest to save them from the concentrated cannonade which the enemy opened upon us as soon as Toombs's regiments succeeded in reaching their main line. But McClellan's anticipation of an overwhelming attack upon his right was so strong that he determined still to press our advance, and sent orders accordingly. The ammunition of Sturgis's and Crook's men had been nearly exhausted, and it was imperative that they should be freshly supplied before entering into another engagement. Sturgis also reported his men so exhausted by their efforts as to be unfit for an immediate advance. On this I sent to Burnside the request that Willcox's division be sent over, with an ammunition train, and that Sturgis's division be replaced by the fresh troops, remaining, however, on the west side of the stream as support to the others. This was done as rapidly as was practicable, where everything had to pass down the steep hill-road and through so narrow a defile as the bridge. Still, it was three o'clock before these changes and preparations could be made. Burnside had personally striven to hasten them, and had come over to the west bank to consult and to hurry matters, and took his share of personal peril, for he came at a time when the ammunition wagons were delivering cartridges, and the road at the end of the bridge where they were was in the range of the enemy's constant and accurate fire. It is proper to mention this because it has been said that he did not cross the stream. The criticisms made by McClellan as to the time occupied in these changes and movements will not seem forcible if one will compare them with any similar movements on the field; such as Mansfield's to support Hooker, or Sumner's or Franklin's to reach the scene of action. About this, however, there is fair room for difference of opinion: what I personally know is that it would have been folly to advance again before Willcox had relieved Sturgis, and that as soon as the fresh troops reported and could be put in line, the order to advance was given. McClellan is in accord with all other witnesses in declaring that when the movement began, the conduct of the troops was gallant beyond criticism.

Willcox's division formed the right, Christ's brigade being north, and Welsh's brigade south of the road leading from the bridge to Sharpsburg. Crook's brigade of the Kanawha division supported Willcox. Rodman's division formed on the left, Harland's brigade having the position on the flank, and Fairchild's uniting with Willcox at the centre. Scammon's brigade was the reserve for Rodman at the extreme left. Sturgis's division remained and held the crest of the hill above the bridge. About half of the batteries of the divisions accompanied the movement, the rest being in position on the hill-tops east of the Antietam. The advance necessarily followed the high ground toward Sharpsburg, and as the enemy made strongest resistance toward our right, the movement curved in that direction, the six brigades of Jones's Confederate division being deployed diagonally across our front, holding the stone fences and crests of the cross-ridges and aided by abundant artillery, in which arm the enemy was particularly strong.

The battle was a fierce one from the moment Willcox's men showed themselves on the open ground. Christ's brigade, taking advantage of all the cover the trees and inequalities of surface gave them, pushed on along the depression in which the road ran, a section of artillery keeping pace with them in the road. The direction of movement brought all the brigades of the first line in echelon, but Welsh soon fought his way up beside Christ, and they together drove the enemy successively from the fields and farm-yards till they reached the edge of the village. Upon the elevation on the right of the road was an orchard in which the shattered and diminished force of Jones made a final stand, but Willcox concentrated his artillery fire upon it, and his infantry was able to push forward and occupy it. They now partly occupied the town of Sharpsburg, and held the high ground commanding it on the southeast, where the National Cemetery now is. The struggle had been long and bloody. It was half-past four in the afternoon, and ammunition had again run low, for the wagons had not been able to accompany the movement. Willcox paused for his men to take breath again and to fetch up some cartridges; but meanwhile affairs were taking a serious turn on the left.

As Rodman's division went forward, he found the enemy before him seemingly detached from Willcox's opponents, and occupying ridges on his left front, so that he was not able to keep his own connection with Willcox in the swinging movement to the right. Still, he made good progress in the face of stubborn resistance, though finding the enemy constantly developing more to his left, and the interval between him and Willcox widening. The view of the field to the south was now obstructed by fields of tall Indian corn, and under this cover Confederate troops approached the flank in line of battle. Scammon's officers in the reserve saw them as soon as Rodman's brigades echeloned, as these were toward the front and right. This hostile force proved to be A. P. Hill's division of six brigades, the last of Jackson's force to leave Harper's Ferry, and which had reached Sharpsburg since noon. Those first seen by Scammon's men were dressed in the National blue uniforms which they had captured at Harper's Ferry, and it was assumed that they were part of our own forces till they began to fire. Scammon quickly changed front to the left, drove back the enemy before him, and occupied a line of stone fences, which he held until he was afterward withdrawn from it. Harland's brigade was partly moving in the corn-fields. One of his regiments was new, having been organized only three weeks, and the brigade had somewhat lost its order and connection when the sudden attack came. Rodman directed Colonel Harland to lead the right of the brigade, while he himself attempted to bring the left into position. In performing this duty he fell, mortally wounded. Harland's horse was shot under him, and the brigade broke in confusion after a brief effort of its right wing to hold on. Fairchild also now received the fire on his left, and was forced to fall back and change front.

Being at the centre when this break occurred on the left, I saw that it would be impossible to continue the movement to the right, and sent instant orders to Willcox and Crook to retire the left of their line, and to Sturgis to come forward into the gap made in Rodman's. The troops on the right swung back in perfect order; Scammon's brigade hung on at its stone wall at the extreme left with unflinching tenacity till Sturgis had formed on the curving hill in rear of them, and Rodman's had found refuge behind. Willcox's left then united with Sturgis, and Scammon was withdrawn to a new position on the left flank of the whole line. That these manoeuvres on the field were really performed in good order is demonstrated by the fact that although the break in Rodman's line was a bad one, the enemy was not able to capture many prisoners, the whole number of missing, out of the 2349 casualties which the Ninth Corps suffered in the battle, being 115, which includes wounded men unable to leave the field.

The enemy were not lacking in bold efforts to take advantage of the check we had received, but were repulsed with severe punishment, and as the day declined were content to entrench themselves along the line of the road leading from Sharpsburg to the Potomac at the mouth of the Antietam, half a mile in our front. The men of the Ninth Corps lay that night upon their arms, the line being one which rested with both flanks near the Antietam and curved outward upon the rolling hill-tops which covered the bridge and commanded the plateau between us and the enemy. With my staff, I lay upon the ground behind the troops, holding our horses by the bridles as we rested, for our orderlies were so exhausted that we could not deny them the same chance for a little broken slumber.

The Ninth Corps occupied its position on the heights west of the Antietam without further molestation, except an irritating picket firing, till the Confederate army retreated on the 19th of September. But the position was one in which no shelter from the weather could be had, nor could any cooking be done; and the troops were short of rations. My division wagon-train, which I had brought from the West, here stood us in good stead, for the corps as a whole was very short of transportation. The energy of Captain Fitch, my quartermaster, forced the train back and forth between us and the nearest depot of supplies, and for several days the whole corps had the benefit of the provisions thus brought forward. Late in the afternoon of Thursday the 18th, Morell's division of Porter's corps was ordered to report to Burnside to relieve the picket line and some of the regiments in the most exposed position. One brigade was sent over the Antietam for this purpose, and a few of the Ninth Corps regiments were enabled to withdraw far enough to cook some rations, of which they had been in need for twenty-four hours. Harland's brigade of Rodman's division had been taken to the east side of the stream to be reorganized, on the evening of Wednesday the 17th. The sounds heard within the enemy's lines by our pickets gave an inkling of their retrograde movement in the night of Thursday, and at break of day on Friday morning the retreat of Lee's whole army was discovered by advancing the picket line. Reconnaissances sent to the front discovered that the whole Confederate army had crossed the Potomac.

The conduct of the battle on the left has given rise to several criticisms, among which the most prominent has been that Porter's corps, which lay in reserve, was not put in at the same time with the Ninth Corps. It has been said that some of them were engaged or in support of the cavalry and artillery at the centre. This does not appear to have been so to any important extent, for no active fighting was going on elsewhere after Franklin's corps relieved Sumner's about noon. McClellan's reports do not urge this. He answered the criticism by saying that he did not think it prudent to divest the centre of all reserve troops. No doubt a single strong division, marching beyond the left flank of the Ninth Corps, would have so occupied A. P. Hill's division that our movement into Sharpsburg could not have been checked, and, assisted by the advance of Sumner and Franklin on the right, would apparently have made certain the complete rout of Lee. As troops are put in reserve, not to diminish the army, but to be used in a pinch, I am convinced that McClellan's refusal to use them on the left was the result of his rooted belief, through all the day after Sedgwick's defeat, that Lee was overwhelmingly superior in force, and was preparing to return a crushing blow upon our right flank. He was keeping something in hand to fill a gap or cover a retreat, if that wing should be driven back. Except in this way, also, I am at a loss to account for the inaction of the right during the whole of our engagement on the left. Looking at our part of the battle as only a strong diversion to prevent or delay Lee's following up his success against Hooker and the rest, it is intelligible. I certainly so understood it at the time, as my report witnesses, and McClellan's original report sustains this view. If he had been impatient to have our attack delivered earlier, he had reason for double impatience that Franklin's fresh troops should assail Lee's left simultaneously with our assault of his other wing, unless he regarded action there as hopeless, and looked upon our movement as a sort of forlorn hope to keep Lee from following up his advantages.

But even these are not all the troublesome questions requiring an answer. It will be remembered that Franklin's corps, after forcing Crampton's Gap, had remained in Pleasant Valley between Rohrersville and Boonsboro until Tuesday night (16th September). McClellan then ordered Couch's division to be sent to occupy Maryland Heights and observe the enemy in Harper's Ferry, whilst Franklin with Smith's and Slocum's divisions should march to the battle-field at daybreak of Wednesday. Why could not Couch be called up and come on our left as well as A. P. Hill's division, which was the last of the Confederate troops to leave the ferry, there being nothing to observe after it was gone? Couch's division, coming with equal pace with Hill's on the other side of the river would have answered our needs as well as one from Porter's corps. Hill came, but Couch did not. Yet even then, a regiment of horse, watching that flank and scouring the country as we swung forward, would have developed Hill's presence and enabled the commanding general either to stop our movement or to take the available means to support it. The cavalry was put to no such use. It occupied the centre of the whole line, only its artillery being engaged during the day. It would have been invaluable to Hooker in the morning, as it would have been to us in the afternoon.

McClellan had marched from Frederick City with the information that Lee's army was divided, Jackson being detached with a large force to take Harper's Ferry. He had put Lee's strength at 120,000 men. Assuming that there was still danger that Jackson might come upon our left with his large force, and that Lee had proven strong enough without Jackson to repulse three corps on our right and right centre, McClellan might have regarded his own army as divided also for the purpose of meeting both opponents, and his cavalry would have been upon the flank of the part with which he was attacking Lee; Porter would have been in position to help either part in an extremity or to cover a retreat; and Burnside would have been the only subordinate available to check Lee's apparent success. Will any other hypothesis intelligibly account for McClellan's dispositions and orders? The error in the above assumption would be that McClellan estimated Lee's troops at nearly double their actual numbers, and that what was taken for proof of Lee's superiority in force on the field was a series of partial reverses which resulted directly from the piecemeal and disjointed way in which McClellan's morning attacks had been made.

The same explanation is the most satisfactory one that I can give for the inaction of Thursday, the 18th of September. Could McClellan have known the desperate condition of most of Lee's brigades, he would also have known that his own were in much better case, badly as they had suffered. I do not doubt that most of his subordinates discouraged the resumption of the attack, for the belief in Lee's great preponderance in numbers had been chronic in the army during the whole year. That belief was based upon the inconceivably mistaken reports of the secret-service organization, accepted at headquarters, given to the War Department at Washington as a reason for incessant demands of reinforcements, and permeating downward through the whole organization till the error was accepted as truth by officers and men, and became a factor in their morale which can hardly be overestimated. The result was that Lee retreated unmolested on the night of the 18th of September, and that what might have been a real and decisive success was a drawn battle in which our chief claim to victory was the possession of the field.

The numbers engaged and the losses on each side have been the subject of unending dispute. If we take the returns of Lee at the beginning of his campaign against Pope, and deduct his acknowledged losses, he crossed the Potomac with over 72,000 men. If we take his returns of September 22, and add the acknowledged losses of the month, he had over 57,000. McClellan's 87,000 present for duty is accepted by all, though various causes considerably reduced the number he brought into action. The best collation of reports of casualties at Antietam gives 12,410 as those on the National side, and 11,172 on the Confederate. Longstreet, comparing the fighting in the fiercest battles of the war, says "on no single day in any one of them was there such carnage as in this fierce struggle."

Chapter 17
McClellan and Politics

When I rode up with Burnside on the afternoon of the 15th September, in the group around McClellan I met Judge Key, whom I had not seen since we parted in the Ohio Senate in April of the preceding year. He was now aide-de-camp on the headquarters staff with the rank of colonel, and doing duty also as judge-advocate. When McClellan directed us to leave the ridge because the display of numbers attracted the enemy's fire, Colonel Key took my arm and we walked a little way down the slope till we found a fallen tree, on which we sat down, whilst he plunged eagerly into the history of his own opinions since we had discussed the causes of the war in the legislature of our State. He told me with earnestness that he had greatly modified his views on the subject of slavery, and he was now satisfied that the war must end in its abolition. The system was so plainly the soul of the rebellion and the tie which bound the seceded States together, that its existence must necessarily depend upon the success of the revolutionary movement, and it would be a fair object of attack, if doing so would help our cause. I was struck by the zeal with which he dashed into the discussion, forgetful of his actual surroundings in his wish to make me quickly understand the change that had come over his views since we parted at Columbus. He was so absorbed that even when a shell burst near us, he only half gave it attention, saying in a parenthetical way that he would change his position, as he would "rather not be hit in the back by one of those confounded things." We had been so sitting that in facing me his back was toward the front and the line of fire.

Colonel Key has been regarded by many as McClellan's evil genius, whose influence had been dominant in the general's political conduct and who was therefore the cause of his downfall. His influence on McClellan was unquestionably great—and what he said to me is an important help in understanding the general's conduct and opinions. It accords with other statements of his which have been made public by Judge William M. Dickson of Cincinnati, who at one time was Colonel Key's partner in the practice of the law.

General McClellan urged me to come to his headquarters without ceremony, and after the battle of Antietam I had several opportunities of unrestrained discussion of affairs in which he seemed entirely frank in giving me his opinions. It was plainly evident that he was subjected to a good deal of pressure by opponents of the administration to make him commit himself to them. On the other hand, Governor Dennison of Ohio, who was his sincere friend, took every opportunity to counteract such influences and to promote a good understanding between him and Mr. Lincoln. McClellan perfectly knew my own position as an outspoken Republican who from the first had regarded the system of slavery as the stake ventured by the Secessionists on their success in the war, and who held to John Quincy Adams's doctrine that the war powers were adequate to destroy the institution which we could not constitutionally abolish otherwise. With me, the only question was when the ripe time had come for action, and I had looked forward to Mr. Lincoln's proclamation with some impatience at the delay.

The total impression left upon me by the general's conversation was that he agreed with Colonel Key in believing that the war ought to end in abolition of slavery; but he feared the effects of haste, and thought the steps toward the end should be conservatively careful and not brusquely radical. I thought, and still think, that he regarded the President as nearly right in his general views and political purposes, but overcrowded by more radical men around him into steps which as yet were imprudent and extreme. Such an attitude on his part made Governor Dennison and myself feel that there was no need of any political quarrel between him and the administration, and that if he would only rebuff all political intriguers and put more aggressive energy into his military operations, his career might be a success for the country as well as for himself. The portions of his correspondence with Burnside which have become public show that the latter also had, as a true friend, constantly urged him to keep out of political controversy. Burnside himself, like Grant and Sherman, began with a dislike of the antislavery movement; but, also like them, his patriotism being the dominant quality, the natural effect of fighting the Secessionists was to beget in him a hearty acceptance of the policy of emancipation to which Mr. Lincoln had been led by the same educational process.

At the time I am speaking of, I knew nothing of McClellan's famous letter to the President from Harrison's Landing, of July 7, but since it has come to light, I have interpreted it much less harshly than many have done. Reading it in the light of his talk during those Antietam days, I think it fair to regard it as an effort to show Mr. Lincoln that they were not far apart in opinion, and to influence the President to take the more conservative course to which he thought him inclined when taking counsel only of his own judgment. McClellan knew that his "change of base" to the James River in June was not accepted as the successful strategy he declared it to be, and that strong influences were at work to remove him. Under the guise of giving advice to the President, he was in fact assuring him that he did not look to the acknowledgment of the Confederacy as a conceivable outcome of the war; that the "contraband" doctrine applied to slaves was consistent with compensated emancipation; that he favoured the application of the principle to the border States so as to make them free States; that concentration of military force as opposed to dispersion of effort was the true policy; that he opposed the rules of warfare which he assumed were announced in General Pope's much criticised orders; and lastly, that he would cordially serve under such general-in-chief as Mr. Lincoln should select.

Compare all this with Mr. Lincoln's known views. It was notorious that he was thought to be too conservative by many of his own party. He had urged a system of compensated emancipation for the border States. He had said that he held the slavery question to be only a part, and an absolutely subordinate part, of the greater question of saving the Union. He had disapproved of a portion of Pope's order regarding the treatment of non-combatants. However ill-advised McClellan's letter was, it may be read between the lines as an attempt to strengthen himself with the President as against Stanton and others, and to make his military seat firmer in the saddle by showing that he was not in political antagonism to Mr. Lincoln, but held, in substance, the conservative views that were supposed to be his. Its purpose seems to me to have been of this personal sort. He did not publish it at the time, and it was not till he was removed from his command that it became a kind of political manifesto. This view is supported by what occurred after the publication of the Emancipation Proclamation, which I shall tell presently; but, to preserve the proper sequence, I must first give another incident.

A few days after the battle of Antietam a prominent clergyman of Hagerstown spent the Sunday in camp, and McClellan invited a number of officers to attend religious services in the parlours of the house where headquarters were. The rooms were well filled, several civilians being also present. I was standing by myself as we were waiting for the clergyman to appear, when a stout man in civilian's dress entered into conversation with me. He stood at my side as we faced the upper part of the suite of rooms, and taking it to be a casual talk merely to pass the time, I paid rather languid attention to it and to him as he began with some complimentary remarks about the army and its recent work. He spoke quite enthusiastically of McClellan, and my loyalty to my commander as well as my personal attachment to him made me assent cordially to what he said. He then spoke of the politicians in Washington as wickedly trying to sacrifice the general, and added, whispering the words emphatically in my ear, "But you military men have that matter in your own hands, you have but to tell the administration what they must do, and they will not dare to disregard it!" This roused me, and I turned upon him with a sharp "What do you mean, sir!" As I faced him, I saw at once by his look that he had mistaken me for another; he mumbled something about having taken me for an acquaintance of his, and moved away among the company.

I was a good deal agitated, for though there was more or less of current talk about disloyal influences at work, I had been sceptical as to the fact, and to be brought face to face with that sort of thing was a surprise. I was a stranger to most of those who were there, and walked a little aside, watching the man who had left me. I soon saw him talking with General Fitz-John Porter, on the opposite side of the room, evidently calling attention to me as if asking who I was. I made inquiries as to who the civilian was, and later came to know him by sight very well. He was John W. Garrett, President of the Baltimore and Ohio Railroad Company.

Mr. Lincoln's Emancipation Proclamation was published on the 24th of September, and within a very few days I was invited to meet General Burnside and General John Cochrane of New York at a camp dinner in McClellan's tent. General Cochrane was a "War Democrat" in politics, and had been active as a politician in his State. He was also the son-in-law of Gerrit Smith, the well-known abolitionist, and had advocated arming the slaves as early as November, 1861. McClellan told us frankly that he had brought us there for the purpose of asking our opinions and advice with regard to the course he should pursue respecting the Proclamation. He said that he was urged to put himself in open opposition to it by politicians not only, but by army officers who were near to him. He named no names, but intimated that they were of rank and influence which gave weight to their advice. He knew that we were all friends of the administration, and his object seemed to be to learn whether we thought he should say anything or should maintain silence on the subject; for he assumed that we would oppose any hostile demonstration on his part.

This naturally led to inquiries as to his actual attitude to the slavery question, and he expressed himself in substance as I have before indicated; repeating with even stronger emphasis his belief that the war would work out the manumission of the slaves gradually and ultimately, and that as to those who came within our lines as we advanced the liberation would be complete and immediate. He thought, however, that the Proclamation was premature, and that it indicated a change in the President's attitude which he attributed to radical influences at Washington.

There had been no previous understanding between us who were his guests. For my part, I then met General Cochrane for the first time, and had conversed with McClellan himself more freely on political subjects than I had with Burnside. We found ourselves, however, in entire accord in advising him that any declaration on his part against the Proclamation would be a fatal error. We could easily understand that he should differ from us in his way of viewing the question of public policy, but we pointed out very clearly that any public utterance by him in his official character criticising the civil policy of the administration would be properly regarded as a usurpation. He intimated that this was his own opinion, but, by way of showing how the matter was thrust at him by others, said that people had assured him that the army was so devoted to him that they would as one man enforce any decision he should make as to any part of the war policy.

I had so recently gone through the little experience on this subject which I have narrated above, that I here spoke out with some emphasis. I said that those who made such assurances were his worst enemies, and in my judgment knew much less of the army than they pretended; that our volunteer soldiers were citizens as well as soldiers, and were citizens more than soldiers; and that greatly as I knew them to be attached to him, I believed not a corporal's guard would stand by his side if he were to depart from the strict subordination of the military to the civil authority. Burnside and Cochrane both emphatically assented to this, and McClellan added that he heartily believed both that it was true and that it ought to be so. But this still left the question open whether the very fact that there was an agitation in camp on the subject, and intrigues of the sort I have mentioned, did not make it wise for him to say something which would show, at least, that he gave no countenance to any would-be revolutionists. We debated this at some length, with the general conclusion that it might be well for him to remind the army in general orders that whatever might be their rights as citizens, they must as soldiers beware of any organized effort to meddle with the functions of the civil government.

I left the Army of the Potomac before McClellan's general order on this subject, dated October 7, was published, but when I read it in the light of the conference in his tent, I regarded it as an honest effort on his part to break through the toils which intriguers had spread for him, and regretted that what seemed to me one of his most laudable actions should have been one of the most misrepresented and misunderstood.

I have always understood that the order was drafted by Colonel Key, who afterward expressed in very strong terms his confidence in the high motives and progressive tendencies of McClellan at the time he issued it.

General Cochrane, some time after the close of the war, in a pamphlet outlining his own military history, made reference to the visit to McClellan which I have narrated, and states that he was so greatly impressed by the anti-slavery sentiments avowed by the general, that he made use of them in a subsequent effort to bring him and Secretary Chase into more cordial relations. It is possible that, in a friendly comparison of views in which we were trying to find how nearly we could come together, the general may have put his opinions with a liberality which outran his ordinary statements of belief; but I am very sure that he gave every evidence of sincerity, and that none of us entertained a doubt of his being entirely transparent with us. He has since, in his *Own Story*, referred to his taking counsel of Mr. Aspinwall of New York at about the same time, and there is evidence that General W. F. Smith also threw his influence against any opposition by McClellan to the Emancipation Proclamation. McClellan's letters show that his first impulse was to antagonism; but there is no fair reason to doubt that his action at last was prompted by the reasons which he avowed in our conversation, and by the honourable motives he professed.

He immediately sent a copy of his order to Mr. Lincoln personally, and this indicates that he believed the President would be pleased with it.

The reference which he made to suggestions that the army would follow him in a *coup d'e'tat* is supported by what he formally declared in his memoirs. He there tells us that in 1861 he was often approached in regard to a "dictatorship," and that when he was finally removed many in the army were in favour of his marching upon Washington to take possession of the government. It would seem that treasonable notions were rife about him to an extent that was never suspected, unless he was made the dupe of pretenders who saw some profit in what might be regarded as a gross form of adulation. He must be condemned for the weakness which made such approaches to him possible; but we are obliged to take the fact as he gives it, and to accept as one of the strange elements of the situation a constant stream of treasonable suggestions from professed friends in the army and out of it. An anecdote which came to me in a way to make it more than ordinarily trustworthy was that in the summer of 1861 McClellan was riding with an older officer of the regular army, and said to him, "I understand there is a good deal of talk of making a dictatorship." "Ah!" said the other, "Mr. Lincoln, I suppose." "Oh, no," replied McClellan, "it's me they're talking of." Bits of evidence from many sources prove that there had been from the first too much such talk about Washington, and whilst McClellan cannot be held responsible for it, there is no proof that he rebuked it as he should have done. It was part of the fermenting political and military intrigue which is found at the seat of government in such a time, if anywhere, and I take satisfaction in testifying that away from that neighbourhood I never even heard the thing mentioned or referred to, that I can recollect. Washington would be spoken of in a general way as a place of intrigues, but I never knew this to have a wider meaning given to it than the ordinary one of political schemes within lawful limits and personal ambitions of no criminal character.

Mr. Lincoln visited our camp on the 1st of October, and remained two or three days. I was with the party of officers invited by McClellan to accompany the President in a ride over the route which Sumner had followed in the battle. We crossed the Antietam in front of Keedysville, followed the hollows and byways to the East Wood, and passed through this and the cornfields which had been the scene of Hooker's and Mansfield's fierce fighting. We visited the Dunker Church and then returned to camp by Bloody Lane and the central stone bridge. The President was observant and keenly interested in the field of battle, but made no display of sentiment. On another day he reviewed the troops which were most accessible from headquarters. As my own corps was among the first on the list, I did not join the escort of the President at the general's quarters, but was with the troops attending to the details of the parade. We were ordered to be under arms at eight o'clock, but it was more than two hours after that when the reviewing cortège came on the ground. The officers were very hilarious over some grotesque story with which Mr. Lincoln had seasoned the conversation, and which seemed to have caused some forgetfulness of the appointment with the troops. We were reviewed by divisions, and I met the party with my staff, riding down the lines with them, and answering the inquiries of the President and the general as to the history and the experience of the different organizations as we passed them. The usual march in review was omitted for lack of time, the President contenting himself with riding along the lines formed in parade. I had missed seeing the President in Washington when I paid my respects at the White House, and this was my first meeting with him after his inauguration. His unpretending cordiality was what first impressed one, but you soon saw with what sharp intelligence and keen humour he dealt with every subject which came up. He referred very pleasantly to his knowledge of me through Secretary Chase, showing the kindly instinct to find some compliment or evidence of recognition for all who approached him.

This geniality in Mr. Lincoln made him avoid personal criticism of the campaign, and gave an air of earnest satisfaction to what he said of the work done by McClellan. There was enough to praise, and he praised it heartily. He was also thankful that the threatened invasion of the North had been defeated, and showed his sense of great relief. He had adopted the rule for himself to limit his direct influence upon his generals to the presentation of his ideas of what was desirable, often taking pains even in his written communications to say that he made no order, and left the definite direction to General Halleck. McClellan gave the most favourable interpretation to all that the President said, but could not ignore the anxiety Mr. Lincoln showed that an energetic campaign should be continued. He wrote home: "I incline to think that the real purpose of his visit is to push me into a premature advance into Virginia."

The President had coupled his earliest telegraphic congratulations with the question, "Can't you beat them some more before they get off?" and McClellan's private correspondence shows that he, on his part, chafed at every suggestion of haste. As early as the 22nd of September, the general had written that he looked upon the campaign as substantially ended, and intended to give some time to the reorganization of the army before beginning a new one. The vicinity of Harper's Ferry or Frederick seemed to him the proper place for the camp meanwhile, and he wished for a rise in the Potomac River which should make it impracticable for Lee to ford it again. He delayed in the neighbourhood of Sharpsburg, waiting for this. To those of us with whom he talked freely, he spoke of the necessity of incorporating into the Army of the Potomac at least a hundred thousand of the new levies to make it really fit for an aggressive campaign, and argued that it would save time in the end to use some of it now in the work of reorganizing.

Mr. Lincoln was plainly troubled with the apprehension that the delays of 1861 were to be repeated, and that the fine October weather of that region would be again wasted and nothing done till the next spring. There were men enough about him at Washington to remind him of this in irritating ways, and to make him realize that as he had personally restored McClellan to the command he would be personally responsible for keeping him moving. McClellan rightly understood Mr. Lincoln's visit as meaning this. He did not refuse to move; on the other hand, he professed to be anxious to do so at the earliest moment when it should be really practicable. His obstinacy was of a feminine sort. He avoided open antagonism which would have been a challenge of strength, but found constantly fresh obstacles in the way of doing what he was determined from the first not to do. The need of clothing for the men and of horses for the cavalry was a fruitful subject for debate, and the debate, if sufficiently prolonged, would itself accomplish the delay that was desired.

The official correspondence shows that the President went back to Washington determined to cut the knot in a peremptory way, if he was forced to do so. McClellan could not have been blind to this. His private letters show that he thought it not improbable that he would be relieved from command. His desire for military success was a ruling one with him on both public and private grounds. We are forced, therefore, to conclude that he actually lacked faith in success, and regarded the crossing of the Potomac as too perilous until he should reorganize the army with the additional hundred thousand recruits. In this we see the ever-recurring effect of his exaggeration of the enemy's force. We now know that this over-estimate was inexcusable, but we cannot deny that he made it, nor, altogether, that he believed in it. It constituted a disqualification for such a command, and led to what must be regarded as the inevitable result—his removal. The political questions connected with the matter cut no important figure in it. If he had had faith in his ability to conquer Lee's army, we should never have heard of them.

Whilst I mean what I say in speaking of McClellan's exaggeration of his enemy as constituting incompetence for such a command, it has reference to the necessity in which we were that our army should be aggressively handled. Few men could excel him in strictly defensive operations. He did not lack personal courage, nor did his intellectual powers become obscured in the excitement of actual war. He showed the ordinary evidences of presence of mind and coolness of judgment under fire. His tendency to see his enemy doubled in force was, however, a constitutional one, and no amount of experience seemed to cure it. Had it not been so he would have devised checks upon the reports of his secret-service agents, and corrected their estimates by those more reliable methods which I have already spoken of. McClellan was, even in those days, often compared to Marshal Daun, whose fair ability but studiously defensive policy was so in contrast with the daring strategy of the great Frederick. The comparison was a fair one. The trouble was that we had need of a Frederick.

It may seem strange that his subordinates so generally accepted his view and supported him in his conduct; but it was a natural result of forces always at work in an army. The old maxim that "Councils of war never fight" is only another way of saying that an army is never bolder than its leader. It is the same as the old Greek proverb, "Better an army of deer with a lion for leader, than an army of lions with a deer for leader." The body of men thus organized relies upon its chief for the knowledge of the enemy and for the plan by which the enemy is to be taken at a disadvantage. It will courageously carry out his plans so long as he has faith in them himself and has good fortune in their execution. Let doubt arise as to either of these things and his troops raise the cry "We are sacrificed," "We are slaughtered uselessly." McClellan's arts of military popularity were such that his army accepted his estimate of the enemy, and believed (in the main) that he had shown great ability in saving them from destruction in a contest at such odds. They were inclined, therefore, to hold the government at Washington responsible for sacrificing them by demanding the impossible. Under such circumstances nothing but a cautious defensive policy could be popular with officers or men. If McClellan's data were true, he and they were right. It would have been folly to cross the Potomac and, with their backs to the river, fight a greatly superior enemy. Because the data were not true there was no solution for the problem but to give the army another commander, and painfully to undo the military education it had for a year been receiving. The process of disillusion was a slow one. The disasters to Burnside and Hooker strengthened the error. Meade's standstill after Gettysburg was very like McClellan's after Antietam, and Mr. Lincoln had to deal with it in a very similar way. When Grant took command the army expected him to have a similar fate, and his reputation was treated as of little worth because he had not yet "met Bobby Lee." His terrible method of "attrition" was a fearfully costly one, and the flower of that army was transferred from the active roster to the casualty lists before the prestige of its enemy was broken. But it was broken, and Appomattox came at last.

It will not do to say that the Confederate army in Virginia was in any sense superior to their army in the West. When the superior force of the National army was systematically applied, General Lee was reduced to as cautious a defensive in Virginia as was General Johnston in Georgia. Longstreet and Hood had no better success when transferred to the West than the men who had never belonged to the Army of Virginia. In fact, it was with Joseph E. Johnston as his opponent that McClellan's career was chiefly run. Yet the Confederate army in the West was broken at Donelson and at Vicksburg. It was driven from Stone's River to Chattanooga, and from Missionary Ridge to Atlanta. Its remnant was destroyed at Franklin and Nashville, and Sherman's March to the Sea nearly completed the traverse of the whole Confederacy. His victorious army was close in rear of Petersburg when Richmond was finally won. Now that we have got rid of the fiction that the Confederate government gave to Lee an enormously larger army than it gave to Bragg or to Joseph Johnston, we have to account for the fact that with much less odds in their favour our Western army accomplished so much more. As a military objective Richmond was in easier reach from the Potomac than Nashville from the Ohio. From Nashville to Chattanooga was fully as difficult a task. The vulnerable lines of communication multiplied in length as we went southward, and made the campaign of Atlanta more difficult still. Vicksburg was a harder nut to crack than Richmond. We must put away our *esprit de corps*, and squarely face the problem as one of military art with the Official Records and returns before us. Our Western army was of essentially the same material as the Eastern. Regiments from nearly all the States were mingled in both. Wisconsin men fought beside those from Maine in the Army of the Potomac, as men who had fought at Antietam and at Gettysburg followed Sherman through the Carolinas. The difference was not in the rank and file, it was not in the subordinates. It was the difference in leadership and in the education of the armies under their leaders during their first campaigns. That mysterious thing, the morale of an army, grows out of its belief as to what it can do. If it is systematically taught that it is hopelessly inferior to its adversary, it will be held in check by a fraction of its own force. The general who indoctrinates his army with the belief that it is required by its government to do the impossible, may preserve his popularity with the troops and be received with cheers as he rides down the line, but he has put any great military success far beyond his reach. In this study of military morale, its causes and its effects, the history of the Army of the Potomac is one of the most important and one of the gravest lessons the world has ever seen.

I have to confess that at Antietam I shared, more or less fully, the opinions of those among whom I was. I accepted McClellan as the best authority in regard to the enemy's numbers, and, assuming that he was approximately right in that, the reasonable prudence of waiting for reinforcements could not be denied. I saw that he had lost valuable time in the movements of the campaign, but the general result seemed successful enough to hide this for the time at least. My own experience, therefore, supports the conclusion I have already stated, that an army's enterprise is measured by its commander's, and, by a necessary law, the army reflects his judgment as to what it can or cannot accomplish.

Mr. Lincoln had told McClellan during his visit to the army that his great fault was "over cautiousness." He had intimated plainly enough that he must insist upon the continuance of the campaign. He had discussed the plans of advance, and urged McClellan to operate upon Lee's communications by marching south on the east side of the Blue Ridge. He had disclaimed any purpose of forcing a movement before the army was ready, but saw no reason why it should take longer to get ready after Antietam than after Pope's last battle. Soon after his return to Washington, Halleck sent a peremptory order to McClellan to cross the Potomac. It was dated October 6th, and said: "The President directs that you cross the Potomac and give battle to the enemy or drive him South. Your army must move now while the roads are good. If you cross the river between the enemy and Washington, and cover the latter by your line of operations, you can be reinforced with 30,000 men. If you move up the valley of the Shenandoah, not more than 12,000 or 15,000 can be sent to you. The President advises the interior line between Washington and the enemy, but does not order it." It also required him to report immediately which line he adopted. Halleck, as General-in-chief, ought to have given his own decision as to the line of operations, but his characteristic indecision was shown in failing to do so. He did not even express an opinion as to the relative merits of the two lines, and limited himself to his concurrence in the order to move in one way or the other.

McClellan replied on the 7th, saying that he had determined to adopt the Shenandoah line, though he wished to "state distinctly" that he should only use that line till the enemy should retire beyond Winchester, as he did not expect to be able to supply his army more than twenty or twenty-five miles beyond a railway or canal depot. If the enemy retreated, he would adopt some new and decisive line of operations. He objected to the interior line because it did not cover Maryland and Pennsylvania from a return of Lee's army, and because (as he said) the army could not be supplied by it. He indicated three days as the time within which he could move. At the end of that time he complained of still lacking clothing. On the 12th he found it "absolutely necessary" that the cavalry should have more horses. The discussion over these things ran on till the 21st.

Mr. Lincoln made a strong effort to save McClellan from the effects of his mental deficiencies. He exhausted advice and exhortation. He even ventured upon mild raillery on the idleness of the army. On the 13th he had written a remarkable letter to McClellan, in which he reminded him of what had occurred between them at the Antietam and argued in favour of the interior line of movement. He showed that Lee at Winchester supplied his army twice as far from his railway depot as McClellan thought possible for the Army of the Potomac. He urged the recognized advantage of operating by a line which attacked the enemy's communications. He pointed out that if Lee should try to cross the Potomac, our army could be in his rear and should destroy him. He showed that McClellan at Harper's Ferry was nearer to Richmond than Lee: "His route is the arc of a circle of which yours is the chord." He analyzed the map and showed that the interior line was the easier for supplying the army: "The chord line, as you see, carries you by Aldie, Haymarket and Fredericksburg, and you see how turnpikes, railroads, and finally the Potomac by Acquia Creek, meet you at all points from Washington." He even gave the figures in miles from gap to gap in the mountains, which would enable McClellan to strike the enemy in flank or rear; and this was of course to be done if Lee made a stand. "It is all easy," his letter concluded, "if our troops march as well as the enemy; and it is unmanly to say they cannot do it." Yet he expressly disclaimed making his letter an order.

As a mere matter of military comprehension and judgment of the strategic situation, the letter puts Mr. Lincoln head and shoulders above both his military subordinates. Halleck saw its force, but would not order it to be carried out. McClellan shrank from the decisive vigour of the plan, though he finally accepted it as the means of getting the larger reinforcements. On the 21st of October the discussion of cavalry horses was pretty well exhausted, and McClellan telegraphed Halleck that in other respects he was nearly ready to move, and inquires whether the President desired him to march on the enemy at once or to wait the arrival of the new horses. Halleck answered that the order of the 6th October remained unchanged. "If you have not been and are not now in condition to obey it, you will be able to show such want of ability. The President does not expect impossibilities, but he is very anxious that all this good weather should not be wasted in inactivity. Telegraph when you will move and on what lines you propose to march." This dispatch was plainly a notice to McClellan that he would be held responsible for the failure to obey the order of the 6th unless he could exonerate himself by showing that he could not obey it. In his final report, however, he says that he treated it as authority to decide for himself whether or not it was possible to move with safety to the army; "and this responsibility," he says, "I exercised with the more confidence in view of the strong assurance of his trust in me, as commander of that army, with which the President had seen fit to honour me during his last visit." Argument is superfluous, in view of the correspondence, to show that orders and exhortations were alike wasted.

The movement began in the last days of October, the Sixth Corps, which was in the rear, crossing the Potomac on the 2d of November. McClellan had accepted Mr. Lincoln's plan, but lack of vigour in its execution broke down the President's patience, and on the 5th of November, upon Lee's re-crossing the Blue Ridge without a battle, he ordered the general to turn over the command to Burnside, as he had declared he would do if Lee's was allowed to regain the interior line. The order was presented and obeyed on the 7th, and McClellan left the army. The fallen general brooded morbidly over it all for twenty years, and then wrote his "Own Story," a most curious piece of self-exposure, in which he unconsciously showed that the illusions which had misguided him in his campaigns were still realities to him, and that he had made no use of the authentic facts which Confederate as well as National records had brought within his reach. He had forgotten much, but he had learned nothing.

Chapter 18
Personal Relations of McClellan, Burnside and Porter

McClellan and Burnside had been classmates at West Point, and had been associated in railway employment after they had left the army, in the years immediately before the war. The intimacy which began at the Academy had not only continued, but they had kept up the demonstrative boyish friendship which made their intercourse like that of brothers. They were "Mac" and "Burn" to each other when I knew them, and although Fitz-John Porter, Hancock, Parker, Reno, and Pleasonton had all been members of the same class, the two seemed to be bosom friends in a way totally different from their intimacy with the others. Probably there was no one outside of his own family to whom McClellan spoke his secret thoughts in his letters, as he did to Burnside. The characteristic lack of system in business which was very noticeable in Burnside, made him negligent, apparently, in discriminating between official letters and private ones, and so it happens that there are a number in the official records which were never meant to reach the public. They show, however, as nothing else could, the relations which the two men sustained to each other, and reveal strong traits in the characters of both.

After Burnside had secured his first success in the Roanoke expedition, he had written to McClellan, then in the midst of his campaign of the peninsula, and this was McClellan's reply on the 21st of May, 1862:

My Dear Burn

Your dispatch and kind letter received. I have instructed Seth (Williams) to reply to the official letter, and now acknowledge the kind private note. It always does me good, in the midst of my cares and perplexities, to see your wretched old scrawling. I have terrible troubles to contend with, but have met them with a good heart, like your good old self, and have thus far struggled through successfully.... I feel very proud of Yorktown: it and Manassas will be my brightest chaplets in history, for I know that I accomplished everything in both places by pure military skill. I am very proud, and very grateful to God that he allowed me to purchase such great success at so trifling a loss of life.... The crisis cannot long be deferred. I pray for God's blessing on our arms, and rely far more on his goodness than I do on my own poor intellect. I sometimes think, now, that I can almost realize that Mahomet was sincere. When I see the hand of God guarding one so weak as myself, I can almost think myself a chosen instrument to carry out his schemes. Would that a better man had been selected.... Good-bye and God bless you, Burn. With the sincere hope that we may soon shake hands, I am, as ever,

Your sincere friend,

McClellan

When McClellan reached the James River after the seven days' battles, the first suggestion as to reinforcing him was that Burnside should bring to his aid the bulk of his little army in North Carolina. This was determined upon, and the Ninth Corps was carried by sea to Fortress Monroe. As soon as the movement was started, Burnside hastened in advance to Washington, and on returning to the fortress wrote McClellan as follows:

Old Point
July 15, 1862
My Dear Mac
I have just arrived from Washington, and have not time to get ready to go up this morning, but will to-morrow.

I've much to say to you and am very anxious to see you.... The President has ordered me to remain here for the present, and when I asked him how long, he said five or six days. I don't know what it means; but I do know, my dear Mac, that you have lots of enemies. But you must keep cool; don't allow them to provoke you into a quarrel. You must come out all right; I'll tell you all tomorrow.
Your old friend
Burn

He went up the river to Harrison's Landing and stayed a couple of days, consulting with McClellan as to the situation. He returned to Old Point Comfort on the 18th, and immediately telegraphed to the War Department for leave to go to Washington and present the results of his conference with McClellan. This was granted, and he again presented himself before the President and Secretary Stanton as the friend of McClellan. He urged the increase of McClellan's army to an extent which would make the general resume the aggressive with confidence. Halleck visited McClellan at once after assuming command as general-in-chief, but satisfied himself that the government could not furnish the thirty thousand additional troops which McClellan then demanded. This led to the decision to bring the Army of the Potomac back by water, and to unite it with Pope's army on the Rappahannock.

On this visit to Washington the President and Secretary of War had offered to Burnside himself the command of the Army of the Potomac. He had refused it, earnestly asserting his faith that McClellan was much fitter for the command than he, and trying hard to restore confidence and a mutual good understanding between his friend and the government. He was discouraged at the result, and after he returned to his command wrote a letter, every line of which shows his sadness and his disinterested friendship, for he does not mention, much less take credit to himself for, the refusal to supersede his friend.

Fort Monroe
Aug. 2, 1862
My Dear Mac
I'm laid up with a lame leg, and besides am much worried at the decision they have chosen to make in regard to your army. From the moment I reached Washington I feared it would be so, and I am of the opinion that your engineers had much to do with bringing about the determination. When the conclusion was arrived at, I was the only one who advocated your forward movement. I speak now as if a positive decision had been arrived at, which I do not know, and you of course do; my present orders indicate it. But you know what they are and all about it, so I will accept it as something that is ordered for the best. Let us continue to give our undivided support to the cause and all will be well. It looks dark sometimes, but a just God will order everything for the best. We can't expect to have it all as we wish. I'm off for my destination, and will write you a long letter from there. The troops are nearly all embarked. Good-bye. God bless you!
Your old friend
A. E. Burnside

Burnside was sent with the Ninth Corps to Falmouth on the Rappahannock. Porter's corps joined him there, and both the corps were sent forward to Warrenton to join Pope. When Pope's communication with Washington was cut, it was only through Burnside that the government could hear of him for several days, and in response to the calls for news he telegraphed copies of Porter's dispatches to him. Like McClellan's private letters, these dispatches told more of the writer's mind and heart than would willingly have been made public. Burnside's careless outspoken frankness as to his own opinions was such that he probably did not reflect what reticences others might wish to have made. Perhaps he also thought that Porter's sarcasms on Pope, coming from one who had gained much reputation in the peninsula, would be powerful in helping to reinstate McClellan.

At any rate, the dispatches were the only news from the battlefield he could send the President in answer to his anxious inquiries, and he sent them. They were the cause of Mr. Lincoln's request to McClellan, on September 1st, that he would write Porter and other friends begging them to give Pope loyal support. They were also the most damaging evidence against Porter in his subsequent court-martial.

Before the Maryland campaign began, Mr. Lincoln again urged upon Burnside the command of the army, and he again declined, warmly advocating McClellan's retention as before. His advocacy was successful, as I have already stated. The arrangement that Burnside and Sumner were to command wings of the army of at least two corps each, was made before we left Washington, and Burnside's subordinates, Hooker and Reno, were, by direction of the President, assigned to corps commands through orders from army headquarters. McClellan did not publish to the Army of the Potomac this assignment of Burnside and Sumner till the 14th of September, though it had been acted upon from the beginning of the campaign. On the evening of the same day Porter's corps joined the army at South Mountain, and before the advance was resumed on the following morning, the order was again suspended and Burnside reduced to the command of a single corps. I have already suggested Hooker's relation to this, and only note at this point the coincidence, if it was nothing more, that the first evidence of any change in McClellan's friendship toward Burnside occurs within a few hours from Porter's arrival, and in connection with a complaint made by the latter.

McClellan and Burnside had slept in the same house the night after the battle of South Mountain. Porter seems to have joined them there. During the evening McClellan dictated his orders for the movements of the 15th which were communicated to the army in the morning. That Porter should be unfriendly to Burnside was not strange, for it had by this time become known that the dispatches of August 27th to 30th were relied upon by General Pope's friends to show Porter's hostile and insubordinate spirit in that campaign. The court-martial was still impending over Porter, and he had been allowed to take the field only at McClellan's special request. Although Burnside had not dreamed of doing Porter an ill service, his transmittal of the dispatches to the President had made them available as evidence, and Porter, not unnaturally, held him responsible for part of his peril. The sort of favouritism which McClellan showed to Porter was notorious in the army. Had the position of chief of staff been given him, it would have sanctioned his personal influence without offending the self-respect of other general officers; but that position was held by General Marcy, the father-in-law of McClellan, and Porter's manifest power at headquarters consequently wore the air of discourtesy toward others. The incident I have narrated of the examination of Lee's position at Sharpsburg from the ridge near Pry's house was an example of this. It was Porter who in the presence of the commandants of the wings of the army was invited by McClellan to continue the examination when the others were sent below the crest of the hill. Governor Sprague testified before the Committee on the Conduct of the War to the notoriety of this from the beginning of the peninsular campaign and to the bad feeling it caused. General Rosecrans testified that in the winter of 1861-62, on his visit to Washington, he found that Porter was regarded as the confidential adviser of McClellan. It was matter of common fame, too well known to be questioned by anybody who served in that army. Mr. Lincoln had discussed it to some extent in his correspondence with McClellan in the month of May, and had warned the general of the mischiefs likely to ensue, even whilst authorizing provisional corps to be organized for Porter and Franklin. He had used such exceptional plainness as to say to the general that "it is looked upon as merely an effort to pamper one or two pets and to persecute and degrade their supposed rivals. The commanders of these corps are of course the three highest officers with you, but I am constantly told that you have no consultation or communication with them; that you consult and communicate with nobody but General Fitz-John Porter and perhaps General Franklin. I do not say these complaints are true or just, but at all events it is proper you should know of their existence."

McClellan's dealing with the division of the army into wings was part of the same persistent method of thwarting the purpose of the administration while ostensibly keeping the letter. It was perfectly easy to advance from South Mountain upon Sharpsburg, keeping Sumner's and Burnside's commands intact. The intermingling of them was unnecessary at the beginning, and was mischievous during the battle of Antietam. No military reason can be given for it, and the history of the whole year makes it plain that the reasons were personal.

The offer of the command of the army to Burnside, though refused, was a sufficiently plain designation of McClellan's successor in case he should be relieved or be disabled. It needed a more magnanimous nature than McClellan's proved to be, to bear the obligation of Burnside's powerful friendship in securing for him again the field command of the army. When he was in personal contact with Burnside, the transparent sincerity of the latter's friendship always brought McClellan to his better self, and to the eye of an observer they were as cordially intimate as they had ever been. Yet unfriendly things which had been done officially could not easily be undone, and the friendship was maintained by the subordinate condoning the sins against it. Hooker was allowed to separate himself from Burnside's command on the morning of the 15th, against the protest of his commander; the order announcing the assignment of the wing command was suspended and was never renewed, though McClellan afterward gave Burnside temporary command of several corps when detached from the rest of the army.

Burnside spent several hours with his chief on Monday morning (15th), and was disturbed and grieved at the course things had taken. It is possible that his pre-occupation of mind made him neglect the prompt issue of orders for moving the Ninth Corps, though I know nothing definite as to this. Porter's corps was to follow us through Fox's Gap, and when his head of column came up the mountain at noon, we certainly were not in motion. My own division was the rear one of the column that day, by way of change, as I had had the advance all the way from Washington. General Porter reported at McClellan's headquarters that the movement of his troops was obstructed by Burnside's, and got at his own special request an order to push by them. The written order Porter preserved, and put upon it an endorsement adding to what it contains the accusation that "Burnside's corps was not moving three hours after the hour designated for him." No doubt there was many a delay in that campaign in divers corps. The significant thing in this one was the pains taken to "make a record" of it against Burnside, and the inclusion in this of unofficial matter by means of the endorsement.

On the 16th another vexatious incident of a similar character occurred. After McClellan's reconnoitring on our left, he orally directed that the divisions of the Ninth Corps should be moved to positions designated by members of his staff. When Burnside had taken his position on a hill-top from which the positions could be seen and the movement accurately directed, another staff officer from McClellan came and requested that the movement be delayed for further consideration by the commanding general. It was this that occasioned a halt and our subsequent march in the dusk of evening, as has been narrated in its place. That evening the following note was written at McClellan's headquarters, but it was not delivered to Burnside till the next day, the day of the battle:

> Headquarters
> Army Of The Potomac
> September 16, 1862.
> Major-General Burnside
> Commanding Ninth Corps, etc.
> *General*
> The General commanding has learned that although your corps was ordered to be in a designated position at 12 M. to-day, at or near sunset only one division and four batteries had reached the ground intended for your troops. The general has also been advised that there was a delay of some four hours in the movement of your command yesterday. I am instructed to call upon you for explanations of these failures on your part to comply with the orders given you, and to add, in view of the im-

portant military operations now at hand, the commanding general cannot lightly regard such marked departure from the tenor of his instructions.

I am, general, very respectfully, your obedient servant,
_____,
Lieutenant-Colonel, Aide-de-camp
Act'g Ass't Adj't. Gen'l.

To this missive Burnside dictated the following answer on the field during the battle:

Headquarters
September 17, 1862.
Brig. Gen. S. Williams
Assistant Adjutant-General.
General

Your dispatch of yesterday this moment received. General Burnside directs me to say that immediately upon the receipt of the order of the general commanding, which was after twelve o'clock, he ordered his corps to be in readiness to march, and instead of having Captain Duane post the divisions in detail, and at the suggestion of Captain Duane, he sent three aides to ascertain the position of each of the three divisions, that they might post them. These aides returned shortly before three o'clock, and they immediately proceeded to post the three columns. The general then went on an eminence above these positions to get a good view of them, and whilst there, during the progress of the movement of his corps, an aide from General McClellan came to him and said that General McClellan was not sure that the proper position had been indicated, and advised him not to hasten the movement until the aide had communicated with the general commanding. He (General Burnside) at once went to General McClellan's headquarters to inform him that he had seen large bodies of the enemy moving off to the right. Not finding the general commanding, General Burnside returned to his command, and the movement was resumed and continued as rapidly as possible. General Burnside directs me to say that he is sorry to have received so severe a rebuke from the general commanding, and particularly sorry that the general commanding feels that his instructions have not been obeyed; but nothing can occur to prevent the general from continuing his hearty co-operation to the best of his ability in any movement the general commanding may direct.

I have the honour to be, general, very respectfully, your obedient servant,
Lewis Richmond
Assistant Adjutant-General

The answer was of course conclusive, but it leaves the difficult problem, how came the reprimand to be written which General McClellan could not have dictated, as the interruption of Burnside's movement was caused by a message from himself? The blank for the name of a staff officer who was to sign it, and the indication of his rank and position point to Lieutenant-Colonel James A. Hardie as the one for whom it was prepared, but Colonel Hardie must have demurred to signing it, since Colonel Richmond's answer implies that General Seth Williams's name was finally attached. All of us who knew General Williams and his methods of doing business will be slow to believe that he volunteered a paper of that kind. He afterward served on Burnside's own staff and had his confidence. The responsibility must fall upon General Marcy, the chief of staff, and most of the officers of that army will be likely to conclude that he also would act only by the direction of McClellan or of some one whom he regarded as having decisive authority to speak for him in his absence.

I have already referred to an error contained in General Porter's report of the battle of Antietam, where he says that "Morell's division in reporting to General Burnside relieved his corps, which was at once recalled from its position in front of Antietam bridge." I mention it again only to say that since this was not only contrary to the fact, but is unsupported by the records, to accept it and to embody it in his official report certainly indicates no friendly disposition toward Burnside. To that extent it supports any other circumstances which point to Porter as the hostile influence which becomes so manifest at McClellan's headquarters after the 14th of September. I know by many expressions uttered by Burnside during those days and afterward, that though he was deeply grieved at some things which had occurred, he did not waver in his loyal friendship to McClellan. He uttered no unkind word in regard to him personally, either then or ever in my hearing. He sometimes spoke of what he believed to be mischievous influences about McClellan and which he thought were too powerful with him, but was earnest and consistent in wishing for him the permanent command of that army till success should give a glorious end to the war. It was after the irritating incidents I have narrated that the visit to McClellan to dine with him occurred, and I saw them frequently together till I left the army on the 5th of October. Their manner toward each other was more than cordial, it was affectionately intimate. Burnside never mentioned to me, although I was next him in command, the reprimand which is copied above. His real unwillingness to supersede McClellan, even when the final order came in November, is abundantly attested. McClellan only by degrees gave outward evidence of the souring of his own feelings toward Burnside, but his private letters show that the process began with the battle of South Mountain. By the time that he wrote his final report in the latter part of 1863 it had advanced far enough to warp his memory of the campaign and to make him try to transfer to Burnside the responsibility for some of his mishaps. When his "Own Story" was written, the process was complete, and no kindly remembrance dictated a word which could give any indication of the friendship that had died.

Those who are not familiar with the customs of military service might see little significance in the fact that the fault-finding with Burnside was put in the form of official communications which thus became part of the permanent documentary history of the war. To military men, however, it would be almost conclusive proof of a settled hostility to him, formally calling his military character in question in a way to make it tell against him for ulterior purposes. Nothing is more common in an active campaign than for a commanding officer to send messages hurrying the movement of a part of his army. These are usually oral, and even when delays are complained of, the commander, in the interests of cordial cooperation and cheerful alacrity, awaits a full opportunity for personal explanation from his immediate subordinates before administering a reprimand. It goes without saying that where intimate friendship exists, still more delicate consideration is used. To send such a letter as that of September 16th, and in the course of such deliberate movements as were McClellan's during those days, would be scarcely conceivable unless there had been a formal breach of personal relations, and it was equivalent to notice that they were henceforth to deal at arm's-length only.

McClellan's "Own Story" shows that in regard to the alleged delay on the morning of the 15th, he had a personal explanation from Burnside. Yet in the night of the 16th the same querulous inquiry was repeated as if it had not been answered, with the addition of the new complaint of a delay on the 16th which was caused by McClellan's personal request, and the whole accompanied by so formal a reprimand that the ordinary reply to it would have been a demand for a court of inquiry. The occurrence was unexampled in that campaign and stands entirely alone, although McClellan's memoirs show that he alleged delays in other cases, notably in Hooker's march that same afternoon to attack the enemy, of which no recorded notice was taken. Considering the personal relations of the men before that time, and as I myself witnessed them from day to day afterward, it is simply incredible that McClellan dictated the letters which went from his headquarters.

Before ending the discussion of matters personal to these officers I will say a few words regarding Burnside's appearance and bearing in the field. He was always a striking figure, and had a dashing way with him which incited enthusiasm among his soldiers. Without seeming to care for his costume, or even whilst affecting a little carelessness, there was apt to be something picturesque about him. He had a hearty and jovial manner, a good-humoured cordiality toward everybody, that beamed in his face as he rode through the camps or along the lines. When not on parade, he often discarded his uniform coat, wearing a light undress jacket, with no indication of his rank except the yellow silk sash about his waist which showed that he was a general officer. On one occasion when I accompanied him in a change of position, we passed the Ninth Corps column in march, and it was interesting to see how he was greeted by the troops which had been with him in his North Carolina campaign. He wore that day a "Norfolk jacket," a brown knit roundabout, fitting close to his person; his hat was the stiff broad-rimmed, high-crowned regulation hat, worn rather rakishly, with gold cord, acorn-tipped; his pistol-belt was a loose one, allowing the holster to hang on his hip instead of being buckled tight about the waist; his boots were the high cavalry boots reaching to the knee; his large buckskin gauntlets covered his forearm; he rode a large bony horse, bob-tailed, with a wall-eye which gave him a vicious look, and suited well the brigandish air of his rider's whole appearance. Burnside's flashing eyes, his beard trimmed to the "Burnside cut" with the moustache running into the side whiskers whilst the square, clean-shaven chin and jaws gave a tone of decision and force to his features, made up a picture that at once arrested the eye. As we went along the roadside at a fast trot, his high-stepping horse seemed to be keeping his white eye on the lookout for a chance to lash out at somebody. The men evidently enjoyed the scene, cheering him loudly. I was particularly amused with one group of soldiers at rest by their stacked muskets. They sat upon their haunches, and clapped their hands as he passed, exclaiming and laughing, "Just see the old fellow! just look at him!" Burnside laughed at their fun as jollily as they did themselves, and took no offence at the free-and-easy way in which they showed their liking for him. There was no affectation in all this, but an honest enjoyment in following his own whim in style and in accoutrement. His sincere earnestness in the cause for which he was fighting was apparent to all who met him, and no one in his presence could question the single-hearted honesty and unselfishness of the man. His bearing under fire was good, and his personal courage beyond question. He shrank from responsibility with sincere modesty, because he questioned his own capacity to deal with affairs of great magnitude. He was not only not ambitious to command a great army, but he honestly sought to put it aside when it was thrust upon him, and accepted it at last from a sense of obligation to the administration which had nominated him to it in spite of his repeated disclaimers. It carafe to him finally, without consulting him, as a military order he could not disobey without causing a most awkward dead-lock in the campaign.

Chapter 19
Return to West Virginia

In war it is the unexpected that happens. On the 4th of October my permanent connection with the Army of the Potomac seemed assured. I was in command of the Ninth Corps, encamped in Pleasant Valley, awaiting the renewal of active operations. My promotion to the rank of Major-General had been recommended by McClellan and Burnside, with the assurance that the permanent command of the corps would be added. On that evening an order came from Washington directing me to return to the Kanawha valley, from which our troops had been driven. I was to report in person at Washington immediately, and would there get detailed directions. The order was as much a surprise to my immediate superiors as it was to me, and apparently as little welcome. We all recognized the necessity of sending some one to the Kanawha who knew the country, and the reasonableness, therefore, of assigning the duty to me. McClellan and Burnside both promised that when matters should be restored to a good footing in West Virginia they would co-operate in an effort to bring me back, and as this was coupled with a strong request to the War Department that my promotion should be made immediate, acquiesced with reasonably good grace.

Going to Washington on the 5th, I received my orders and instructions from Halleck, the General-in-Chief. They were based upon the events which had occurred in the Kanawha valley since I left it in August. The information got by General Stuart from Pope's captured quartermaster had led to a careful examination of the letter-books captured at the same time, and Lee thus learned that I had left 5000 men, under Colonel Lightburn, to garrison the posts about Gauley Bridge. The Confederate forces were therefore greater than ours in that region, and General Loring, who was in command, was ordered to make at once a vigorous aggressive campaign against Lightburn, to "clear the valley of the Kanawha and operate northwardly to a junction" with the army of Lee in the Shenandoah valley. Loring marched, on the 6th of September, with a column which he reported about 5000 strong, expecting to add to it by organizing recruits and militia as Floyd had done in the previous year. His line of operations was by way of Princeton, Flat-top Mountain and Raleigh C. H. to Fayette C. H. His forces do not seem to have been noticeably increased by recruiting till ours had retreated out of the valley.

Lightburn's advanced positions were two—a brigade under Colonel Siber of the Thirty-seventh Ohio being at Raleigh C. H. and another under Colonel Gilbert of the Forty-fourth Ohio, near the Hawk's Nest, and at Alderson's on the Lewisburg road. A small post was kept up at Summersville and one at Gauley Bridge, where Lightburn had his headquarters, and some detachments guarded trains and steamboats in the lower valley. Gauley Bridge was, as in the preceding year, the central point, and though it was necessary to guard both the Lewisburg and the Raleigh roads on the opposite sides of the New River gorge, a concentration on the line the enemy should take was the plain rule of action when the opposing armies were about equal. Or, by concentrating at Gauley Bridge, my experience had proved that we could hold at bay three or four times our numbers. In either case, fighting in detail was to be avoided, and rapid concentration under one leader to be effected.

On the approach of the enemy Siber was withdrawn from Raleigh C. H. to Fayette, and Gilbert to Tompkins farm, three miles from Gauley Bridge, but the brigades were not united. On the 10th of September Loring attacked Siber at Fayette, in the entrenchments made by Scammon in the winter. Siber repulsed the efforts of Loring to drive him out of his position, and held it during the day. Three companies of the Fourth Virginia under Captain Vance, and a squad of horse were sent by Lightburn from Gauley Bridge to Siber's assistance, but the latter, being without definite orders and thinking he could not hold the position another day, retreated in the night, setting fire to a large accumulation of stores and abandoning part of his wagons. He halted on the ridge of Cotton Hill, covering the road to Gauley Bridge, and was there joined by five companies of the Forty-seventh Ohio, also sent to his assistance by Lightburn. Loring followed and made a partial attack, which was met by the rear-guard under Captain Vance and repulsed, whilst Siber's principal column marched on to Montgomery's ferry on the Kanawha.

Meanwhile Lightburn had called in Gilbert's force to Gauley Bridge during the night of the both, and placed them opposite the ferry connecting with Siber, which was just below Kanawha Falls and in the lower part of the Gauley Bridge camp. On Siber's appearance at the ferry, Lightburn seems to have despaired of having time to get him over, and directed him to march down the left bank of the river, burning the sheds full of stores which were on that side of the stream. When Captain Vance with the rear-guard reached the ferry, the buildings were blazing on both sides of the narrow pass under the bluff, and his men ran the gantlet of fire, protecting their heads with extra blankets which they found scattered near the stores. Vance easily held the enemy at bay at Armstrong's Creek, and Siber marched his column, next morning, to Brownstown, some twenty-five miles below Kanawha Falls, where steamboats met him and ferried him over to Camp Piatt. There he rejoined Lightburn.

Gilbert's artillery was put in position on the right bank at Montgomery's Ferry, and checked the head of Loring's column when it approached the Kanawha in pursuit of Siber. Lightburn had ordered the detachment in post at Summersville to join him at Gauley, and Colonel Elliot of the Forty-seventh Ohio, who commanded it, marched down the Gauley with his ten companies (parts of three regiments) and a small wagon train. He approached Gauley Bridge on the 11th, but Lightburn had not waited for him, and the enemy were in possession. Elliot burned his wagons and took to the hills with his men, cutting across the angle between the Gauley and the Kanawha and joining Gilbert's column near Cannelton. A smaller detachment, only a little way up the Gauley, was also left to its fate in the precipitate retreat, and it also took to the hills and woods and succeeded in evading the enemy. It was about ten o'clock in the morning when Loring's head of column approached the Kanawha and drew the fire of Gilbert's guns. After about an hour's cannonade across the river, Lightburn gave the order to retreat down the right bank, after burning the stores and blowing up the magazine at Gauley Bridge. Loring found men to swim across the river and extinguish the fires kindled on the ferry-boats, which were soon put in use to ferry Echols's brigade across. This followed Lightburn down the right bank, whilst Loring himself, with Williams's and Wharton's brigades, marched after Siber down the left. The over-hanging cliffs and hills echoed with the cannonade, and the skirmishers exchanged rifle-shots across the rapid stream; but few casualties occurred, and after Elliot joined the column, it marched with little interruption to Camp Piatt, thirteen miles from Charleston, where Siber met them, and the steamboats he had used passed down the river to the Ohio.

Siber's brigade continued its retreat rapidly to Charleston, passed through the town and crossed the Elk River. Gilbert's brigade also retired, but in better order, and it kept up a skirmish with the advance-guard of Echols's column which was following them. When Gilbert reached the outskirts of Charleston, he checked the advance of the enemy long enough to enable the quartermasters at the post to move their trains across the Elk; but the haste of the evacuation was so great that the stores in depot there were not removed, and were burned to prevent their falling into the enemy's hands. Gilbert retired across the Elk, and the suspension bridge was destroyed. Loring's artillery made a dash for a hill on the left bank of the Kanawha, which commanded the new position taken up by Lightburn's troops, and the Confederate battery soon opened an enfilade fire across the river, taking the line of breastworks along the Elk in flank and in reverse. The trains and the stragglers started in direst confusion on the road to Ravenswood on the Ohio, which offered a line of retreat not subject to the enemy's fire. Siber's brigade followed, Gilbert's continued to bring up the rear. The road down the Kanawha was abandoned because it was in range of artillery from the opposite side of the river throughout its whole course down the valley. The road to Ripley and Ravenswood was therefore taken, and the flying troops were met at those towns on the Ohio by steamboats which conveyed part of them to Point Pleasant at the mouth of the Kanawha, where the whole command was concentrated in the course of a few days. Siber's loss was 16 killed, 87 wounded, and over 100 missing. Gilbert reported 9 men killed and 8 wounded, with about 75 missing; but as the enemy do not enumerate any captured prisoners in their reports except a lieutenant and 10 men, it is evident that the missing were mostly men who outran the others. Loring's losses as reported by his surgeon were 18 killed and 89 wounded. The enemy claim to have captured large numbers of wagons, horses, mules, and stores of all kinds which Loring estimated at a million dollars' worth, besides all that were burned.

It was a panicky retreat after the hot little fight by Siber's brigade at Fayette C. H., and it is not worth while to apply to it any military criticism, further than to say that either of the brigades entrenched at Gauley Bridge could have laughed at Loring. The river would have been impassable, for all the ferry-boats were in the keeping of our men on the right bank, and Loring would not dare pass down the valley leaving a fortified post on the line of communications by which he must return. The topography of the wild mountain region was such that an army could only pass from the lower Kanawha to the headwaters of the James River by the road Loring had used in his advance, or by that leading through the post of Gauley Bridge to Lewisburg and beyond. The Confederate War Department seem to have thought that their forces might have passed from Charleston to the Ohio, thence to Parkersburg, and turning east from this town, have made their way to Beverly and to the Valley of Virginia by the route Garnett had used in the previous year. They would have found, however, as Loring told them, that it would have been easy for the National forces to overwhelm them with numbers while they were making so long and so difficult a march in a vast region most of which was a wilderness.

Lightburn's position had been made more embarrassing by the fact that a cavalry raid under Brigadier-General Jenkins was passing around his left flank while Loring came upon him in front. Jenkins with a light column of horse moved from Lewisburg by way of the Wilderness Road to north-western Virginia, captured posts and destroyed stores at Weston, Buckhannon, and Roane C. H., and made a circuit to the lower Kanawha, rejoining Loring after Lightburn's retreat. Little real mischief was done by this raid, but it added to the confusion, and helped to disturb the self-possession of the commanding officer. In this way it was one of the causes of the precipitate retreat.

Several circumstances combined to make Lightburn's disaster embarrassing to the government. West Virginia had not been connected with any military department after Pope's command had been broken up. McClellan's authority did not extend beyond his own army and its theatre of operations. Halleck could hardly take personal charge of the affairs of remote districts. Thus the Kanawha valley had dropped out of the usual system and was an omitted case. The embarrassment was increased by the fact that Buell was retreating out of Tennessee before Bragg, Morgan had evacuated Cumberland Gap and was making a painful and hazardous retreat to the Ohio, and the Confederate forces under Kirby Smith were moving directly upon Cincinnati. Lightburn's mishap, therefore, was only the northern extremity of a line of defeats extending through the whole length of the Ohio valley from Parkersburg to Louisville. The governors of West Virginia and Ohio were naturally alarmed at the events in the Kanawha valley, and were earnest in their calls upon the War Department for troops to drive Loring back beyond the mountains and for an officer to command them who knew something of the country.

Halleck seems to have been puzzled at the condition of things, not having realized that Pope's retirement had left West Virginia "in the air." It took a week, apparently, to get satisfactory details of the actual situation, and on the 19th of September the first important step was taken by annexing the region to the Department of the Ohio, then commanded by Major-General Horatio G. Wright, whose headquarters were at Cincinnati. Wright was directed to provide for the recovery of lost ground in West Virginia as rapidly as possible, but the campaign in Kentucky was the more important and urgent, so that no troops could be spared for secondary operations until the Confederates had ceased to threaten Cincinnati and Louisville.

On the 1st of October Halleck again called General Wright's attention to the need of doing something for West Virginia. Governor Peirpoint, of that State, represented the Confederates under Loring as about 10,000 in number, and this reflected the opinion which Lightburn had formed during his retreat. It became the basis of calculation in the campaign which followed, though it greatly exaggerated Loring's force. Three days later Brigadier-General George W. Morgan was known to have reached the Ohio River with the division he had brought from Cumberland Gap, and General Halleck outlined a plan of action. He ordered Morgan's division to be sent to Gallipolis to take part in the advance into the Kanawha valley, where some new Ohio regiments were also to join them. He at the same time called me to Washington to receive instructions under which I was to take command of the whole force operating on the Kanawha line. Brigadier-General Milroy had already (September 25th) been ordered to proceed thither with his brigade, which was in Washington and was part of Banks's forces garrisoning the capital. He was moved through Pennsylvania to Wheeling by rail, and thence down the Ohio River to Point Pleasant at the mouth of the Kanawha.

My order to leave the Army of the Potomac reached me on Saturday evening. Much business had to be closed up before I could properly turn over the command of the Ninth Corps, but I was able to complete it and make the journey to Washington so as to report to General Halleck on Monday morning. He received me very kindly, and explained the necessity they were under to send some one to the Kanawha valley who knew the country. He was complimentary as to my former service there, and said my return to that region would meet the earnest wishes of the governors of West Virginia and Ohio, as well as the judgment of the War Department and of himself. To compensate for separating me from the command of the Ninth Corps, it had been decided to make my promotion at once and to put the whole of West Virginia under my command as a territorial district. He inquired into some details of the topography of the Kanawha valley and of my experience there, and concluded by saying that reinforcements would be sent to make the column I should lead in person stronger than the 10,000 attributed to Loring. My task would then be to drive back the enemy beyond the mountains. When that was accomplished, part of the troops would probably be withdrawn. The actual position of Milroy's brigade was not definitely known, and Governor Peirpoint of West Virginia had asked to have it sent to Clarksburg. This gave me the opportunity to urge that my own Kanawha division be detached from the Ninth Corps and sent back to Clarksburg, where with Milroy they would make a force strong enough to take care of that part of the State and to make a co-operative movement toward Gauley Bridge. This also was granted, and immediate promotion was given to Colonel Crook so that he might command the division, and a promise was made to do the like for Colonel Scammon, who would then be available for the command of the division still under Lightburn, whose retreat was strongly condemned as precipitate. No soldier could object to an arrangement so satisfactory as this, and though I still preferred to remain with the Army of the Potomac, I could only accept the new duty with sincere thanks for the consideration shown me. The General-in-Chief accompanied me to the room of the Secretary of War, and Mr. Stanton added to my sense of obligation by warm expressions of personal good-will. His manner was so different from the brusque one commonly attributed to him that I have nothing but pleasant remembrances of my relations to him, both then and later. My own appointment as major-general was handed me by him, the usual promotions of my personal staff were also made, and directions were given for the immediate appointment of Crook to be brigadier.

I called to pay my respects to the President, but he was in Cabinet meeting and could not be seen. I had a short but warmly friendly visit with Mr. Chase later in the day, and was ready to leave town for my new post of duty by the evening train. The Secretary of War directed me to visit Wheeling and Columbus on my way, and then to report to General Wright at Cincinnati before going to the Kanawha valley. This was in fact the quickest way to reach the mouth of the Kanawha River, for the fall rains had not yet come to make the Ohio navigable, and from Columbus to Cincinnati, and thence by the Marietta Railway eastward, was, as the railway routes then ran, the best method of joining my command. The Baltimore and Ohio Railroad was interrupted between Harper's Ferry and Hancock (about fifty miles) by the Confederate occupation of that part of Virginia. General Crook was ordered to march the division from its camp in Pleasant Valley to Hancock, where trains on the western division of the railway would meet him and transport the troops to Clarksburg. For myself and staff, we took the uninterrupted railway line from Washington to Pittsburg, and thence to Wheeling, where we arrived on the evening of October 8th. The 9th was given to consultation with Governor Peirpoint and to communication with such military officers as were within reach. We reached Columbus on the both, when I had a similar consultation with Governor Tod and his military staff in regard to new regiments available for my use. Leaving Columbus in the afternoon, we arrived at Cincinnati late the same night, and on Saturday, the 11th, I reported to General Wright.

He was an officer of the engineer corps of the regular army, a man of fine acquirements and of a serious and earnest character, whose military service throughout the war was marked by solidity and modesty. If there seemed at first a little *hauteur* in his manner, one soon saw that it was a natural reserve free from arrogance. The sort of confusion in which everything was, is indicated by the fact that he knew nothing of my whereabouts when informed from Washington that I would be ordered to the Kanawha, and on the same day (6th October) addressed a dispatch to me at Point Pleasant whilst I was receiving instructions from General Halleck in Washington. Our personal consultation established a thoroughly good understanding at once, and as long as I remained under his orders, I found him thoroughly considerate of my wishes and appreciative of my suggestions and of the conduct of my own part of the work to be done.

Morgan's division, after reaching the Ohio River, had been moved to Portland on the Marietta Railroad, the nearest point to Gallipolis, which was twenty-five miles away and nearly opposite the mouth of the Great Kanawha. His retreat had been through a sparsely settled country, much of which was a wilderness, rugged and broken in the extreme. His wagons had broken down, his teams were used up, his soldiers were worn out, ragged, and barefoot. Many arms and accoutrements had been lost, and the command was imperatively in need of complete refitting and a little rest. The men had been largely recruited in East Tennessee and Kentucky, and were unwilling to serve in any other theatre of war. The Tennesseans, indeed, were reported to be mutinous at the news that they were to be sent to the Kanawha valley. General Wright issued orders for the refitting of the command, and promised such delay and rest as might be found practicable. He detached three regiments to serve in Kentucky, and directed their place to be made good by three new Ohio regiments then organizing. The division was permitted to remain at Portland till imperatively needed for my movement.

There were no trains running on the railroad on Sunday, and Monday morning, the 13th October, was the earliest possible start on the remainder of my journey. I left Cincinnati at that time, and with my personal staff reached Portland in the afternoon. Morgan's division was found to be in quite as bad condition as had been reported, but he was in daily expectation of the new equipments and clothing, as well as wagons for his baggage-train and fresh horses for his artillery. It was stated also that a paymaster had been ordered to join the division, with funds to pay part at least of the large arrears of pay due to the men. This looked hopeful, but still implied some further delay. Uneasy to learn the actual condition of affairs with Lightburn's command, I determined to reach Gallipolis the same night. Our horses had been left behind, and being thus dismounted, we took passage in a four-horse hack, a square wagon on springs, enclosed with rubber-cloth curtains. Night fell soon after we began our journey, and as we were pushing on in the dark, the driver blundered and upset us off the end of a little sluiceway bridge into a mud-hole. He managed to jump from his seat and hold his team, but there was no help for us who were buttoned in. The mud was soft and deep, and as the wagon settled on its side, we were tumbled in a promiscuous heap into the ooze and slime, which completely covered us. We were not long in climbing out, and seeing lights in a farm-house, made our way to it. As we came into the light of the lamps and of a brisk fire burning on the open hearth, we were certainly as sorry a military spectacle as could be imagined. We were most kindly received, the men taking lanterns and going to our driver's help, whilst we stood before the fire, and scraped the thick mud from our uniforms with chips from the farmer's wood yard, making rather boisterous sport of our mishap. Before the wagon had been righted and partly cleaned, we had scraped and sponged each other off and were ready to go on. We noticed, however, that the room had filled with men, women, and children from the neighbourhood, who stood bashfully back in the shadows, and who modestly explained that they had heard there was a "live general" there, and as they had never seen one, they had "come over." They must have formed some amusing ideas of military personages, and we found at least as much sport in being the menagerie as they did in visiting it. Our mishap made us wait for the moon, which rose in an hour or so, and we then took leave of our entertainers and our audience and drove on, with no desire, however, to repeat the performance. We made some ten miles more of the road, but found it so rough, and our progress so slow, that we were glad to find quarters for the rest of the night, finishing the journey in the morning.

On reaching my field of duty, my first task was to inspect the forces at Point Pleasant, and learn what was necessary to make a forward movement as soon as Morgan's troops should reach me. General Wright had originally expected that inclusive of

Milroy's and Morgan's troops, I should find at the mouth of the Kanawha, on arriving there, some 20,000 men. In fact, however, Lightburn's diminished command had only been reinforced by three new Ohio regiments (the Eighty-ninth, Ninety-first, and Ninety-second) and a new one from West Virginia (the Thirteenth), and with these his strength was less than 7300, officers and men, showing that his original command was sadly reduced by straggling and desertion during his retreat. The new regiments were made up of good material, but as they were raw recruits, their usefulness must for some time be greatly limited.

Two regiments of infantry and a squadron of cavalry with a howitzer battery were at Guyandotte, under Colonel Jonathan Cranor of the Fortieth Ohio, and the Fifth West Virginia was at Ceredo near the mouth of the Big Sandy River. They had been stationed at these points to protect the navigation of the Ohio and to repel the efforts of the Confederate Cavalry General Jenkins to "raid" that region in which was his old home. They formed, a little later, the Third Brigade of the Kanawha division under Crook.

I found General Milroy in command as the ranking officer present, and he had sent Cranor's command down the river. When Governor Peirpoint learned that Milroy's brigade had passed Wheeling on his way to the Kanawha, he applied urgently to General Wright to send him, instead, from Parkersburg by rail to Clarksburg to form the nucleus of a column to move southward from that point upon the rear of Loring's forces. Wright assented, for both he and Halleck accepted the plan of converging columns from Clarksburg and Point Pleasant, and regarded that from the former place as the more important. If directions were sent to Milroy to this effect, they seem to have miscarried. Besides his original brigade, some new Indiana regiments were ordered to report to him. He had, with characteristic lack of reflection and without authority, furloughed the Fifth West Virginia regiment in mass and sent the men home. I gave him a new one in place of this, ordered him to reassemble the other as soon as possible, and to march at once to Parkersburg, proceeding thence to Clarksburg by rail. The new troops added to his command enabled him to organize them into a division of two brigades, and still other regiments were added to him later. Milroy was a picturesque character, with some excellent qualities. A tall man, with trenchant features, bright eyes, a great shock of grey hair standing out from his head, he was a marked personal figure. He was brave, but his bravery was of the excitable kind that made him unbalanced and nearly wild on the battle-field. His impulsiveness made him erratic in all performances of duty, and negligent of the system without which the business of an army cannot go on. This was shown in his furlough of a regiment whilst *en route* to reinforce Lightburn, who was supposed to be in desperate straits. It is also seen in the absence of Official Records of the organization of his command at this time, so that we cannot tell what regiments constituted it when his division was assembled at Clarksburg. He is described, in the second Battle of Bull Run, as crazily careering over the field, shouting advice to other officers instead of gathering and leading his own command, which he said was routed and scattered. Under the immediate control of a firm and steady hand he could do good service, but was wholly unfit for independent responsibility. His demonstrative manner, his boiling patriotism, and his political zeal gave him prominence and made him a favourite with the influential war-governor of Indiana, Oliver P. Morton, who pushed his military advancement.

The Kanawha division left the Army of the Potomac on the 8th of October and reached Hancock on the 10th. There it crossed the track of a raid of the Confederate cavalry into Pennsylvania, under Stuart. By McClellan's order one brigade was sent to McConnelsville to intercept the enemy, and the other was halted. By the 13th Crook had been allowed to concentrate the division at Hancock again, but was kept waiting for orders, so that he was not able to report to me his arrival at Clarksburg till the 20th. Colonel Scammon was on a short leave of absence during this march, and was promoted. He reported to me in person in his new rank of brigadier a little later. The brigades of the Kanawha division were commanded by the senior colonels present.

The increase of troops in the district made immediate need of transportation and munitions and supplies of all kinds. The Kanawha division had not been allowed to bring away with it its admirably equipped supply train, but its energetic quartermaster, Captain Fitch, came with the troops, and I immediately made him chief quartermaster of the district. Milroy's division had no wagons, neither had Morgan's. The fall rains had not yet raised the rivers, and only boats of lightest draught could move on the Ohio, whilst navigation on the Kanawha was wholly suspended. Four hundred wagons and two thousand mules were estimated as necessary to supply two moving columns of ten thousand men each, in addition to such trains as were still available in the district. Only one hundred wagons could be promised from the depot at Cincinnati, none of which reached me before the enemy was driven out of the Kanawha valley. I was authorized to contract for one hundred more to be built at Wheeling, where, however, the shops could only construct thirty-five per week, and these began to reach the troops only after the 1st of November. We hoped for rains which would give us navigation in the Kanawha in spite of the suffering which wet weather at that season must produce, and I ordered wagons and teams to be hired from the country people as far as this could be done. Similar delays and trouble occurred in procuring advance stores and equipments. Part of Morgan's men were delayed at the last moment by their new knapsacks coming to them without the straps which fasten them to the shoulders. General Wright blamed the depot officers for this, and took from me and my subordinates all responsibility for the delays; but the incidents make an instructive lesson in the difficulty of suddenly organizing a new and strong military column in a region distant from large depots of supply. It also shows the endless cost and mischief that may result from an ill-advised retreat and destruction of property at such posts as Gauley Bridge and Charleston. To put the local quartermasters at Gallipolis and other towns on the Ohio side of the river under my command, General Wright enlarged the boundaries of my district so as to include the line of Ohio counties bordering on the river.

On visiting Lightburn's command at Point Pleasant, I ordered a brigade to be sent forward next day (15th) to Ten-mile Creek, repairing the road and bridges, whilst a scouting party of experienced men started out at once to penetrate the country by circuitous ways and to collect information. In two or three days bits of news began to arrive, with rumours that Loring was retreating. The truth was that he in fact withdrew his infantry, leaving Jenkins with the cavalry and irregular forces to hold the valley for a time, and then to make a circuit northward by way of Bulltown, Sutton, etc., gaining the Beverly turnpike near the mountains and rejoining the infantry, which would march to join Lee by roads intersecting that highway at Monterey. Such at least was the purpose Loring communicated to the Confederate War Department; but he was not allowed to attempt it. His instructions had been to march his whole command by the route Jenkins was taking and at least to hold the valley stubbornly as far as Charleston. On receipt of the news that he was retreating, orders were sent him to turn over the command to Brigadier-General John Echols, the next in rank, and to report in person at Richmond. Echols was ordered immediately to resume the positions which had been abandoned, and did so as rapidly as possible. Loring had in fact begun his retreat on the 11th, three days before I reached Gallipolis, but the first information of it was got after the scouting had been begun which is mentioned above. By the 18th I was able to give General Wright confirmation of the news and a correct outline of Loring's plan, though we had not then learned that Echols was marching back to Charleston. We heard of his return two or three days later. As evidence of the rapidity with which information reached the enemy, it is noteworthy that Lee knew my command had left the Army of the Potomac for West Virginia on the 11th October, three days after Crook marched from camp in Pleasant Valley. He reported to Richmond that four brigades had gone to that region, which was accurate as to the number, though only half right as to identification of the brigades. On the 13th he sent further information that I had been promoted and assigned to command the district.

By the 20th there had been a slight rise in the Kanawha River, so that it was possible to use small steamboats to carry supplies for the troops, and Lightburn was ordered to advance his whole division to Red House, twenty-five miles, and to remove obstructions to navigation which had been planted there. One brigade of Morgan's division was in condition to move, and it was ordered from Portland to Gallipolis. The rest were to follow at the earliest possible moment. The discontent of the East Tennessee regiments had not been lessened by the knowledge they had that powerful political influences were at work to second their desire to be moved back into the neighbourhood of their home. On the 10th of October a protest against their being sent into West Virginia was made by Horace Maynard, the loyal representative of East Tennessee in Congress, a man of marked character and ability and deservedly very influential with the government. Maynard addressed Halleck a second time on the subject on the 22d, and on the 29th Andrew Johnson, then military governor of Tennessee, wrote to President Lincoln for the same purpose. It hardly need be said that the preparation of those regiments would proceed slowly, pending such negotiations. Their distant homes and families were at the mercy of the enemy, and it seemed to them intolerable that their faces should be turned in any other direction. I suggested an exchange for new Ohio regiments, but as these were not yet filled up, it could not be done. General Wright assured them that they should be sent to Kentucky as soon as we were again in possession of West Virginia. Most of these regiments came under my command again later in the war, and I became warmly attached to them. Their drill and discipline were always lax, but their courage and devotion to the national cause could not be excelled.

It was not till the 23d that any of Morgan's men really entered into the forward movement in the valley. On that day the brigade of Colonel John F. DeCourcey (Sixteenth Ohio), composed of Ohio and Kentucky troops, reached Ten-mile Creek and was ordered to march to Red House the day after. Lightburn was busy clearing the river of obstructions and preparing to move to Pocataligo River as the next step in advance. Of the other brigades belonging to Morgan, that of Brigadier-General Samuel P. Carter, composed partly of Tennesseans, was at Gallipolis, intending to enter the valley on the 24th. The remaining brigade, under Brigadier-General James G. Spears, was entirely Tennessean, and was still at Portland where the paymaster had just arrived and was giving the regiments part payment.

My purpose was to concentrate the force at Pocataligo, assume the command in person, and attack the enemy in the positions in front of Charleston, in which Wise had resisted me in the previous year. I should have been glad to make the expected movement of a column from Clarksburg under Crook and Milroy co-operate directly with my own, but circumstances made it impracticable. The operations of the Confederate cavalry under Jenkins were keeping the country north of the Kanawha in a turmoil, and reports had become rife that he would work his way out toward Beverly. The country was also full of rumours of a new invasion from East Virginia. Milroy's forces were not yet fully assembled at Clarksburg on the 20th, but he was ordered to operate toward Beverly, whilst Crook, with the old Kanawha division, should move on Summersville and Gauley Bridge. Both had to depend on hiring wagons for transportation of supplies. Separated as they were, they would necessarily be cautious in their movements, making the suppression of guerrillas, the driving out of raiders, and the general quieting of the country their principal task. Their role was thus, of course, made subordinate to the movement of my own column, which must force its own way without waiting for results from other operations.

Half of Carter's brigade was, at the last moment, delayed at Gallipolis, the clothing and equipments sent to them there being found incomplete. Just half of Morgan's division with two batteries of artillery were in motion on the 24th. On that day Lightburn was moved to Pocataligo, about forty miles from the river mouth, where I joined him in person on the 27th. A cold storm of mingled rain and snow had made the march and bivouac very uncomfortable for a couple of days. General Morgan accompanied me, and during the 28th the active column of three and a half brigades was concentrated, two or three other regiments being in echelon along the river below. Tyler Mountain behind Tyler Creek was, as formerly, the place at which the enemy was posted to make a stand against our further progress, though he had no considerable force on the south side of the river at the mouth of Scary Creek. Reconnaissances showed nothing but cavalry in our immediate front, and it afterwards appeared that Echols began a rapid retreat from Charleston on that day. He had called to him Jenkins with the greater part of the cavalry, and entrusted to the latter the duty of holding us back as much as possible. Suspecting this from evidence collected at Pocataligo, I determined to put Siber's brigade and a battery, all in light marching order, on the south side of the river, accompanied by a light-draught steamboat, which the rise in the river after the storm enabled us to use as far as Charleston. This brigade could turn the strong position at Tyler Mountain, and passing beyond this promontory on the opposite side of the river, could command with artillery fire the river road on the other bank behind the enemy in our front. The steamboat would enable them to make a rapid retreat if the belief that no great force was on that side of the river should prove to be a mistake. Siber was also furnished with a battery of four mountain howitzers, which could be carried to the edge of the water or anywhere that men could march.

On the right bank of the river (north side) the principal column of two brigades (Toland's and DeCourcey's) advanced on the turnpike near the stream, having one six-gun battery and a section of twenty-pounder Parrots with them. What was present of Carter's brigade was sent by the mountain road further from the stream, to cover our left and to turn the flank of the Tyler Mountain position, if a stubborn stand should be made there. A light six-gun battery accompanied it. All moved forward simultaneously on the morning of the 29th. The dispositions thus made rendered it vain for the enemy's cavalry to offer any stubborn resistance, and Jenkins abandoned Tyler Mountain on our approach, thus giving us certain knowledge that he was not closely supported by the infantry. Our advance-guard reached the Elk River opposite Charleston in the afternoon, and I made personal reconnaissance of the means of crossing. The suspension bridge had been ruined in Lightburn's retreat, and the enemy had depended upon a bridge of boats for communication with their troops in the lower valley. These boats had been taken to the further bank of the river and partly destroyed, but as the enemy had continued his retreat, we soon had a party over collecting those that could be used, and other flatboats used in the coal trade, and a practicable bridge was reconstructed before night of the 30th. Meanwhile I entered the town with the advance-guard as soon as we had a boat to use for a ferry, and spent the night of the 29th there. We had friends enough in the place to put us quickly in possession of all the news, and I was soon satisfied that Echols had no thought of trying to remain on the western side of the mountains.

The column crossed the Elk late in the afternoon of the 30th, and I pushed Toland's and Carter's brigades to Malden and Camp Piatt that evening, Siber's brigade advancing to Brownstown on the other side of the Kanawha River. Lightburn's division was ordered forward next day to Gauley Bridge, Carter's brigade at Malden was ordered to send strong parties southward into Boone County, to reconnoitre and to put down guerrilla bands. DeCourcey's brigade was halted at Charleston, and Spears' Tennessee brigade was directed to remain at Gallipolis till further orders. Communication was opened with Crook, who was ordered to press forward via Summersville to Gauley Bridge as quickly as possible. The retreating enemy had burned the bridges, obstructed the roads with fallen timber, and cut and destroyed the flatboats along the river; so that the first and most pressing task was to reopen roads, make ferries and bridges, and thus renew the means of getting supplies to the troops. The river was still low, unusually so for the season, and the water was falling. Every energy was therefore necessary to get forward supplies to Gauley Bridge and the other up-river posts, for if the river should freeze whilst low, the winter transportation would be confined to the almost impassable roads. I reported to General Wright the re-occupation of the valley, our lack of wagon-trains for further advance, and all the facts which would assist in deciding whether anything further should be attempted. I did not conceal the opinion which all my experience had confirmed, that no military advantage could be secured by trying to extend operation by this route across the mountains into the James River valley.

On the 2d of November Brigadier-General Scammon reported for duty, and I ordered him to Gauley Bridge to assume command of the division which was then under Colonel Lightburn, who resumed the command of his brigade. Scammon was directed to inspect carefully all our old positions as far as Raleigh C. H., to report whether the recent retreat of troops from Fayetteville had been due to any improper location of the fortifications there, to examine the road up Loup Creek, and any others which might be used by the enemy to turn our position at Gauley Bridge, to state the present conditions of buildings at all the upper posts, and whether any storehouses had escaped destruction. In short, we needed the material on which to base intelligent plans for a more secure holding of the region about the falls of the Kanawha, or for a further advance to the eastward if it should be ordered.

The information which came to me as soon as I was in actual contact with the enemy, not only satisfied me that Loring's forces had been greatly exaggerated, but led me to estimate them at a lower figure than the true one. In reporting to General Wright on 1st November, I gave the opinion that they amounted to about 3500 infantry, but with a disproportionate amount of artillery, some twenty pieces. The cavalry under Jenkins numbered probably 1000 or 1500 horse. About the first of October Loring, in a dispatch to Richmond, stated his force at "only a little more than 4000," which probably means that the 5000 with which he entered the valley were somewhat reduced by the sick and by desertions. He seems to refer to his infantry, for Jenkins's command had been an independent one. It would be reasonable, therefore, to put his total strength at some 6000 or a little higher. On our side, the column with which I actually advanced was just about 9000 men, with 2000 more of Morgan's command within reach, had there been need to call them up from the Ohio River.

On the 8th of November Halleck telegraphed to General Wright that no posts need be established beyond Gauley Bridge, and that about half of my command should be sent to Tennessee and the Mississippi valley. On the same day General Wright formally approved my views as submitted to him, and ordered Morgan's division to be sent to Cincinnati at once. It was thus definitively settled that my task for the winter would be to restore the condition of affairs in West Virginia which had existed before Loring's invasion, and organize my district with a view to prompt and easy supply of my posts, the suppression of lawlessness and bushwhacking, the support of the State authorities, and the instruction and discipline of officers and men. My first attention was given to the question of transportation, for the winter was upon us and wagons were very scarce. The plan of using the river to the utmost was an economy as well as a necessity, and I returned to my former arrangement of using *batteaux* for the shallow and swift waters of the upper river, connecting with the movable head of steamboat navigation. A tour of inspection to Gauley Bridge and the posts in that vicinity satisfied me that they were in good condition for mutual support, and for carrying on a system of scouting which could be made a useful discipline and instruction to the troops, as well as the means of keeping thoroughly informed of the movements of the enemy.

The line of the Baltimore and Ohio Railroad was kept under the control of General Kelley, and his authority extended to active co-operation with the Army of the Potomac in keeping open communication with Washington. In case of need, the commander of that army was authorized to give orders to General Kelley direct, without waiting to transmit them through my headquarters. General Milroy was established on the Beverly front, communicating on his left with General Kelley and on his right with General Crook, at Gauley Bridge. General Scammon had his station at Fayette C. H., covering the front on the south side of New River, whilst Crook watched the north side and extended his posts in Milroy's direction as far as Summersville. Colonel Cranor remained on the Ohio near Guyandotte, scouting the valley of the Guyandotte River and communicating with Charleston and other posts on the Kanawha.

On the 12th of November reports were received from General Kelley that authentic information showed that Jackson was advancing from the Shenandoah valley upon West Virginia. Similar information reached army headquarters at Washington, and in anticipation of possible necessity for it, I directed Milroy to hold himself in readiness to march at once to join Kelley, if the latter should call upon him. I telegraphed General Wright that I did not think the report would prove well founded, but it put everybody upon the alert for a little while. Kelley had beaten up a camp of Confederates under Imboden about eighteen miles above Moorefield on the south branch of the Potomac, causing considerable loss to the enemy in killed and wounded and capturing fifty prisoners. Some movement to support Imboden probably gave rise to the story of Jackson's advance, but Lee kept both corps of his army in hand and moved the whole down the Rappahannock soon afterward, to meet Burnside's advance upon Fredericksburg.

The invasion of the Kanawha valley by Loring had stirred up much bitter feeling again between Union men and Confederates, and was followed by the usual quarrels and recriminations among neighbours. The Secessionists were stimulated to drop the prudent reserve they had practised before, and some of them, in the hope that the Confederate occupation would be permanent, persecuted loyal men who were in their power. The retreat of the enemy brought its day of reckoning, and was accompanied by a fresh emigration to eastern Virginia of a considerable number of the more pronounced Secessionists. I have said that Mr. George Summers, formerly the leading man of the valley, had studiously avoided political activity after the war began; but this did not save him from the hostility of his disloyal neighbours. Very shortly after my re-occupation of Charleston he called upon me one evening and asked for a private interview. He had gone through a painful experience, he said, and as it would pretty surely come to my ears, he preferred I should hear it from himself, before enemies or tale-bearers should present it with such colouring as they might choose. During the Confederate occupation he had maintained his secluded life and kept aloof from contact with the military authorities. Their officers, however, summoned him before them, charged him with treason to Virginia and to the Confederate States, and demanded of him that he take the oath of allegiance to the Southern government. He demurred to this, and urged that as he had scrupulously avoided public activity, it would be harsh and unjust to force him to a test which he could not conscientiously take. They were in no mood to listen to argument, and charged that his acquiescence in the rule of the new state government of West Virginia was, in his case, more injurious to the Confederate cause than many another man's active unionism. Finding Mr. Summers disposed to be firm, they held him in arrest; and as he still refused to yield, he was told that he should be tied by a rope to the tail of a wagon and forced to march in that condition, as a prisoner, over the mountains to Richmond.

He was an elderly man, used to a refined and easy life, somewhat portly in person, and, as he said, he fully believed such treatment would kill him. The fierceness of their manner convinced him that they meant to execute the threat, and looking upon it as a sentence of death, he yielded and took the oath. He said that being in duress of such a sort, and himself a lawyer, he considered that he had a moral right to escape from his captors in this way, though he would not have yielded to anything short of what seemed to him an imminent danger of his life. The obligation, he declared, was utterly odious to him and was not binding on his conscience; but he had lost no time in putting himself into my hands, and would submit to whatever I should decide in the matter. It would be humiliating and subject him to misconstruction by others if he took conflicting oaths, but he was willing to abjure the obligation he had taken, if I demanded it, and would voluntarily renew his allegiance to the United States with full purpose to keep it.

He was deeply agitated, and I thoroughly pitied him. My acquaintance with him in my former campaign gave me entire confidence in his sincerity, and made me wish to spare him any fresh embarrassment or pain. After a moment's reflection, I replied that I did not doubt anything he had told me of the facts or of his own sentiments in regard to them. His experience only confirmed my distrust of all test oaths. Either his conscience already bound him to the National government, or it did not. In either case I could not make his loyalty more sure by a fresh oath, and believing that the one he had taken under duress was void in fact as well as in his own conscience, I would leave the matter there and ask nothing more of him. He was greatly relieved by my decision, but bore himself with dignity. I never saw any reason to be sorry for the course I took, and believe that he was always afterward consistent and steady in his loyalty to the United States.

CHAPTER 20
Winter Quarters, 1862-63

Early in December I established my winter headquarters at Marietta on the Ohio River, a central position from which communication could be had most easily with all parts of the district and with department headquarters. It was situated at the end of the railway line from Cincinnati to the Ohio River near Parkersburg, where the Baltimore and Ohio Railroad met the Cincinnati line. The Baltimore road, coming from the east, forked at Grafton in West Virginia and reached Wheeling, as has been described in an earlier chapter. The river was usually navigable during the winter and made an easy communication with Wheeling as with the lower towns. I was thus conveniently situated for most speedily reaching every part of my command, in person or otherwise. It took but a little while to get affairs so organized that the routine of work ran on quietly and pleasantly. No serious effort was made by the enemy to re-enter the district during the winter, and except some local outbreaks of "bush-whacking" and petty guerrilla warfare, there was nothing to interrupt the progress of the troops in drill and instruction.

A good deal of obscurity still hangs about the subject of guerrilla warfare, and the relation of the Confederate government to it. There was, no doubt, a good deal of loose talk that found its way into print and helped form a popular opinion, which treated almost every scouting party as if it were a lawless organization of "bush-whackers." But there was an authoritative and systematic effort of the Richmond government to keep up partisan bodies within our lines which should be soldiers when they had a chance to do us a mischief, and citizens when they were in danger of capture and punishment. When Fremont assumed command of the Mountain Department, he very early called the attention of the Secretary of War to the fact that Governor Letcher was sending commissions into West Virginia, authorizing the recipients to enlist companies to be used against us in irregular warfare.

The bands which were organized by the Confederate Government under authority of law, but which were free from the control of army commanders and unrestrained by the checks upon lawlessness which are found in subordination to the operations of organized armies, were called "Partisan Rangers," and protection as legitimate soldiers was promised them. They were not required to camp with the army, or to remain together as troops or regiments. They wore uniforms or not, as the whim might take them. They remained, as much as they dared, in their home region, and assembled, usually at night, at a preconcerted signal from their leaders, to make a "raid." They were not paid as the more regular troops were, but were allowed to keep the horses which they captured or "lifted." They were nominally required to turn over the beef-cattle and army stores to the Confederate commissariat, but after a captured wagon-train had been looted by them, not much of value would be found in it. Their raids were made by such numbers as might chance to be got together. Stuart, the brilliant Confederate cavalry commander, whilst crediting Mosby with being the best of the partisans, said of him, "he usually operates with only one-fourth of his nominal strength. Such organizations, as a rule, are detrimental to the best interests of the army at large." General Lee, in forwarding one of Mosby's reports, commended his boldness and good management, but added: "I have heard that he has now with him a large number of men, yet his expeditions are undertaken with very few, and his attention seems more directed to the capture of sutlers' wagons, etc., than to the injury of the enemy's communications and outposts.... I do not know the cause for undertaking his expeditions with so few men; whether it is from policy or the difficulty of collecting them. I have heard of his men, among them officers, being in rear of this army, selling captured goods, sutlers' stores, etc. This had better be attended to by others. It has also been reported to me that many deserters from this army have joined him. Among them have been seen members of the Eighth Virginia Regiment." In the "Richmond Examiner" of August 18, 1863 (the same date as General Lee's letter), was the statement that "At a sale of Yankee plunder taken by Mosby and his men, held at Charlottesville last week, thirty-odd thousand dollars were realized, to be divided among the gallant band."

The injury to the discipline of their own army gradually brought leading officers of the Confederates to the conviction that the "Partisan Rangers" cost more than they were worth. In January, 1864, General Rosser, one of the most distinguished cavalry officers of the South, made a formal communication to General Lee on the subject. "During the time I have been in the valley," he said, "I have had ample opportunity of judging of the efficiency and usefulness of the many irregular bodies of troops which occupy this country, known as partisans, etc., and am prompted by no other feeling than a desire to serve my country, to inform you that they are a nuisance and an evil to the service. Without discipline, order, or organization, they roam broadcast over the country, a band of thieves, stealing, pillaging, plundering, and doing every manner of mischief and crime. They are a terror to the citizens and an injury to the cause. They never fight; can't be made to fight. Their leaders are generally brave, but few of the men are good soldiers, and have engaged in this business for the sake of gain." After classifying the mischiefs to the regular service, he continues: "It is almost impossible to manage the different companies of my brigade that are from Loudoun, Fauquier, Fairfax, etc., the region occupied by Mosby. They see these men living at their ease and enjoying the comforts of home, allowed to possess all that they capture, and their duties mere pastime pleasures compared with their own arduous ones, and it is a natural consequence, in the nature of man, that he should become dissatisfied under these circumstances. Patriotism fails, in a long and tedious war like this, to sustain the ponderous burdens which bear heavily and cruelly upon the heart and soul of man." General Rosser recommended the absorption of the partisan bodies into the ordinary brigades, using their supposed talents for scouting by sending them on expeditions as regular patrols and reconnoitring parties, reporting to their proper command as soon as the duty was done.

It was upon Rosser's communication that Stuart made the endorsement already quoted, and Lee sent it forward to the War Department, further endorsed thus: "As far as my knowledge and experience extend, there is much truth in the statement of General Rosser. I recommend that the law authorizing these partisan corps be abolished. The evils resulting from their organization more than counterbalance the good they accomplish." The Secretary of War, Mr. Siddon, drafted a bill to abolish them, and it passed the Confederate House. Delay occurring in the Senate, the matter was compromised by transferring all the Rangers except Mosby's and McNeill's to the line. As it was to Mosby's that the reported facts applied, and all agreed that his was the best of the lot, we may imagine what must have been the character of the rest.

In the first two winters of the war, these organizations were in the height of their pernicious activity, and the loyal West Virginians were their favourite victims. We knew almost nothing of their organization, except that they claimed some Confederate law for their being. We seldom found them in uniform, and had no means of distinguishing them from any other armed horse-stealers and "bush-whackers." We were, however, made unpleasantly certain of the fact that in every neighbourhood where secession sentiments were rife, our messengers were waylaid and killed, small parties were ambushed, and all the exasperating forms of guerrilla warfare were abundant. Besides all this, the Confederate authorities assumed to call out the militia of counties into which they were intending to make an expedition, so that they might have the temporary co-operation of local troops. They claimed the right to do this because they had not recognized the separation of West Virginia, and insisted that the whole was subject to the laws of Virginia. The result was that the Union men formed companies of "Home Guards" for self-protection, and the conflict of arms was carried into every settlement in the mountain nooks and along the valleys. In this kind of fighting there was no quarter given, or if prisoners were taken, they were too often reported as having met with fatal accidents before they could be handed over to the regular authorities. As all this could have no effect upon the progress of the war, the more cool and intelligent heads of both sides opposed it, and gradually diminished it. Severe measures against it were in fact merciful, for the horrors of war are always least when the fighting is left to the armies of responsible belligerents, unprovoked by the petty but exasperating hostilities of irregulars. The trouble from this source was less during the winter of 1862-63 than it had been the year before, but it still gave occupation to small movable columns of our troops from time to time.

The organization of my staff was somewhat increased with the enlargement of responsibilities. Lieutenant-Colonel McElroy, who had been my adjutant-general in the campaign of 1861, returned to me as inspector-general and took the whole supervision of the equipment, drill, and instruction of the troops of the district. Major Bascom, who had received his promotion at the same time with mine, continued to be adjutant-general. The increased work in looking after supplies made more force in the commissariat a necessity, and Captain Barriger of the regular army was sent to me, my former commissary, Captain Treat, continuing on the staff. Barriger was a modest, clear-headed officer of admirable business qualifications, whom I had the good fortune to be again associated with late in the war. Three principal depots of supply were established at the bases of the principal lines of communication in the district—Wheeling, Parkersburg, and Gallipolis. At each of these, depot commissaries and quartermasters were located, and the posts and commands at the front drew their supplies from them. Captain Fitch, my quartermaster, supervised his department in a similar way to that of the commissariat. My aides were Captain Christie and Lieutenant

Conine, as before, and I added to them my brother, Theodore Cox, who served with me as volunteer aide without rank in the battles of South Mountain and Antietam, and was then appointed lieutenant in the Eleventh Ohio Infantry. He was my constant companion from this time till peace was established. The medical department remained under the care of Major Holmes, Brigade-Surgeon, who combined scientific with administrative qualities in a rare measure.

There was no military movement during the winter of sufficient importance to be told at length. Constant scouting and reconnoissances were kept up, slight skirmishes were not infrequent, but these did not prevent our sense of rest and of preparation for the work of the next spring. General Crook, with a brigade, was transferred temporarily to the command of Rosecrans in Tennessee, and Kelley, Milroy, and Scammon divided the care of the three hundred miles of mountain ranges which made our front. My own leisure gave me the opportunity for some systematic and useful reading in military history and art. An amusing interlude occurred in a hot controversy which arose between General Milroy and one of his subordinates which would not be worth mentioning except for the fact that the subordinate had afterward a world-wide notoriety as military chief of the Paris Commune in 1870.

Gustave Cluseret was a Frenchman, who was appointed in the spring of 1862 an aide-de-camp with the rank of colonel upon the staff of General Frémont, who (with questionable legality) assigned him to command a brigade, and recommended his appointment as brigadier for good conduct in the May and June campaign against Jackson. The appointment was made on October 14th, and during the fall and winter he had a brigade in Milroy's division. Milroy was, for a time, loud in his praises of Cluseret as the *beau ideal* of an officer, and their friendship was fraternal. In the winter, however, their mutual admiration was nipped by a killing frost, and a controversy sprung up between them which soon led to mutual recrimination also in the superlative degree. They addressed their complaints to General Halleck, and as the papers passed through my headquarters, I was a witness of their berating of each other. They made a terrible din, on paper, for a while, but I cannot recall anything very serious in their accusations. Halleck pigeon-holed their correspondence, but Milroy had powerful political friends, and Cluseret, learning that his appointment would not be confirmed by the Senate, anticipated their action, and terminated his military career in the United States by resigning two days before the close of the session of Congress.

This brings me to the subject of Congressional action in the matter of the promotions and appointments in the army during this winter session which closed the Thirty-seventh Congress. By it I was myself to suffer the one severe disappointment of my military career. The time was one of great political excitement, for the fall elections had resulted in a great overturning in the Congressional delegations. The Democrats had elected so many representatives for the Thirty-eighth Congress that it was doubtful whether the administration would be able to command a majority in the House. The retirement of McClellan from the command had also provoked much opposition, and in the lack of full knowledge of the reasons for displacing him, political ones were imagined and charged. Public policy forbade the President to make known all his grounds of dissatisfaction with the general, and many of his own party openly questioned his wisdom and his capacity to govern. Men whose patriotism cannot be questioned shared in this distrust, and in their private writings took the most gloomy view of the situation and of the future of the country. This was intensified when Burnside was so bloodily repulsed at Fredericksburg at the close of the first week of the session.

As is usual in revolutionary times, more radical measures were supposed by many to be the cure for disasters, and in caucuses held by congressmen the supposed conservatism of Mr. Lincoln and part of his cabinet was openly denounced, and the earnestness of the army leaders was questioned. Much of this was a misunderstanding of the President and of events which time has corrected, but at the moment and in the situation of the country it was natural. It strongly affected the conduct of the federal legislators, and must be taken into the account when we try to understand their attitude toward the army and the administration of military affairs.

In the Senate, at a very early day after the opening of the session, Mr. Wilson, chairman of the Committee on Military Affairs, offered a resolution (which passed without opposition) calling upon the Secretary of War for "the number and names of the major-generals and brigadier-generals in the service of the United States, and where and how they are employed." This was, no doubt, the offspring of an opinion in vogue in Congress, that the President had gone beyond the authority of law in the number of these officers he had appointed. If this were true, the course taken was not a friendly one toward the administration. The whole list of appointments and promotions would be submitted to the Senate for confirmation, and if the statutory number had been exceeded, that body could stop confirming when it reached the legal limit. There were, of course, frequent consultations between the Congressional committees or the individual members and the Secretary of War; but whatever efforts there may have been to reach a quiet understanding failed. On the 21st of January, the Secretary not having responded to Mr. Wilson's resolution, Mr. Rice of Minnesota offered another (which also passed by unanimous consent), directing the Secretary of War "to inform the Senate whether any more major and brigadier generals have been appointed and paid than authorized by law; and if so, how many; give names, dates of appointment and amounts paid."

Two days later the Secretary sent in his reports in response to both resolutions. To the first he replied that the interests of the public service would not permit him to state "where and how" the general officers were employed, but he gave the list of names. He gave also a separate list of six major-generals who were not assigned to any duty. To the second resolution he replied that "It is believed by this Department that the law authorizing the increase of the volunteer and militia forces necessarily implied an increase of officers beyond the number specified in the Act of July 17, 1862, to any extent required by the service, and that the number of appointments is not beyond such limit." If the limit of the statute named were strictly applied, he said there would be found to be nine major-generals and forty-six brigadier-generals in excess. There had been no payments of increased salary to correspond with the increased rank, except in one instance. The list submitted showed fifty-two major-generals in service, and one (Buford) was omitted, so that if forty should prove to be the limit, there would be thirteen in excess. This, however, was only apparently true, for the Secretary's list included the four major-generals in the regular army, whose case was not covered by the limitation of the statute. This seems to have been overlooked in the steps subsequently taken by members of Congress, and as the action was unwelcome to the President, he did not enlighten the legislators respecting their miscalculation. The business proceeded upon the supposition that the appointments in the highest rank were really thirteen in excess of the number fixed by the statute.

The state of the law was this. The Act of July 22, 1861, authorized the President to call for volunteers, not exceeding half a million, and provided for one brigadier-general for four regiments and one major-general for three brigades. The Act of 25th July of the same year authorized a second call of the same number, and provided for "such number of major-generals and brigadier-generals as may in his (the President's) judgment be required for their organization." In the next year, however, a "rider" was put upon the clause in the appropriation bill to pay the officers and men of the volunteer service, which provided "that the President shall not be authorized to appoint more than forty major-generals, nor more than two hundred brigadier-generals," and repealed former acts which allowed more. This limit just covered those who had been appointed up to the date of the approval of the appropriation bill. Two questions, however, were still open for dispute. First, whether a "rider" upon the appropriation should change a general law on the subject of army organization, and second, whether the new limit might not allow appointments to be *thereafter* made to the extent of the numbers stated. The report of Mr. Stanton evidently suggests such questions.

The matter was now in good shape for what politicians call "a deal," and negotiations between members of Congress and the executive were active. The result appears to have been an understanding that a bill should be passed increasing the number of general officers, so as not only to cover the appointments already made, but leaving a considerable margin of new promotions to be filled by arrangement between the high contracting parties. On the 12th of February, 1863, the Senate passed a bill providing for the appointment of twenty major-generals of volunteers and fifty brigadiers. This was not acceptable to the House. The battle of Stone's River had lately been fought in Tennessee, and representatives from the West were urgent in arguing that affairs near Washington unduly filled the view of the administration. There was some truth in this. At any rate the House amended the bill so as to increase the numbers to forty major-generals and one hundred brigadiers, to be made by promotions, for meritorious service, from lower grades. As soon as it was known that the Military Committee of the House would report such an amendment, it was assumed that the Senate would concur, and a "slate" was made up accordingly. On the hypothesis that the list of major-generals was thirteen in excess of the forty fixed by statute, a new list of twenty-seven was made out, which would complete the forty to be added by the new bill. A similar list was prepared for the brigadiers and precisely similar negotiations went on, but for brevity's sake I shall confine myself to the list for the highest rank, in which I was personally concerned.

The House passed the amended bill on the 27th of February, and it went back to the Senate for concurrence in the amendments. But now an unexpected difficulty arose. The Senate refused to concur in the changes made by the House. It matters little whether the senators were offended at the determination of the lower House to have so large a share in the nominations, or desired to punish the President for having gone beyond the letter of the law in his promotions of 1862; the fact was that they voted down the amendments. A committee of conference between the two houses was appointed, and a compromise report was made fixing the additional number of major-generals at thirty and of brigadiers at seventy-five. Both Houses finally concurred in the report, the bill went to the President on the 1st of March, and he signed it on the next day.

There was but a single working-day of the session left, for the session must end at noon of the 4th of March. The list must be reduced. The manner in which this was done clinches the proof, if there had been any doubt before, that the list of twenty-seven was the result of negotiations with congressmen. No meddling with that list was permitted, though the use of patronage as "spoils" had some very glaring illustrations in it. The President had to make the reduction from his own promotions made earlier, and which were therefore higher on the list and in rank, instead of dropping those last added, as had seemed to be demanded by the earlier action of Congress. The only exception to this was in the case of General Schofield, whose even-handed administration of the District of Missouri and army of the frontier had excited the enmity of extreme politicians in that State and in Kansas, led by Senator "Jim" Lane, the prince of "jayhawkers." Schofield was dropped from the twenty-seven.

A few changes had occurred in the original roster of officers, making additional vacancies. Governor Morgan of New York, who had a complimentary appointment as major-general, but had never served, resigned. Schuyler Hamilton also resigned, and Fitz-John Porter was cashiered.

The number to be sacrificed was thus reduced to six, and the lot fell on Generals N. B. Buford, G. W. Morell, W. F. Smith, H. G. Wright, J. M. Schofield, and myself. The last four won their promotion a second time and were re-appointed and confirmed at varying intervals; but of that later. Of course, in such a scramble it was only a question as to who had or had not powerful friends on the spot who would voluntarily champion his cause. No one at a distance could have any warning. The passage of the bill and action under it came together. For myself, I had gone quietly on in the performance of duty, never dreaming of danger, and it was long years after the war before I learned how the thing had in fact been done. My place had been near the top of the list, the commands which I had exercised and the responsibilities entrusted to me had been greater than those of the large majority of the appointees, and I had conclusive evidence of the approval of my superiors. The news was at first, therefore, both astonishing and disheartening. As a result of political "influences," it is sufficiently intelligible. I had at that time a barely speaking acquaintance with Senator Wade of Ohio. It was the same with Senator Sherman, but with the added disadvantage that in the senatorial contest of 1860 between him and Governor Dennison I had warmly espoused the cause of the latter. Mr. Hutchins, the representative from my district, had not been re-nominated, and Garfield, who was elected in his place, had not yet taken his seat, but was still in the military service in the field. Mr. Chase had been a constant friend, but this was just the time when his differences with Mr. Lincoln had become acute, and since the 20th of December the President had in his hands the resignations of both Seward and Chase, which enabled him to refuse both, and to baffle the party in the Senate which was trying to force him to reorganize his cabinet by excluding Seward and those who were thought the more conservative. As he expressed it, "he had a pumpkin in each end of his bag, and could now ride." If, on the theory of apportioning the promotions to States, it were held that Ohio must lose one of the six nominated, it was easy to see where the balance of influence would be. General Halleck was well known to be persistent in favouring appointments from the regular army, and would urge that the reduction should be made from those originally appointed from civil life. These were Schenck and myself. But General Schenck was a veteran member of the House of Representatives and had now been elected to the next house, in which it was known he would be a prominent character. It goes without saying, therefore, that on such a basis the black ball would come to me. To complete the story of the promotions made at this time, it may be added that a short executive session of the Senate was held after the regular adjournment of Congress on the 4th of March, and that the President sent in the names of Carl Schurz and Julius Stahel to be made major-generals. For one of these a vacancy was made by the arrangement that Cassius M. Clay was reappointed minister to St. Petersburg and resigned the military rank which he had never used. The other seems to have been made by a resignation to take effect the next month. General Sumner died on the 21st of March, making another vacancy, but it is difficult to fix with accuracy the exact date of the changes which occurred. In the case of the last two promotions Mr. Lincoln openly declared that he made them in recognition of the German element in the army and in politics.

It would be unjust to assume that members of Congress and the President were not guided by patriotic motives. The reform of the public service in matters of appointment had not then attracted much attention. Patronage was used for political purposes with complete frankness and openness. In civil offices this custom was boldly defended and advocated. There was some consciousness shown that promotions in the army ought to be controlled by a somewhat different rule, but it seemed to be thought that enough was done in the way of safeguard when the choice was confined to officers already in service, and appointments for the highest grades were not given to entirely new men from civil life. Each aspirant could find friends to sound his praises, and it was easy to assert that it was only giving preference to one's friends among officers of equal merit. Many excellent appointments were in fact made, and the proportion of these would have been greater if the judgment of military superiors had been more controlling in determining the whole list. Mr. Lincoln's humorous way of explaining his actions may give an impression of a lower standard than he actually acknowledged; but it cannot be denied that he allowed himself to be pressed into making military promotions, at times, upon purely political or personal reasons.

It did not seem to occur to the authorities that the judgment of superior officers in the field should be called for and carefully considered when it was a question of promoting one of their subordinates. An instance which occurred in General Buell's army carried this beyond the verge of the grotesque. Colonel Turchin, of an Illinois regiment, was a Russian, an educated officer who had served in the Russian staff corps. An excellent soldier in many respects, his ideas of discipline were, unfortunately, lax, and in the summer of 1862 he was court-martialled for allowing his men to pillage a town in Tennessee. The court was an intelligent one, of which General Garfield was president. The story current in the army at the time, and which I believe to be true, is that after the court had heard part of the testimony it became apparent that they must convict, and Mrs. Turchin, who usually accompanied her husband in the field, started to the rear to procure political "influences" to save him. With various recommendations she went to Washington, and was so successful that although the sentence of the court dismissing him from the service was promulgated on the 6th of August, he had been appointed a brigadier-general of volunteers on the 5th, and he was not one of those who were dropped from the list on March 3, 1863. The trial was one of considerable notoriety, yet it is probable that it was overlooked by the President and Secretary of War at the time the appointment was made; but it cannot need to be said that whatever grounds for leniency might have existed, it turns the whole business into a farce when they were made the basis of a promotion in the revised list six months later. To add to the perfection of the story, Mrs. Turchin had acted on her own responsibility, and the colonel did not know of the result till he had gone home, and in an assembly of personal friends who called upon him ostensibly to cheer him in his doleful despondency, his wife brought the little drama to its *dénouement* by presenting him with the appointment in their presence.

One of the worst features of the method of appointment by "slate" made up between congressmen and the executive was that it filled up every place allowed by law, and left nothing to be used as a recognition for future services in the field, except as vacancies occurred, and these were few and far between. The political influences which determined the appointment were usually powerful enough to prevent dismissal. Whoever will trace the employment of officers of the highest grades in the last half of the war, will find large numbers of these on unimportant and nominal duty, whilst their work in the active armies was done by men of lower grade, to whom the appropriate rank had to be refused. The system was about as bad as could be, but victory was won in spite of it. It was fortunate, on the whole, that we did not have the grades of lieutenant-general and general during the war, as the Confederates had. They made the one the regular rank of a corps commander and the other of the commander of an army in the field. With us the assignment of a major-general by the President to command a corps gave him a temporary precedence over other major-generals not so assigned, and in like manner for the commander of an army. If these were relieved, they lost the precedence, and thus there was a sort of temporary rank created, giving a flexibility to the grade of major-general, without which we should have been greatly embarrassed. Grant's rank of lieutenant-general was an exceptional grade, made for him alone, when, after the battle of Missionary Ridge, he was assigned to the command of all the armies.

These opinions of mine are not judgments formed after the fact. The weak points in our army organization were felt at the time, and I took every means in my power to bring them to the attention of the proper authorities, State and National. At the close of 1862 a commission was appointed by the Secretary of War to revise the articles of war and army regulations. Of this commission Major-General Hitchcock was chairman. They issued a circular calling for suggestions as to alterations supposed to be desirable, and a copy was sent to me among others. I took occasion to report the results of my own experience, and to trace the evils which existed to their sources in our military system. I called attention to the striking parallel between our practices and those that had been in use in the first French Republic, and to the identical mischiefs which had resulted. Laxity of discipline, straggling, desertion, demagoguery in place of military spirit, giving commissions as the reward of mere recruiting, making new regiments instead of filling up the old ones, absence of proper staff corps—every one of these things had been suffered in France till they could no longer be endured, and we had faithfully copied their errors without profiting by the lesson.

In the freedom of private correspondence with Mr. Chase I enlarged upon the same topics, and urged him to get the serious attention of the President and the cabinet to them. I gave him examples of the mischiefs that were done by the insane efforts to raise new regiments by volunteering when we ought to apply a conscription as the only fair way of levying a tax on the physical strength of the nation. I said: "I have known a lieutenant to be forced by his captain (a splendid soldier) to resign on account of his general inefficiency. I have seen that same lieutenant take the field a few months later as lieutenant-colonel of a new regiment, whilst the captain still stood at the head of his fraction of a company in the line. This is not a singular instance, but an example of cases occurring literally by the thousand in our vast army during the year past.... Governor Tod (of Ohio) said to me some time ago, with the deepest sorrow, that he was well aware that in raising the new regiments by volunteering, the distribution of offices to the successful recruiters was filling the army with incompetent men whom we should have to sift out again by such process as we could!.... Have we time for the sifting process? Even if we had, how inefficient the process itself when these officers have their commissions in their pockets, and cannot be brought before a court or a military commission till much of the mischief they can do is accomplished, bad habits amongst the soldiers formed, and the work of training them made infinitely more difficult than with absolutely raw recruits. It was in view of such probable results that I expressed the hope that no more new regiments would be raised by volunteering, when, in July last, the levy of an additional force was mooted. It seemed to me that the President could well say to the world, 'Our people have shown abundant proof of their enthusiasm in support of the government by volunteering already to the number of more than half a million, a thing unprecedented in the world's history: we now, as a matter of military expediency, call for a draft to fill up the broken battalions.'"

I urged with equal frankness the need of giving unity to the army by abolishing the distinction between regulars and volunteers, and by a complete reorganization of the staff. I said it seemed absurd that with nearly a million of men in the field, the Register of the Army of the United States should show an organization of some twenty regiments only, of which scarce a dozen had been in active service. "If a volunteer organization is fit to decide the *great* wars of the nation, is it not ridiculous to keep an expensive organization of regulars for the petty contests with Indians or for an ornamental appendage to the State in peace?" The thing to be aimed at seemed to me to be to have a system flexible enough to provide for the increase of the army to any size required, without losing any of the advantage of character or efficiency which, in any respect, pertained to it as a regular army. Circumstances to which I have already alluded, probably prevented Mr. Chase from taking any active part again in the discussion of army affairs in the cabinet. Probably many of the same ideas were urged upon the President from other quarters, for there was much agitation of the subject in the army and out of it. But nothing came of it, for even the draft, when it became the law, was used more as a shameful whip to stimulate volunteering than as an honourable and right way to fill the ranks of the noble veteran regiments. General Sherman found, in 1864, the same wrong system thwarting his efforts to make his army what it should be, and broke out upon it in glorious exasperation.

Chapter 21
Farewell to West Virginia

My purpose to get into active field service had not slept, and soon after the establishment of a winter organization in the district, I had applied to be ordered to other duty. My fixed conviction that no useful military movements could be made across the mountain region implied that the garrisons of West Virginia should be reduced to a minimum and confined to the duty of defending the frontier of the new State. The rest of the troops might properly be added to the active columns in the field. McClellan had been relieved of command whilst I was conducting active operations in the Kanawha valley, and Burnside suffered his repulse at Fredericksburg within a few days after I was directed to make my headquarters at Marietta and perfect the organization of the district. I was therefore at a loss to choose where I would serve, even if I had been given *carte blanche* to determine my own work. Enough was known of the reasons for the President's dissatisfaction with McClellan to make me admit that the change of command was an apparent necessity, yet much was unknown, and the full strength of the President's case was not revealed till the war was over. My personal friendship for McClellan remained warm, and I felt sure that Hooker as a commander would be a long step downward. In private I did not hesitate to express the wish that McClellan should still be entrusted with the command of the Potomac army, that it should be strongly reinforced, and that by constant pressure upon its commander his indecision of character might be overcome.

Those who were near to McClellan believed that he was learning greater self-confidence, for the Antietam campaign seemed a decided improvement on that of the Chickahominy. The event, in great measure, justified this opinion, for it was not till Grant took command a year later that any leadership superior to McClellan's was developed. Yet it must be confessed that we did not know half the discouragements that were weighing upon the President and his Secretary of War, and which made the inertia of the Eastern army demand a desperate remedy.

My personal affairs drifted in this way: the contest over the lists of promotions, of which I knew next to nothing, prevented any action on the request for a change of duty, and the close of the session of Congress brought the official notice that the promotion had expired by legal limitation. The first effect was naturally depressing, and it took a little time and some philosophy to overcome it; but the war was not ended yet, and reflection made the path of duty appear to be in the line of continued active service.

To form a new department for General Schenck, West Virginia was detached from the Department of the Ohio and annexed to Maryland. This was a mistake from a military point of view, for not only must the posts near the mountains be supplied and reinforced from the Ohio as their base, toward which would also be the line of retreat if retreat were necessary, but the frequent advances of the Confederate forces, through the Shenandoah valley to the Potomac, always separated the West from any connection with Baltimore, and made it impossible for an officer stationed there (as General Schenck was) to direct affairs in the western district at the very time of greatest necessity.

Another important fact was overlooked. The river counties of Ohio formed part of the district, and the depots on the river were supplied from Cincinnati. Not only was Gallipolis thus put in another department from the posts directly dependent on that depot as a base of supplies and the principal station for hospitals, but the new boundary line left me, personally, and my headquarters in the Department of the Ohio. I at once called the attention of the War Department to these results, sending my communication in the first instance through General Wright. He was in the same boat with myself, for his rank had also been reduced on the 4th of March, but he thought the intention must have been to transfer me with the district to the Eastern Department. On this I wrote to Washington direct, asking for definite orders. I also wrote to General Schenck, telling him of General Wright's supposition that I was transferred with the district, and inquiring if he had any definite decision of the question.

About the 3rd of April I was directed to report in person to General Schenck at Baltimore, and reached that city on the 4th. My relations with General Schenck had been, personally, cordial, and our friendship continued till his death, many years after the war. Whatever plans he may have had were set aside by orders from Washington, which met me at his headquarters, ordering me to report at Columbus, Ohio, to assist the governor in organizing the troops to be called out under the new enrolment and conscription law. This was accompanied by the assurance that this duty would be but temporary, and that my desire to be assigned to active field duty would then be favourably considered. It is not improbable that my report on army organization, which has been mentioned, had something to do with this assignment; but I did not ask permission to visit Washington, though within a couple of hours' ride of the capital, and hastened back to my assigned post. Besides my wish to cut my connection with West Virginia on general military theories of its insignificance as a theatre of war, my stay there would have been intolerable, since General Milroy, in whose judgment I had less confidence than in that of any of my other subordinates, was, by the curious outcome of the winter's promotions, the one of all others who had been put over my head. I could not then foresee the cost the country would pay for this in the next summer's campaign in the Shenandoah, but every instinct urged me to sever a connection which could bode no good. The reasonableness of my objection to serving as a subordinate where I had been in command was recognized, and the arrangement actually made was as acceptable as anything except a division in an active army.

It greatly added to my contentment to learn that General Burnside had been ordered to the Department of the Ohio, and would be my immediate superior. I hastened back to Marietta, closed up the business pending there, and went to Columbus on the 9th of April. The arrangement between Governor Tod and General Burnside proved to be the formation of the Military District of Ohio, including the whole State. I was placed in command of this district, reporting directly to the general, who himself conferred with the governor. My own relations to my superiors were thus made strictly military, which was a much pleasanter thing for me than direct connection with the civil authorities would be; for this involved a danger of cross-purposes and conflicting orders. Brigadier-General John S. Mason, an excellent officer, was ordered to report to me as my immediate subordinate in command of the camps and the post at Columbus, and before the end of the month Burnside directed me to fix my own headquarters at Cincinnati, where I could be in constant communication with himself. All this was done with the most cordial understanding between Burnside and the governor. Indeed, nothing could be more perfect than the genial and reasonable tone of Governor Tod's intercourse with the military officers stationed in Ohio.

My duties under the Enrolment Act turned out to be very slight. The Act (passed March 3, 1863) made, in general, each congressional district an enrolment district under charge of a provost-marshal with the rank of captain. A deputy provost-marshal supervised the enrolment and draft for the State, and the whole was under the control of the provost-marshal-general at Washington, Colonel James B. Fry. The law provided for classification of all citizens capable of military duty between the ages of twenty and forty-five, so as to call out first the unmarried men and those not having families dependent on them. The exemptions on account of physical defects were submitted to a board of three, of which the local provost-marshal was chairman, and one was a medical man. Substitutes might be accepted in the place of drafted men, or a payment of three hundred dollars would be taken in place of personal service, that sum being thought sufficient to secure a voluntary recruit by the government. The principal effect of this provision was to establish a current market price for substitutes.

The general provisions of the law for the drafting were wise and well matured, and the rules for the subordinate details were well digested and admirably administered by Colonel Fry and his bureau. It was a delicate and difficult task, but it was carried out with such patience, honesty, and thoroughness that nothing better could be done than copy it, if a future necessity for like work should arise. There was no good ground for complaint, and in those cases where, as in New York, hostile political leaders raised the cry of unfairness and provoked collision between the mob and the National authorities, the victims were proved to be the dupes of ignorance and malice. The administration of the law was thoroughly vindicated, and if there were to be a draft at all, it could not be more fairly and justly enforced.

There was room for difference of opinion as to some of the provisions of the law regarding exemption and substitution, but the most serious question was raised by the section which applied to old regiments and which had nothing to do with the enrolment and draft. This section directed that when regiments had become reduced in numbers by any cause, the officers of the regiment should be proportionately diminished. As new regiments were still received and credited upon the State's liability under the draft, it of course resulted that the old regiments continued to decay. A public sentiment had been created which looked upon the draft as a disgrace, and the most extraordinary efforts were made to escape it. Extra bounties for volunteering were paid by counties and towns, and the combination of influences was so powerful that it was successful in most localities, and very few men were actually put in the ranks by the draft.

The offer of extra bounties to induce volunteering brought into existence "bounty-jumping," a new crime analogous to that of "repeating" at elections. A man would enlist and receive the bounty, frequently several hundred dollars, but varying somewhat in different places and periods. He would take an early opportunity to desert, as he had intended to do from the first.

Changing his name, he would go to some new locality and enlist again, repeating the fraud as often as he could escape detection. The urgency to get recruits and forward them at once to the field, and the wide country which was open to recruiting, made the risk of punishment very small. Occasionally one was caught, and he would of course be liable to punishment as a deserter. The final report of the provost-marshal-general mentions the case of a criminal in the Albany penitentiary, New York, who confessed that he had "jumped the bounty" thirty-two times.

Another evil incidental to the excessive stimulus of volunteering was a political one, which threatened serious results. It deranged the natural political balance of the country by sending the most patriotic young men to the field, and thus giving an undue power to the disaffected and to the opponents of the administration. This led to the State laws for allowing the soldiers to vote wherever they might be, their votes being certified and sent home. In its very nature this was a makeshift and a very dubious expedient to cure the mischief. It would not have been necessary if we had had at an early day a system of recruiting that would have drawn more evenly from different classes into the common service of the country.

The military officers of the department and district had nothing to do with the enrolment and drafting, unless resistance to the provost-marshals should make military support for these officers necessary. We had hoped to have large camps of recruits to be organized and instructed, but the numbers actually drafted in Ohio, in 1863, were insignificant, for reasons already stated. Three or four very small post garrisons were the only forces at my command, and these were reduced to the minimum necessary to guard the prison camps and the depots of recruiting and supply.

General Burnside had not come West with a purpose to content himself with the retiracy of a department out of the theatre of actual war. His department included eastern Kentucky, and afforded a base for operations in the direction of East Tennessee. Mr. Lincoln had never lost his eagerness and zeal to give assistance to the loyal mountaineers, and had arranged with Burnside a plan of co-operation with Rosecrans by which the former should move from Lexington, Ky., upon Knoxville, whilst the latter marched from Murfreesboro, Tenn., upon Chattanooga. This was better than the impracticable plan of 1861, which aimed at the occupation of East Tennessee before Chattanooga had been taken, and the task was at last accomplished by the method now used. It was by no means the best or most economical method, which would have been to have but one strong army till Chattanooga were firmly in our hands, and then direct a subordinate column upon the upper Holston valley. It was utterly impossible to keep up a line of supply for an army in East Tennessee by the wagon roads over the mountains. The railroad through Chattanooga was indispensable for this purpose. But Mr. Lincoln had not fully appreciated this, and was discontented that both Buell and Rosecrans had in turn paid little attention, as it seemed, to his desire to make the liberation of East Tennessee the primary and immediate aim of their campaigns. He had therefore determined to show his own faith in Burnside, and his approval of the man, by giving him a small but active army in the field, and to carry out his cherished purpose by having it march directly over the Cumberland Mountains, whilst Rosecrans was allowed to carry out the plan on which the commanders of the Cumberland army seemed, in the President's opinion, too stubbornly bent.

Burnside's old corps, the Ninth, was taken from the Army of the Potomac and sent to Kentucky, and a new corps, to be called the Twenty-third, was soon authorized, to contain the Tennessee regiments which had been in General Morgan's command, and two divisions made up of new regiments organized in Ohio, Indiana, and Illinois under the last call for volunteers. To these were added several Kentucky regiments of different ages in service. General Parke, so long Burnside's chief of staff, was to command the Ninth Corps, and Major-General George L. Hartsuff was assigned to the Twenty-third. In a former chapter I have spoken of Hartsuff's abilities as a staff officer in West Virginia. His qualities as a general officer had not been tried. He was wounded at the beginning of the engagement at Antietam, where he commanded a brigade in Hooker's corps. That was his first service under his appointment as brigadier, and he had necessarily been out of the field since that time. My own expectation was that he would make an excellent reputation as a corps commander, but it was not his fortune to see much continuous field service. His health was seriously affected by his wounds, and after a short trial of active campaigning he was obliged to seek more quiet employment.

The establishment of my headquarters at Cincinnati threw me once more into close personal relations with Burnside, and enabled me to learn his character more intimately. His adjutant-general's office was on East Fourth Street, and most of the routine work was done there. The general had his own quarters on Ninth Street, where he had also an office for himself and his aides-de-camp. My own office and the official headquarters of the district were on Broadway below Fourth, in the house now occupied by the Natural History Society. There was thus near half a mile between us, though I was but a little way from the adjutant-general of the department, through whose office my regular business with the general went. Burnside, however, loved to discuss department affairs informally, and with the perfect freedom of unrestrained social intercourse. When he gave his confidence he gave it without reserve, and encouraged the fullest and freest criticism of his own plans and purposes. His decisions would then be put in official form by the proper officers of the staff, and would be transmitted, though I was nearly always personally aware of what was to be ordered before the formal papers reached me. He had very little pride of opinion, and was perfectly candid in weighing whatever was contrary to his predilections; yet he was not systematic in his business methods, and was quite apt to decide first and discuss afterward. He never found fault with a subordinate for assuming responsibility or acting without orders, provided he was assured of his earnest good purpose in doing so. In such cases he would assume the responsibility for what was done as cheerfully as if he had given the order. In like manner he was careless of forms himself, in doing whatever seemed necessary or proper, and might pass by intermediate officers to reach immediately the persons who were to act or the things to be done. There was no intentional slight to any one in this: it was only a characteristic carelessness of routine. Martinets would be exasperated by it, and would be pretty sure to quarrel with him. No doubt it was a bad business method, and had its mischiefs and inconveniences. A story used to go the rounds a little later that soldiers belonging to the little army in East Tennessee were sometimes arrested at their homes and sent back as deserters, when they would produce a furlough written by Burnside on a leaf of his pocket memorandum-book, which, as they said, had been given by him after hearing a pitiful story which moved his sympathies. Such inventions were a kind of popular recognition of his well-known neglect of forms, as well as of his kind heart. There was an older story about him, to the effect that, when a lieutenant in the army, he had been made post-quartermaster at some little frontier garrison, and that his accounts and returns got into such confusion that after several pretty sharp reminders the quartermaster-general notified him, as a final terror, that he would send a special officer and subject him and his papers to a severe scrutiny. As the story ran, Burnside, in transparent honesty, wrote a cordial letter of thanks in reply, saying it was just what he desired, as he had been trying hard to make his accounts up, but had to confess he could do nothing with them, but was sure such an expert would straighten them. In my own service under him I often found occasion to supply the formal links in the official chain, so that business would move on according to "regulations;" but any trouble that was made in this way was much more than compensated by the generous trust with which he allowed his name and authority to be used when prompt action would serve the greater ends in view.

My habit was to go to his private quarters on Ninth Street, when the regular business of the day was over, and there get the military news and confer with him on pending or prospective business affecting my own district. His attractive personality made him the centre of a good deal of society, and business would drop into the background till late in the evening, when his guests voluntarily departed. Then, perhaps after midnight, he would take up the arrears of work and dictate letters, orders, and dispatches, turning night into day. It not infrequently happened that after making my usual official call in the afternoon, I had gone to my quarters and to bed at my usual hour, when I would be roused by an orderly from the general begging that I would come up and consult with him on some matter of neglected business. He was always bright and clear in those late hours, and when he buckled to work, rapidly disposed of it.

He did not indulge much in retrospect, and rarely referred to his misfortunes in the Army of the Potomac. On one or two occasions he discussed his Fredericksburg campaign with me. The delay in sending pontoons from Washington to Falmouth, which gave Lee time to concentrate at Fredericksburg, he reasonably argued, was the fault of the military authorities at Washington; but I could easily see that if his supervision of business had been more rigidly systematic, he would have made sure that he was not to be disappointed in his means of crossing the Rappahannock promptly. As to the battle itself he steadily insisted that the advance of Meade's division proved that if all the left wing had acted with equal vigour and promptness, Marye's heights would have been turned and carried. It is due to him to repeat that in such discussions his judgment of men and their motives was always kind and charitable. I never heard him say anything bitter, even of those whom I knew he distrusted.

At the time I am speaking of, Cincinnati was in a curious political and social condition. The advance through Kentucky of Bragg and Kirby Smith in the preceding year had made it a centre for "rebel sympathizers." The fact that a Confederate army had approached the hills that bordered the river had revived the hopes and the confidence of many who, while wishing success to the Southern cause, had done so in a vague and distant way. Now it seemed nearer to them, and the stimulus to personal activity was greater. There was always, in the city, a considerable and influential body of business men who were of Southern families; and besides this, the trade connections with the South, and the personal alliances by marriage, made a ground of sympathy which had noticeable effects. There were two camps in the community, pretty distinctly defined, as there were in Kentucky. The loyal were ardently and intensely so. The disloyal were bitter and not always restrained by common prudence. A good many Southern women, refugees from the theatre of active war, were very open in their defiance of the government, and in their efforts to aid the Southern armies by being the bearers of intelligence. The "contraband mail" was notoriously a large and active one.

Burnside had been impressed with this condition of things from the day he assumed command. His predecessor had struggled with it without satisfactory results. It was, doubtless, impossible to do more than diminish and restrain the evil, which was the most annoying of the smaller troubles attending the anomalous half-military and half-civil government of the department. Within three weeks from his arrival in Cincinnati, Burnside was so convinced of the widespread and multiform activity of the disloyal element that he tried to subdue it by the publication of his famous General Order No. 38[1]. The reading of the order gives a fair idea of the hostile influences he found at work, for of every class named by him there were numerous examples.

---

1. General Orders. No. 38. HEADQUARTERS DEPARTMENT OF THE OHIO, CINCINNATI, OHIO, April 13, 1863. The commanding general publishes, for the information of all concerned, that hereafter all persons found within our lines who commit acts for the benefit of the enemies of our country, will be tried as spies or traitors, and, if convicted, will suffer death. This order includes the following classes of persons: Carriers of secret mails; writers of letters sent by secret mails; secret recruiting officers within the lines; persons who have entered into an agreement to pass our lines for the purpose of joining the enemy; persons found concealed within our lines, belonging to the service of the enemy; and, in fact, all persons found improperly within our lines who could give private information to the enemy; and all persons within our lines who harbour, protect, conceal, feed, clothe, or in any way aid the enemies of our country. The habit of declaring sympathy for the enemy will not be allowed in this department. Persons committing such offences will be at once arrested with a view to being tried as above stated, or sent beyond our lines into the lines of their friends. It must be distinctly understood that treason, expressed or implied, will not be tolerated in this department. All officers and soldiers are strictly charged with the execution of this order, By command of Major-General Burnside,
Lewis Richmond
Assistant Adjutant General

It was no doubt true that the Confederate authorities had constant correspondence with people in the Northern States, and that systematic means were used to pass information and contraband merchandise through the lines. Quinine among drugs, and percussion caps among ordnance stores were the things they most coveted, and dealers in these carried on their trade under pretence of being spies for each side in turn. But besides these who were merely mercenary, there were men and women who were honestly fanatical in their devotion to the Confederate cause. The women were especially troublesome, for they often seemed to court martyrdom. They practised on our forbearance to the last degree; for they knew our extreme unwillingness to deal harshly with any of their sex. Personally, I rated the value of spies and informers very low, and my experience had made me much more prone to contempt than to fear of them. But examples had to be made occasionally; a few men were punished, a few women who belonged in the South were sent through the lines, and we reduced to its lowest practical terms an evil and nuisance which we could not wholly cure. The best remedy for these plots and disturbances at the rear always was to keep the enemy busy by a vigorous aggressive at the front. We kept, however, a species of provost court pretty actively at work, and one or two officers were assigned to judge-advocate's duty, who ran these courts under a careful supervision to make sure that they should not fall into indiscretions.

So long as the hand of military power was laid only on private persons who were engaged in overt acts of giving aid and comfort to the rebellion in the ways specified in Order No. 38, there was little criticism. But the time came when General Burnside seemed to be challenged by a public character of no little prominence to enforce his order against him. The Vallandigham case became the sensation of the day, and acquired a singular historical importance. The noise which was made about it seemed to create a current opinion that Burnside's action was a new departure, and that his Order No. 38 was issued wholly on his own responsibility. This was not so. In the preceding year, and about the time of his Emancipation Proclamation, the President had also proclaimed against treasonable practices in very emphatic terms. He had declared that "all rebels and insurgents, their aiders and abettors, within the United States, and all persons discouraging volunteer enlistments, resisting militia drafts, or guilty of any disloyal practice, affording aid and comfort to rebels against the authority of the United States, shall be subject to martial law and liable to trial and punishment by courts-martial or military commission."

Burnside's order was in strict accordance with this authority, and he had no ultimate responsibility for the policy thus proclaimed. He was simply reiterating and carrying out in his department the declared purpose of the administration. Even in the matter of newspaper publications, his predecessor, General Wright, had felt obliged, upon Bragg and Kirby Smith's invasion of Kentucky, to put a stop to treasonable editorials and to the publication of military information likely to benefit the enemy. He issued a circular on September 13, 1862, notifying the publishers of the Cincinnati papers that the repetition of such offence would be immediately followed by the suppression of the paper and the arrest and confinement of the proprietors and writers. It is necessary to keep these facts in mind if we would judge fairly of Burnside's responsibility when it was his fortune to apply the rule to a case attracting great public attention.

CHAPTER 22

The Vallandigham Case—
The Holmes County War

Clement L. Vallandigham had been representative in Congress of the Montgomery County district of Ohio, and lived at Dayton. He was a man of intense and saturnine character, belligerent and denunciatory in his political speeches, and extreme in his views. He was the leader in Ohio of the ultra element of opposition to the administration of Mr. Lincoln, and a bitter opponent of the war. He would have prevented the secession of the Southern States by yielding all they demanded, for he agreed with them in thinking that their demands for the recognition of the constitutional inviolability of the slave system were just. After the war began he still advocated peace at any price, and vehemently opposed every effort to subdue the rebellion. To his mind the war was absolutely unconstitutional on the part of the national government, and he denounced it as tyranny and usurpation. His theory seemed to be that if the South were "let alone," a reconstruction of the Union could be satisfactorily effected by squelching the anti-slavery agitation, and that the Western States, at any rate, would find their true interest in uniting with the South, even if the other Northern States should refuse to do so. Beyond all question he answered to the old description of a "Northern man with Southern principles," and his violence of temper made it all a matter of personal hatred with him in his opposition to the leaders of the party in power at the North. His denunciations were the most extreme, and his expressions of contempt and ill-will were wholly unbridled. He claimed, of course, that he kept within the limits of a "constitutional opposition," because he did not, in terms, advise his hearers to combine in armed opposition to the government.

About the first of May he addressed a public meeting at Mount Vernon in central Ohio, where, in addition to his diatribes against the Lincoln administration, he denounced Order No. 38, and Burnside as its author. His words were noted down in short-hand by a captain of volunteers who was there on leave of absence from the army, and the report was corroborated by other reputable witnesses. He charged the administration with designing to erect a despotism, with refusing to restore the Union when it might be done, with carrying on the war for the liberation of the blacks and the enslavement of the whites. He declared that the provost-marshals for the congressional districts were intended to restrict the liberties of the people; that courts-martial had already usurped power to try citizens contrary to law; that he himself would never submit to the orders of a military dictator, and such were Burnside and his subordinates; that if those in authority were allowed to accomplish their purposes, the people would be deprived of their liberties and a monarchy established. Such and like expressions, varied by "trampling under his feet" Order No. 38, etc., made the staple of his incendiary speech.

When the report was made to Burnside and he had satisfied himself of its substantial truth, he promptly accepted the challenge to test the legality of his order, and directed the arrest of Mr. Vallandigham. It was characteristic of him that he did not consult with his subordinates or with lawyers. He did not even act through my district organization, but sent his own aide-de-camp with a guard to make the arrest at Dayton. My recollection is that I did not know of the purpose till it was accomplished. His reason for direct action, no doubt, was that if there were many links in the chain of routine, there were multiplied chances of failure. He did not want to be baffled in the arrest, or to give the opportunity for raising a mob, which there would be if his purposes were to become known in advance,

The arrest was made in the early morning of the 5th of May, before dawn, and the prisoner was brought to Cincinnati. He was at first taken under guard to the Burnet House, where he breakfasted, and was then put in the military prison connected with the houses used as barracks for the troops in the city. A military commission had been ordered on the 21st of April from Department Headquarters for the trial of the classes of offenders named in Order No. 38, and of this commission Brigadier-General R. B. Potter of the Ninth Corps was President. General Potter was a distinguished officer throughout the war. He was a brother of Clarkson N. Potter, the prominent lawyer and Democratic member of Congress later, and both were sons of the Episcopal Bishop Potter of Pennsylvania. The character of the whole court was very high for intelligence and standing. Before this court Mr. Vallandigham was arraigned on the charge of publicly expressing sympathy with those in arms against the government, and uttering disloyal sentiments and opinions with intent to weaken the power of the government in its efforts to suppress the rebellion.

Vallandigham consulted with the Hon. George E. Pugh and others as his counsel, and then adopted the course of protesting against the jurisdiction of the court and against the authority for his arrest. His grounds were that he was not amenable to any military jurisdiction, and that his public speech did not constitute an offence known to the Constitution and laws. To avoid the appearance of waiving the question of jurisdiction, his counsel did not appear, though offered the opportunity to do so, and Mr. Vallandigham cross-examined the witnesses himself, and called those who testified for him. The question of fact raised by him was that he had not advised forcible resistance to the government, but had urged action at the elections by defeating the party in power at the polls. That he did not in terms advocate insurrection was admitted by the judge advocate of the court, but the commission were persuaded that the effect of his speech was intended and well calculated to be incendiary, and to arouse any kind of outbreak in sympathy with the armed enemies of the country. The trial ended on the 7th of May, but the judgment was not promulgated till the 16th, proceedings in *habeas corpus* having intervened. The finding of the court was that the prisoner was guilty, as charged, and the sentence was close confinement in Fort Warren, Boston harbour, during the continuance of the war.

On the 9th of May Mr. Pugh made application to the United States Circuit Court, Judge Leavitt sitting, for a writ of *habeas corpus* directed to General Burnside, in order that the lawfulness of Mr. Vallandigham's arrest and trial might be tested. The court directed notice of the application to be given to the general, and set the 11th for the hearing. The case was elaborately argued by Mr. Pugh for the prisoner, and by Mr. Aaron F. Perry and the District Attorney Flamen Ball for General Burnside. The hearing occupied several days, and the judgment of the court was given on the morning of the 16th. Judge Leavitt refused the writ on the ground that, civil war being flagrant in the land, and Ohio being under the military command of General Burnside by appointment of the President, the acts and offences described in General Order No. 38 were cognizable by the military authorities under the powers of war.

General Burnside had awaited the action of the court, and now promulgated the sentence under the judgment of the military commission. Three days later (May 19th) the President commuted the sentence by directing that Mr. Vallandigham be sent "under secure guard, to the headquarters of General Rosecrans, to be put by him beyond our military lines, and that in case of his return within our line, he be arrested and kept in close custody for the term specified in his sentence." This was done accordingly. The Confederate officials adopted a careful policy of treating him courteously without acknowledging that he was one of themselves, and facilities were given him for running the blockade and reaching Canada. There he established himself on the border and put himself in communication with his followers in Ohio, by whom he was soon nominated for the Governorship of the State.

The case, of course, excited great public interest, and was, no doubt, the occasion of considerable embarrassment to the administration. Mr. Lincoln dealt with it with all that shrewd practical judgment for which he was so remarkable, and in the final result it worked to the political advantage of the National cause. Sending Vallandigham beyond the lines took away from him the personal sympathy which might have been aroused had he been confined in one of the casemates of Fort Warren, and put upon him an indelible badge of connection with the enemies of the country. The cautious action of the Confederates in regard to him did not tend to remove this: for it was very apparent that they really regarded him as a friend, and helped him on his way to Canada in the expectation that he would prove a thorn in Mr. Lincoln's side. The President's proposal to the leading politicians who applied to him to rescind the sentence, that as a condition of this they should make certain declarations of the duty to support the government in a vigorous prosecution of the war, was a most telling bit of policy on his part, and took the sting entirely out of the accusations of tyranny and oppression.

It must be admitted, however, that the case was one in which the administration ought to have left Burnside wholly untrammelled in carrying out the proclamation of September 25, 1862, or should have formulated a rule for its military officers, so that they would have acted only in accordance with the wishes of the government, and in cases where the full responsibility would be assumed at Washington. When Burnside arrested Mr. Vallandigham, the Secretary of War telegraphed from Washington his approval, saying, "In your determination to support the authority of the government and suppress treason in your department, you may count on the firm support of the President." Yet when a little later Burnside suppressed the "Chicago Times" for similar utterances, the President, on the request of Senator Trumbull, backed by prominent citizens of Chicago, directed Burnside to revoke his action. This the latter did by General Order No. 91, issued on the 4th of June. He read to me on June 7th a letter from Mr. Stanton, which practically revoked the whole of his Order No. 38 by directing him not to arrest civilians or suppress newspapers without conferring first with the War Department. This would have been very well if it had been done at the beginning; but to have it come after political pressure from the outside, and in so marked contradiction to the approval first expressed, shows that there was no well-considered policy. It put Burnside himself in an intolerable position, and, of course, made him decline further responsibility for such affairs in his department.

The whole question as to the right and the policy of military arrests and orders in such a time bristles with difficulties. Had I been consulted before Burnside took action, I should have advised him to collect carefully the facts and report them to Washington, asking for specific instructions. The subject called for directions which would be applicable in all the military departments which included States out of the theatre of active warlike operations; and such general directions should be given by the government. But Burnside was apt to act impulsively, and his impulse was to follow the bent of his ardent patriotism. He was stirred to burning wrath by what seemed to him an intent to give aid and comfort to the rebellion, and meant to punish such conduct without stopping to ask what complications might come of it.

I had found it desirable to form a judgment of my own with reference to the extent or limitation of military authority in the actual circumstances, and I quote the form in which I then cast it, so that I may not seem to be giving opinions formed after my own military duties were ended. I concluded, "First: That martial law operates either by reason of its proclamation by competent authority, or *ex necessitate rei* in the immediate theatre of military operations. Second; That when the struggle is in the nature of a revolution, and so long as the attempted revolution is in active progress, no definite limits can be given to the 'theatre of operations,' but the administration must be regarded as possessing a limited discretionary power in the use of martial law." As to the practical application of this power, "the presumptions are always in favour of the established civil law of the land, whenever and wherever it has a reasonable chance of unobstructed operation. In a State or portion of the country not the theatre of actual fighting, and where the civil courts are actually organized and working, there must be some strong reason for sending criminals or State prisoners before a military tribunal; such as that the government had reason to believe that a conspiracy was so powerful as to make an actual present danger of its overthrowing the loyal governments in some of the States before the civil courts could act in the ordinary process of business. In such a case, the arrest and admission to bail of the conspirators might be only the signal for their adherents to seize the reins of civil power, overthrow the courts, and consummate a revolution. The quick and summary action of military power would then be the only thing which could avert the danger. The justification of the use of a military tribunal depends on the existence of 'probable cause' for believing the public danger to be great."

I see no reason to change the form of stating the principle I then adopted. The limitations given it seem sufficient to secure proper caution in applying it, and will show that I thought then, as I do now, that the administration ought to have laid down rules by which the commandants of military departments could be guided, and which would have saved us from the weakness of acting with seeming vigour on one day, only to retreat from our position the next.

In Vallandigham's case the common argument was used by his friends that he was not exceeding a lawful liberty of speech in political opposition to the administration. When, however, a civil war is in progress, it is simply a question of fact whether words used are intended to give aid and comfort to the enemy and are evidence of conspiracy with the public enemy. If so, it is too clear for argument that the overt acts of the enemy are brought home to all who combine and confederate with them, and all are involved in the same responsibility. This question of fact and intent was officially settled by the findings of the military court. But there was another connection of the speech with overt acts, which the public mind took firm hold of. Among the most incendiary of Vallandigham's appeals had been those which urged the people to resist the provost-marshals in the several districts. It is nonsense to say that resisting the draft or the arrest of deserters only meant voting for an opposition party at the elections. There had been armed and organized resistance to arrest of deserters in Noble County just before his speech, and soon after it there was a still more formidable armed organization with warlike action against the enrolling officers in Holmes County, in the same region in which the speech was made. This last took the form of an armed camp, and the insurgents did not disperse till a military force was sent against them and attacked them in fortified lines, where they used both cannon and musketry. It did not seem plausible to the common sense of the people that we could properly charge with volleying musketry upon the barricades of the less intelligent dupes, whilst the leader who had incited and counselled the resistance was to be held to be acting within the limits of proper liberty of speech. Law and common sense are entirely in harmony in regarding the conspiracy as a unit, the speech at Mount Vernon and the armed collision on the Holmes County hill being parts of one series of acts in which the instigator was responsible for the natural consequences of the forces he set in motion.

To complete the judicial history of the Vallandigham case, it may be said that he applied to the Supreme Court of the United States a few months afterward for a writ to revise and examine the proceedings of the military commission and to determine their legality. The court dismissed his application on the ground that the writ applied for was not a legal means of bringing the proceedings of the military court under review. The charges and specifications and the sentence were all set forth in the application, so that the court was made officially aware of the full character of the case. This was naturally accepted at the time as practically sustaining the action of the President and General Burnside. When, however, the war was over, there was taken up to the Supreme Court the case of Milligan from Indiana, who had been condemned to death for treasonable conduct in aid of the rebellion, done as a member of the Knights of the Golden Circle, an organization charged with overt acts in attempting to liberate by force the Confederate prisoners of war in the military prisons, and otherwise to assist the rebellion. The current public sentiment in regard to executive power had unquestionably changed with the return to peace, and Lincoln having been assassinated and Johnson being in the presidential chair, the tide was running strongly in favour of congressional rather than executive initiative in public affairs. It cannot be denied that the court responded more or less fully to the popular drift, then as in other important historical junctures. In the opinion as delivered by Judge Davis, it went all lengths in holding that the military commission could not act upon charges against a person not in the military service, and who was a citizen of the State where tried, when in such State the civil courts were not actually suspended by the operations of war. Chief Justice Chase and three of the justices thought this was going too far, and whilst concurring in discharging Milligan, held that Congress could authorize military commissions to try civilians in time of actual war, and that such military tribunals might have concurrent jurisdiction with the civil courts.

We must not forget that whilst the judicial action determines the rights of the parties in a suit, the executive has always asserted his position as an independent co-ordinate branch of the government, authorized by the Constitution to determine for himself, as executive, his duties, and to interpret his powers, subject only to the Constitution as he understands it. Jefferson, Jackson, and Lincoln in turn found themselves in exigencies where they held it to be their duty to decide for themselves on their high political responsibility in matters of constitutional power and duty. Lincoln suspended the privilege of *habeas corpus* by his own proclamation, and adhered to his view, although Judge Taney in the Circuit Court for Maryland denied his power to do so. When Congress passed a regulating act on the subject which seemed to him sufficient, he signed the statute because he was quite willing to limit his action by the provisions embodied in it, and not because he thought the act necessary to confer the power.

An incident in the history of the treasonable organizations believed to exist in Indiana emphasizes the change of mental attitude of Judge Davis between 1863 and 1866. During the progress of the Vallandigham case, General Burnside conceived a distrust of the wisdom of the course pursued by Brigadier-General Carrington, who commanded at Indianapolis, and sent Brigadier-General Hascall there to command that district. Carrington had been the right hand of Governor Morton in ferreting out the secrets of the Golden Circle, and applying Order No, 38 to them, but Burnside's lack of confidence in the cool-headed caution and judgment of his subordinate led him to make the change. Hascall was a brave and reliable Indiana officer, who had seen much active field service, and with whom I was associated in the Twenty-third Corps during the Atlanta campaign. He was ardently loyal, but an unexcitable, matter-of-fact sort of person. He did not suit Governor Morton, who applied to the Secretary of War to have him removed from command, declaring that immediate action was important. Judge Davis, who was in Indianapolis, was induced to co-operate with the governor in the matter, and telegraphed to Mr. Stanton that Hascall's removal was demanded by the honour and interests of the government. Hascall was sent to the field, and after a short interval Carrington was restored to duty at Indianapolis. In the continued investigation and prosecution of the Golden Circle, and finally in the trial of Milligan, General Carrington was, under Governor Morton, the most active instrument; and it was, of course, to keep him at work on that line that the changes in command were secured. Yet it was the fruit of this very work of Carrington that was so strongly and sweepingly declared to be illegal by the Supreme Court, Judge Davis himself delivering the opinion and going beyond the chief-justice and others in denying all power and authority to military courts in such cases. Had Mr. Lincoln lived, he would no doubt have avoided any question before the Supreme Court in regard to his authority, by pardoning Milligan as he granted amnesty to so many who had been active in the rebellion. But Mr. Johnson was so much hampered by his quarrel with Congress over reconstruction that he was disposed to avoid interference with criminal cases where his action could subject him to the charge of sympathy with the accused. He carefully abstained from meddling with Jefferson Davis as he did with Milligan, and left the responsibility with the courts.

The final development of the investigation of the Society of the Golden Circle took place after I had again obtained a field command, and I was glad to have no occasion to form a personal judgment about it. The value of evidence collected by means of detectives depends so greatly on the character of the men employed and the instructions under which they act, that one may well suspend judgment unless he has more than ordinarily full knowledge on these points. The findings of the military commission must stand as a *prima facie* historical determination of the facts it reported, and the burden of proof is fairly upon those who assert that the conclusions were not sustained by trustworthy evidence.

I have mentioned the open resistance to the draft and to the arrest of deserters in Noble and in Holmes counties. The first of these was scarcely more than a petty riotous demonstration, which melted away before the officers as soon as they were able to show that they were backed by real power. The second looked for a time more formidable, and assumed a formal military organization. Governor Tod issued a proclamation warning the offenders of the grave consequences of their acts, and exhorting them for their own sake and the sake of their families to disperse and obey the laws. I directed General Mason at Columbus to be sure, if military force had to be used, that enough was concentrated to make stubborn resistance hopeless. The insurgents maintained a bold face till the troops were close upon them; but when they saw a strong line of infantry charging up toward the stone fences on the hillside where they had made their camp, and heard the whistling of bullets from the skirmishers, their courage gave way and they fled, every man for himself. Only two or three were seriously wounded, and comparatively few arrests were made. Submission to law was all that was demanded, and when this was fully established, the prisoners were soon released without further punishment. The fear of further prosecutions operated to preserve the peace, and the men who had been allowed to go at large were a guaranty, in effect, for the good behaviour of the community.

Before dropping the subject, I may properly add that the arrest of Mr. Vallandigham very naturally raised the question how far we were willing to go in bringing disloyal men before the military courts. Prominent citizens, and especially men in official position, often found themselves urged to ask for the arrest of the more outspoken followers of Vallandigham in every country neighbourhood. In answer to inquiries which had come through the Hon. Martin Welker, member of Congress for the Wayne County district, I wrote him a letter which shows the efforts we made to be prudent and to avoid unnecessary collisions. Judge Welker had served as Judge Advocate on my staff in the three months' service in the spring of 1861, and my intimacy with him made me speak as to our policy without reserve.

"We are hopeful," I wrote, "now that the United States Circuit Court has refused to release Mr. Vallandigham on *habeas corpus*, that his followers will take warning and that their course will be so modified that there may be no occasion to make many more arrests.

"I am persuaded that our policy should be to repress disloyalty and sedition at home rather by punishment of prominent examples than by a general arrest of all who may make themselves obnoxious to General Order No. 38, as the latter course will involve a more frequent application of military authority than we choose to resort to, unless circumstances should make it imperatively necessary... I am full of hope that the seditious designs of bad men will fail by reason of the returning sense of those who have been their dupes, and that the able and patriotic opinion of Judge Leavitt in the *habeas corpus* case will cause great numbers to take positive ground in favour of the government, who have hitherto been more or less under the influence of our northern traitors. If such shall be the result we can afford to overlook bygones, and I am inclined to await the development of public sentiment before following up Vallandigham's arrest by many others."

This letter was written before the Secretary of War made any limitation of Burnside's authority in enforcing his famous order, and shows that in the District of Ohio, at least, there was no desire to set up a military despotism, or to go further in applying military methods to conduct in aid of the rebellion than we might be forced to go.

Burnside's action in suppressing disloyal newspapers was not peculiar to himself. General Wright, his predecessor, had done the same, and other military commandants, both before and after and in other parts of the country, had felt obliged to take the same course. These facts only make more clear the desirability of a well-considered system of action determined by the government at Washington, and applicable to all such cases.

CHAPTER 23

Burnside and Rosecrans— The Summer's Delays

Burnside was not a man to be satisfied with quasi-military duty and the administration of a department outside of the field of active warfare. He had been reappointed to the formal command of the Ninth Corps before he came West, and the corps was sent after him as soon as transportation could be provided for it. He reached Cincinnati in person just as a raid into Kentucky by some 2000 Confederate cavalry under Brigadier-General John Pegram was in progress. Pegram marched from East Tennessee about the middle of March, reaching Danville, Ky., on the 23d. He spread reports that he was the advance-guard of a large force of all arms intending a serious invasion of the State. These exaggerations had their effect, and the disturbance in the Department of the Ohio was out of proportion to the strength of the hostile column. The troops belonging to the post at Danville retreated to the hither side of the Kentucky River at Hickman's Bridge, where they took up a defensive position. They saved the railway bridge from destruction, and Brigadier-General Quincy A. Gillmore, who commanded the District of Central Kentucky with headquarters at Lexington, was able to concentrate there a sufficient force to resume the offensive against Pegram.

Burnside ordered reinforcements to Gillmore from the other parts of Kentucky, and Pegram, whose report indicates that a foray for beef, cattle, and horses was the principal object of his expedition, commenced his retreat. Gillmore followed him up vigorously, recapturing a considerable part of the cattle he had collected, and overtaking his principal column at Somerset, routed him and drove him beyond the Cumberland River.

The month of March had begun with pleasant spring weather, and on the 15th General Wright had written to Halleck that an invasion of Kentucky was probable, especially as Rosecrans showed no signs of resuming the aggressive against Bragg's army in middle Tennessee. In Halleck's letter of instructions to Burnside as the latter was leaving Washington to relieve Wright, the general plan of an advance on East Tennessee in connection with that of Rosecrans toward Chattanooga was outlined, but the General-in-Chief acknowledged that the supply of an army in East Tennessee by means of the wagon roads was probably impracticable. He pointed out the necessity of reducing the number and size of garrisons in the rear, and making everything bend to the great object of organizing the army for active initiative against the enemy. He recommended building blockhouses to protect the principal bridges on the railroads, where very small garrisons could give comparative security to our lines of communication. This plan was ultimately carried out on a large scale, and was the necessary condition of Sherman's Atlanta campaign of 1864. Taken as a whole, Halleck's instructions to Burnside presented no definite objective, and were a perfunctory sort of introduction to his new command, which raises a doubt whether the organization of a little army in the Department of the Ohio met his approval.

The fact was that Burnside was acting on an understanding with President Lincoln himself, whose ardent wish to send a column for the relief of the loyal people of East Tennessee never slumbered, and who was already beginning to despair of its accomplishment by Rosecrans's army. The uneasiness at Washington over Rosecrans's inaction was becoming acute, and Mr. Lincoln was evidently turning to Burnside's department in hope of an energetic movement there. In this hope Burnside was sent West, and the Ninth Corps was detached from the Army of the Potomac and sent after him. The project of following up his advance by the construction of a railroad from Danville, then the terminus of the railway line reaching southward from Cincinnati, was discussed, and the President recommended it to Congress, but no appropriation of money was made. The scheme was hardly within the limits of practicable plans, for the building of a railway through such difficult country as the Cumberland mountain region implied laborious engineering surveys which could only be made when the country was reduced to secure possession, and the expenditure of time as well as of money would be likely to exceed the measure of reasonable plans for a military campaign. The true thing to do was to push Rosecrans's army to Chattanooga and beyond. With the valley of the Tennessee in our possession, and Chattanooga held as a new base of supply for a column in East Tennessee as well as another in Georgia, the occupation of Knoxville and the Clinch and Holston valleys to the Virginia line was easy. Without it, all East Tennessee campaigns were visionary. It was easy enough to get there; the trouble was to stay. Buell's original lesson in logistics, in which he gave the War Department a computation of the wagons and mules necessary to supply ten thousand men at Knoxville, was a solid piece of military arithmetic from which there was no escape.

When Burnside reached Cincinnati and applied himself practically to the task of organizing his little army for a march over the mountains, his first requisitions for wagons and mules were a little startling to the Quartermaster-General and a little surprising to himself. He began at once an engineering reconnaissance of the country south of Lexington and Danville, as far as it was within our control, and employed an able civil engineer, Mr. Gunn, to locate the preliminary line for a railway. These surveys were the starting-points from which the actual construction of the road between Cincinnati and Chattanooga was made after the close of the war.

Burnside also urged that the troops in Kentucky, exclusive of the Ninth Corps, be organized into a new corps with General Hartsuff as its commander. Halleck demurred to this, but the President directed it to be done, and the order was issued by the War Department on 27th April. Burnside also applied himself earnestly to procuring from Rosecrans a plan of active co-operation for an advance. As soon as Hartsuff assumed command of the new Twenty-third Corps, Burnside sent him, on May 3rd, to visit Rosecrans in person, giving him authority to arrange an aggressive campaign. Hartsuff's old relations to Rosecrans made him a very fit person for the negotiation. Rosecrans hesitated to decide, and called a council of his principal officers. He suggested that the Ninth Corps be sent down the Louisville and Nashville Railroad to Glasgow, near the Tennessee line, but did not indicate any immediate purpose of advancing. Burnside meant to take the field with both corps of his command, which he had organized under the name of the Army of the Ohio; but to reassure Rosecrans, he wrote that if in co-operation the two armies should come together, he would waive his elder rank and serve under Rosecrans whilst he should remain in middle Tennessee. It was now the 15th of May, and he sent a confidential staff officer again to Rosecrans to try to settle a common plan of operations. On the 18th Halleck had heard of Bragg's army being weakened to give General Joseph E. Johnston a force with which to relieve Pemberton at Vicksburg, and he became urgent for both Rosecrans and Burnside to advance. He thought it probable that raids would be attempted by the enemy to distract attention from his real object, and pointed out concentration and advance as the best way to protect the rear as well as to reach the enfeebled adversary. Burnside hastened in good faith his preparations for movement. He was collecting a pack mule train to supply the lack of wagons, and put his detachments in motion to concentrate. He begged for the third division of his corps (Getty's), which had been detained in the Army of the Potomac and could not yet be spared, but did not wait for it. By the 1st of June he was ready to leave in person for the front, and on the 3rd was at Lexington, definitely committed to the movement into East Tennessee. There he was met by an order from Halleck to send 8000 men at once to reinforce General Grant at Vicksburg. The promise was made that they should be returned as soon as the immediate exigency was over, but the order was imperative. Burnside never hesitated in obedience. The two divisions of the

Ninth Corps made about the number required, and they were immediately turned back and ordered to the Ohio River to be shipped on steamboats. Sorely disappointed, Burnside asked that he might go with his men, but was told that his departmental duties were too important to spare him from them. Major-General Parke was therefore sent in command of the corps. Burnside returned to Cincinnati, grieving at the interruption of his plans, yet hoping it would not be for long. His duties at the rear were not agreeable, especially as this was just the time when he was directed to recall his order suppressing disloyal newspapers, and to refrain from arrests of civilians without explicit authority from Washington.

We may safely assume that the President and his War Secretary were as little pleased at having to order the Ninth Corps away as Burnside was to have them go. In fact the order was not made till they entirely despaired of making Rosecrans advance with the vigour necessary to checkmate the Confederates. On the receipt of Halleck's dispatch of the 18th May, Rosecrans entered into a telegraphic discussion of the probable accuracy of Halleck's information, saying that whatever troops were sent by the enemy to Mississippi were no doubt sent from Charleston and Savannah and not from Bragg. He insisted that it was not good policy to advance at present. On the 21st he said, "If I had 6000 cavalry in addition to the mounting of the 2000 now waiting horses, I would attack Bragg within three days." He also interposed the unfavourable judgment of his corps commanders in regard to an advance. Military history shows that this is pretty uniformly an excuse for a delay already fully resolved on by a commanding general. Halleck had no more cavalry to send, and could only say so. Burnside notified Rosecrans on the 22nd that his columns had begun the movements of concentration and that they would be complete in three or four days. On the 28th Mr. Lincoln himself telegraphed Rosecrans, "I would not push you to any rashness, but I am very anxious that you do your utmost, short of rashness, to keep Bragg from getting off to help Johnston against Grant." Rosecrans curtly answered, "Dispatch received. I will attend to it." In his dispatches to Mr.

Stanton of similar date there is no intimation of any purpose whatever to move. In telegraphing to Burnside, Rosecrans said that he was only waiting for the development of the former's concentration, and that he wished to advance by the 4th of June. Burnside had already informed him that he would be ready by June 2nd, and repeated it. On the date last named Rosecrans telegraphed Burnside that his movement had already begun, and that he wanted the Army of the Ohio to come up as near and as quickly as possible. Still he gave no intimation to the authorities at Washington of an advance, for none had in fact been made by his army, nor even of any near purpose to make one. On June 3rd, Halleck telegraphed him: "Accounts received here indicate that Johnston is being heavily reinforced from Bragg's army. If you cannot hurt the enemy now, he will soon hurt you." He followed this by his dispatch to Burnside ordering reinforcements to be sent to Grant, and the remainder of the troops in the Department of the Ohio to be concentrated defensively in Kentucky. The only move that Rosecrans made was to send on the 8th to his general officers commanding corps and divisions, a confidential circular asking their opinion in writing in answer to the following questions, in substance—

1. Has the enemy been so materially weakened that this army could advance on him at this time with strong reasonable chances of fighting a great and successful battle?

2. Is an advance of our army likely to prevent additional reinforcements being sent against General Grant by Bragg?

3. Is an immediate or early advance of our army advisable?

With substantial unanimity they answered that it was not advisable to move, though they seem generally to have been aware that Breckinridge with about 10,000 men of all arms had gone from Bragg to Johnston. When Rosecrans reported the result of this council to Halleck, the latter reminded him of the maxim that "councils of war never fight," and that the responsibility for his campaign rests upon a commanding general and cannot be shared by a council of war.

The careful study of the correspondence elicited by Rosecrans's circular would make a most valuable commentary upon the theme, "*Why* Councils of War never fight." The three questions were addressed to sixteen general officers commanding corps and divisions. In reading the responses the impression grows strong that there was what may be called a popular feeling among these officers that their duty was to back up their commanding general in a judgment of his on the subjects submitted, which could hardly be other than well known. On the question as to the probable reduction of Bragg's army by detachments sent to Johnston, whilst they nearly all have some knowledge of the diminution of the Confederate army to about the extent mentioned above, most of them answer that they do not think it a *material* weakening, that being the tenor of the inquiry put to them. Some of them, however, say very naturally that as the secret service is managed from headquarters and all the information received is forwarded there, General Rosecrans should be much better able to answer this question than his subordinates. As to the second part of that question, nearly all seem to assume that the battle would be in the nature of a direct attack on the fortifications at Shelbyville and are not sanguine of a successful result. The few who speak of turning manoeuvres feel that the further retreat of Bragg would only lengthen their own line of communications and do no good. Strangely, too, they argue, many of them, that an advance would not prevent further depletion of Bragg to strengthen Johnston. They consequently and almost unanimously advise against an immediate or early advance.

It is instructive to compare these opinions with the actual facts. The inaction of the summer had led directly to the detachment of two divisions of infantry and artillery and one of cavalry to reinforce Johnston, just as the inactivity of Meade later in the season encouraged the Richmond government to send Longstreet to Bragg from Virginia. If Rosecrans had moved early in the season, not only must Bragg have kept his army intact, but the battle of Chickamauga, if fought at all, must have been decided without Longstreet, and therefore most probably with brilliant success for our arms. It was delay in advancing, both in

Tennessee and in Virginia, that thus directly led to disaster. If a brilliant victory at Chickamauga had been coincident with the fall of Vicksburg and Lee's defeat at Gettysburg, it does not seem rash to believe that the collapse of the Confederacy would have been hastened by a year.

Two of the generals who answered these questions attained afterward to such distinction that their replies are an interesting means of learning their mental character and gauging their development. Sheridan answered briefly that he believed Bragg had no more than 25,000 or 30,000 infantry and artillery, with a "large" cavalry force. In this he was very close to the mark. Bragg's report for the latter part of May, before sending reinforcements to Johnston, showed his forces present for duty to be 37,000 infantry, a little less than 3000 artillery, and 15,000 cavalry, in round numbers. Deduct 10,000 from these, and Sheridan is found to be sufficiently accurate. He did not think Bragg would fight, but would retreat, and thought that in such a case he would not be hindered from sending more help to Johnston. Again, as forage in the country was scarce, he voted against an early advance.

Thomas did not believe Bragg had been materially weakened, for if any troops had been sent away, he thought they had returned or their places had been supplied. He concluded that Bragg was ready to fight with an army at least as large as that of Rosecrans; that to hold our army where it was would sufficiently prevent further reduction of Bragg's; that an advance would give the latter the advantage and was not advisable. His preference for defensive warfare was very evident. He said it was true that Bragg might be reinforced and take the initiative, but that he "should be most happy to meet him here with his reinforcements." In conclusion he indicated the necessity of 6000 more cavalry to be added to the army.

When the answers were all received, Garfield summed them up in a paper, which must be admitted to be a remarkable production for a young volunteer officer deliberately controverting the opinions of such an array of seniors. He gave, as the best information at headquarters, the force of Bragg, before sending help to Johnston, as 38,000 infantry, 2600 artillery, and 17,500 cavalry. This made the infantry about 1000 too many, the artillery nearly exactly right, and the cavalry 2500 too many—on the whole a very close estimate. From these he deducted 10,000, which was right. He stated Rosecrans's force at 82,700 "bayonets and sabres" with about 3000 more on the way, but deducted 15,000 for necessary posts and garrisons. The balancing showed 65,000 to throw against Bragg's 41,500. He further showed that delay would give time for the enemy's detachments to return, whilst we could hope for no further increase during the rest of the season. He then analyzed the military and civil reasons for activity, declared that he believed we could be victorious, and that the administration and the country had the right to expect the army to try.

The result was a curious but encouraging result of bold and cogent reasoning. Although Rosecrans reported to General Halleck on the 11th of June the opinion of his corps and division commanders against an early advance, the logic and the facts pressed upon him by his chief of staff evidently took strong hold of his active intellect, so that when Halleck on the 16th asked for a categorical answer whether he would make an immediate movement forward, he replied, "If it means to-night or to-morrow, no. If it means as soon as all things are ready, say five days, yes." No doubt the rather plain intimation that a categorical "no" would be followed by action at Washington helped the decision; but it would have helped it to a decided negative if Garfield's paper, reinforced by the personal advice and oral discussions which we now know were of daily occurrence between them, had not had a convincing weight with him, both as to the feasibility of the campaign of turning manoeuvres which he devised and adopted, and as to its probable success. The result is reckoned one of his chief claims to military renown.

But to judge properly the relations of the government to both the commanding generals in Kentucky and Tennessee, it is necessary to go back to the days immediately after the battle of Stone's River, and to inquire what were the tasks assigned these commanders and the means furnished to perform them. The disappointment of the administration at Washington with Rosecrans's conduct of his campaign dated, indeed, much earlier than the time indicated. He had succeeded Buell at the end of October when Bragg was in full retreat to the Tennessee River. The continuance of a vigorous pursuit and the prompt reoccupation of the country held by us in the early summer was regarded as of the utmost importance for political, quite as much as for military reasons. It was not a time to halt and reorganize an army. The question of foreign intervention was apparently trembling in the balance, and to let European powers rest under the belief that we had lost most of what had been gained in the advance from Donelson to Shiloh and Corinth, was to invite complications of the most formidable character. The Washington authorities had therefore a perfect right to decide that to press Bragg vigorously and without intermission was the imperative duty of the commander of the Army of the Cumberland. He would be rightly held to have disappointed the expectations of his government if he failed to do so. Rosecrans had been chosen to succeed Buell because of the belief that his character was one of restless vehemence better adapted to this work than the slower but more solid qualities of Thomas, who was already second in command in that army. Halleck was obliged very soon to remind Rosecrans of this, and to claim the right of urging him onward because he himself had given the advice which had been decisive when the question of the choice was under consideration.

Yet as soon as the army was again concentrated about Nashville, Rosecrans's correspondence took the form of urgent demands for the means of reorganization. He insisted that his cavalry force must be greatly increased, that he must have repeating arms for his horsemen, that he must organize a selected corps of mounted infantry and obtain horses for them—in short, that he must take months to put his army in a condition equal to his desires before resuming the work of the campaign. His energy seemed to be wholly directed to driving the administration to supply his wants, whilst Bragg was allowed not only to stop his rather disorganized flight, but to retrace his steps toward middle Tennessee.

On the 4th of December Halleck telegraphed that the President was so disappointed and dissatisfied that another week of inaction would result in another change of commanders. Rosecrans replied detailing his necessities, but taking a high tone and declaring himself insensible to threats of removal. The next day Halleck patiently but decidedly gave the reasons which made the demand for activity a reasonable one, adding the reminder that no one had doubted that Buell would eventually have succeeded, and that Rosecrans's appointment had been made because they believed he would move more rapidly. Meanwhile every effort was made to furnish him with the arms, equipments, and horses he desired.

The battle of Stone's River had many points of resemblance to that of Antietam, and like that engagement was indecisive in itself, the subsequent retreat of the Confederates making it a victory for the national arms. The condition of the Army of the Cumberland after the battle was a sufficient reason for some delay, and a short time for recuperation and reinforcement was cordially accepted by everybody as a necessity of the situation. Congratulations and thanks were abundantly showered on the army, and promotions were given in more than common number. It was not concealed, however, that the government was most anxious to follow up the success and to make the delays as short as possible. An aggressive campaign was demanded, and the demand was a reasonable one because the means furnished were sufficient for the purpose.

At the close of the month of January, Rosecrans's forces present for duty in his department numbered 65,000, the Confederates under Bragg were 40,400. The end of February showed the National forces to be 80,000, the enemy 43,600. After this Bragg's army gradually increased till midsummer, when it reached a maximum of about 57,000, and Rosecrans's grew to 84,000. The Confederates had a larger proportion of cavalry than we, but this was at the expense of being much weaker in infantry, the decisive arm in serious engagements. In fact this disproportion was another reason for active work, since experience showed that the enemy kept his cavalry at home when he was vigorously pushed, and sent them on raids to interrupt our communications when we gave him a respite. Our superiority in numbers was enough, therefore, to make it entirely reasonable and in accord with every sound rule of conducting war, that the government should insist upon an active and aggressive campaign from the earliest day in the spring when the weather promised to be favourable. Such weather came at the beginning of March, and the Confederates took advantage of it, as we have seen, by sending Pegram into Kentucky. Their cavalry under Wheeler attacked also Fort Donelson, but were repulsed. A reconnaissance by a brigade under Colonel Coburn from Franklin toward Spring Hill resulted in the capture of the brigade by the Confederates under Van Dorn. In the same month Forrest made a daring raid close to Nashville and captured Colonel Bloodgood and some 800 men at Brentwood. Rosecrans organized a raid by a brigade of infantry mounted on mules, commanded by Colonel Streight, with the object of cutting the railroad south of Chattanooga. It was delayed in starting till near the end of April, and was overtaken and captured near Rome in Georgia. These exasperating incidents were occurring whilst the Army of the Cumberland lay still about Murfreesboro, and its commander harassed the departments at Washington with the story of his wants, and intimated that nothing but carelessness as to the public good stood between him and their full supply. He was assured that he was getting his full share of everything which could be procured—rifles, revolvers, carbines, horses, and equipments—but the day of readiness seemed as far off as ever.

On the 1st of March the President, feeling that the time had come when his armies should be in motion, and plainly discouraged at the poor success he had had in getting Rosecrans ready for an advance, authorized General Halleck to say to him that there was a vacant major-generalcy in the regular army which would be given to the general in the field who should first win an important and decisive victory. The appeal to ambition was treated as if it had been an insult. It was called an "auctioneering of honour," and a base way to come by a promotion. Halleck retorted conclusively that Rosecrans himself had warmly advocated giving promotion in the lower grades only for distinguished services in the field, and said: "When last summer, at your request, I urged the government to promote you for success in the field, and, again at your request, urged that your commission be dated back to your services in West Virginia, I thought I was doing right in advocating your claim to honours for services rendered." In view of this unique correspondence it is certainly curious to find Rosecrans a few days later enumerating his personal grievances to Mr. Lincoln, and putting among them this, that after the battle of Stone's River he had asked "as a personal favour" that his commission as major-general of volunteers should be dated back to December, 1861, and that it was not granted. It was considerably antedated, so as to make him outrank General Thomas, much to the disgust of the latter when he learned it; but the date was not made as early as Rosecrans desired, which would have made him outrank Grant, Buell, and Burnside as well as Thomas.

Persuasion and exhortation having failed, Grant must either be left to take the chances that part of Bragg's army would be concentrated under Johnston in Mississippi, or he must be strengthened by sending to him that part of our forces in Kentucky and Tennessee which could most easily be spared. There can be no doubt that it was well judged to send the Ninth Corps to him, as it would be less mischievous to suspend Burnside's movement into East Tennessee than to diminish the Army of the Cumberland under existing circumstances. It is, however, indisputably clear that the latter army should have been in active campaign at the opening of the season, whether we consider the advantage of the country or the reputation of its commander.

If we inquire what means the administration gave Burnside to perform his part of the joint task assigned him, we shall find that it was not niggardly in doing so. His forces were at their maximum at the end of May, when they reached but little short of 38,000 present for duty in his whole department. This included, however, all the great States of Ohio, Indiana, Illinois, and Michigan as well as the eastern half of Kentucky, and there were several camps of prisoners and posts north of the Ohio which demanded considerable garrisons. Eight thousand men were used for this purpose, and nobody thought this an excess. Thirty thousand were thus left him for such posts in Kentucky as would be necessary to cover his communications and for his active column. He expected to make his active army about 25,000, and the advance movements had begun when, as has been stated, he was ordered to suspend, and to send the Ninth Corps to Grant.

The enemy in East Tennessee were under the command of General Dabney Maury at first, but when he was sent to Mobile, General S. B. Buckner was made the commandant. His returns of forces for May 31st show that he had 16,267 present for duty, with which to oppose the advance of Burnside. The information of the latter was that his opponent had 20,000, and he reckoned on having to deal with that number. The passes of the Cumberland Mountains were so few and so difficult that it was by no means probable that his campaign would be an easy one; yet the difficulties in the first occupation were not so serious as those which might arise if Bragg were able to maintain an interior position between the two National armies. In that case, unless he were kept thoroughly employed by Rosecrans, he might concentrate to crush Burnside before his decisive conflict with the Army of the Cumberland. This was the inherent vice of a plan which contemplated two independent armies attempting to co-operate; and if Rosecrans had been willing to open his campaign on the 1st of March, it is almost certain that the troops in Kentucky would have been ordered to him. The President did not determine to send Burnside to the West and to give him a little army of his own till he despaired of the liberation of East Tennessee in that season by any activity of Rosecrans. This cannot be overlooked in any candid criticism of the summer's work.

CHAPTER 24

The Morgan Raid

The departure of General Burnside and his staff for active service in the field was quite an event in Cincinnati society. The young men were a set of fine fellows, well educated and great social favourites. There was a public concert the evening before they left for Lexington, and they were to go by a special train after the entertainment should be over. They came to the concert hall, therefore, not only booted and spurred, but there was perhaps a bit of youthful but very natural ostentation of being ready for the field. Their hair was cropped as close as barber's shears could cut it, they wore the regulation uniform of the cavalry, with trim round-about jackets, and were the "cynosure of all eyes." Their parting words were said to their lady friends in the intervals of the music, and the pretty dramatic effect of it all suggested to an onlooker the famous parting scene in "Belgium's capital" which "Childe Harold" has made so familiar.

It was quite an anti-climax, however, when the gay young officers came back, before a week was over, crestfallen, the detaching of the Ninth Corps having suspended operations in Kentucky. They were a little quizzed about their very brief campaign, but so good-humouredly that they bore it pretty well, and were able to seem amused at it, as well as the fair quizzers.

In preparation for a lengthened absence, Burnside had turned over to me some extra duties. He ordered the District of Michigan to be added to my command, and gave general directions that the current business of the department headquarters should pass through my hands. As General Parke, his chief of staff, had gone to Vicksburg in command of the Ninth Corps, Burnside made informal use of me to supply in some measure his place. Our relations therefore became closer than ever. He hoped his troops would soon come back to him, as was promised, and in resuming business at the Cincinnati headquarters, he tried to keep it all in such shape that he could drop it at a moment's notice.

To keep the enemy occupied he organized two expeditions, one under Brigadier-General Julius White into West Virginia, and the other under Colonel W. P. Sanders into East Tennessee. The latter was one of the boldest and longest raids made during the war, and besides keeping the enemy on the alert, destroying considerable military stores and a number of important railway bridges, it was a preliminary reconnaissance of East Tennessee and the approaches to it through the mountains, which was of great value a little later. The force consisted of 1500 mounted men, being detachments from different regiments of cavalry and mounted infantry, among which were some of the loyal men of East Tennessee under Colonel R. K. Byrd. Sanders was a young officer of the regular army who was now colonel of the Fifth Kentucky Cavalry. He rapidly made a first-class reputation as a bold leader of mounted troops, but was unfortunately killed in the defence of Knoxville in November of this same year. His expedition started from Mount Vernon, Kentucky, on the 14th of June, marched rapidly southward sixty miles to Williamsburg, where the Cumberland River was fordable. Thence he moved southwest about the same distance by the Marsh Creek route to the vicinity of Huntsville in Tennessee. Continuing this route southward some fifty miles more, he struck the Big Emory River, and following this through Emory Gap, he reached the vicinity of Kingston on the Clinch River in East Tennessee, having marched in all rather more than two hundred miles. Avoiding Kingston, which was occupied by a superior force of Confederates, he marched rapidly on Knoxville, destroying all the more important railway bridges. Demonstrating boldly in front of Knoxville, and finding that it was strongly held and its streets barricaded for defence, he passed around the town and advanced upon Strawberry Plains, where a great bridge and trestle crosses the Holston River, 2100 feet in length, a place to become very familiar to us in later campaigning. Crossing the Holston at Flat Creek, where other bridges were burned, he moved up the left (east) bank of the river to attack the guard at the big bridge, the Confederate forces being on that side. He drove them off, capturing 150 of the party and five cannon. He not only destroyed the bridge, but captured and burnt large quantities of military stores and camp equipage. On he went along the railway to Mossy Creek, where another bridge 300 feet long was burned. He now turned homeward toward the north-west, having greatly injured a hundred miles of the East Tennessee Railroad. Turning like a fox under the guidance of his East Tennessee scouts, he crossed the Clinch Mountains and the valley of the Clinch, and made his way back by way of Smith's Gap through the Cumberland Mountains to his starting-place in Kentucky. He had captured over 450 prisoners, whom he paroled, had taken ten cannon and 1000 stands of small arms which he destroyed, besides the large amounts of military stores which have been mentioned. He marched about five hundred miles in the whole circuit, and though frequently skirmishing briskly with considerable bodies of the enemy, his losses were only 2 killed, 4 wounded, and 13 missing. Of course a good many horses were used up, but as a preliminary to the campaign which was to follow and in which Sanders was to have a prominent place, it was a raid which was much more profitable than most of them. He was gone ten days.

The expedition under Brigadier-General Julius White was sent to beat up the Confederate posts in the Big Sandy valley and to aid incidentally the raid under Sanders into East Tennessee. Burnside sent another southward in the direction of Monticello, Kentucky. The object of these was to keep the enemy amused near home and prevent the raids his cavalry had been making on the railway line by which Rosecrans kept up his communication with Louisville. They seem rather to have excited the emulation of the Confederate cavalryman Brigadier-General John H. Morgan, who, a few days before Rosecrans's advance on Tullahoma, obtained permission to make a raid, starting from the neighbourhood of McMinnville, Tenn., crossing the Cumberland near Burkesville, and thence moving on Louisville, which he thought he might capture with its depots of military stores, as it was supposed to be almost stripped of troops. His division consisted of about 3000 horsemen, and he took the whole of it with him, though Wheeler, his chief, seems to have limited him to 2000. His instructions were to make a rapid movement on the line of the Louisville and Nashville Railroad in Kentucky and to get back to his place in Bragg's army as quickly as possible.

Morgan's reputation as a soldier was a peculiar one. He had made a number of raids which showed a good deal of boldness in the general plan and a good deal of activity in the execution, but it cannot be said that he showed any liking for hard fighting. Like boys skating near thin ice, he seemed to be trying to see how close he could come to danger without getting in. A really bold front showed by a small body of brave men was usually enough to turn him aside. It is instructive to compare his career with Forrest's. They began with similar grade, but with all the social and personal prestige in Morgan's favour. Forrest had been a local slave-trader, a calling which implied social ostracism in the South, and which put a great obstacle in the way of advancement. Both were fond of adventurous raids, but Forrest was a really daring soldier and fought his way to recognition in the face of stubborn prejudice. Morgan achieved notoriety by the showy temerity of his distant movements, but nobody was afraid of him in the field at close quarters.

The official order to Morgan to start on his expedition was dated on the 18th of June, but he did not get off till the close of the month. It would seem that he remained in observation on the flank of Rosecrans's army as the left wing moved upon Manchester, and began his northward march after Bragg had retreated to Decherd on the way to Chattanooga. At any rate, he was first heard of on the north side of the Cumberland on the 2nd of July, near Burkesville and marching on Columbia. Burnside immediately ordered all his cavalry and mounted infantry to concentrate to meet him, but his route had been chosen with full knowledge of the positions of our detachments and he was able to get the start of them. Brigadier-General H. M. Judah, who commanded the division of the Twenty-third Corps which covered that part of our front, seems to have wholly misconceived the situation, and refused to listen to the better information which his subordinates gave him. After a slight skirmish at Columbia, Morgan made for the Green River bridge at Tebb's Bend, an important crossing of the Louisville Railroad. The bend was occupied by Colonel O. H. Moore of the Twenty-fifth Michigan Infantry, who, under previous instructions from Brigadier-General E. H. Hobson, entrenched a line across the neck of the bend, some distance in front of the stockade at the bridge. Morgan advanced upon the 4th of July, and after a shot or two from his artillery, sent in a flag demanding the surrender of Moore's little force, which amounted to only 200 men. Moore did not propose to celebrate the national anniversary in that way, and answered accordingly. The enemy kept up a lively skirmishing fight for some hours, when he withdrew. Moore had beaten him off with a loss of 6 killed and 23 wounded of the brave Michigan men. He reported Morgan's loss at 50 killed and 200 wounded. The Confederate authorities admit that they had 36 killed, but put their wounded at only 46, an incredibly small proportion to the killed.

The raiders continued their route to Lebanon, where was the Twentieth Kentucky Infantry under Lieutenant-Colonel Charles S. Hanson, numbering less than 400 men, without artillery. A brigade ordered to reinforce the post delayed its advance, and Hanson was left to his own resources. After several hours of a lively skirmishing fight without much loss, he surrendered to save the village from destruction by fire, which Morgan threatened. The loss in the post was 4 killed and 15 wounded. Hanson reported 29 rebel dead left on the field and 30 wounded, also abandoned. No doubt others of the wounded were taken care of and concealed by their sympathizers in the vicinity. Some military stores had been burned with the railway station-house before Hanson surrendered. He and his men were paroled in the irregular way adopted by Morgan on the raid.

Bardstown was the next point reached by the enemy, but Morgan's appetite for Louisville seems now to have diminished, and he turned to the westward, reaching the Ohio River on the 8th, at Brandenburg, some thirty miles below the city. The detachments of mounted troops which were in pursuit had been united under the command of General Hobson, the senior officer present, and consisted of two brigades, commanded by Brigadier-General J. M. Shackelford and Colonel F. Wolford. They approached Brandenburg on the evening of the 8th and captured the steamboat "McCombs" with a remnant of Morgan's men and stores the next morning when they entered the town. They saw on the opposite bank the smoking wreck of the steamboat "Alice Dean" which Morgan had set on fire after landing his men on the Indiana shore. The steamboat "McCombs" was sent to Louisville for other transports. A delay of twenty-four hours thus occurred, and when Hobson's command was assembled in Indiana, Morgan had the start by nearly two days.

It is claimed by Morgan's intimate friend and chronicler that he intended to cross the Ohio from the day he left camp in Tennessee, although it would be contrary to his orders; and that he had made investigations in advance in regard to fords on the upper Ohio and particularly at Buffington Island, where he ultimately tried to cross into West Virginia. If true, this would forfeit every claim on his part to the character of a valuable and intelligent subordinate; for operations on a large scale would be absolutely impossible if the commander of a division of cavalry may go off as he pleases, in disobedience to the orders which assign him a specific task. Except for this statement, it would be natural to conclude that when he approached Louisville he began to doubt whether the city were so defenceless as he had assumed, and knowing that twenty-four hours' delay would bring Hobson's forces upon his back, he then looked about for some line of action that would save his prestige and be more brilliant than a race back again to Tennessee. It is quite probable that the feasibility of crossing the Ohio and making a rapid ride through the country on its northern bank had been discussed by him, and conscious as he was that he had thus far accomplished nothing, he might be glad of an excuse for trying it. This interpretation of his acts would be more honourable to him as an officer than the deliberate and premeditated disobedience attributed to him. But whether the decision was made earlier or later, the capture of the steamboats at Brandenburg was at once made use of to ferry over his command, though it was not accomplished without some exciting incidents. A party of the Confederates under Captain Hines had crossed into Indiana a few days before without orders from Morgan, being as independent of him, apparently, as he was of General Bragg. Hines's party had roused the militia of the State, and he had made a rapid retreat to the Ohio, reaching it just as Morgan entered Brandenburg. It may be that the lucky daredevilry of Hines's little raid fired his commander's heart to try a greater one; at any rate, Morgan forgave his trespass against his authority as he prayed to be forgiven by Bragg, and turned his attention to driving off the Indiana militia who had followed Hines to the bank of the river and now opened fire with a single cannon. Morgan's artillery silenced the gun and caused the force to retreat out of range, when he put over two of his regiments, dismounted, to cover the ferrying of the rest. At this point one of the "tin-clad" gunboats of the river fleet made its appearance and took part in the combat. The section of Parrot guns in Morgan's battery proved an overmatch for it, however, and it retired to seek reinforcements. The interval was used to hasten the transport of the Confederate men and horses, and before further opposition could be made, the division was in the saddle and marching northward into Indiana.

At the first news of Morgan's advance into Kentucky, Burnside had directed General Hartsuff, who commanded in that State, to concentrate his forces so as to capture Morgan if he should attempt to return through the central part of it. Judah's and Boyle's divisions were put in motion toward Louisville, and the remainder of the mounted troops not already with Hobson were also hurried forward. These last constituted a provisional brigade under Colonel Sanders. It may help to understand the organization of the National troops to note the fact that all which operated against Morgan were parts of the Twenty-third Corps, which was composed of four divisions under Generals Sturgis, Boyle, Judah, and White. The brigades were of both infantry and mounted troops, united for the special purposes of the contemplated campaign into East Tennessee. For the pursuit of Morgan the mounted troops were sent off first, and as these united they formed a provisional division under Hobson, the senior brigadier present. Quite a number of the regiments were mounted infantry, who after a few months were dismounted and resumed their regular place in the infantry line. For the time being, however, Hobson had a mounted force that was made up of fractions of brigades from all the divisions of the corps; and Shackelford, Wolford, Kautz, and Sanders were the commanders of the provisional brigades during the pursuit. Its strength did not quite reach 3000 men.

Morgan's first course was due north, and he marched with some deliberation. On the 10th he reached Salem, about forty miles from the river, on the railway between Louisville and Chicago. A small body of militia had assembled here, and made a creditable stand, but were outflanked and forced to retreat after inflicting on him a score of casualties. The evidences Morgan here saw of the ability of the Northern States to overwhelm him by the militia, satisfied him that further progress inland was not desirable, and turning at right angles to the road he had followed, he made for Madison on the Ohio. There was evidently some understanding with a detachment he had left in Kentucky, for on the 11th General Manson, of Judah's division, who was on his way with a brigade from Louisville to Madison by steamboats under naval convoy, fell in with a party of Morgan's men seeking to cross the river at Twelve-mile Island, a little below Madison. Twenty men and forty-five horses were captured. If any of this party had succeeded in crossing before (as was reported) they would of course inform their chief of the reinforcements going to Madison, and of the gunboats in the river. Morgan made no attack on Madison, but took another turn northward in his zigzag course, and marched on Vernon, a railway-crossing some twenty miles from Madison, where the line to Indianapolis intersects that from Cincinnati to Vincennes. Here a militia force had been assembled under Brigadier-General Love, and the town was well situated for defence. Morgan, declining to attack, now turned eastward again, his course being such that he might be aiming for the river at Lawrenceburg or at Cincinnati.

The deviousness of his route had been such as to indicate a want of distinct purpose, and had enabled Hobson greatly to reduce the distance between them. Hanson's brigade on the steamboats was now about 2500 strong, and moved on the 12th from Madison to Lawrenceburg, keeping pace as nearly as possible with Morgan's eastward progress. Sanders's brigade reached the river twenty miles above Louisville, and General Boyle sent transports to put him also in motion on the river. At the request of Burnside, Governor Tod, of Ohio, called out the militia of the southern counties, as Governor Morton had done in Indiana. Burnside himself, at Cincinnati, kept in constant telegraphic communication with all points, assembling the militia where they were most likely to be useful and trying to put his regular forces in front of the enemy. It would have been easy to let the slippery Confederate horsemen back into Kentucky. The force in the river, both naval and military, unquestionably prevented this at Madison, and probably at Lawrenceburg. On the 13th Morgan was at Harrison on the Ohio State line, and it now became my turn as district commander to take part in the effort to catch him. I had no direct control of the troops of the Twenty-third Corps, and the only garrisons in Ohio were at the prison camps at Columbus and Sandusky. These of course could not be removed, and our other detachments were hardly worth naming. Burnside declared martial law in the counties threatened with invasion, so that the citizens and militia might for military purposes come directly under our control. The relations between the general and myself were so intimate that no strict demarcation of authority was necessary. He authorized me to give commands in his name when haste demanded it, and we relieved each other in night watching at the telegraph. A small post had been maintained at Dayton, since the Vallandigham disturbance, and Major Keith, its commandant, was ordered to take his men by rail to Hamilton. He went at once and reported himself holding that town with 600 men, including the local militia, but only 400 were armed. Lieutenant-Colonel Neff commanded at Camp Dennison, thirteen miles from Cincinnati, and had 700 armed men there, with 1200 more of unarmed recruits. At both these posts systematic scouting was organized so as to keep track of the enemy, and their active show of force was such that Morgan did not venture to attack either, but threaded his way around them. At Cincinnati there was no garrison. A couple of hundred men formed the post at Newport on the Kentucky side of the river, but the main reliance was on the local militia. These were organized as soon as the governor's call was issued on the evening of the 12th. Batteries were put in position covering the approaches to the city from the north and west, and the beautiful suburban hills of Clifton and Avondale afforded excellent defensive positions.

The militia that were called out were of course infantry, and being both without drill and unaccustomed to marching, could only be used in position, to defend a town or block the way. In such work they showed courage and soldierly spirit, so that Morgan avoided collision with all considerable bodies of them. But they could not be moved. All we could do was to try to assemble them at such points in advance as the raiders were likely to reach, and we especially limited their task to the defensive one, and to blockading roads and streams. Particular stress was put on the orders to take up the planking of bridges and to fell timber into the roads. Little was done in this way at first, but after two or three days of constant reiteration, the local forces did their work better, and delays to the flying enemy were occasioned which contributed essentially to the final capture.

No definite news of Morgan's crossing the Ohio line was received till about sunset of the 13th when he was marching eastward from Harrison. Satisfied that Lawrenceburg and lower points on the Ohio were now safe, Burnside ordered the transports and gunboats at once to Cincinnati. Manson and Sanders arrived during the night, and the latter with his brigade of mounted men was, at dawn of the 14th, placed on the north of the city in the village of Avondale. Manson with the transports was held in readiness to move further up the river.

Feeling the net drawing about him, Morgan gave his men but two or three hours' rest near Harrison, and then took the road toward Cincinnati. He reached Glendale, thirteen miles northwest of the city, late in the night, and then turned to the east, apparently for Camp Dennison, equally distant in a northeast direction. His men were jaded to the last degree of endurance, and some were dropping from the saddle for lack of sleep. Still he kept on. Colonel Neff, in accordance with his orders, had blockaded the principal roads to the west, and stood at bay in front of his camp. Morgan threw a few shells at Neff's force, and a slight skirmish began, but again he broke away, forced to make a detour of ten miles to the north. We had been able to warn Neff of their approach by a message sent after midnight, and he had met them boldly, protecting the camp and the railroad bridge north of it. The raiders reached Williamsburg in Clermont County, twenty-eight miles from Cincinnati, in the afternoon of the 14th, and there the tired men and beasts took the first satisfactory rest they had had for three days. Morgan had very naturally assumed that there would be a considerable regular force at Cincinnati, and congratulated himself that by a forced night march he had passed round the city and avoided being cut off. He had, in truth, escaped by the skin of his teeth. Could Burnside have felt sure that Lawrenceburg was safe a few hours earlier, Manson and Sanders might have been in Cincinnati early enough on the 13th to have barred the way from Harrison. He had in fact ordered Manson up at two o'clock in the afternoon, but the latter was making a reconnaissance north of the town, and was detained till late in the night. As soon as it was learned on the 14th that Morgan had passed east of the Little Miami River, Sanders was ordered to join Hobson and aid in the pursuit. Hobson's horses were almost worn out, for following close upon Morgan's track, as he was doing, he found only broken down animals left behind by the rebels, whilst these gathered up the fresh animals as they advanced. Still he kept doggedly on, seldom more than ten or fifteen miles behind, but unable to close that gap till his opponent should be delayed or brought to bay.

After entering Clermont County, the questions as to roads, etc, indicated that Morgan was making for Maysville, hoping to cross the river there. Manson's brigade and the gunboats were accordingly sent up the river to that vicinity. The militia of the Scioto valley were ordered to destroy the bridges, in the hope that that river would delay him, but they were tardy or indifferent, and it was a day or two later before the means of obstruction were efficiently used. Judah's forces reached Cincinnati on the 14th, a brigade was there supplied with horses, and they were sent by steamers to Portsmouth. Judah was ordered to spare no effort to march northward far enough to head off the enemy's column. On the 16th General Scammon, commanding in West Virginia, was asked to concentrate some of his troops at Gallipolis or Pomeroy on the upper Ohio, and promptly did so. The militia were concentrated at several points along the railway to Marietta. Hobson was in the rear, pushing along at the rate of forty miles a day.

Morgan had soon learned that the river was so patrolled that no chance to make a ferry could be trusted, and he made his final effort to reach the ford at Buffington Island, between Marietta and Pomeroy. He reached Pomeroy on the 18th, but Scammon was occupying it, and the troops of the Kanawha division soon satisfied Morgan that he was not dealing with militia. He avoided the roads held by our troops, and as they were infantry, could move around them, though a running skirmish was kept up for some miles. Hobson was close in rear, and Judah's men were approaching Buffington. Morgan reached the river near the ford about eight o'clock in the evening. The night was pitchy dark, and his information was that a small earthwork built to command the ford was occupied by a permanent garrison. He concluded to wait for daylight. The work had in fact been abandoned on the preceding day, but at daybreak in the morning he was attacked. Hobson's men pushed in from west and north, and Judah from the south. The gunboats came close up to the island, within range of the ford, and commanded it. Hobson attacked vigorously and captured the artillery. The wing of the Confederate forces, about 700 in number, surrendered to General Shackelford, and about 200 to the other brigades under Hobson. The rest of the enemy, favoured by a fog which filled the valley, evaded their pursuers and fled northward. Hobson ordered all his brigades to obey the commands of Shackelford, who was in the lead, and himself sought Judah, whose approach had been unknown to him till firing was heard on the other side of the enemy. Judah had also advanced at daybreak, but in making a reconnaissance he himself with a small escort had stumbled upon the enemy in the fog. Both parties were completely surprised, and before Judah could bring up supports, three of his staff were captured, Major Daniel McCook, paymaster, who had volunteered as an aide, was mortally wounded, ten privates were wounded, and twenty or thirty with a piece of artillery captured. Morgan hastily turned in the opposite direction, when he ran into Hobson's columns; Judah's prisoners and the gun were recaptured, and the enemy driven in confusion, with the losses above stated.

As Hobson was regularly a brigade commander in Judah's division, the latter now asserted command of the whole force, against Hobson's protest, who was provisionally in a separate command by Burnside's order. Fortunately, Shackelford had already led Hobson's men in rapid pursuit of the enemy, and as soon as Burnside was informed of the dispute, he ordered Judah not to interfere with the troops which had operated separately. By the time this order came Shackelford was too far away for Hobson to rejoin him, and continued in independent command till Morgan's final surrender. He overtook the flying Confederates on the 20th, about sixty miles further north, and they were forced to halt and defend themselves. Shackelford succeeded in getting a regiment in the enemy's rear, and after a lively skirmish between 1200 and

1300 surrendered. Morgan himself again evaded with about 600 followers. Shackelford took 500 volunteers on his best horses and pressed the pursuit. The chase lasted four days of almost continuous riding, when the enemy was again overtaken in Jefferson County, some fifteen miles northwest of Steubenville. General Burnside had collected at Cincinnati the dismounted men of Hobson's command, had given them fresh horses, and had sent them by rail to join Shackelford. They were under command of Major W. B. Way of the Ninth Michigan Cavalry and Major G. W. Rue of the Ninth Kentucky Cavalry. They brought five or six hundred fresh men to Shackelford's aid, and their assistance was decisive. Morgan's course to the river at Smith's Ferry on the border of Columbiana County was intercepted, and near Salineville he was forced to surrender with a little less than 400 men who still followed him. About 250 had surrendered in smaller bodies within a day or two before, and stragglers had been picked up at many points along the line of pursuit. Burnside reported officially that about 3000 prisoners were brought to Cincinnati. General Duke states that some 300 of Morgan's command succeeded in crossing the Ohio about twenty miles above Buffington, and escaped through West Virginia. He also gives us some idea of the straggling caused by the terrible fatigues of the march by telling us that the column was reduced by nearly 500 effectives when it passed around Cincinnati. It is probable that these figures are somewhat loosely stated, as the number of prisoners is very nearly the whole which the Confederate authorities give as Morgan's total strength. Either a considerable reinforcement must have succeeded in getting to him across the river, or a very small body must have escaped through West Virginia. Burnside directed the officers to be sent to the military prison camp for officers on Johnson's Island in Sandusky Bay, and the private soldiers to go to Camp Chase at Columbus and Camp Morton at Indianapolis. Soon afterward, however, orders came from Washington that the officers should be confined in the Ohio penitentiary, in retaliation for unusual severities practised on our officers who were prisoners in the South. Morgan's romantic escape from the prison occurred just after I was relieved from the command of the district in the fall, for the purpose of joining the active army in East Tennessee.

A glance at the raid as a whole, shows that whilst it naturally attracted much attention and caused great excitement at the North, it was of very little military importance. It greatly scattered for a time and fatigued the men and horses of the Twenty-third Corps who took part in the chase. It cost Indiana and Ohio something in the plunder of country stores and farmhouses, and in the pay and expenses of large bodies of militia that were temporarily called into service. But this was all. North of the Ohio no military posts were captured, no public depots of supply were destroyed, not even an important railway bridge was burned. There was no fighting worthy of the name; the list of casualties on the National side showing only 19 killed, 47 wounded, and 8 missing in the whole campaign, from the 2nd of July to the final surrender. For this the whole Confederate division of cavalry was sacrificed. Its leader was never again trusted by his government, and his prestige was gone forever. His men made simply a race for life from the day they turned away from the militia at Vernon, Indiana. Morgan carefully avoided every fortified post and even the smaller towns. The places he visited after he crossed the Ohio line do not include the larger towns and villages that seemed to lie directly in his path. He avoided the railroads also, and these were used every day to convey the militia and other troops parallel to his route, to hedge him in and finally to stop him. His absence was mischievous to Bragg, who was retreating upon Chattanooga and to whom the division would have been a most welcome reinforcement. He did not delay Burnside, for the latter was awaiting the return of the Ninth Corps from Vicksburg, and this did not begin to arrive till long after the raid was over. None of the National army's communications were interrupted, and not a soldier under Rosecrans lost a ration by reason of the pretentious expedition. It ended in a scene that was ridiculous in the extreme. Morgan had pressed into his service as guides, on the last day of his flight, two men who were not even officers of the local militia, but who were acting as volunteer homeguards to protect their neighbourhood. When he finally despaired of escape, he begged his captive guides to change their role into commanders of an imaginary army and to accept his surrender upon merciful and favourable terms to the vanquished! He afterward claimed the right to immediate liberation on parole, under the conditions of this burlesque capitulation. Shackelford and his rough riders would accept no surrender but an unconditional one as prisoners of war, and were sustained in this by their superiors. The distance by the river between the crossing at Brandenburg and the ferry above Steubenville near which Morgan finally surrendered, was some six hundred miles. This added to the march from Tennessee through Kentucky would make the whole ride nearly a thousand miles long. Its importance, however, except as a subject for an entertaining story, was in an inverse ratio to its length. Its chief interest to the student of military history is in its bearing on the question of the rational use of cavalry in an army, and the wasteful folly of expeditions which have no definite and tangible military object.

CHAPTER 25

The Liberation of East Tennessee

During the Morgan Raid and whilst we in Ohio were absorbed in the excitement of it, events were moving elsewhere. Lee had advanced from Virginia through Maryland into Pennsylvania and had been defeated at Gettysburg by the National army under Meade. Grant had brought the siege of Vicksburg to a glorious conclusion and had received the surrender of Pemberton with his army of 30,000 Confederates. These victories, coming together as they did and on the 4th of July, made the national anniversary seem more than ever a day of rejoicing and of hope to the whole people. We did not get the news of Grant's victory quite so soon as that of Meade's, but it came to us at Cincinnati in a way to excite peculiar enthusiasm.

An excellent operatic company was giving a series of performances in the city, and all Cincinnati was at Pike's Opera House listening to *I Puritani* on the evening of the 7th of July. General Burnside and his wife had one of the proscenium boxes, and my wife and I were their guests. The second act had just closed with the famous trumpet song, in which Susini, the great basso of the day, had created a *furore*. A messenger entered the box where the general was surrounded by a brilliant company, and gave him a dispatch which announced the surrender of Vicksburg and Pemberton's army. Burnside, overjoyed, announced the great news to us who were near him, and then stepped to the front of the box to make the whole audience sharers in the pleasure. As soon as he was seen with the paper in his hand, the house was hushed, and his voice rang through it as he proclaimed the great victory and declared it a long stride toward the restoration of the Union. The people went almost wild with excitement, the men shouted hurrahs, the ladies waved their handkerchiefs and clapped their hands, all rising to their feet. The cheering was long as well as loud, and before it subsided the excitement reached behind the stage. The curtain rose again, and Susini came forward with a national flag in each hand, waving them enthusiastically whilst his magnificent voice resounded in a repetition of the song he had just sung, and which seemed as appropriate as if it were inspired for the occasion—

"Suoni la tromba, e intrepido Io pugnerò da forte, Bello è affrontar la morte, Gridando libertà!"

The rejoicing and the cheers were repeated to the echo, and when at last they subsided, the rest of the opera was only half listened to, suppressed excitement filling every heart and the thought of the great results to flow from the victories absorbing every mind.

Burnside reckoned with entire certainty on the immediate return of the Ninth Corps, and planned to resume his expedition into East Tennessee as soon as his old troops should reach him again. The Morgan raid was just beginning, and no one anticipated its final scope. In the dispatch from the Secretary of War which announced Grant's great victory, Burnside was also told that the corps would immediately return to him. In answering it on the 8th July, he said, "I thought I was very happy at the success of General Grant and General Meade, but I am still happier to hear of the speedy return of the Ninth Corps." He informed Rosecrans of it on the same day, adding, "I hope soon to be at work again."

The Washington authorities very naturally and very properly wished that the tide of success should be kept moving, and Secretary Stanton had exhorted Rosecrans to further activity by saying, on the 7th, "You and your noble army now have the chance to give the finishing blow to the rebellion. Will you neglect the chance?" Rosecrans replied: "You do not appear to observe the fact that this noble army has driven the rebels from middle Tennessee, of which my dispatches advised you. I beg in behalf of this army that the War Department may not overlook so great an event because it is not written in letters of blood." He, however, did not intimate any purpose of advancing. No doubt the manoeuvring of Bragg out of his fortified positions at Shelbyville and Tullahoma had been well done; but its chief value was that it forced Bragg to meet the Army of the Cumberland in the open field if the advantage should be promptly followed up. If he were allowed to fortify another position, nothing would be gained but the ground the army stood on. Had Rosecrans given any intimation of an early date at which he could rebuild the Elk River bridge and resume active operations, it would probably have relieved the strain so noticeable in the correspondence between him and the War Department. He did nothing of the kind, and the necessity of removing him from the command was a matter of every-day discussion at Washington, as is evident from the confidential letters Halleck sent to him. The correspondence between the General-in-Chief and his subordinate is a curious one. A number of the most urgent dispatches representing the dissatisfaction of the President and the Secretary were accompanied by private and confidential letters in which Halleck explains the situation and strongly asserts his friendship for Rosecrans and the error of the latter in assuming that personal hostility to himself was at bottom of the reprimands sent him on account of his delays. It was with good intentions that Halleck wrote thus, but the wisdom of it is very questionable. It gave Rosecrans ground to assume that the official dispatches were only the formal expression of the ideas of the President and Secretary whilst the General-in-Chief did not join in the condemnation of his dilatory mode of conducting the campaign. To say to Rosecrans, as Halleck did on July 24th, "Whether well founded or without any foundation, the dissatisfaction really exists, and I deem it my duty as a friend to represent it to you truly and fairly," is to neglect his duty as commander of the whole army to express his own judgment and to give orders which would have the weight of his military position and presumed knowledge in military matters. When, therefore, a few days later he gave peremptory orders to begin an active advance, these orders were interpreted in the light of the preceding correspondence, and lost their force and vigour. They were met by querulous and insubordinate inquiries whether they were intended to take away all discretion as to details from the commander of an army in the field. It has been argued that Rosecrans's weakness of character consisted in a disposition to quarrel with those in power over him, and that a spirit of contradiction thwarted the good military conduct which his natural energy might have produced. I cannot help reading his controversial correspondence in the light of my personal observation of the man, and my conviction is that his quarrelsome mode of dealing with the War Department was the result of a real weakness of will and purpose which did not take naturally to an aggressive campaign that involved great responsibilities and risks. Being really indecisive in fixing his plan of campaign and acting upon it, his infirmity of will was covered by a belligerence in his correspondence. A really enterprising commander in the field would have begun an active campaign in the spring before any dissatisfaction was exhibited at Washington; and if he had a decided purpose to advance at any reasonably early period, there was nothing in the urgency shown by his superiors to make him abandon his purpose. He might have made testy comments, but he would have acted.

Halleck's correspondence with Burnside in July is hard to understand, unless we assume that it was so perfunctory that he did not remember at one time what he said or did earlier. In a dispatch to the General-in-Chief dated the 11th, Rosecrans had said, "It is important to know if it will be practicable for Burnside to come in on our left flank and hold the line of the Cumberland; if not, a line in advance of it and east of us." It was already understood between Rosecrans and Burnside that the latter would do this and more as soon as he should have the Ninth Corps with him; and the dispatch must be regarded as a variation on the form of excuses for inaction, by suggesting that he was delayed by the lack of an understanding as to co-operation by the Army of the Ohio. On receipt of Rosecrans's dispatch,

Halleck answered it on the 13th, saying, "General Burnside has been frequently urged to move forward and cover your left by entering East Tennessee. I do not know what he is doing. He seems tied fast to Cincinnati." On the same day he telegraphed Burnside, "I must again urge upon you the importance of moving forward into East Tennessee, to cover Rosecrans's left." It is possible that Burnside's telegraphic correspondence with the Secretary of War was not known to Halleck, but it is hard to believe that the latter was ignorant of the proportions the Morgan raid had taken after the enemy had crossed the Ohio River. The 13th of July was the day that Morgan marched from Indiana into Ohio and came within thirteen miles of Cincinnati. Burnside was organizing all the militia of southern Ohio, and was concentrating two divisions of the Twenty-third Corps to catch the raiders. One of these was on a fleet of steamboats which reached Cincinnati that day, and the other, under Hobson, was in close pursuit of the enemy. Where should Burnside have been, if not at Cincinnati? If the raid had been left to the "militia and home guards," as Halleck afterward said all petty raids should be, this, which was not a petty raid, would pretty certainly have had results which would have produced more discomfort at Washington than the idea that Burnside was "tied fast to Cincinnati." Burnside was exactly where he ought to be, and doing admirable work which resulted in the capture of the division of 3000 rebel cavalry with its officers from the general in command downward. That the General-in-Chief was entirely ignorant of what was going on, when every intelligent citizen of the country was excited over it and every newspaper was full of it, reflects far more severely upon him than upon Burnside.

But this was by no means the whole. He forgot that when he stopped Burnside's movement on 3rd June to send the Ninth Corps to Grant, it was with the distinct understanding that it prevented its resumption till the corps should return. He had himself said that this should be as early as possible, and meanwhile directed Burnside to concentrate his remaining forces as much as he could. Burnside had been told on the 8th of July, without inquiry from him, that the corps was coming back to him, and had immediately begun his preparation to resume an active campaign as soon as it should reach him. Not hearing of its being on the way, on the 18th he asked Halleck if orders for its return had been given. To this dispatch no answer was given, and it was probably pigeonholed and forgotten. Burnside continued his campaign against Morgan, and on the 24th, when the last combinations near Steubenville were closing the career of the raider, Halleck again telegraphs that there must be no further delay in the movement into East Tennessee, and orders an immediate report of the position and number of Burnside's troops organized for that purpose! He was still ignorant, apparently, that there had been any occasion to withdraw the troops in Kentucky from the positions near the Cumberland River.

Burnside answered temperately, reciting the facts and reminding him of the actual state of orders and correspondence, adding only, "I should be glad to be more definitely instructed, if you think the work can be better done." Morgan's surrender was on the 26th, and Burnside immediately applied himself with earnest zeal to get his forces back into Kentucky. Judah's division at Buffington was three hundred miles from Cincinnati and five hundred from the place it had left to begin the chase. Shackelford's mounted force was two hundred miles further up the Ohio. This last was, as has been recited, made up of detachments from all the divisions of the Twenty-third Corps, and its four weeks of constant hard riding had used up men and horses. These all had to be got back to the southern part of central Kentucky and refitted, returned to their proper divisions, and prepared for a new campaign. The General-in-Chief does not seem to have had the slightest knowledge of these circumstances or conditions.

On the 28th another Confederate raid developed itself in southern Kentucky, under General Scott. It seemed to be intended as a diversion to aid Morgan to escape from Ohio, but failed to accomplish anything. Scott advanced rapidly from the south with his brigade, crossing the Cumberland at Williamsburg and moving through London upon Richmond. Colonel Sanders endeavoured to stop the enemy at Richmond with about

500 men hastily collected, but was driven back. He was ordered to Lexington and put in command of all the mounted men which could be got together there, 2400 in all, and advanced against Scott, who now retreated by Lancaster, Stanford, and Somerset. At Lancaster the enemy was routed in a charge and 200 of them captured. Following them up with vigour, their train was destroyed and about 500 more prisoners were taken. At the Cumberland River Sanders halted, having been without rations for four days. The remnant of Scott's force had succeeded in crossing the river after abandoning the train. Scott claimed to have taken and paroled about 200 prisoners in the first part of his raid, but such irregular paroles of captured men who could not be carried off were unauthorized and void. The actual casualties in Sanders's command were trifling.

The effect of this last raid was still further to wear out Burnside's mounted troops, but he pressed forward to the front all his infantry and organized a column for advance. In less than a week, on August 4, he was able to announce to the War Department that he had 11,000 men concentrated at Lebanon, Stanford, and Glasgow, with outposts on the Cumberland River, and that he could possibly increase this to 12,000 by reducing some posts in guard of the railway. Upon this, Halleck gave to Rosecrans peremptory orders for the immediate advance of the Army of the Cumberland, directing him also to report daily the movement of each corps till he should cross the Tennessee. On the next day Burnside was ordered in like manner to advance with a column of 12,000 men upon Knoxville, on reaching which place he was to endeavour to connect with the forces under Rosecrans. The dispatch closed with what was called a repetition of a former order from the Secretary of War for Burnside to leave Cincinnati and take command of his moving column in person. Burnside had never dreamed of doing anything else, as everybody near him knew, though he had in fact been quite ill during the latter part of July. The mention of a former order was another sheer blunder on General Halleck's part, and Burnside indignantly protested against the imputation contained in it. The truth seems to be that Halleck was in such a condition of irritation over his correspondence with Rosecrans, that nothing pertaining to the Department of the Ohio was accurately placed in his mind or accurately stated when he had occasion to refer to it. In cutting the knot by peremptory orders to both armies to move, he was right, and was justified in insisting that the little column of 12,000 under Burnside should start although it could only be got together in greatest haste and with the lack of equipment occasioned by the "wear and tear" of the operations against Morgan. If, in insisting on this, he had recognized the facts and given Burnside and his troops credit for the capture of the rebel raiders and the concentration, in a week, of forces scattered over a distance of nearly a thousand miles, no one would have had a right to criticise him. The exigency fairly justified it. But to treat Burnside as if he had been only enjoying himself in Cincinnati, and his troops all quietly in camp along the Cumberland River through the whole summer—to ignore the absence of the Ninth Corps and his own suspension of a movement already begun when he took it away—to assume in almost every particular a basis of fact absolutely contrary to the reality and to telegraph censures for what had been done, under his own orders or strictly in harmony with them—all this was doing a right thing in as absurdly wrong a way as was possible. A gleam of humour and the light of common sense is thrown over one incident, when Mr. Lincoln, seeing that Burnside had full right from the dispatches to suppose the Ninth Corps was to come at once to him from Vicksburg and that no one had given him any explanation, himself telegraphed that the information had been based on a statement from General Grant, who had not informed them why the troops had not been sent. "General Grant," the President quaintly added, "is a copious worker and fighter, but a very meagre writer or telegrapher. No doubt he changed his purpose for some sufficient reason, but has forgotten to notify us of it." The reference to copious work as contrasted with the *copia verborum* gains added point from a dispatch of Halleck to Rosecrans, quite early in the season, in which the latter is told that the cost of his telegraph dispatches is "as much or perhaps more than that of all the other generals in the field."

The form of the reference to Grant enables us also to read between the lines the progress he was making in reputation and in the President's confidence. He kept "pegging away," and was putting brains as well as energy into his work. The records show also that Burnside took the hint, whether intended or not, and in this campaign did not err on the side of copiousness in dispatches to Washington.

To avoid the delay which would be caused by the distribution of his mounted force to the divisions they had originally been attached to, Burnside organized these into a division under Brigadier-General S. P. Carter, and an independent brigade under Colonel F. Wolford. He also reorganized the infantry divisions of the Twenty-third Corps. The first division, under Brigadier-General J. T. Boyle, was to remain in Kentucky and protect the lines of communication. The second was put under command of Brigadier-General M. D. Manson, and the third under Brigadier-General M. S. Hascall. Each marching division was organized into two brigades with a battery of artillery attached to each brigade. Three batteries of artillery were in reserve.

On the 11th of August General Burnside went to Hickman's Bridge, and the forward movement was begun. At this date the Confederate forces in East Tennessee under General Buckner numbered 14,733 "present for duty," with an "aggregate present" of 2000 or 3000 more. Conscious that the column of 12,000 which Halleck had directed him to start with was less than the hostile forces in the Holston valley, Burnside reduced to the utmost the garrisons and posts left behind him. Fortunately the advanced division of the Ninth Corps returning from Vicksburg reached Cincinnati on the 12th, and although the troops were wholly unfit for active service by reason of malarial diseases contracted on the "Yazoo," they could relieve some of the Kentucky garrisons, and Burnside was thus enabled to increase his moving column to about 15,000 men. The earlier stages of the advance were slow, as the columns were brought into position to take up their separate lines of march and organize their supply trains for the road. On the 20th Hanson's division was at Columbia, Hascall's was at Stanford, Carter's cavalry division was at Crab Orchard, and independent brigades of cavalry under Colonels Wolford and Graham were at Somerset and Glasgow. On that day orders were issued for the continuous march. General Julius White relieved Manson in command of the second division, and the two infantry divisions were to move on Montgomery, Tenn., Hascall's by way of Somerset, Chitwoods, and Huntsville, and White's by way of Creelsboro, Albany, and Jamestown. Carter's cavalry, which covered the extreme left flank, marched through Mt. Vernon and London to Williamsburg, where it forded the Cumberland, thence over the Jellico Mountains to Chitwoods where it became the advance of Hascall's column to Montgomery. At this point the columns were united and all moved together through Emory Gap upon Kingston. Burnside accompanied the cavalry in person, and sent two detachments, one to go by way of Big Creek Gap to make a demonstration on Knoxville, and the other through Winter's Gap for the same purpose of misleading the enemy as to his line of principal movement.

Nothing could be more systematic and vigorous than the march of Burnside's columns. They made from fifteen to twenty or twenty-five miles a day with the regularity of clock-work, though the route in many parts of it was most difficult. There were mountains to climb and narrow gorges to thread. Streams were to be forded, roads were to be repaired and in places to be made anew. On the 1st of September Burnside occupied Kingston, having passed through Emory Gap into East Tennessee and communicated with Crittenden's corps of Rosecrans's army. Here he learned that upon the development of the joint plan of campaign of the National commanders, Bragg had withdrawn Buckner's forces south of the Tennessee at Loudon, there making them the right flank of his army about Chattanooga. There was, however, one exception in Buckner's order to withdraw. Brigadier-General John W. Frazer was left at Cumberland Gap with 2500 men, and though Buckner had on August 30th ordered him to destroy his material and retreat into Virginia, joining the command of Major-General Samuel Jones, this order was withdrawn on Frazer's representation of his ability to hold the place and that he had rations for forty days. There being therefore no troops in East Tennessee to oppose its occupation, Burnside's advance-guard entered Knoxville on the 3rd of September. Part of the Twenty-third Corps had been sent toward London on the 2nd, and upon their approach the enemy burned the great railroad bridge at that place. A light-draught steamboat was building at Kingston, and this was captured and preserved. It played a useful part subsequently in the transportation of supplies when the wagon-trains were broken down and the troops were reduced nearly to starvation. No sooner was Burnside in Knoxville than he put portions of his army in motion for Cumberland Gap, sixty miles northward. He had already put Colonel John F. DeCourcey (Sixteenth Ohio Infantry) in command of new troops arriving in Kentucky, and ordered him to advance against the fortifications of the gap on the north side. General Shackelford was sent with his cavalry from Knoxville, but when Burnside learned that DeCourcey and he were not strong enough to take the place, he left Knoxville in person with Colonel Samuel Gilbert's brigade of infantry and made the sixty-mile march in fifty-two hours. Frazer had refused to surrender on the summons of the subordinates; but when Burnside arrived and made the demand in person, he despaired of holding out and on the 9th of September surrendered the garrison. A considerable number got away by scattering after the flag was hauled down, but 2,205 men laid down their arms, and twelve pieces of cannon were also among the spoils. DeCourcey's troops were left to garrison the fortifications, and the rest were sent to occupy the upper valley of the Holston toward the Virginia line.

On the 10th, and while still at Cumberland Gap, Burnside received a dispatch from General Crittenden with the news that he was in possession of Chattanooga, that Bragg had retreated toward Rome, Ga., and that Rosecrans hoped with his centre and right to intercept the enemy at Rome, which was sixty miles south of Chattanooga. Everything was therefore most promising on the south, and Burnside had only to provide for driving back the Confederates under Jones, at the Virginia line, a hundred and thirty miles northeast of Knoxville.

It becomes important here to estimate these distances rightly. Knoxville is a hundred and eleven miles distant from Chattanooga by the railroad, and more by the country roads. From Bristol on the northeast to Chattanooga on the southwest is two hundred and forty-two miles, which measures the length of that part of the Holston and Tennessee valley known as East Tennessee. If Rosecrans were at Rome, as General Crittenden's dispatch indicated, he was more than a hundred and seventy miles distant from Knoxville, and nearly three hundred miles from the region about Greeneville and the Watauga River, whose crossing would be the natural frontier of the upper valley, if Burnside should not be able to extend his occupation quite to the Virginia line. It will be seen therefore that the progress of the campaign had necessarily made Rosecrans's and Burnside's lines of operation widely divergent, and they were far beyond supporting distance of each other, since there was no railway communication between them, and could not be for a long time. Burnside captured some locomotives and cars at Knoxville; but bridges had been destroyed to such an extent that these were of little use to him, for the road could be operated but a short distance in either direction and the amount of rolling stock was, at most, very little. Complete success for Rosecrans, with the reopening and repair of the whole line from Nashville through Chattanooga, including the rebuilding of the great bridge at London, were the essential conditions of further co-operation between the two armies, and of the permanent existence of Burnside's in East Tennessee.

Efforts had been made to extend the lines of telegraph as Burnside advanced, but it took some time to do this, and even when the wires were up there occurred a difficulty in making the electric circuit, so that through all the critical part of the Chickamauga campaign, Burnside had to communicate by means of so long a line of couriers that three days was the actual time of transmittal of dispatches between himself and Washington. The news from Rosecrans on the 10th was so reassuring that Burnside's plain duty was to apply himself to clearing the upper valley of the enemy, and then to further the great object of his expedition by giving the loyal inhabitants the means of self-government, and encouraging them to organize and arm themselves with the weapons which his wagon trains were already bringing from Kentucky. He had also to provide for his supplies, and must use the good weather of the early autumn to the utmost, for the long roads over the mountains would be practically impassable in winter. The route from Kentucky by way of Cumberland Gap was the shortest, and, on the whole, the easiest, and a great system of transportation by trains under escort was put in operation. The camp at Cumberland Gap could give this protection through the mountain district, and made a convenient stopping-place in the weary way when teams broke down or had to be replaced. Other roads were also used whilst they seemed to be safe, and the energies and resources of the quartermaster's department were strained to the utmost to bring forward arms, ammunition for cannon and muskets, food and medical supplies, and all the munitions of war. The roads were covered with herds of beeves and swine, and feeding stations for these were established and the forage had to be drawn to them, for nothing could be got, along the greater part of the route. Burnside hoped that the railway by Chattanooga would be put in repair and be open before winter should shut in, but he very prudently acted on the principle of making the most of his present means. It was well he did so, for otherwise his little army would have been starved before the winter was half over.

From Cumberland Gap the courier line was sixty miles shorter than from Knoxville, and the first dispatches of Burnside announcing his capture of Frazer's troops reached Washington more quickly than later ones. At noon of the 11th Mr. Lincoln answered it with hearty congratulations and thanks. This was quickly followed by a congratulatory message from Halleck accompanied by formal orders. These last only recapitulated the points in Burnside's further operations and administration which were the simplest deductions from the situation. Burnside was to hold the country eastward to the gaps of the North Carolina mountains (the Great Smokies) and the valley of the Holston up to the Virginia line. Halleck used the phrase "the line of the Holston," which would be absurd, and was probably only a slip of the pen. The exact strength of General Jones, the Confederate commander in southwestern Virginia, was not known, but, to preserve his preponderance, Burnside could not prudently send less than a division of infantry and a couple of brigades of cavalry to the vicinity of Rogersville or Greeneville and the railroad crossing of the Watauga. This would be just about half his available force. The other division was at first divided, one of the two brigades being centrally placed at Knoxville, and the other at Sevierville, thirty miles up the French Broad River, where it covered the principal pass over the Smokies to Asheville, N. C. The rest of his cavalry was at London and Kingston, where it covered the north side of the Tennessee River and communicated with Rosecrans's outposts above Chattanooga.

Halleck further informed Burnside that the Secretary of War directed him to raise all the volunteers he could in East Tennessee and to select officers for them. If he had not already enough arms and equipments he could order them by telegraph. As to Rosecrans, the General-in-Chief stated that he would occupy Dalton or some other point south of Chattanooga, closing the enemy's line from Atlanta, and when this was done, the question would be settled whether the whole would move eastward into Virginia or southward into Georgia and Alabama. Burnside's present work being thus cut out for him, he set himself about it with the cordial earnestness which marked his character. He had suggested the propriety of his retiring as soon as the surrender of Frazer had made his occupation of East Tennessee an assured success, but he had not formally asked to be relieved. His reasons for doing so dated back to the Fredericksburg campaign, in part; for he had believed that his alternative then presented to the government, that he should be allowed to dismiss insubordinate generals or should himself resign, ought to have been accepted. His case had some resemblance to Pope's when the administration approved his conduct and his courage but retired him and restored McClellan to command, in deference to the supposed sentiment of the Army of the Potomac. Halleck's persistent ignoring of the officially recorded causes of the delay in this campaign, and his assumption that the Morgan raid was not an incident of any importance in Burnside's responsibilities, had not tended to diminish the latter's sense of discomfort in dealing with army head-quarters. A debilitating illness gave some added force to his other reasons, which, however, we who knew him well understood to be the decisive ones with him. Mr. Lincoln's sincere friendship and confidence he never doubted, but his nature could not fully appreciate the President's policy of bending to existing circumstances when current opinion was contrary to his own, so that he might save his strength for more critical action at another time. Burnside had now the *éclat* of success in a campaign which was very near the heart of the President and full of interest for the Northern people. This, he felt, was a time when he could retire with honour. Mr. Lincoln postponed action in the kindest and most complimentary words, and when he finally assigned another to command the department, did not allow Burnside to resign, but laid out other work for him where his patriotism and his courage could be of use to the country.

The advent of the army into East Tennessee was, to its loyal people, a resurrection from the grave. Their joy had an exultation which seemed almost beyond the power of expression. Old men fell down fainting and unconscious under the stress of their emotions as they saw the flag at the head of the column and tried to cheer it! Women wept with happiness as their husbands stepped out of the ranks of the loyal Tennessee regiments when these came marching by the home. These men had gathered in little recruiting camps on the mountain-sides and had found their way to Kentucky, travelling by night and guided by the pole-star, as the dark-skinned fugitives from bondage had used to make their way to freedom. Their families had been marked as traitors to the Confederacy, and had suffered sharpest privations and cruel wrong on account of the absence of the husband and father, the brother, or the son. Now it was all over, and a jubilee began in those picturesque valleys in the mountains, which none can understand who had not seen the former despair and the present revulsion of happiness. The mountain coves and nooks far up toward the Virginia line had been among the most intense in loyalty to the nation. Andrew Johnson's home was at Greeneville, and he was now the loyal provisional governor of Tennessee, soon to be nominated Vice-President of the United States. General Carter, who had asked to be transferred from the navy to organize the refugee loyalists into regiments, was a native of the same region. It was at the Watauga that the neighbouring opponents of secession had given the first example of daring self-sacrifice in burning the railway bridge. For this they were hanged, and their memory was revered by the loyal men about them, as was Nathan Hale's by our revolutionary fathers. East Tennessee was full of such loyalty, but here were good reasons why Burnside should push his advance at least to the Watauga, and if possible to the Virginia line. His sympathies were all alive for this people. The region, he telegraphed the President, is as loyal as any State of the North. It threw off all disguise, it blossomed with National flags, it took no counsel of prudence, it refused to think of a return of Confederate soldiers and Confederate rule as a possibility. It exulted in every form of defiance to the Richmond government and what had been called treason to the Confederate States. The people had a religious faith that God would not abandon them or suffer them to be again abandoned. If such an incredible wrong were to happen, they must either leave their country in mass, or they must be ready to die. They could see no other alternative.

Chapter 26
Burnside in East Tennessee

For a week after the capture of Cumberland Gap Burnside devoted himself to the pleasing task of organizing the native loyalists into a National Guard for home defence, issuing arms to them upon condition that they should, as a local militia, respond to his call and reinforce for temporary work his regular forces whenever the need should arise. The detailed reports from the upper valley reported the enemy under Jones at first to be 4000, and later to be 6000 strong. These estimates came through cool-headed and prudent officers, and were based upon information brought in by loyal men who had proven singularly accurate in their knowledge throughout the campaign. Point was added to these reports by the experience of one of his regiments. A detachment of 300 men of the One Hundredth Ohio had been sent to support a cavalry reconnaissance near Limestone Station on the railroad, whilst Burnside was investing Cumberland Gap, and these had been surrounded and forced to surrender by the enemy. This showed the presence of a considerable body of Confederates in the upper valley, and that they were bold and aggressive. It was the part of prudence to act upon this information, and Burnside ordered all his infantry except one brigade to march toward Greeneville. Two brigades of cavalry were already there, and his purpose was to concentrate about 6000 infantry, try to obtain a decisive engagement with the Confederates, and to punish them so severely that the upper valley would be safe, for a time at least, from invasion by them, so that he might be free to withdraw most of his troops to co-operate with Rosecrans in a Georgia campaign, if that alternative in Halleck's plans should be adopted. He felt the importance of this the more, as the news received from Virginia mentioned the movement of railway rolling-stock to the East to bring, as rumour had it, Ewell's corps from Lee to reinforce Jones. The sending of the railway trains was a fact, but the object, as it turned out, was to transport Longstreet's corps to reinforce Bragg. Of this, however, Burnside had no intimation, and must act upon the information which came to him.

The Ninth Corps began to arrive at Cincinnati from Vicksburg on the 12th of August, half of it coming then, and the second division arriving on the 20th. It was reduced to 6000 by casualties and by sickness, and was in a pitiable condition. Being made up of troops which had served in the East, the men were not acclimated to the Mississippi valley, and in the bayous and marshes about Vicksburg had suffered greatly. Malarial fevers ate out their vitality, and even those who reported for duty dragged themselves about, the mere shadows of what they had been. General Parke reported their arrival and was then obliged to go upon sick-leave himself. General Welsh, who had distinguished himself at Antietam, reported that his division must recuperate for a few weeks before it could take the field. He made a heroic effort to remain on duty, but died suddenly on the 14th, and his loss was deeply felt by the corps. Potter's division was as badly off as Welsh's, and both were for a short time scattered at healthful camps in the Kentucky hills. Each camp was, at first, a hospital; but the change of climate and diet rapidly restored the tone of the hardy soldiery.

General Willcox, who commanded the Indiana district, belonged to the corps, and asked to be returned to duty with it. He was allowed to do so on the 11th of September, and the War Department sent with him a new division of Indiana troops which had been recruited and organized during the summer. Burnside had ordered recruits and new regiments to rendezvous in Kentucky, and prepared to bring them as well as the Ninth Corps forward as soon as the latter should be fit to march. Every camp and station at the rear was full of busy preparation during the last of August and the beginning of September, and at the front the general himself was now concentrating his little forces to strike a blow near the Virginia line which would make him free to move afterward in any direction the General-in-Chief should determine.

On the 16th of September Hascall's division was echeloned along the road from Morristown back toward Knoxville; White's division passed Knoxville, moving up the valley to join Hascall. Hartsuff, who commanded the Twenty-third Corps, had been disabled for field work by trouble from his old wounds and was at Knoxville. Burnside was also there, intending to go rapidly forward and overtake his infantry as soon as they should approach Greeneville. In the night the courier brought him a dispatch from Halleck, dated the 13th, directing a rapid movement of all his forces in Kentucky toward East Tennessee, where the whole Army of the Ohio was to be concentrated as soon as possible. He also directed Burnside to move his infantry toward Chattanooga, giving as a reason that Bragg might manoeuvre to turn Rosecrans's right, and in that case Rosecrans would want to hand Chattanooga over to Burnside so that he himself could move the whole Army of the Cumberland to meet Bragg.

There was nothing in this dispatch which intimated that Rosecrans was in any danger, nor was Burnside informed that Bragg had been reinforced by Longstreet's corps. On the other hand, his information looked to Ewell's joining Jones against himself. The object Halleck had in view seemed to be to get the Ninth Corps and other troops now in Kentucky into East Tennessee as rapidly as possible, and then to move the whole Army of the Ohio down toward Rosecrans. It certainly could not be that he wished Cumberland Gap abandoned, and the trains and detachments coming through it from Kentucky left to the tender mercies of Jones and his Confederates, who could capture them at their leisure and without a blow. It was equally incredible that the government could wish to stop the organization of the loyalists just as weapons were being distributed to them, and to abandon them to the enemy when their recent open demonstrations in favour of the Union would make their condition infinitely worse than if our troops had never come to them. The rational interpretation, and the one Burnside gave it, was that the alternative which had been stated in the earlier dispatch of the 11th had been settled in favour of a general movement southward instead of eastward, and that this made it all the more imperative that he should disembarrass himself of General Jones and establish a line on the upper Holston which a small force could hold, whilst he with the rest of the two corps should move southward as soon as the Ninth Corps could make the march from Kentucky. This was exactly what General Schofield did in the next spring when he was ordered to join Sherman with the Army of the Ohio; and I do not hesitate to say that it was the only thing which an intelligent military man on the ground and knowing the topography would think of doing. To make a panicky abandonment of the country and of the trains and detachments *en route* to it, would have been hardly less disgraceful than a surrender of the whole. To Burnside's honour and credit it should be recorded that he did not dream of doing it. He strained every nerve to hasten the movement of his troops so as to get through with his little campaign against Jones by the time the Ninth Corps could come from Kentucky, and if he could accomplish it within that limit, he would have the right to challenge the judgment of every competent critic, whether he had not done that which became a good soldier and a good general.

On the 17th of September the concentration of Burnside's infantry toward Greeneville had so far progressed that he was preparing to go personally to the front and lead them against the enemy. It is noticeable in the whole campaign that he took this personal leadership and activity on himself. In Hartsuff's condition of health it would have been within the ordinary methods of action that the next in rank should assume command of the Twenty-third Corps, and that the department commander should remain at his headquarters at Knoxville. But Hartsuff was able to attend to office business, and so Burnside practically exchanged places with him, leaving his subordinate with discretion to direct affairs in the department at large, whilst he himself did the field work with his troops. He had done it at Cumberland Gap when he received the surrender of Frazer; he was doing it now, and he was to do it again, still later, when he met Longstreet's advance at the crossing of the Holston River.

In preparation for an absence of some days, he wrote, on the date last mentioned, a long dispatch to General Halleck, in the nature of a report of the state of affairs at that date. He explained the failure of the telegraph and the efforts that were making to get it in working order. He gave the situation of the troops and stated his purpose to attack the enemy. He noticed the report of Ewell's coming against him and promised stout resistance, finding satisfaction in the thought that it would give Meade the opportunity to strike a decisive blow against Lee's reduced army. He reported the condition of his trains and cattle droves on the road from Kentucky, and the contact of his cavalry in the south part of the valley with Rosecrans's outposts. The bridge over the Hiwassee at Calhoun, he said, could be finished in ten days, and the steamboat at Kingston would soon be completed and ready for use. All this promised better means of supply at an early day, though at present "twenty-odd cars" were all the means of moving men or supplies on the portion of the railroad within his control.

Later in the same day he received Halleck's dispatch of the 14th, which said it was believed the enemy would concentrate to give Rosecrans battle, and directed him to reinforce the latter with all possible speed.

Still, no information was given of the movement of Longstreet to join Bragg, and indeed it was only on the 15th that Halleck gave the news to Rosecrans as reliable. Burnside must therefore regard the enemy concentrating in Georgia as only the same which Rosecrans had been peremptorily ordered to attack and which he had been supposed to be strong enough to cope with. No time was stated at which the battle in Georgia would probably occur. To hasten the work in hand, to put affairs at the Virginia line in condition to be left as soon as might be, and then to speed his forces toward Chattanooga to join in the Georgia campaign, was plainly Burnside's duty. If it would be too rash for Rosecrans to give battle without reinforcements, that officer was competent to manoeuvre his army in retreat and take a defensible position till his reinforcements could come. That course would be certainly much wiser than to abandon East Tennessee to the enemy, with all the consequences of such an act, quite as bad as the loss of a battle. As matters turned out, even such instantaneous and ruinous abandonment would not have helped Rosecrans. It was now the afternoon of the 17th of September. The battle of Chickamauga was to begin in the early morning of the 19th and to end disastrously on the 20th. One full day for the marching of troops was all that intervened, or two at most, if they were only to reach the field upon the second day of the battle. And where were Burnside's men? One division at Greeneville and above, more than two hundred miles from Chattanooga, and the other near New Market and Morristown, a hundred and fifty miles. Burnside's "twenty-odd cars" were confined to a section of the railroad less than eighty miles long, and could hardly carry the necessary baggage and ammunition even for that fraction of the way. The troops must march, and could not by any physical possibility make a quarter of the distance before Rosecrans's fate at Chickamauga should be decided. The authorities at Washington must bear the responsibility for complete ignorance of these conditions, or, what would be equally bad, a forgetfulness of them in a moment of panic.

But Burnside did not know and could not guess that a battle was to be fought so soon. All he could do was to prepare to carry out the wishes of the War Department as speedily as could be, without the total ruin of East Tennessee and all he had accomplished. Such ruin might come by the fate of war if he were driven out by superior force, but he would have been rightly condemned if it had come by his precipitate abandonment of the country. He did more to carry out Halleck's wish than was quite prudent. He stopped the troops which had not yet reached Greeneville and ordered a counter-march. He hastened up the country to make the attack upon the Confederates with the force he already had in their presence, and then to bring the infantry back at once, hoping the cavalry could hold in check a defeated enemy.

The necessity of delivering a blow at General Jones was afterwards criticised by Halleck, but it was in accordance with the sound rules of conducting war. To have called back his troops without a fight would have been to give the enemy double courage by his retreat, and his brigades would have been chased by the exulting foe. They would either have been forced to halt and fight their pursuers under every disadvantage of loss of prestige and of the initiative, or have made a precipitate flight which would have gone far to ruin the whole command as well as the Tennessee people they had just liberated. It is true that this involved an advance from Greeneville upon Jonesboro, but the cavalry were already in contact with the enemy near there, and this was the only successful mode of accomplishing his purpose.

Making use of the portion of the railroad which could be operated, Burnside reached Greeneville on the 18th and rode rapidly to Jonesboro. On the 19th a brigade of cavalry under Colonel Foster attacked the enemy at Bristol, defeated them, tore up the railroad, and destroyed the bridges two miles above the town. Foster then returned to Blountsville, and marched on the next day to Hall's Ford on the Watauga, where, after a skirmishing fight lasting several hours, he again dislodged the enemy, capturing about fifty prisoners and a piece of artillery with slight loss to himself. These were flanking movements designed to distract the attention of the enemy whilst Burnside concentrated most of his force in front of their principal position at Carter's Station, where the most important of the railway bridges in that region crosses the Watauga. To impress his opponent with the belief that he meant to make an extended campaign, Burnside, on the 22nd, notified Jones to remove the non-combatants from the villages of the upper valley. Foster's brigade of cavalry was again sent to demonstrate on the rear, whilst Burnside threatened in front with the infantry. The enemy now evacuated the position and retreated, first burning the bridge. This was what Burnside desired, and the means of resuming railway communication to support an advance toward Knoxville being taken from the Confederates for a considerable time, he was now able to put all his infantry except two regiments in march for Knoxville. A brigade of cavalry with this small infantry support at Bull's Gap was entrusted with the protection of this region, and by the help of the home guards of loyal men, was able to hold it during the operations of the next fortnight. Burnside's purpose had been, if he had not been interrupted, to have pressed the Confederates closely with a sufficient force in front to compel a retreat, whilst he intercepted them with the remainder of his army, moving by a shorter line from Blountsville. He made, however, the best of the situation, and having driven the enemy over the State line and disengaged his own troops, he was free to concentrate the greater part of them for operations at the other end of the valley.

The Ninth Corps was now beginning to arrive, and was ordered to rendezvous first at Knoxville. Willcox had assembled his division of new troops, mostly Indianans, and marched with them to Cumberland Gap, where he relieved the garrison of that post, and was himself entrusted by Burnside with the command of that portion of the department, covering the upper valleys of the Clinch and Holston as well as the lines of communication with Cincinnati and the Ohio River.

In the days immediately preceding the battle of Chickamauga, Halleck had urged reinforcements forward toward Rosecrans from all parts of the West. Pope in Minnesota, Schofield in Missouri, Hurlbut at Memphis, and Sherman at Vicksburg had all been called upon for help, and all had put bodies of troops in motion, though the distances were great and the effect was a little too much like the proverbial one of locking the stable door after the horse had been stolen. As there was no telegraphic communication with Burnside, the General-in-Chief gave orders through the adjutant-general's office in Cincinnati directly to the Ninth Corps and to the detachments of the Twenty-third Corps remaining or assembling in Kentucky, to march at once into East Tennessee. An advisory supervision of the department offices in Cincinnati had been left with me, and Captain Anderson, the assistant adjutant-general, issued orders in General Burnside's name after consultation with me. General Parke cut short his sick-leave, and, though far from strong, assumed command of the Ninth Corps and began the march for Cumberland Gap. The guards for the railways and necessary posts were reduced to the lowest limits of safety, and every available regiment was hurried to the front.

By the end of September Burnside's forces were pretty well concentrated between Knoxville and Loudon, the crossing of the Holston River. It had now been learned that Bragg's army had suffered even more than Rosecrans's in the battle of Chickamauga, and notwithstanding the rout of the right wing of the Cumberland Army, the stubborn fighting of the centre and left wing under Thomas had made the enemy willing to admit that they had not won a decisive victory. Our army was within its lines at Chattanooga, and these had been so strengthened that General Meigs, who had been sent out in haste as a special envoy of the War Department, reported to Mr. Stanton on the 27th of September that the position was very strong, being practically secure against an assault, and that the army was hearty, cheerful, and confident. Meigs was himself a distinguished officer of the Engineer Corps as well as quartermaster-general, and the weight of his opinion at once restored confidence in Washington. He saw at a glance that the only perilous contingency was the danger of starvation, for the wagon roads over the mountains on the north side of the Tennessee were most difficult at best, and soon likely to become impassable. The army was safe from the enemy till it chose to resume the offensive, provided it could be fed. He concluded his dispatch by saying, "Of the rugged nature of this region I had no conception when I left Washington. I never travelled on such roads before." It was only too evident that Halleck shared this ignorance, and had added to it a neglect to estimate the distances over these mountains and through these valleys, and the relations of the points, he directed Burnside to hold, with the immediate theatre of Rosecrans's operations.

On the same date as Meigs's report, Burnside was also sending a full statement of his situation and an explanation of his conduct. The telegraphic communication was opened just as he finished his dispatch, and for the first time he had the means of rapid intercourse with army headquarters. He patiently explained the misconceptions and cross purposes of the preceding fortnight, and showed how impossible and how ruinous would have been any other action than that which he took. Halleck had said that it would now be necessary to move the Army of the Ohio along the north side of the Tennessee till it should be opposite Chattanooga and reinforce Rosecrans in that way. Burnside pointed out that this would open the heart of East Tennessee to Bragg's cavalry or detachments from his army. He offered to take the bolder course of moving down the south side of the rivers, covering Knoxville and the valley as he advanced.

Mr. Lincoln replied by authorizing Burnside to hold his present positions, sending Rosecrans, in his own way, what help he could spare. Halleck's answer was an amazing proof that he had never comprehended the campaign. He reiterated that Burnside's orders, before leaving Kentucky and continuously since, had been "to connect your right with General Rosecrans's left, so that if the enemy concentrated on one, the other would be able to assist." If this meant anything, it meant that Burnside was to keep within a day's march of Rosecrans; for two days was more than enough to fight out a battle like Chickamauga. Yet he and everybody else knew that Burnside's supply route from Kentucky was through Cumberland Gap, and he had warmly applauded when Burnside turned that position, and by investing it in front and rear, had forced Frazer to surrender. He had explicitly directed Burnside to occupy and hold the upper Holston valley nearly or quite to the Virginia line, and one gets weary of repeating that between these places and Chattanooga was a breadth of two hundred miles of the kind of country Meigs had described and more than ten days of hard marching. His present orders are equally blind. Burnside is directed to reinforce Rosecrans with "all your available force," yet "East Tennessee must be held at all hazards, if possible." To "hold at all hazards" might be understood, but what is the effect of the phrase "if possible"? It must amount in substance to authority to do exactly what Burnside was doing—to hold East Tennessee with as small means as he thought practicable, and to reinforce Rosecrans with what he could spare.

It was, on the whole, fortunate for the country that Burnside was not in telegraphic communication with Washington sooner. Had he been actually compelled to abandon East Tennessee on the 13th or 14th of September, incalculable mischief would have followed. The Ninth Corps was *en route* for Cumberland Gap, and it with all the trains and droves on the road must either have turned back or pushed on blindly with no probability of effecting a junction with the Twenty-third Corps. Even as it was, the terror in East Tennessee, when it became known that they were likely to be abandoned, was something fearful. Public and private men united in passionate protests, and the common people stood aghast. Two of the most prominent citizens only expressed the universal feeling when, in a dispatch to Mr. Lincoln, they used such language as this:

> In the name of Christianity and humanity, in the name of God and liberty, for the sake of their wives and children and everything they hold sacred and dear on earth, the loyal people of Tennessee appeal to you and implore you not to abandon them again to the merciless dominion of the rebels, by the withdrawal of the Union forces from East Tennessee.

With the evidence of the ability of the Army of the Cumberland to hold its position at Chattanooga, there came a breathing spell and a quick end of the panic. It was seen that there was time to get all desirable reinforcements to Rosecrans from the West, and Hooker was sent with two corps from the East, open lines of well-managed railways making this a quicker assistance than could be given by even a few days' marches over country roads. The culmination of the peril had been caused by the inactivity of the Army of the Potomac, which had permitted the transfer of Longstreet across four States; and now Hooker was sent from that army by a still longer route through the West to the vicinity of Bridgeport, thirty miles by rail below Chattanooga on the Tennessee River, but nearer fifty by the circuitous mountain roads actually used. It became evident also that Burnside's army could only subsist by making the most of its own lines of supply through Kentucky. To add its trains to those which were toiling over the mountains between Chattanooga and Bridgeport, would risk the starvation of the whole. Until a better line could be opened, Burnside was allowed to concentrate most of his forces in the vicinity of Loudon, where he guarded the whole valley. His cavalry connected with Rosecrans on the north side of the Tennessee, and also held the line of the Hiwassee on the left.

On the last day of September Burnside reported the concentration of his forces and submitted three alternate plans of assisting Rosecrans: First, to abandon East Tennessee and move all his forces by the north bank of the Tennessee River to Chattanooga. This was what Halleck had seemed to propose. Second, to cross the Holston and march directly against Bragg's right flank whilst Rosecrans should attack in front. This was essentially what Grant afterward did, putting Sherman in a position similar to that which Burnside would have taken. Third, to march with 7000 infantry and 5000 cavalry entirely around Bragg by the east, and strike his line of communications at Dalton or thereabouts. This had a strong resemblance to the strategy of Sherman next spring, when he forced Johnston out of Dalton by sending McPherson to his rear at Resaca. Burnside added to it the plan of a march to the sea, proposing that if Bragg pursued him, he should march down the railroad to Atlanta, destroying it as thoroughly as possible, and then make his way to the coast, living on the country.

The last of these plans was that which Burnside preferred and offered to put into immediate execution. Neither of them was likely to succeed at that moment, for Rosecrans was so far demoralized by the effects of his late battle that he was in no condition to carry out any aggressive campaign with decisive energy. He declared in favour of the first (for they were communicated to him as well as to Halleck), and this only meant that he wanted his army at Chattanooga reinforced by any and every means, though he could not supply them, and the fortifications were already so strong that General Meigs reported that 10,000 men could very soon hold them against all Bragg's army. The plans, however, give us interesting light on Burnside's character and abilities, and show that he was both fertile in resources and disposed to adopt the boldest action. Halleck in reply said that distant expeditions into Georgia were not now contemplated, nor was it now necessary to join Rosecrans at Chattanooga. It was sufficient for Burnside to be in position to go to Rosecrans's assistance if he should require it. He was, however, to "hold some point near the upper end of the valley," which kept alive the constant occasion for misunderstanding, since it implied the protection and occupation of all East Tennessee, and the general there in command was the only one who could judge what was necessary to secure the object. The necessity for activity soon showed itself. About the 6th of October General Jones was reported to be showing a disposition to be aggressive, and Burnside determined to strike a blow at him again and with more force than that which had been interrupted a fortnight before. Willcox was ordered from Cumberland Gap to Morristown with his four new Indiana regiments; the Ninth Corps (having now only about 5000 men present for duty) was moved up the valley also, whilst the Twenty-third Corps, with two brigades of cavalry, was left in its positions near Loudon. The rest of the cavalry, under Shackelford, accompanied the movement up the valley of which Burnside took command in person. Leaving the cavalry post at Bull's Gap and advancing with his little army, he found the enemy strongly posted about midway between the Gap and Greeneville. Engaging them and trying to hold them by a skirmishing fight, he sent Foster's cavalry brigade to close the passage behind them. Foster found the roads too rough to enable him to reach the desired position in time, and the enemy retreating in the night escaped. The pursuit was pushed beyond the Watauga River, and a more thorough destruction was made of the railroad to and beyond the Virginia line. Considerable loss had been inflicted on the enemy and 150 prisoners had been captured, but no decisive engagement had been brought about, Jones being wary and conscious of inferiority of force. Willcox was left at Greeneville with part of the cavalry, while Burnside brought back the Ninth Corps to Knoxville. The activity was good for the troops and was successful in curbing the enemy's enterprise, besides encouraging the loyal inhabitants. There was now a lull in affairs till November, broken only by a mishap to Colonel Wolford's brigade of cavalry on the south of the Holston, where he was watching the enemy's advanced posts in the direction of Athens and Cleveland. Burnside had sent a flag of truce through the lines on the 19th of October, and the enemy taking advantage of it, delivered an unexpected blow upon Wolford, capturing 300 or 400 of his men and a battery of mountain howitzers, together with a wagon train which was several miles from camp.

ALSO FROM LEONAUR
AVAILABLE IN SOFTCOVER OR HARDCOVER WITH DUST JACKET

SEPOYS, SIEGE & STORM *by Charles John Griffiths*—The Experiences of a young officer of H.M.'s 61st Regiment at Ferozepore, Delhi ridge and at the fall of Delhi during the Indian mutiny 1857.

CAMPAIGNING IN ZULULAND *by W. E. Montague*—Experiences on campaign during the Zulu war of 1879 with the 94th Regiment.

THE STORY OF THE GUIDES *by G. J. Younghusband*—The Exploits of the Soldiers of the famous Indian Army Regiment from the northwest frontier 1847 - 1900..

ZULU: 1879 *by D.C.F. Moodie & the Leonaur Editors*—The Anglo-Zulu War of 1879 from contemporary sources: First Hand Accounts, Interviews, Dispatches, Official Documents & Newspaper Reports.

THE RECOLLECTIONS OF SKINNER OF SKINNER'S HORSE *by James Skinner*—James Skinner and his 'Yellow Boys' Irregular cavalry in the wars of India between the British, Mahratta, Rajput, Mogul, Sikh & Pindarree Forces.

TOMMY ATKINS' WAR STORIES 14 FIRST HAND ACCOUNTS—Fourteen first hand accounts from the ranks of the British Army during Queen Victoria's Empire Original & True Battle Stories Recollections of the Indian Mutiny With the 49th in the Crimea With the Guards in Egypt The Charge of the Six Hundred With Wolseley in Ashanti Alma, Inkermann and Magdala With the Gunners at Tel-el-Kebir Russian Guns and Indian Rebels Rough Work in the Crimea In the Maori Rising Facing the Zulus From Sebastopol to Lucknow Sent to Save Gordon On the March to Chitral Tommy by Rudyard Kipling

CHASSEUR OF 1914 *by Marcel Dupont*—Experiences of the twilight of the French Light Cavalry by a young officer during the early battles of the great war in Europe.

TROOP HORSE & TRENCH *by R. A. Lloyd*—The experiences of a British Lifeguardsman of the household cavalry fighting on the western front during the First World War 1914-18.

THE EAST AFRICAN MOUNTED RIFLES *by C. J. Wilson*—Experiences of the campaign in the East African bush during the First World War.

THE FIGHTING CAMELIERS *by Frank Reid*—The exploits of the Imperial Camel Corps in the desert and Palestine campaigns of the First World War.

AVAILABLE ONLINE AT
www.leonaur.com
AND OTHER GOOD BOOK STORES

www.ingramcontent.com/pod-product-compliance
Lightning Source LLC
Chambersburg PA
CBHW031306150426
43191CB00005B/101